"For companies who want to confidently step into the AI age, *The CIO's Guide to Enterprise FinOps* off[illegible] and practical roadmap for CIOs and CXOs to harness IT as [illegible] Enterprise FinOps framework can overcome the[illegible] hold companies from their true poten[illegible]

Subroto Muke[illegible]

"I just wanted to share my thoughts on *The CIO's Guide to Enterprise FinOps*, authored by Vineet Sawant. The book offers a refreshing look at the evolving role of the CIO as a key driver for business transformation, highlighting how enterprise FinOps can significantly impact business outcomes. It provides a thorough framework for implementing and measuring enterprise FinOps, which is very insightful. The principles of collaboration across different business entities to achieve positive financial results are particularly compelling. Overall, it's a great read and comes highly recommended."

Ushasri Tirumala, *EVP & GM, Manhattan Associates*

"The framework content and mental models deliver a timely and essential perspective on FinOps, showing how these tools strengthen decision-making in an AI-driven era. As frontier AI firms balance fiscal discipline with bold innovation, this book provides the clarity, structure, and cultural mindset needed to invest wisely while driving meaningful, scalable transformation."

Luke Fangman, *Cloud & AI MD Oil, Gas & Energy, Microsoft*

"Vineet Sawant's *The CIO's Guide to Enterprise FinOps* tackles the 'CIO's Dilemma', balancing operational stability with innovation. His accessible style simplifies complex concepts, providing a pragmatic framework for leaders to drive business value."

Maz Zaheer, *SVP and CIO, McKesson Oncology & Multispecialty*

"This book is a manifesto for CIOs. The Run-Transform-Innovate (RTI360) model and Enterprise FinOps framework presented in this book offer a practical roadmap for CIOs to navigate the competing demands of operational resilience and strategic growth."

Mark Collins, *Former President and Chief Operating Officer, MV Transportation*

"Vineet Sawant's book on CIOs and FinOps is a reflection of someone who has fought in the trenches of tech debt, cost optimization and revenue enablement and has lived to tell the tale. Through thorough explanation, he makes a strong case for the myriad conflicting priorities a CIO juggles. Where the book truly becomes a page turner is when Vineet turns prescriptive, using hard numbers and proven tactics to tell you exactly how you could go about both 'learning how to fish' and 'landing the big one'."

Razab Chowdury, *Former Cloud Ops Practice Leader, Slalom Consulting*

"*The CIO's Guide to Enterprise FinOps* captures the tension every technology leader faces; balancing operational excellence with the relentless push for innovation. This book distills that challenge with clarity and offers a pragmatic roadmap for transforming IT from a cost center into a strategic engine for growth. As someone who has led large scale digital and AI transformations across global enterprises, I found its insights both timely and deeply resonant. A must-read for CIOs and business leaders navigating the next era of enterprise modernization."

Ashish Barve, *Digital Transformation, Former McKesson VP*

"This book clearly captures the modern CIO's dilemma, balancing operational stability with transformation and innovation, while offering a practical framework grounded in real-world complexity. Its articulation of Enterprise FinOps as both a mindset and execution model makes the narrative especially relevant for CIOs navigating SaaS, AI and cloud-driven cost pressures."

Shyam Kumar, *Founder and CEO, CloudNuro*

The CIO's Guide to Enterprise FinOps

A practical guide to help unlock potential savings of over 30% in IT spend, this book presents a framework for IT executives to identify hidden cost reduction opportunities, improve business alignment, and redirect savings toward critical digital transformation and innovation initiatives while maintaining operational stability.

Unlike books that focus solely on financial optimization of public cloud services like AWS, Azure, and Google, this one expands the scope to address cost savings across all types of enterprise IT assets, whether hardware, software, or even services. Readers will gain concrete strategies to assess FinOps maturity, understand IT spend factors, and implement optimization levers across their entire technology landscape. Through real-world case studies and a flexible Enterprise FinOps framework, the book provides actionable methods to reduce technology debt, fuel innovation, and align IT investments with business objectives, potentially unlocking millions in savings that can be redirected to strategic priorities like innovation and transformation. It positions IT from a cost center to becoming a driver of business growth.

This guide is primarily designed for IT practitioners with budget decision-making authority, particularly CIOs and their executive management teams responsible for enterprise IT services. It also serves middle and senior managers seeking departmental cost optimization, independent consultants specializing in IT financial management, and students interested in this emerging field.

Vineet Sawant brings over 25 years of technology leadership experience, working extensively with CIOs and other C-level executives to spearhead strategic digital and cloud transformations. At roles such as Divisional VP Technology Operations at Corning and VP Professional Services at Rackspace, he has driven Enterprise FinOps, IT, and process optimization and operations modernization initiatives, reduced technology debt, delivered AI innovations, and scaled global delivery centers and ecosystems.

The CIO's Guide to Enterprise FinOps

Unlock Operational Savings to Bootstrap Your Innovation and Transformation

Vineet Sawant

Routledge
Taylor & Francis Group
NEW YORK AND LONDON

Designed cover image: Getty Images

First published 2027
by Routledge
605 Third Avenue, New York, NY 10158

and by Routledge
4 Park Square, Milton Park, Abingdon, Oxon, OX14 4RN

Routledge is an imprint of the Taylor & Francis Group, an informa business

ISBN: 9781041159889 (hbk)
ISBN: 9781041159872 (pbk)
ISBN: 9781003682196 (ebk)

DOI: 10.4324/9781003682196

Typeset in Sabon
by Deanta Global Publishing Services, Chennai, India

To my father, whose wisdom taught me to look at every challenge from multiple angles; my mother, whose poetry and resilience ignited my creative spirit; and to my sisters, Simi and Vidya, who showed me the true power of determination and perseverance.

To my wonderful wife, Jo, and our amazing children, Ronak and Kanak, whose love and support inspire me every day to raise the bar and bring this book to life. To our loyal dog, Muffin, for unwavering company during the long nights of writing.

To the colleagues across the globe who have challenged and inspired me; to my mentors, teams, and co-workers whose guidance and diverse perspectives shaped my career; to the clients who shared their experiences with grace; and to the innovators and thinkers worldwide, upon whose shoulders we stand.

Contents

Foreword

As someone who has spent decades navigating the complexities of information technology, leading global teams, and driving transformation across industries, I have witnessed closely the transformative power of aligning IT investments with organizational goals. Over the past 30 years, I have had the privilege of supporting global clients across industries ranging from automotive, manufacturing, and healthcare to telecommunications and financial services.

My journey has been defined by a relentless pursuit of operational excellence and a commitment to innovation. There is an immutable truth that I have realized over these years: that the success of any initiative hinges not just on the tools we use, but on the people who wield them. Over the course of my career, I have had the privilege of leading cross-functional teams at companies like EDS, Hewlett-Packard, DXC Technology, and MV Transportation, and I have witnessed firsthand how the interplay between strategy, technology, and people can either propel an organization forward or stall its progress.

It is with this perspective that I am both honored and compelled to write this foreword for *The CIO's Guide to Enterprise FinOps*, by Vineet Sawant. This is a book that encapsulates the very principles that have guided my career. Vineet was part of my leadership team when I was the Vice President of Americas Delivery for Hewlett Packard Enterprise Services (HPE) and DXC Technology. The period of transition from HPE to DXC was an extraordinary time of change for one of the biggest and most innovative companies in the world, and took place at a stage where cloud, data, and AI were starting to be strategic drivers for our customers. The successful transformation into one of the largest IT services companies in the world was principally due to our people who embraced this change and the opportunities it offered, and took on the challenges to make it happen. This principle of human capital lies at the heart of *The CIO's*

Guide to Enterprise FinOps, a book that offers a practical framework for optimizing costs and realizing business alignment.

This book is a manifesto for CIOs. As the book elaborates, in an era where digital and AI transformation is no longer a choice but a necessity, IT leaders are tasked with a paradox: to deliver stability and efficiency while simultaneously driving innovation and agility. It provides a clear and actionable framework for resolving this through the lens of Enterprise FinOps. As someone who has faced these situations, I can attest to the challenges of this balancing act. The Run-Transform-Innovate (RTI360) model and Enterprise FinOps framework presented in this book offer a practical roadmap for CIOs to navigate the competing demands of operational resilience and strategic growth.

Whether I was overseeing the global delivery of services supporting General Motors or driving operational strategy as the President and COO at MV Transportation, I have always emphasized the importance of aligning IT spending with business outcomes. The concept that operational efficiencies can fund transformation and innovation is a principle that this book elevates to a strategic imperative. In my experience, the most successful transformations are those that begin with a rigorous and realistic examination of existing processes, technologies, and costs. They are fueled by the collective intelligence and collaboration of teams that are empowered to innovate and adapt. This is where the Enterprise FinOps framework becomes a powerful tool for CIOs and IT executives. By applying the principles of cost management, combining it with modern technology like analytics, AI, and automation, and harnessing the power of collaboration, CIOs can unlock hidden value and reinvest in the future.

I saw firsthand over the years of working with multiple clients in the Americas how technology debt, like outdated infrastructure and inefficient workflows, could stifle innovation. As pioneers of IT services such as outsourcing and transformations, our teams helped enterprises focus back on their core competencies and let them repurpose underutilized assets to free up capital for innovation. In my experience, the most effective CIOs are those who translate technical complexity into business value, using the strength of their teams to build consensus and secure buy-in from stakeholders. Technologies like AI and analytics are tools that, when used effectively, can amplify the capabilities of teams and enable organizations to achieve greater efficiency and innovation. One lesson I have learned throughout my career is that the most successful organizations are those that invest in their people as much as they invest in their technology. This book talks about the cognitive biases and cultural barriers that can hinder progress, and they provide practical strategies for overcoming these obstacles. This aligns with my own belief that the most effective leaders are those who understand the psychology of their teams and create environments where innovation can thrive.

Finally, I want to emphasize that *The CIO's Guide to Enterprise FinOps* is a call to action. The book's focus on the FinOps framework, expanding its scope to all IT expenditures, is particularly relevant in today's dynamic business environment. The book reflects the author's decades of experience, insight, and leadership in the world of IT. It presents a roadmap to not only survive but thrive in an era of relentless disruption. Technologies like AI can unlock tremendous value, but can also consume and overwhelm your budget and attention, opening up perils on other fronts. To the CIOs, CXOs, practitioners, executives, and leaders who will read this book, I encourage you to embrace its principles, apply its strategies, and lead your organizations into a future where operational excellence and innovation are complementary forces that drive sustainable success when combined with the right people and the right mindset. This book is a valuable companion on that journey, and I am confident that it will inspire readers to lead with purpose, empower their teams, and achieve outcomes that go far beyond.

Mark Collins
Former President and Chief Operating Officer, MV Transportation
Former Vice President of America's Delivery, DXC Technology & Hewlett-Packard
Former Executive at Electronic Data Systems

Preface

In today's fast-paced digital landscape, CIOs and IT leaders face an unprecedented challenge of balancing the demands of operational stability, innovation, and business alignment while navigating complex, heterogeneous IT environments. The pressure to reduce costs, eliminate technology debt, and drive transformative change has never been greater.

The CIO's Guide to Enterprise FinOps is a practical guide that lets CIOs and other IT decision-makers leverage Enterprise Financial Optimization (Enterprise FinOps) to resolve challenges faced in the modern IT landscape. It offers a transformative roadmap to turn these challenges into opportunities and offers a holistic, actionable framework to align IT spending with strategic business goals, optimize operations, reduce technology debt, and unlock sustainable innovation. It lets you consistently deliver increased business value from your IT investments while simultaneously reducing operational costs.

This book is also relevant to business leaders across the enterprise, as well as CFOs and other CXOs who are looking to partner and better align with IT to leverage technology as a driver for their business growth. With its coverage of contemporary issues like the challenges facing CIOs, technology debt reduction, and the role of modern technologies like AI, the book also serves as a practical resource for IT practitioners aspiring to leadership roles and IT executives who would like to leverage Enterprise FinOps to bring dynamic change.

When technology and people are aligned, IT teams can execute complex projects with ease. But there is still misalignment with business goals. IT functions as a cost center. Even when the two circles representing business and people are aligned, but technology is not, you get a process-centric culture. Everyone knows their business well, but execution is manual and slow.

As illustrated in Figure 0.1, Enterprise FinOps brings business, technology, and people together. When they are fully aligned, the whole is greater than the sum of the parts. It unleashes business alignment; it unlocks business value and develops a culture of continuous optimization and

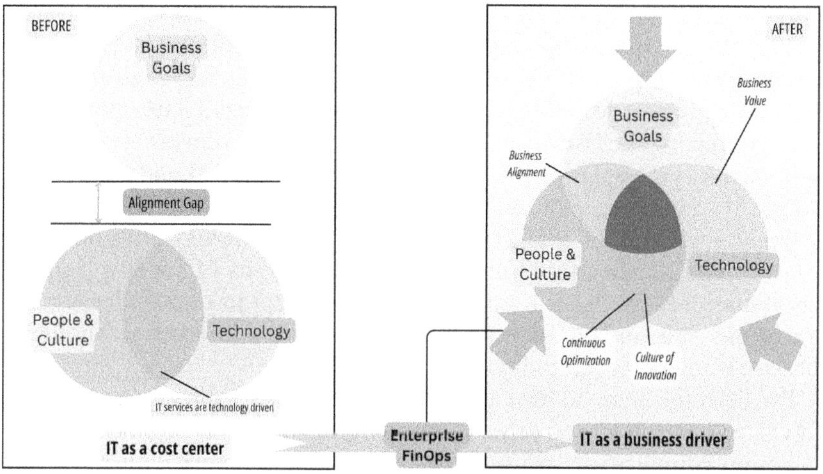

Figure 0.1 Enterprise FinOps aligns technology, business, and people and turns IT into a business driver

innovation. The resulting intersection at the center is the engine that flexes as needed, even if the individual circles spin at different speeds. It keeps driving continuous optimization and transformation forward and acts as the catalyst for innovation.

The origins of this book are from several years back, when I was in a consulting role with Hewlett Packard Enterprise (HPE) Services, helping customers on modernization and transformation initiatives. I've participated in enterprise-wide mega-digital transformation programs, seen the havoc that indiscriminate cost-cutting measures can do, designed technology-led innovations that promised to change the industry status quo, and led massive cloud transformations. The concepts in this book have been further refined through subsequent executive leadership roles in leading companies like DXC, a global leader in IT services; Rackspace, a pioneer in managed infrastructure and multi-cloud services; Nabors, a global leader in leveraging innovation for drilling optimization; and Corning, where I led enterprise-wide AIOps and FinOps initiatives. The idea of a holistic framework that addresses challenges across operations, transformations, and innovations was developed further through the opportunity of working with several customers, companies, and enterprises, and has resulted in the ideas, pathways, and roadmap outlined in this book.

While transformation and modernization were the natural solution to reducing technology debt, a few bold CIOs took on holistic digital transformations that changed not just the IT landscape, but also the way business operated. Some preferred a more phased approach or lowered costs by outsourcing maintenance for legacy systems and other services, transferring the risk to external providers. The cloud triggered a large-scale exodus from on-premises hosted systems to SaaS and IaaS platforms. But the root causes of technology debt continued to accumulate. While they were addressing the cost issue, the over-consumption dimension remained as it was. It is a similar problem that is surfacing with AI and data today, where AI, data-lake, and analytics platforms start off small but rapidly consume the entire IT budget. The problems of yesterday have not been resolved and are further multiplied by the demands of today's technology. Enterprise FinOps is a solution that works not just across legacy and operations systems, but also for AI, data, cloud, and other technologies that are being deployed today.

I've been fortunate to have the opportunity to work directly with CEOs, CTOs, COOs, CIOs, and other decision makers either as part of an executive team supporting them or a partner working closely with them and their teams to resolve their challenges. This book reflects over 30 years of hands-on work in leading, strategizing, designing, and executing solutions on how to keep moving ahead with innovation while unlocking inefficiencies and keeping operations stable.

Currently, many organizations are operating with a lack of true visibility into their IT spend. This leads to wasted resources, ambiguous prioritization, unpredictable costs, and a disconnect between IT investments and business goals. Enterprise FinOps is a strategic approach that fundamentally shifts how we manage IT spend. It reduces IT costs, drives efficiency, optimizes the IT environment, aligns IT investments with business goals, and develops a mindset of accountability and responsible technology usage.

By implementing Enterprise FinOps, you'll gain the following benefits:

- Cost optimization ensures that every dollar spent delivers maximum value and increases ROI, while unlocking costs that can be leveraged elsewhere.
- Reduced risk by eliminating operational inefficiencies and reducing technology debt.
- Greater agility by optimizing investments that are aligned with business goals to support innovation and growth.
- Improved governance through streamlined controls and consistent decision-making.

The audience for this book includes the following:

- CIOs and CDIOs leading IT organizations.
- IT executives responsible for sections of the IT portfolio, such as the VPs for Infrastructure, Cloud, or Business Systems, who would like to

drive cost optimization within their groups and better business alignment with their stakeholders.
- Business unit leaders, CMOs, CFOs, and other CXOs who are interested in partnering with IT to harness technology to unlock business value for their businesses.
- IT practitioners at all levels who would like to understand the synergistic relationship between business and technology better and leverage programs like Enterprise FinOps.

This book aims to help organizations transform their IT spend from a cost center into a strategic asset. Key themes that are explored in this book are the following:

- What are the dilemmas faced by CIOs responsible for modern heterogeneous technology landscapes, such as the challenges of balancing operational stability with business flexibility, reducing technology debt and inefficiencies, and driving innovation?
- How can IT become a driver for business growth rather than just be a provider or enabler for technology?
- How Enterprise FinOps addresses these challenges to bring about cost optimization, business alignment, and value realization from IT, and results in a mindset of responsible technology usage across the enterprise?
- How does the momentum created by Enterprise FinOps through small operational savings result in bigger exponential savings and bring about other benefits to create a strong foundation for transformations and innovations?
- Explores how AI, automation, and emerging technologies can further accelerate and optimize the IT operational landscape.

I hope you enjoy reading this book and using the techniques and roadmap shown here to launch or augment your own Enterprise FinOps program to transform your organization into a driver for business value.

Vineet Sawant
https://www.enterprisefinops.com
Visit the website for related articles on Enterprise FinOps and an extensive library of mental models for IT that you can apply in your IT scenarios.
https://www.linkedin.com/in/sawantvineet/
Houston, TX, USA, January 2026

Author Biography – Vineet Sawant

Over the past 25 years, I've navigated the ever-evolving landscape of enterprise IT, transforming from a hands-on technologist into a strategic leader who bridges the gap between innovation and operational excellence. My career has been defined by a relentless focus on solving the most pressing challenges of modern enterprises, scaling digital transformation, modernizing IT operations, and driving innovation at scale. Today, as a thought leader, adviser, and author, I'm on a mission to help organizations not only survive but thrive in an era defined by rapid technological change, rising costs, and the urgent need for sustainable growth.

My journey as an IT explorer started from working on the ground to build and maintain the technology fabric that powered some of the world's most complex enterprises. Over time, I transitioned from a hands-on engineer to a leader who could perceive the broader implications of technology on business outcomes. This shift was driven by a growing realization that technology alone isn't enough; it's how you leverage it to meet your challenges. Without alignment between IT, finance, operations, and business strategy, even the most cutting-edge solutions fail to deliver value. This insight became the foundation of my work in Enterprise FinOps. As enterprises increasingly moved to the cloud and adopted SaaS platforms, I saw firsthand how misaligned spending and poor governance could derail even the most promising initiatives. My role has been to turn these challenges into opportunities, building frameworks that empower organizations to optimize costs and gain from the investments that are being made.

At Corning, one of the world's leading innovators in materials science, as the Divisional VP for Technology Operations, the dynamics between operational stability and business flexibility were at the forefront. My team successfully implemented several transformative programs, such as bringing in operational improvements to key IT processes, laying the foundations for an AIOps platform, vendor consolidations that unlocked strategic partnerships, and a FinOps model that redefined how we aligned IT spending with business KPIs. These initiatives not only saved millions in annual costs but also set new standards for how IT can balance financial discipline with strategic growth. At Rigcloud, a pioneering platform in real-time data optimization, I spearheaded the design and deployment of next-generation cloud infrastructures that transformed our legacy system into an agile, scalable solution. At Rackspace, a global leader in managed cloud services, I led a company-wide initiative to redefine the company's application and cloud services offerings for enterprise clients.

At Hewlett-Packard Enterprise Services (HPE), I played a pivotal role in driving innovative projects for clients like Starbucks and led large-scale IT consulting and managed services initiatives for global clients. My work centered on helping enterprises modernize their IT infrastructure while aligning spending with business objectives. At DXC Technology, a global IT services leader, I contributed to a large digital initiative that redefined the business model for our client through ERP, CRM, and other transformations.

Whether you're an IT leader looking to implement an Enterprise FinOps framework, a strategist navigating the challenges of digital transformation, or an innovator seeking to future-proof your organization through innovations in AI, I'm here to help. My goal is to build a community of leaders who are not just reacting to change but shaping it together. My experiences have reinforced my belief that the most successful enterprises are those that can anticipate the future and build systems that adapt to it. As I write this book, I'm reminded of the journey that brought me here, a career spent at the intersection of technology, business, strategies, and people. It's a journey that's been defined by challenges, breakthroughs, and the unwavering belief that the right strategies can transform entire industries. I'm excited to share that journey with you and help build something that creates lasting value.

Vineet Sawant
https://www.enterprisefinops.com
Visit the website for related articles on Enterprise FinOps and an extensive library of mental models for IT that you can apply in your IT scenarios.
https://www.linkedin.com/in/sawantvineet/

Introduction

PART I: THE CHALLENGES FACING CIOS TODAY

Why Do We Need a Holistic Approach to Tackle Today's IT Challenges?

Today, the Chief Information Officer's (CIO) role is more complex and strategic than ever. CIOs balance not only technical leadership and risk management but also business acumen and strategic innovation. Today's CIOs are confronted by several conflicting paradoxes due to the multifaceted goals facing IT, complex heterogeneous environments, and a plethora of modern technology choices. There are ample opportunities to harness technology; however, accumulated constraints often hold them back from realizing the true value of technology in a timely manner.

CIOs have adopted several methodologies and frameworks over the years, such as ITIL/ITSM, Business Scorecard Framework, COBIT, and SEI-CMM for IT that undertook to resolve inefficiencies and build business alignment. There are still existing gaps to be addressed. Part I of this book defines the interconnected challenges that CIOs face and introduces how Enterprise Financial Optimization (Enterprise FinOps) can help them unlock operational savings and bootstrap transformations and innovations.

Chapter 1: The CIO's Dilemma

Modern IT landscapes are defined by a complex and heterogeneous mix of the old and the new. CIOs must balance operational stability with business flexibility and maintain a resilient workforce and operating structure that supports both objectives. There is constant change driven by the adoption of new technologies, increasing cost pressures, and changing business objectives. IT strives to transform from being viewed

DOI: 10.4324/9781003682196-1

as cost centers for the enterprise to becoming business value drivers. This chapter addresses how these and other inherent tensions are the heart of the "CIO's dilemma."

The chapter explores the evolution of the modern CIO, from operations leaders to today's business enablers. It proposes a foundational Run-Transform-Innovate (RTI360) model where "Run" lets IT operate and maintain services across the enterprise, "Transform" reduces technology debt through modernization, and "Innovate" lets IT create value. The chapter provides a framework for systematically resolving operational inefficiencies that limit our ability to deliver true business value.

It explores the emergence of Enterprise FinOps as a mindset and practical methodology that can be applied to your entire IT portfolio to drive cost optimization and business alignment. While a primary goal is to reduce costs and optimize IT operations, Enterprise FinOps connects IT investments to tangible business outcomes. Today, the promise of artificial intelligence, the risks posed by inadequate cybersecurity, and the benefits of digital transformation have moved them from being discretionary investments to strategic imperatives. These engines are driving business competitiveness across industries. Embracing Enterprise FinOps is a necessity today for organizations seeking to thrive in today's dynamic digital environment.

PART II: ENTERPRISE FINOPS PROVIDES A FRAMEWORK FOR RESOLVING THE CIO'S DILEMMAS

How Does Enterprise FinOps Resolve the Challenges?

The next three chapters dive deeper into how Enterprise FinOps can address the challenges outlined in Part I. It describes the philosophy behind Enterprise FinOps and lays out a foundational framework, and then looks at technology debt reduction, a key priority that underlies any transformation efforts. Finally, we look at how Enterprise FinOps can be a catalyst to bootstrap transformation and innovation efforts.

Chapter 2: Enterprise FinOps

Enterprise FinOps lets CIOs and IT decision makers align their IT spend expenses with their business objectives. It lets you see the full picture across every expense, team, and decision, and its potential impact. It aligns them all toward the same goal of a business that's agile, efficient, and future-ready. The chapter introduces a structured framework for Enterprise FinOps and outlines the core pillars. The "Principles" pillar outlines the philosophy behind Enterprise FinOps. This chapter defines the role that Enterprise FinOps plays in augmenting traditional IT financial management and budgeting. It analyzes typical cost factors and drivers for IT spend areas across infrastructure, applications, software, and services, and shows how Enterprise FinOps can optimize this spend. It proposes ways to integrate cost optimization into the everyday fabric of IT governance. The chapter looks at how FinOps lets CIOs not just save money but also drive innovation, sustainability, and alignment with business goals. The chapter also comments on industry frameworks that have evolved from the cloud.

Chapter 3: Technology Debt Reduction

Technology debt refers to the accumulated technical inefficiencies and out dated systems that organizations continue to use due to their critical role in business operations. This chapter explores the factors that lead to the accumulation of technology debt and its impact. It dives into the risks of under-investing in modernization and the gradual buildup of technology debt. Debt differs in different areas of IT, such as software and application development, infrastructure, and IT services. The chapter debunks the myth that cloud and Software as a Service (SaaS) offerings are immune to tech debt. It then details ways to mitigate tech debt, starting with application rationalization that provides the assessment that underlies digital transformation and looks at the "7R"s of legacy modernization for mitigating tech debt. While zero tech debt is unrealistic, Enterprise FinOps offers a way to maintain continuous tech debt management, keeping it down to manageable levels. The chapter then proposes a single Key Performance Indicator (KPI) that can let you measure tech debt to establish a baseline and guide future transformation efforts.

Chapter 4: Bootstrapping Transformations and Innovations

The chapter shows how Enterprise FinOps acts as a catalyst for change and illustrates how Run savings from Enterprise FinOps can bootstrap efforts across Transform and Innovate. It describes how operational inefficiencies are like potential energy waiting to be converted into dynamic motion. Enterprise FinOps develops momentum through carefully prioritized transformation and innovation initiatives. The chapter explores the Return on Investment (ROI) of transformations and the role of innovations in achieving long-term goals. It proposes a practical matrix for prioritizing innovation initiatives. The chapter discusses the need to balance short-term needs with long-term investments. It explores the traps of quick-fix, reactive decisions that so often happen in IT. The chapter compares the pros and cons of newer organizational structures often seen in IT teams, such as flat hierarchies, outsourcing, bimodal teams, and product-led teams, and describes how Enterprise FinOps can drive technology-led optimization regardless of which hierarchy an IT organization has adopted. It explores the risks inherent in digital transformations and proposes mitigation actions that can be applied. It investigates the importance of management of change to enable successful transformations. It concludes with how Enterprise FinOps provides a solid foundation for digital transformation initiatives. Enterprise FinOps brings visibility and business alignment that determine what innovation initiatives matter the most to the business, and provides a solid rationale for the business case and prioritization of transformation projects.

PART III: HOW CAN YOU IMPLEMENT ENTERPRISE FINOPS?

What Actions Are Needed to Implement and Sustain Enterprise FinOps?

Previous chapters outlined the philosophy and rationale behind Enterprise FinOps and introduced a robust framework that works across your entire IT portfolio. This part outlines a practical methodology and roadmap that you can customize as needed for your own Enterprise FinOps implementation. It describes the overall steps for implementing Enterprise FinOps through a phased approach. Cost optimization, business alignment, and technical levers are elaborated in subsequent chapters. The chapter on monitoring and measurements describes how you can arrive at Enterprise FinOps KPIs and metrics that are aligned with your IT strategy and business goals. Organizations often struggle with too many KPIs that lead to chaos and reporting inefficiencies. It shows how to derive a single KPI that represents the value provided by Enterprise FinOps. The chapter on mental models lets you create a culture of accountability and describes a few models that can play a big role in decision-making, prioritization, and lets you avoid common biases in IT decision-making.

Chapter 5: Implementing Enterprise FinOps

Previous chapters outlined the philosophy behind Enterprise FinOps and introduced a comprehensive framework. This chapter provides a practical and structured methodology for implementing it in your organization.

It brings together the various strategies we have discussed so far and establishes a clear roadmap for implementing Enterprise FinOps. The chapter emphasizes a phased approach for implementing the framework. It describes key activities that can help you build an Enterprise FinOps strategy that is aligned with your overall IT strategy and business goals. It then describes a critical activity that launches your implementation, the Enterprise FinOps assessment. The chapter shows how you can prioritize your assessment findings to execute optimization activities. It then dives into how you can expand your Enterprise FinOps to cover the entire IT organization and continue on your journey toward continuous cost optimization and business alignment. Finally, it describes strategies for mitigating potential risks and how to build a continuous FinOps culture.

Chapter 6: Cost Optimization Levers

This chapter outlines strategies for cost optimization. It illustrates through an energy optimization analogy how cost optimization is a combination of cutting costs as well as optimizing consumption to exactly what you need, and avoiding waste. It expands the analogy to typical scenarios seen in a corporate environment. The chapter details techniques in vendor management and procurement for various types of IT assets, including hardware, software, cloud and SaaS, and IT outsourced services. These strategies also provide insights into how to reduce lock-in and leverage benchmarking for insight-driven procurement. Next, the chapter explores consumption patterns for IT assets and how user behavior and needs can lead to a personalized experience and lead to further opportunities for optimizing consumption patterns and costs. The chapter explores strategies like software harvesting and product licensing that can reduce IT spend with minimal technology changes and result in quick wins for your Enterprise FinOps implementation. It then outlines capital allocation strategies, starting with a detailed look at Capex vs. Opex, and the role of Enterprise FinOps in striking a balance. Finally, the chapter dives into strategies for reducing Shadow IT.

Chapter 7: Technical Levers for Enterprise FinOps

This chapter outlines technical levers used in Enterprise FinOps in a way that even business or non-technical executives can relate to. Most of the cost optimization strategies mentioned in the prior chapter, and the Enterprise Architecture (EA) levers in this chapter, are process and workflow-driven. In contrast, technical levers for cost optimization are mostly iterative activities that need technical expertise. The chapter first describes Enterprise Architecture and its role in Enterprise FinOps in optimizing design, engineering, and governance. EA levers can reduce IT waste before anything is spent on development or licensing. EA techniques like Business Capability Mapping can play a significant role in ensuring business alignment of IT initiatives. The chapter then looks at the most impactful technical levers used in Enterprise FinOps, across both on-premises infrastructure as well as public cloud and SaaS implementations. It provides a short but concise explanation of techniques like workload and rate optimization, service optimization, performance tuning, and rightsizing. These techniques are mainly used in the "Optimize phase" by operations and engineering teams. It also looks at unique models in the public cloud space, such as spot instances and capacity exchange programs. There are several tools and platforms in the market that can be used to automate these levers.

Chapter 8: Measuring and Monitoring Success

This chapter discusses KPIs for measuring and monitoring Enterprise FinOps. It goes through key metrics like Return on Investment (ROI) that align IT investments with business goals. It then discusses various methods to structure a business value framework. The chapter looks at typical metrics and KPIs relevant at the CIO level. Enterprise FinOps KPIs are derived from this. The chapter proposes a single KPI, "IT Value Delivered," that can be used to measure the value and effectiveness of your Enterprise FinOps program. The chapter explores the power of analytics, transparent communication, and trust development to enable better decision-making. Various analytics techniques are highlighted, each building a layer that complements other techniques to provide visibility and insights into your IT spend data. The chapter talks about how analytics can enable financial modeling for future scenarios, including economic fluctuations. This chapter emphasizes that successful FinOps is fundamentally about building trust and transparency through consistent and reliable information. Regular, objective reporting fosters a sense of confidence within your organization. Building strong relationships alongside robust reporting is presented as the key to unlocking the full potential of Enterprise FinOps. It builds resilience and a collaborative, trusted partnership with business stakeholders.

Chapter 9: Mental Models for Enterprise FinOps

The chapter explores the significance of mental models for complex IT programs and reflects on how they offer us a way to shape our decision-making in the context of the Run-Transform-Innovate RTI 360 model introduced in Chapter 1. Enterprise FinOps is a mindset shift. Mental models serve as essential building blocks for leaders who want to create a culture of unbiased but informed decision-making, continuous improvement, and accountability. The chapter also discusses cognitive biases. Decisions regarding IT spending are often made quickly, with limited data points. Understanding and overcoming biases can lead to better decision-making on IT spend. As an example, one of the models, the Sunk Cost fallacy, explains how people might continue to invest in solutions due to emotional or financial investment in the past. The chapter illustrates how mental models and the visibility offered by Enterprise FinOps can help you recognize and avoid biases. This chapter offers only a small subset of mental models. They have been curated and selected based on their contextual relevance to complex IT initiatives and Enterprise FinOps. I highly recommend that all practitioners involved in your company's Enterprise FinOps continue to enhance and add to this list based on your unique context and environment.

PART IV: THE EVOLUTION OF ENTERPRISE FINOPS

This part looks at the next steps in the evolution of Enterprise FinOps. Leveraging technologies like AI and automation can take you further up the maturity scale and accelerate the benefits from Enterprise FinOps. Enterprise FinOps becomes a silent but powerful engine ensuring continuous cost optimization and business alignment.

Chapter 10: The Future of Enterprise FinOps

This chapter provides an overview of the future of Enterprise FinOps and the use of modern technologies in supporting its continued evolution and added value. It explores traditional versus modern approaches for IT and the redefined role of FinOps as an essential IT strategy. The chapter explores how key Enterprise FinOps processes such as budgeting and forecasting can be augmented by the use of AI/ML technology. It discusses how AI tools and techniques like GenAI, chatbots, agentic AI, and AIOps can be used to amplify and augment cost optimization and operational efficiency. The chapter looks at automation techniques and how they can accelerate Enterprise FinOps processes by enforcing policy-as-code or enabling a continuous optimization environment. Finally, the chapter looks at emerging technologies like blockchain, AR/VR, and digital twins, and the role they can play in the future of Enterprise FinOps. The chapter also provides a realistic view of what technologies are feasible today and what still needs to be developed to create the cost, efficiency, and business alignment-savvy and intelligent Enterprise FinOps nervous system of the modern enterprise.

SUPPLEMENTARY MATERIAL

This part provides additional information that complements your Enterprise FinOps journey. The FinOps framework gives you a ready framework that originated in the cloud and can now be adapted to other parts of the IT portfolio.

Appendix 1: The FinOps Foundation Framework

The chapter provides a concise primer on the FinOps framework provided by the FinOps Foundation. This is a practical framework that can be leveraged to implement Enterprise FinOps in your organization. This is an industry framework that originated from guidelines and practices to optimize public cloud spending. Since then, the scope has expanded to other areas of IT spend, including SaaS, AI, and datacenters. This framework encompasses the principles of Enterprise FinOps elaborated earlier in this book. The FinOps Foundation provides detailed guidance on the phases, domains, and activities that make up this framework. It also offers structured training and certification paths so that users involved in an organization's effort can become familiar with the concepts and activities that are used to implement, monitor, and govern this initiative.

Part I

The Challenges Facing CIOs Today

Why Do We Need a Holistic Approach to Tackle Today's IT Challenges?

Today, the CIO role is more complex and strategic than ever. CIOs balance not only technical leadership and risk management, but also business acumen and strategic innovation. Today's CIOs are confronted by several conflicting paradoxes due to the multifaceted goals facing IT, complex heterogeneous environments, and a plethora of modern technology choices. There are ample opportunities to harness technology; however, accumulated constraints often hold them back from realizing the true value of technology in a timely manner.

CIOs have adopted several methodologies and frameworks over the years, such as ITIL/ITSM, Business Scorecard Framework, COBIT, and SEI-CMM for IT that undertook to resolve inefficiencies and build business alignment. There are still existing gaps to be addressed. Part I of this book defines the interconnected challenges that CIOs face and introduces how enterprise financial optimization (Enterprise FinOps) can help them unlock operational savings and bootstrap transformations and innovations.

DOI: 10.4324/9781003682196-2

Chapter 1

The CIO's Dilemma

DOI: 10.4324/9781003682196-3

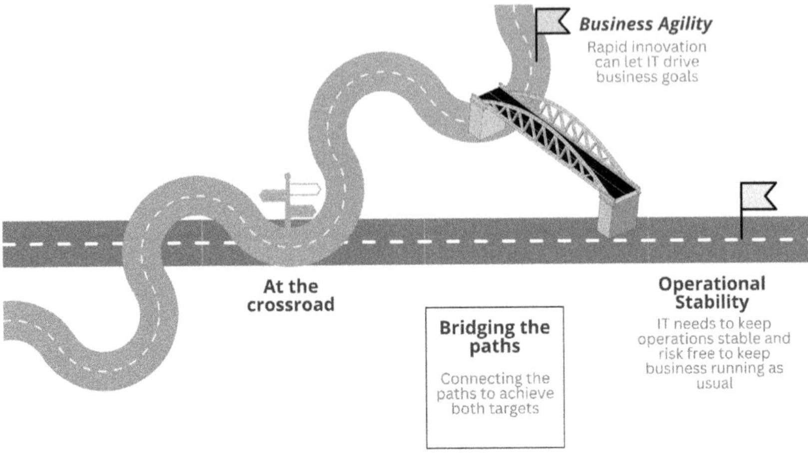

Figure 1.1 CIOs are at the crossroads of operational stability and business agility

1.1 The CIO's Dilemma

Chief Information Officers (CIOs) are at a critical junction. As shown in Figure 1.1, on one hand, there's a well-trodden and proven path that meets operational goals and keeps the business running smoothly. On the other hand, there's a path where pursuing innovation can make you the heroes of the boardroom, driving business goals at an unprecedented pace. Often, the two destinations seem conflicting. Your challenge is to make these journeys coincide, weaving technology into the fabric of business goals and sparking innovation while also keeping systems lean and spinning smoothly. You navigate a complex path bridging IT and business to maintain efficient and scalable Information Technology (IT) operations across the entire enterprise. At the same time, you are driving digital transformation and modernization initiatives and creating a competitive advantage through innovation. The *CIO's Dilemma* is what you face every single day, a set of often contradictory challenges, decisions, and paradoxes that span across IT strategy, delivery, technology, people, and organizational structures.

CIOs have multiple priorities on their minds and face conflicting choices, as shown in Figure 1.2. You may be cutting costs, launching a new AI or data platform, or dealing with a major upgrade to your Enterprise Resource Planning (ERP) system that has a risk of business disruption.

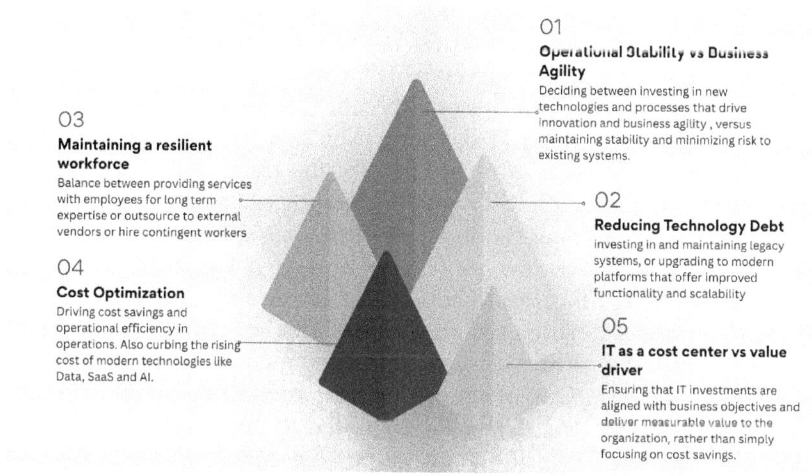

Figure 1.2 The CIO's dilemmas are often conflicting choices that they must make and decision points that determine the way ahead

While you may have cloud costs under control, the AI private "ChatGPT" equivalent chatbot that you launched recently is exponentially becoming popular across the company, but so are its costs. It's an everyday task to motivate the workforce and keep the data center from collapsing under its own weight. Signing off on the cloud migration that your Customer Resource Management (CRM) team has been pushing for could save millions, but also risks breaking sensitive data integrations and risking security breaches. It's up to you to convince the rest of the C-suite that the new SaaS platform isn't just a nice-to-have but a must-have for supply chain resilience. You are constantly responding to board and executive expectations around cybersecurity, AI adoption, and meeting customer, regulator, and partner demands to keep pace with competitive and technological shifts.

The pressure is also internal. You have a great team. Your engineers want to build the future. Your procurement team wants to negotiate better deals. Your operations leaders want to invest in advanced monitoring and self-healing systems. But none of them sees the full picture. You do.

Often, CIOs fail not because they lack vision, but because they try to do too much. They chase promising technology trends, only to find their teams pursuing endless experimentation without delivering any business outcomes. They slash budgets and scramble to contain the operational impact. They prioritize speed over sustainability and end up with a fractured IT organization, a combination of short-term wins that faded away, and a legacy of missed opportunities. The fix starts with a simple question on what's holding you back. Maybe it's the way you measure success. Maybe it's the silos you can't seem to break. Maybe it's the fact that your business stakeholders think IT costs are a black box. But you don't need to fix everything at once. You need to fix the thing that's holding you down the most. You're the CIO who bridges the crossroads and redefines the paths. You're holding the keys that can accelerate the future of the business.

In the book *Organizational Culture and Leadership* (Schein & Schein, 2010), the authors describe the engineering mindset that IT traditionally has and contrast it with an executive subculture focused on financial health and business growth. One of the CIO's roles is to bridge these two subcultures successfully. Martha Heller explored the complexities facing IT leaders in the book *The CIO Paradox: Battling the Contradictions of IT Leadership* (Heller, 2012). While the term "the CIO's dilemma" may have appeared in articles before this, this book formalized the unique challenges CIOs face in balancing business leadership with technological stewardship. In *Strategic Information Technology* (Langer & Yorks, 2010), Arthur Langer and Lyle Yorks further elaborated on the challenges and dilemmas facing CIOs in the 2010s, with cloud technologies disrupting traditional on-premises models and accelerating the need for modernization.

The modern CIO must juggle multiple streams without compromising risk. Let's consider the key dimensions of strategy, delivery, and people. Companies led by agile CIOs create a culture where technology fuels competitive advantage. The best CIOs balance the books and the blueprints. Armed with their own Rosetta Stone, they have decoded the secret to translating technology into business outcomes. They set clear priorities and measure impact with real numbers that perfectly align with business and IT strategy. The payoff is a resilient organization that both explores and exploits. It adapts quickly, keeps customers delighted, and stays ahead of rivals while keeping ongoing business humming smoothly. The CIO's dilemmas are not traps but choices that let you lead the organization into tomorrow.

1.1.1 Operational Focus vs Business Flexibility

A defining dilemma for today's CIO is balancing operational rigor with business flexibility, as illustrated in Figure 1.3. You need to deliver IT services efficiently, make timely modernizations, and introduce innovations that add value to the business. Your peers in the executive leadership and other business unit leaders expect IT to drive business growth through

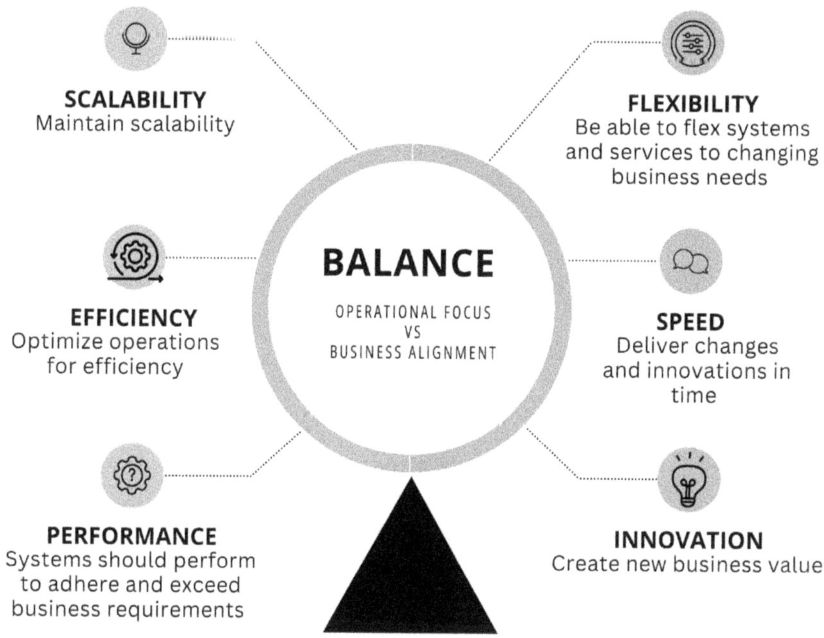

Figure 1.3 Operational focus vs. business flexibility is a defining dilemma for CIOs

innovation. Cost reduction is always a driver. IT can streamline its own costs and use technology to reduce enterprise-wide expenses by streamlining production, inventory, and supply chain operations, and automating business and manufacturing processes. Most business leaders believe strongly that IT can truly drive competitive advantage. The optimal use of technology can let the business respond faster to market changes and improve customer experience by delivering personalized services and engagement.

But IT is often considered a cost center. You have a few opportunities to generate revenue directly. Technology debt and rising operational costs limit the ability and appetite to fund expansive transformations and innovations. Harnessing the value of data and information is often a key priority. Company boards and investors are also pushing for companies to remain competitive and profitable through innovations. At its very heart, this dilemma manifests as a budget allocation challenge: how to balance spending across Run (maintaining and operating existing systems), Transform (modernizing platforms and processes), and Innovate (investing in new capabilities that create future value). A large part of traditional IT budgets goes in maintaining and upgrading existing infrastructure, applications, and services. However, just maintaining the status quo does little toward advancing business goals of growth, improved customer experiences, and rapid changes. CIOs need to prioritize investments that lead to transformation and innovation. IT budgets are always limited, typically being no more than 3% to 10% of the overall enterprise revenue. This leads to difficult decisions on where to apply scarce resources, people, and money. CIOs must balance these competing priorities to remain relevant and succeed in today's fast-paced environment.

1.1.2 Delivering to Business Expectations

While innovation is exciting, business leaders expect CIOs to maintain business continuity as a top priority. I've seen firsthand how outdated systems can grind operations to a halt. How often have you seen a factory floor go from a swirl of humming machines to total silence because a single server crashed due to a rushed update the previous night? Downtime is a revenue leak that results in missed deadlines and frustrated customers. Business leaders don't want to hear about "technical challenges." They want solutions that cut downtime, reduce manual interventions, and replace guesswork with predictive models. The old way of doing things, with patchworks, siloed data, and paper trails, has a shelf life. It's time to replace it with modular and flexible platforms that integrate data across the enterprise into a single pane of glass.

Another critical business expectation is supply chain resilience. Supply chains are a minefield of risks. Disruptions cause stockouts, overstocking, and delays, leading to customer dissatisfaction and lost revenue from production delays. A storm in Southeast Asia, a geopolitical snarl, or a supplier's server outage can ripple through your inventory like a stone skipping across a pond. Real-time visibility proves essential, supported by an AI-powered inventory optimization program to reduce overstocking. AI and ML can predict delays before they happen. IoT sensors can transmit locations and machine performance data. Place them on warehouse shelves to track inventory; embed them inside pumps, tanks, and motors. Use predictive algorithms to analyze supplier performance. Analytics in centralized dashboards can show inventory levels across continents. Reducing overstocking and increasing inventory turn can also have a positive impact on the company's cash flow.

Cybersecurity is a relentless and continuous war against hackers who can compromise your systems and sensitive data. Ransomware doesn't care, and in fact would prefer that your systems are secure by last year's standards so that they can slip in new exploits. Zero-trust architecture is like a fortress. Lock down Information Technology (IT)/Operational

Technology (OT) networks by treating every device like an intruder until proven otherwise. Real-time threat detection, automated response protocols, and strict access controls are the difference between a ten-minute incident and a ten-day disaster.

Modernization of legacy systems not only reduces downtime but also increases business agility through modular and cloud-based systems that offer scalability and real-time data integration. Businesses can respond quickly to changing requirements, whether a new product line, a new territory, or a sudden influx of orders. Working with modular and cloud-based systems, they can reshape workflows, ramp up production lines, or even commission entirely new factories. It also eliminates the need for costly on-premises infrastructure. Modular solutions let companies implement new features and revise functionality incrementally, reducing the risk and cost associated with a complete overhaul of existing systems.

Innovation from IT is a powerful business enabler and essential for long-term value creation. Your systems and sensors produce vast amounts of data every second. Historical records and production logs contain a wealth of information. AI and ML can analyze this data to identify patterns, predict equipment failures, and optimize production schedules. Real-time integration and edge-level AI can detect anomalies and schedule maintenance before failures occur. Digital twins provide visibility into the production workflow. You can simulate changes and estimate the impact before they are actually implemented. It results in reduced downtime and maintenance costs and faster adaptability. Challenges of high upfront costs, user adoption, and upskilling can be tackled through a strategic approach to innovation that aligns IT with business objectives.

1.1.3 Exponential Costs of Modern IT

AI and data are driving a monumental increase in IT spending. Most companies are turning to the cloud to fuel their AI initiatives. AI usage ranges from simple use cases like private LLMs for secure chatbots to fully featured platforms that allow users to upload data, run algorithms, and create custom applications to derive their own insights. This is causing unprecedented pressure on IT budgets that were already groaning from the rising costs of maintaining legacy systems. What started as pilots and experiments is now in full-fledged production, causing significant strain as the amount of data processing, storage, model training, and usage grows. It is a similar story with data lakes and data marts in the cloud. As the amount of data being transferred to the cloud grows, the cost of maintaining data lakes and analytical engines is also growing. AI, cloud services, and investments in data center infrastructure are driving increased IT spending in 2026. Various groups publish detailed reports on the state of IT spending.

CIOs need to control and curb the costs of modern technologies before they take over their budgets. Spiceworks recently published its 2026 State of IT report (Aberdeen, n.d.). BCG released its IT Spending Pulse report in late 2025 (BCG, n.d.) .

1.1.4 Explore or Exploit

Brian Christian and Tom Griffiths elaborated the "Exploit/Explore" paradigm in their book *Algorithms to Live By* (Brian Christian, 2016). The authors comment that exploring gives the ability to seek opportunities such as revenue growth, margin improvement, and time to market that can be of exponential value, but never exploiting will deny you the fruits of a successful exploration. In the context of IT, with technology changing so rapidly, technology vendors are churning a seemingly limitless onslaught of new releases, upgrades, and versions, month after month. If organizations are too biased toward exploitation mainly, rising technology debt can mire teams in maintaining older and legacy systems. CIOs can strike a balance between the two by creating an environment where innovation is encouraged, but safeguarded through sandboxes, Center of Excellence-type organizational models, carefully designed pilots, and iterative and agile methodologies. Exploitation of your established systems is important, as constant change is detrimental to user adoption and productivity. Users and entities such as business units need time to get adjusted to changes in processes and systems and maximize their productive potential. While user adoption, operational stability and continuity, and predictable results follow exploitation, exploration is critical for creating new business value. It can result in breakthroughs that improve or optimize processes and make tedious work easier for users. It can drive business growth, improve competitiveness, and create or increase revenue streams.

Adopting a product management mindset for IT services and platforms can let CIOs blend exploration with exploitation. Encourage feature development and technology exploration through concepts such as a Minimum Viable Product (MVP) and iterative releases. Strong adherence to a clear understanding of business outcomes and prioritization based on user requests ensures that unnecessary exploration is delayed or discouraged. An iterative roadmap with clearly established timeframes for releases lets you exploit the core base while keeping exploration ongoing for new features.

1.1.5 Maintaining a Resilient Workforce

CIOs have several choices, as shown in Figure 1.4, when it comes to maintaining a resilient workforce. Often, CIOs must adopt a hybrid approach

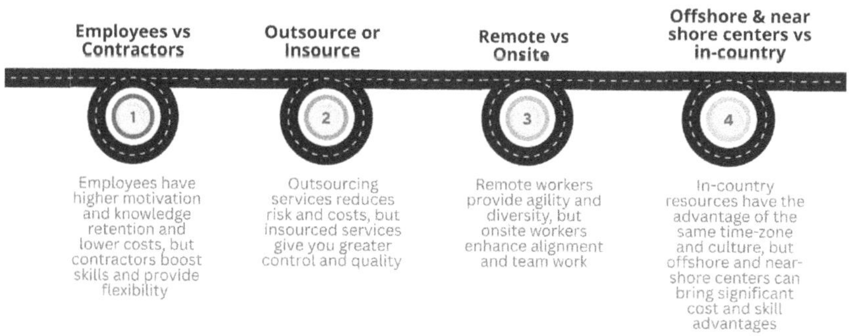

Figure 1.4 Maintaining a resilient workforce

to balance these models into one cohesive team that works together, in perfect alignment with the CIOs' IT and the company's business strategy.

1.1.5.1 Employees vs Contractors

There are multiple dilemmas embedded in maintaining a resilient and productive workforce. One is the balance you drive between employees and contingent workers in your team. Employees have higher motivation and knowledge retention, while contractors give you flexibility to ramp your workforce up or down as needed, and also boost skills quickly in hard-to-find talent areas. Organizations need to train their staff for new skills or hire employees who already have these abilities when they implement new technology platforms. You can acquire new skills through contingent resources. Staffing consolidators let you onboard short-term and consulting resources quickly. Organizations can use freelancers, contractors, and temporary workers to handle unexpected project needs without making permanent hiring commitments.

Contingent resources are typically more expensive than employees, even when the total cost to the company, including benefits and training, is factored in. Further, there is more risk of a contractor leaving suddenly midway through a critical project. Organizations that use contingent workers need to address any issues that affect their ability to maintain work quality consistency and achieve proper performance standards. The lack of access to company knowledge and cultural understanding could be an unintended impact that limits contingent workers in their work performance. Investing in employee skills and development provides long-term flexibility and scalability. Organizations that demonstrate their commitment to employee development create higher motivation and employee engagement, and enable them to make decisions that align with company objectives.

The CIO can create an agile workforce that is capable of adapting quickly to changing business conditions by blending a contingent workforce with an active program to upskill employees. To ensure knowledge retention, transition knowledge and work from contingent workers to employees in a timely manner. Strong governance policies should be established to ensure your IT leaders are clear when to use employees vs. contractors. A typical policy would be to ensure contractors are engaged only for a limited period, and renewals trigger off exception approvals. I've seen many organizations where it's not uncommon to see contractors who have been working in the same team for years on end, even when the original project or initiative was completed successfully.

1.1.5.2 Insourcing vs. Outsourcing

CIOs face a constant challenge to determine which IT services should remain internal versus being outsourced to external providers. With vendor management as part of your responsibilities, this is an area where you are constantly striving for the right balance. You can develop a core competency map that aligns with your IT strategy and business targets. Organizations often choose to outsource their non-core operations, including help desk support and infrastructure management. But models have matured where even vital IT operations like application development and maintenance can be successfully outsourced through managed services.

Insourcing gives you better control, security, and innovation, but outsourcing gives you lower costs, fast scaling of talent, and access to specialized skills. CIOs must evaluate organizational needs against data loss risks, security threats, and operational disruptions when conducting their assessment.

Organizations can access external expertise through outsourcing to stay innovative, but they need to trust their third-party service providers to fulfill their commitments. Organizations need to evaluate their specific requirements and danger levels and business objectives to decide between internal IT service delivery and external service acquisition. CIOs need to participate in strategic discussions about service delivery methods by evaluating the advantages and disadvantages of both models, assessing factors like expenses, service quality, security, scalability, and the flexibility to innovate quickly.

1.1.5.3 Remote vs Onsite

The COVID pandemic highlighted the tug-of-war between flexibility and focus. It forced the trade-off between the freedom of remote work and the advantages of people working face-to-face together in the office. Enterprises were pleasantly surprised when remote teams came together during the pandemic and maintained productivity levels to the same level as before. When your team can work from a mountain cabin or an apartment in the Bahamas, you're saving on office space today, and also building a resilient workforce that can outlast a hurricane, a pandemic, or a sudden shift in market demand. You have access to a global workforce, with access to talent whether on the East Coast of the United States, or in France or Turkey. But this is a calculated gamble. Collaboration tools can make distance a non-issue, but on-site face-to-face work is the glue that holds many IT teams together. Help or advice is just a desk away. Team productivity is enhanced when they norm and storm constantly in the same environment. Innovations spark in the middle of a whiteboard session, where a half-baked idea gets refined over a coffee or a lunch break.

While many companies have mandated "back to office" policies, many companies post-pandemic are trying out versions where people work out of the office two or three days a week. Your choice has to match your goals for a resilient workforce. If you're a startup or in the midst of a massive transformation that needs close coordination between the business and IT, maybe the chaos and spontaneous creativity of on-site collaboration is your fuel. If you have a decentralized team with people in various global locations, a hybrid approach could be a good solution. You are building a workforce that can pivot, adapt, and keep going no matter where they are.

1.1.5.4 Offshore or Nearshore vs Onshore

One of my responsibilities in many prior roles has been to create a hybrid IT workforce that balances the advantages of remote IT centers with nearshore and onshore locations. Onshore is the obvious choice as there are no time zone gaps or language barriers, and similar cultural norms. But that same team could cost 30% or more than a nearshore group, and access to talent is limited. And if your talent pool is spread thin, scaling becomes a nightmare. For IT teams in the USA, nearshore locations such as Mexico, Canada, Costa Rica, or Brazil are like the "Goldilocks" of talent management. For European companies, nearshore locations include countries like Egypt, Hungary, and Poland. Nearshore is close enough to avoid the chaos and disconnectedness of offshore, but also offers a lower cost basis for IT talent. I recently onboarded a nearshore IT center in Mexico for operations in the US. Time zones were a two-hour difference. But getting the right leadership talent and ensuring they adopted our remote work policy of at least three days in the office was still a challenge. Offshore locations such as India, the Philippines, Malaysia, or Eastern Europe represent a double-edged sword. You get access to expert talent and substantial cost savings. You can introduce models like multiple shifts offering 24×7×365 support or follow-the-sun continuous development where teams in the USA wind down for the day, and teams offshore pick up the flow. But you're also dealing with a cultural gap and the need to ensure your on-site and offshore teams work seamlessly together. Language and timing are rarely the barrier. An integrated global development and support methodology should be developed where teams follow consistent delivery processes, no matter where in the world they are.

Resilience is diversifying your ability and capability. I've seen companies that split their work with nearshore for mission-critical tasks where communication and speed matter and offshore for scalable projects that don't need constant oversight. You don't outsource; rather, you integrate. You build bridges between teams across rigid, hierarchical systems and bind together teams from different locations and values. The trade-off is between cost and culture. Your choice has to match your goals.

1.1.6 Bimodal IT

In many IT teams, teams that manage datacenters and virtualized servers, operational services, and on-premises hosted enterprise systems operate traditionally. Their focus is on stable operations and involves careful planning, strict governance, and change management processes, and methodical risk mitigation. This mode may be different from teams that handle cloud infrastructure, cloud-native development, and SaaS platforms. Here, rapid experimentation, flexibility, and risk-taking take precedence. Depicted in Figure 1.5, this situation is often referred to as bimodal IT, where teams consciously or subconsciously run in both these two modes in the same organization.

These methods can introduce conflict between teams. The bimodal model also creates issues for organizational governance and staff accountability, especially when applications span across both traditional and cloud infrastructure. Both models are necessary in today's complex and rapidly changing environment, but the CIO needs to create a system that unites these methods seamlessly. A model that is often adopted is to leverage a fast, flexible mode when developing and onboarding applications on the cloud and then transition it to a cloud operations team, which works in a more traditional mode, or uses DevOps to combine operations in an agile mode.

In the article "Juggling the Paradoxes – Governance Mechanisms in Bimodal IT Organizations" (Jöhnk et al., Oesterle, Winkler, & Nørbjerg, 2019), the authors mention that effective governance mechanisms are necessary to resolve this paradox.

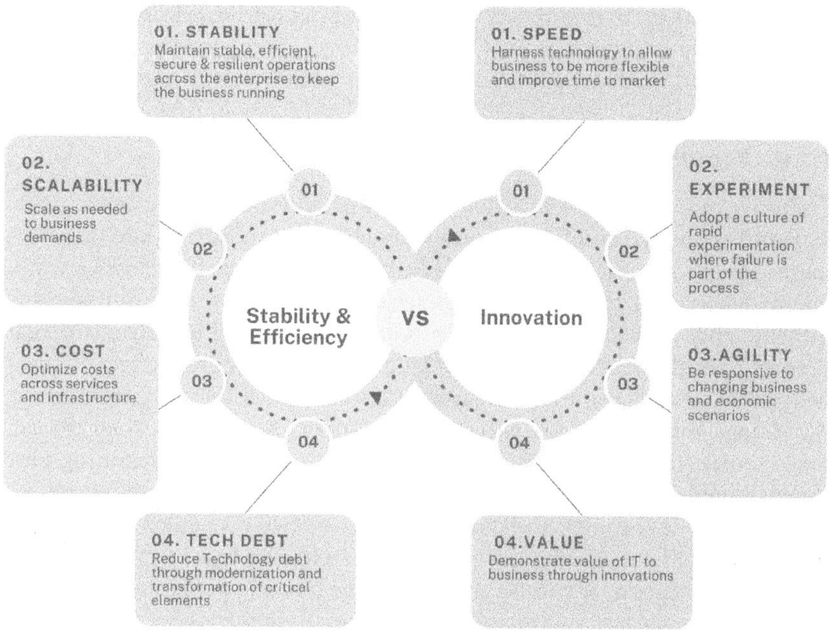

Figure 1.5 Differing priorities driving bimodal teams

1.1.7 Cost Center vs Value Driver

For years, IT has been cleaning up messes, not building the future. Naveen Zutshi's *Forbes* article (Zutshi, 2025) hit the nail on the head. CIOs are stuck in a loop where budgeting systems treat IT like a fixed expense. You're fighting for a seat at the table where the real decisions are made. CIOs spend months trimming fat, only to realize the real problem was the lack of alignment with business goals. They focused on reducing costs by 15%, but innovation output dropped by 40%. When success is measured by how much you're saving, it's easy to forget that you're here to drive growth. This results in a narrowed focus on operational efficiency, often at the expense of strategic initiatives that could have a greater impact on business outcomes. But the business is starting to listen. Technology isn't simply a tool anymore. It's the engine of competition. Stop talking about IT as a function and start treating it as a lever. When you align your budget with business outcomes, you stop being the cost center and become the catalyst. The question isn't whether you can afford to innovate. It's whether you can afford not to. You're managing the future, but the future isn't waiting.

But the tide is turning. Organizations are starting to see IT as a strategic asset. Companies that embrace AI, IoT, and data-driven decision-making are outpacing competitors. CIOs can position themselves as key drivers of value creation, driving innovation and growth for their organizations.

1.1.8 *Tackling These Dilemmas*

There are many more dilemmas and new ones coming up as business, political, and economic conditions constantly change. Innovation and transformation projects need a considerable upfront investment in technology and talent. Measuring the Return on Investment (ROI) for such initiatives is difficult and cumbersome. While you can come up with metrics on cost savings over the years, it is difficult to quantify the rippling effect of business value adds that a major transformation can deliver. Any technological change invariably introduces new vulnerabilities and security threats that require further investment in cybersecurity measures. Integrating new technologies into your IT landscape, especially when maintaining legacy systems, can be complex and costly. Then you have your talent challenges. With limited IT talent who have experience with the latest technology systems and platforms, it can be challenging to hire the personnel needed to make these initiatives successful. Finally, there is stakeholder alignment as new systems trigger significant changes to business processes and employee behavior that need carefully designed user adoption and change management initiatives.

Implementation of *Enterprise FinOps* (Enterprise Financial Optimization) techniques, as outlined in this book, can enable organizations to optimize their operations across their entire IT portfolio of cloud, SaaS, data centers, AI, enterprise systems, and IT services. It is quite realistic to achieve over *30% reduction* in your operational spend over a period of 8 to 24 months. The gains also flow through to transformations and innovations, by bringing the same efficiencies to newer projects as well as improving business alignment and value creation. Even a modest reduction in your run costs can unlock funding for bootstrapping innovation and transformation initiatives. While this cost optimization is underway, other Enterprise FinOps techniques let you focus on aligning your IT services with business objectives and addressing the other challenges and dilemmas presented here.

1.2 The Evolving Role of the CIO

Technology has been an indispensable tool that has driven the evolution of human progress. From rudimentary stone-age Oldowan tools used by early humans to the sophisticated space-age laser weaponry of today, from inventions like the printing press that democratized knowledge to virtual

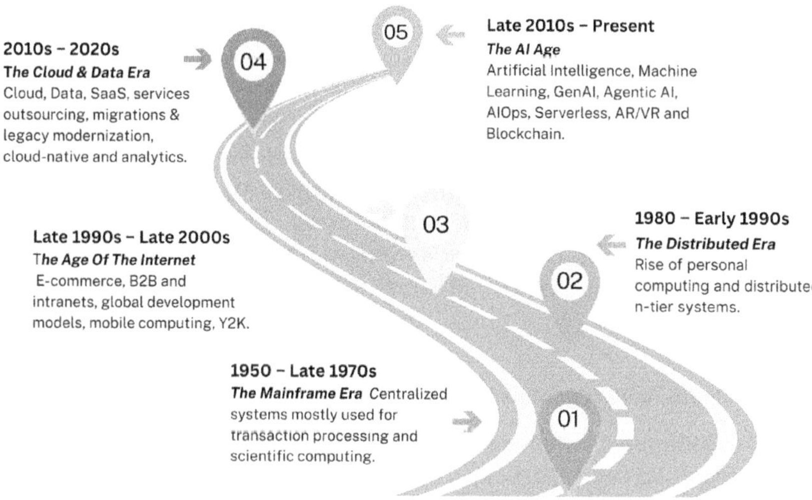

Figure 1.6 The evolution of the CIO through the last few decades

metaverses, from the earliest abacuses to modern quantum computers, technology has let humans live better and fuller lives.

Let's explore how IT has impacted business in the past few decades. The CIO's role has evolved significantly over the past seven decades, as shown in Figure 1.6. From managing batch processing systems, today's CIOs are strategic business leaders driving organizational innovation. Synnott and Gruber talked about the CIO's role in their groundbreaking publication *Information Resource Management: Opportunities and Strategies for the 1980s* (Synnott & Gruber, 1981). From their definition to today's strategic business leaders indicates a shift from technology management to transformational leadership. CIOs are now recognized as drivers of competitive advantage, innovation, and business strategy. Their leadership role is even more critical as artificial intelligence, cybersecurity, and digital transformation become leading technologies to power organizational success in an increasingly technology-dependent business environment. Today, the CIO is a powerful influencer of the enterprise's executive strategy.

1.2.1 From Operations Leader to Business Enabler

The leadership role originated in the 1950s–1970s, when IT professionals managed huge centralized computing systems.

1.2.1.1 The Mainframe Era (1950s–late 1970s)

Early computing was based on large centralized systems that took up entire rooms. IT was like a hidden space somewhere in the deep innards of the building, quiet, isolated, and mostly invisible to the rest of the organization. A small team of technicians, operators, and programmers would spend their days wrestling with mainframes, handling batch processing, payroll, and basic data management with punch cards and codes that none outside a small select group really understood. The IT leader's job was mostly administrative, focused on keeping the systems running. This was a largely reactive, cost-control-oriented function focused on maintaining existing systems.

1.2.1.2 The Distributed Computing Era (1980s–Early 1990s)

Personal computers exploded on the scene. Generations of young aspiring tinkerers and developers experimented with gaming and programming. PCs made their way to desktops and revolutionized office productivity with document processing and spreadsheets. Desktops turned into workstations that could connect to remote servers across the world. It transformed CIOs from operational resource leaders to executive entrepreneurs, as they adapted from managing massive mainframes to supporting diverse computing platforms. This era democratized computing power and transformed technology infrastructure. As stated in a 1981 paper, "Manager or Technician? The Nature of the Information Systems Manager's Job" (Ives & Olson, 1981), the role of the information systems manager evolved in 20 years from that of a technician managing a relatively unimportant service function into that of a general manager whose department could substantially empower the entire organization.

It led to massive decentralization of computer tasks and also led to the rise of local information managers within business groups who were responsible for maintaining their own systems. With the emergence of PCs and client/server computing, the CIO began to gain strategic influence as legacy mainframes started to age and more sophisticated supply chain and financial systems began to appear, especially around new models of client-server computing and three-tier models with distinct layers for servers, databases, and front-end clients. There was a shift from pure operations to managing increasingly complex and distributed systems. The term "CIO" began to gain traction. The role continued to be largely focused on operational improvement. This was also the start of modernization, as aging mainframes started to be replaced by more modern client-server systems, although critical business systems were still based on powerful centralized minicomputers with networked workstations, especially in business-critical processes.

1.2.1.3 *The Internet Era (Late 1990s–Late 2000s) and the Start of Digital Transformation*

The internet and dot com era of the 2000s led to CIOs becoming business partners focused on aligning technology initiatives with core business goals and adapting to the opportunities of the internet age. The focus shifted from building in-house systems to implementing specialized systems offered by vendors in the areas of Enterprise Resource Planning (ERP), Customer Resource Management (CRM), and Supply Chain Management (SCM). I recollect the challenges of implementing ERP systems in the US Midwest during this time. Y2K was a pivotal, high-risk event that drove urgent remediation initiatives worldwide, a massive global exercise on catching up with urgent and necessary, but relatively simple issues caused by format incompatibility in legacy applications and hardware.

The internet boom continued in the 2000s. The "dot-com" thinkers envisaged a brand-new world. They created new ways of doing business and disrupted many established players. There was a rise in fragmentation of technology adoption as business units embraced the internet but carved out technology according to their specific needs. Articles like HBR's "IT Doesn't Matter" (Carr, 2003) questioned the value that IT provided to its organization. Then the pace of technology changes increased. CIOs now had the attention of the boardroom. Organizations were able to adopt radically new digital business models. The web's public launch in 1991 (History of the Internet, n.d.) fundamentally changed how organizations conducted business and managed information. Most mainframe-based business systems that were developed in-house began to be replaced by specialist systems developed by product vendors, especially in ERP, manufacturing, and supply chain.

This era also saw the rise of outsourcing, with several functions previously done by in-house IT staff now done by external service providers. The rise of better and faster networking and communication technology also led to the rise of development centers and remote offices, often in locations far from the central offices of the company. There was a need for centralized decision-making with CIOs once again rising to the front on large implementations, outsourcing, and complex modernization projects. As e-commerce became commonplace, organizations needed CIOs who could navigate this new landscape and ensure that their IT systems were adapted to support online business and marketing models. CIOs were given the responsibility of working with the business closely to adopt Business-to-Consumer (B2C), Business-to-Employee (B2E), and Business-to-Business (B2B) systems, transmitting data securely across company lines, integrating them with existing infrastructure, and managing the rapid flow of information. I was the proud owner of a Palm VII and a Sharp Mobilon tablet that let me log into and work on ERP systems in our remote offices, even while on a train racing toward downtown Chicago. I was busy leading teams developing innovative mobile and e-commerce interfaces to ERP systems that freed up users from their desks and let them create shopping websites with integrated inventory management. CIOs were charged with leveraging the internet for business advantage, dealing with significant security challenges, and incorporating strategic planning. Cyberattacks shifted the focus on information security to a more strategic level, as inadequate measures could stifle the entire company. Data protection, compliance, and risk management were now on the minds of the company leaders. Services vendors began specializing in modernization and outsourced services, and mega-outsourcing of IT became an everyday reality.

1.2.1.4 The Cloud Computing and Data Era (2010–2020) and the Rise of Data Analytics

The 2010s–2020s witnessed the emergence of CIOs as transformation strategists. Server virtualization meant that you could run multiple applications on the same physical hardware, saving costs and reducing complexity. Companies like Rackspace pioneered early cloud-like models where customers could commission virtual servers without needing to maintain their own data centers. Major industry players accelerated transformation initiatives. Cloud computing exploded into the world like a force of nature. Google, Microsoft, and Amazon dismantled the old guard and built something entirely new. Suddenly, the playing field was level. A solo developer with a laptop could access the same enterprise-grade computing power as a Fortune 500 company. It felt like handing every builder a toolbox and telling them, "Go build something."

For CIOs, this was a double-edged sword. True agility was now within reach. No more waiting years for hardware upgrades. No more locking money into depreciating servers. It offered pay-as-you-go models that turned IT budgets from rigid, upfront costs into flexible, usage-based expenses. But then the shadows of trust, control, and risk caught up. Moving sensitive data out of on-premises infrastructure felt like handing over the keys to a vault. How do you ensure compliance when your data is scattered across multiple jurisdictions? How do you protect intellectual property when it's hosted in someone else's data center? These weren't hypothetical questions, but a daily battle.

But the cloud changed the pace. Agile development has now become the new standard. Teams that had adopted the cloud could deploy updates in minutes instead of months. SaaS platforms like Salesforce or Microsoft 365 were accelerants. Rather than being a year-long project, modernization was now a sprint. The cloud democratized innovation. And for CIOs, that meant a new kind of pressure. CIOs were now expected to be a strategist and a catalyst for change. The journey hasn't been smooth. Legacy systems still cling to the past. Hybrid infrastructures are complex to govern and maintain. Still, the momentum is unstoppable. The cloud unshackled what was possible. And for those willing to embrace the chaos, the rewards are huge.

1.2.1.5 The AI and Data Transformation Era (Late 2010's–Present)

CEOs and business leaders today are keenly aware of the competitive advantages that the timely adoption of the right technology can provide, and also of the mercurial change that a capable CIO can achieve. Just like the many advances in technology over the decades, today we have AI and IoT rewriting the rules. While AI has always been evolving since the early 1950s, the 2020s is the true age of AI, with Generative AI (GenAI), agentic AI, and Machine Learning (ML) making their way into every aspect of life. Today, the CIO's role is more complex and strategic than ever. CIOs balance not only technical leadership and risk management, but also business acumen and strategic innovation. CIOs are now expected to drive innovation and support new business models, aim for data-driven revenue generation, integrate technology quickly into business processes, and manage the ethical implications of new technologies. CIOs also need to tackle how to integrate and operationalize technologies back into the operational cadence while maintaining the speed and flexibility offered by newer, non-traditional ways of delivering services through methodologies such as agile, DevOps, and product-centric teams. The exponentially rising cost of modern technologies is another challenge that CIOs are tackling to prevent data, storage, and computing costs from overwhelming their IT spend.

1.3 The "Run, Transform, Innovate" Model (RTI360)

This section proposes a foundational model that helps set the context for the rest of the book and is especially useful for laying out the foundations of Enterprise FinOps as an enabler of cost optimization and business alignment.

As illustrated in Figure 1.7, the IT portfolio of services, platforms, initiatives, projects, and products that you offer your enterprise users (internal customers) can be broadly categorized into Run, Transform, and Innovate, and extended further through continuous improvement. It offers a 360-degree view of the main services, activities, and initiatives that your organization does. There may be several services, such as Project Management or Enterprise Architecture, that may not strictly align with these pillars, or overlap across all three categories, or simply be support functions for the rest of the portfolio.

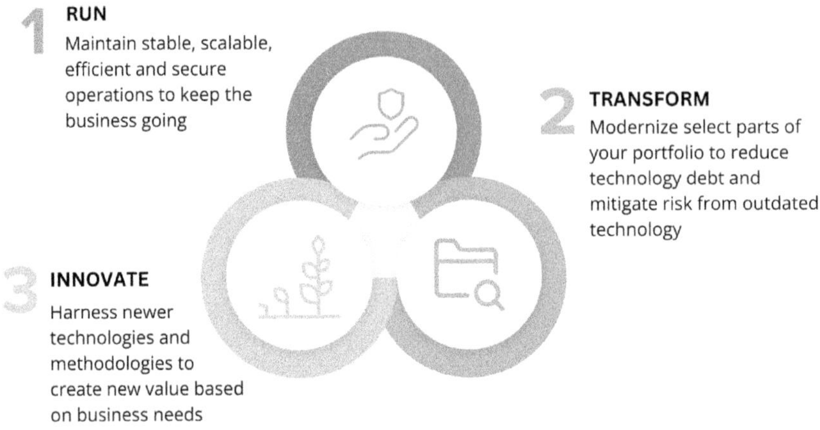

Figure 1.7 The run-transform-innovate (RTI360) model

Services across these categories occur concurrently. While maintaining Run operations, you may have a major initiative underway that aims to modernize your e-commerce platform to deliver an omnichannel experience. At the same time, you may be introducing innovations such as an AI chatbot that improves your customer service experience. Often, teams from the same IT portfolio or group will be responsible for all three categories: operating the environment, modernizing it through migrations, as well as developing customizations or integrations that further add business value.

The RTI360 model offers us a practical way to visualize and strategize about the IT landscape that you oversee. It offers a simple lens helping leaders make clearer prioritization and investment decisions. It does not seek to restrict or limit other established frameworks that may already be in place at your organization, such as ITIL/ITSM, SEI-CMMi, COBIT, or methodologies such as DevOps or Scrum. It is just a convenient way to demarcate the various services that your team provides along dimensions of cost, organization, and impact.

You will likely have other popular frameworks and operating models such as the ones shown in Figure 1.8, at play in your IT organization. IT frameworks offer a set of best practices, guidelines, instructions, or principles. They ensure the technology and processes that your team adopts align with industry regulations, and offer a practical and feasible way to operate your organization based on a set of widely accepted industry best practices. An IT operating model similarly lets you organize resources and

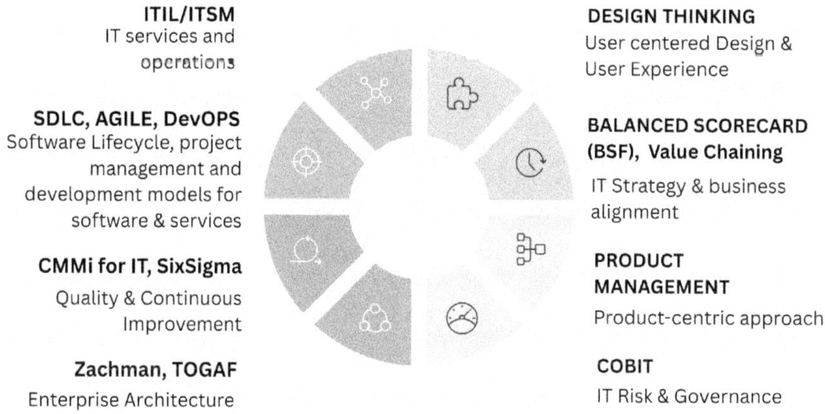

Figure 1.8 Different frameworks and operating models for IT

the way they work or perform and accomplish tasks. The RTI360 model and Enterprise FinOps can operate seamlessly with other models that you may have implemented in your IT organization.

1.3.1 Run (or Maintain)

Run, put simply, is keeping the lights on and making the business function smoothly and efficiently. It's mostly reactive and focused on minimizing risk, although predictive techniques and Artificial Intelligence for Operations (AIOps) are making maintenance more proactive. Running operations is *the* biggest ongoing expense for most IT departments, often up to 60% of the total IT budget, as shown in Figure 1.9. It's a predictable and necessary cost, but it's often undervalued. Day-to-day operations of IT include core business and mission-critical systems that enable the enterprise, such as ERP, SCM, CRM, Human Resources Information Systems (HRIS), financial systems, marketing and e-commerce websites, Manufacturing Engineering Systems (MES), and other critical business applications. Another key area of Run is the underlying infrastructure and operations, such as server maintenance, network management, data center operations, and supporting manufacturing systems at factories. Run extends to services that employees and customers depend on, such as IT Help Desk & Support, and providing technical support on-site at company office locations and factories. Security operations include monitoring for threats, patching vulnerabilities, and ensuring data protection.

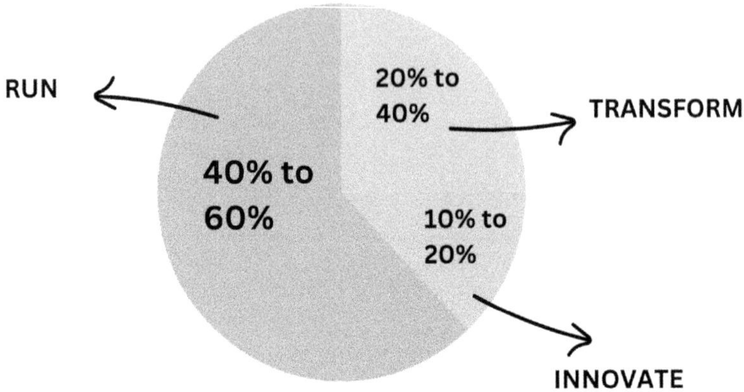

Figure 1.9 Typical distribution of IT spend across Run, Innovate and Transform

So, what does Run spend on? It includes infrastructure costs for equipment such as servers, storage, network routers, and firewalls, data centers (including utilities), software licensing and support for existing software, often being renewed year after year. IT staff salaries and benefits for core IT operations, help desk, and support personnel are a big part. Maintenance and support contracts with major product, SaaS, cloud, and services vendors are another component, much needed to ensure Service Level Agreements (SLAs) that bring assurance and reliability to IT services.

1.3.1.1 A Seismic Shift from Traditional to Modern Run Operations

The Run category is evolving into something entirely different. Ten years ago, our focus was on servers, switches, and the physical weight of IT infrastructure. Today we're juggling hybrid cloud environments, APIs that multiply rapidly, and data lakes that swallow entire departments. Containers, microservices, and data fabrics are everyday words. We're herding cats across multiple landscapes, each with its own service provider, compliance rules, and deployment quirks. DevOps rewired the entire playbook. Analytics infrastructure is the backbone of decision-making. Manual processes are relics. You can't keep up with the velocity of modern business using spreadsheets, telephone calls, and coffee-stained sticky notes.

The people running operations now are system admins, architects, and engineers who have mastered the tools offered by modern technology. These tools are as diverse as the problems we solve. It means your Run operations are no longer a silo but a cross-functional dance, where every step requires coordination, every decision has downstream consequences, and every failure is a potential risk to stable business as usual.

1.3.1.2 *Key Challenges in the Modern "Run" Category*

The old playbook of rigid processes, siloed teams, and quarterly patch cycles crumbles under the weight of today's demands. Today's Run ecosystems of microservices, APIs, and cloud environments breathe, evolve, and demand constant vigilance. Private clouds (your on-premises datacenters) must adopt cloud-like services, tools, and automation to make it easier to provision, scale, and optimize resources, and offer DevOps models to operate in alignment with business and product teams. It's an attitude change to adapt to being in a hybrid cloud.

I've spent years interviewing candidates, and the numbers are sobering. IT professionals come armed with certifications in cloud administration and architecture, but few have hands-on experience with cloud cost optimization, security configurations, migrations, or real-time implementations. That's a crisis. When you deploy a service in a cloud environment, you're opening a door to your citadel. Every API endpoint, every Identity and Access Management (IAM) policy, every auto-scaling rule is a potential vulnerability. Last year, one of the departments in the company I worked for slashed their AWS bill by over 20% just by switching to Reserved Instances (RIs), but struggled to patch up security issues. The rising use of the cloud elsewhere swallowed up the savings. Nevertheless, that is cost savings that require tools, processes, and people who understand the connection between performance and expenditure. Then there's the data. Modern environments generate terabytes of logs, metrics, and traces daily. Without AIOps, you're drowning in noise. We undertook a pilot in AIOps to extend our ITSM platform, and teams were on their way to predict outages before they happen.

The CIO's role is like being the conductor of a symphony where security, cost, speed, and agility must harmonize. The future of IT isn't in the past. It's in the people who can navigate this chaos with clarity. It's in the tools that turn data into decisions, and the leaders who see "Run" operations not as a burden, but as the engine of transformation.

1.3.2 *Transform (or Modernize)*

Systems gradually outlive their designated lives and come to the point where they cannot be operated reliably anymore. The reasons are myriad. It could be due to unsupported or end-of-life software, vendors going out of business, lack of hardware parts or replacements, or simply because they do not integrate well with other enterprise systems. Sometimes, technologies age to the point where you cannot find skilled resources that know how to maintain them, or simply lack the scalability and feature set to meet current or future business goals. Technology debt cripples and slows down the ability of IT to advance.

Transformation lets you adopt new technologies or processes to modernize systems and reduce technology debt. As further elaborated in the chapter on technology debt, transformation can take many paths. You can strategically upgrade and optimize existing systems and processes with selective changes to improve efficiency, productivity, and agility, minimizing business disruption, or switch them out to completely different platforms. These could be large business-wide initiatives, such as a major digital transformation program, or could be limited to strategic projects that impact only a few sections of IT or the business. Legacy modernization deals with the phase out of older systems. Cloud migrations are at a level of maturity and executed routinely to move applications and data to the cloud for scalability and cost savings, although the actual migration itself can be a high cost. Transformation projects require investments in software, hardware, and skilled resources and could typically take up 20–40% of the IT budget. Transformation demands significant organizational change and stakeholder engagement to be successful. Besides the cost of the transformation itself, you also have to account for related costs for data migration, system integration, and user training. Normally, the transformed environment would be handed back to the operations teams and often results in reduced Run costs. Automation and migration tools can drastically reduce the cost of modernization, and carefully executed pilots can mitigate the risk.

1.3.3 Innovate (or Create)

Exploration and adoption of new technologies, processes, and systems are the lifeline that keeps the enterprise alive and ready to adapt to changing business scenarios. Innovation results in the creation of entirely new products, services, or business models. It can add significant business value to the enterprise by accelerating processes and improving user productivity.

Innovation can push the boundaries of what's possible and disrupt existing markets to fundamentally change how the business operates. But this is also where the biggest risks and uncertainties lie. In their very nature, new technologies are unproven – they need to be seasoned, and that takes time. Failures are common. Sometimes technology just can't live up to its promises. CIOs need to encourage a culture where teams can afford to take controlled risks and learn from mistakes. While the adoption of Generative AI has been quite fast, enterprises are still rolling out reliable AI/ML models and agentic AI solutions. Technologies such as blockchain are being leveraged in the financial sector and increasingly across other industry sectors, exploring potential applications in supply chain management, legal services, healthcare, and vendor management. The Internet of Things (IoT) is a stepping stone for advancing to more sophisticated solutions such as digital twins and simulations, connecting devices across IT and business, and collecting data for insights. Quantum computing has advanced tremendously in recent months and has exciting potential for advanced processing that would normally take supercomputer-level computing.

Innovation pilots can consume 10–20% or more of the assigned IT budget, and even more based on the enterprise's appetite for gaining from the latest technologies and their willingness to experiment with newer business models. When there is a solid business case, the Innovate budget can also be directly funded outside traditional IT spend, as special projects. Innovate is also the most visible part of IT. Run is often taken for granted, while Transform is deemed necessary to mitigate risks. But Innovate is where IT can leapfrog itself as a strategic enabler for the business. It's also the riskiest, with a high chance of failure if not managed carefully. But where there is high risk, there are often high rewards. Innovation risks can be mitigated through frequent experimentation, prototyping, and collaboration with external partners, funding for pilot projects, proof of concept, and experimentation. SaaS platforms, APIs and Platform-as-a-Service (PaaS) services, agile methodologies, and cloud computing have provided a fast and practical environment for Innovate today.

1.4 Typical IT Spends

When it comes to balancing operational efficiency with strategic transformation and innovation, IT budget management is where most leaders start. Many dilemmas arise because resources are always finite. Effective budget management forces prioritization and aligns spending with strategic objectives, and ultimately, demonstrates the value of IT to business stakeholders. For this, a competent and effective Business Value Framework is absolutely essential. We'll talk more about this in the next section.

A well-defined IT budget and a complementary IT strategy signal to the business what IT considers most important. The budget creates accountability for IT's performance in the coming year. You can derive your own IT budgeting using concepts like rolling forecasts or zero-based budgeting, where each expense is justified from scratch. Value-based budgeting is often used to prioritize investments based on their potential value to the business. The type of industry and growth targets for the enterprise make a significant impact on your Run-Transform-Innovate distribution. A mature retailer could have a high Run investment for security and operational efficiency, moderate Transform investment for CRM integration and customer experience imperatives such as e-commerce platform upgrades. The maturity of their customer processes may lead to low Innovation investment, such as in exploring AR/VR for customer engagement or blockchains. On the other hand, a disruptive Fintech startup would have high Innovation investment in developing blockchain-based contracts and payment methods and API integrations across major platforms, moderate Transform as they are likely already built cloud-native services, and low Run with systems mostly in the cloud or SaaS or outsourced to external providers.

1.4.1 RTI360 – A Balancing Act

Business leaders often gravitate toward prioritizing immediate needs over long-term investments in transformation or innovation. Most business cases for transformations or innovations cannot demonstrate ROI because these benefits are often accumulated over several years. A majority of IT resources are typically dedicated to running operations and are difficult to free up to focus on transformative work, simply because Run needs immediate and urgent attention when things break or threaten to break. Figure 1.10 discusses conflicting tensions for the CIO while allocating resources and funding. Another operational challenge is managing the scale and complexity of the data being processed across the enterprise. The volume, velocity, and variety of data need continuous refinement of infrastructure. Table 1.1 discusses characteristics and differences between

Figure 1.10 Conflicting tensions for the CIO

Table 1.1 Characteristics of run, transform and innovate

Feature	*Run*	*Transform*	*Innovate*
Objective	Maintain current operations	Change existing operations	Create new operations/ value
Focus	Stability, efficiency, cost control	Strategic shift, disruption	Experimentation, discovery
Risk level	Low – minimal disruption	Medium – significant changes	High – uncertain outcomes
Time horizon	Short-term (0–3 years)	Medium-term (3–5 years)	Long-term (5+ years)
Key metrics	Uptime, cost per transaction, efficiency	Revenue growth, market share, customer satisfaction	New revenue streams, intellectual property, competitive advantage
IT role	Operational support, system maintenance	Strategic alignment, agile delivery	Research and development, prototyping
Examples	Server patching, database backups, help desk support	Implementing a new CRM system, cloud migration, redesigning the website	Developing a blockchain solution, exploring AR/ VR applications, creating a new digital product

Run-Transform & Innovate areas. A large portion of operational efforts is dedicated to reactive maintenance and optimization.

There are intricate synergies between the categories of IT spend. Run naturally feeds and leads to transformation. Any migration relies on a stable and well-maintained IT infrastructure. Without a stable, well-maintained IT infrastructure, transformation projects will invariably face delays, cost overruns, and ultimately, failure. Successful transformation projects create the environment and the capabilities needed to support innovation. Transformation brings fresh insights and ideas that can lead to Innovation. Successful innovation needs to be handed over to Run for ongoing operations, or leverage a DevOps model that blends maintenance and development into a single team through continuous operations.

1.4.2 Addressing Operational Inefficiencies

Operational inefficiencies are hidden drains on IT resources and budgets, eating away resources, time, and money slowly but surely. Figure 1.11

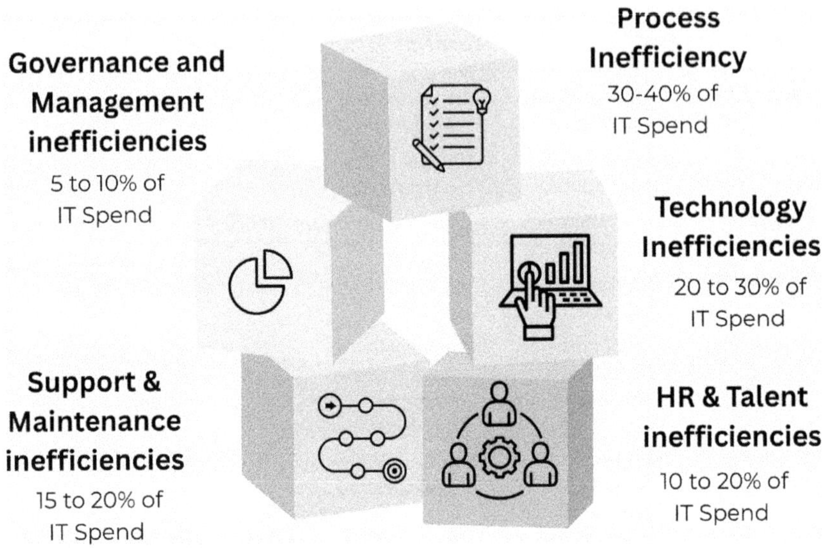

Figure 1.11 Categories of operational inefficiencies

depicts some of these inefficiencies. Identifying and resolving these inefficiencies is an important step for cost optimization.

In any IT organization that has grown organically, you will find several manual processes even in everyday activities. In incident management or vendor procurement, agents route tickets manually through email or use cumbersome approval processes to get something done. Siloed teams lead to communication gaps and errors that further cause delays.

Unresolved technology debt leads to inefficient systems. Legacy systems may have been depreciated, so the natural tendency is to continue exploiting your investment as long as possible. However, legacy systems could be quite expensive to maintain. Out-of-standard support products have additional costs for support and licensing and may require specialized and more expensive talent. Underutilized resources such as servers, storage, and network capacity are another hidden opportunity for optimization. Poorly integrated systems or a lack of integration between systems cause data silos, with manual data transfer and reporting further exacerbating process-related inefficiencies. Cumbersome backup processes, excessive retention policies, inadequate disaster recovery plans, and unnecessary data redundancy lead to huge amounts of storage and clog up reporting and analytics. Another example is where teams overspend on cloud contracts and ignore cost optimization tools.

People and talent management inefficiencies are mostly due to skill gaps. IT teams may lack the necessary skills for modern technologies such as cloud, automation, or DevOps, and this leads to excessive spending on contingent resources. Not taking advantage of upskilling or hiring employees with these skills leads to contingent workers being retained well beyond the initial project or initiative. The pursuit of endless and indefinite experimentation, especially in the absence of clear ROI targets, can lead to low accountability and overstaffing. Constant turnover rates lead to increased recruitment and training costs.

Operational inefficiencies can also result from a lack of the right tools or skills. Many teams still don't have efficient knowledge and case management tools. This leads to reactive incident resolution, wasted user time, and longer system downtime.

Governance and management inefficiencies arise from issues like a lack of alignment when IT projects are not aligned with business objectives. Despite having frameworks and standards like agile or PMI PMBOK, poor project management leadership can cause projects to be over budget and behind schedule. If you don't track and measure risks actively, the project can suffer from high mitigation costs. Excessive data and manual data flows create unnecessary information overload.

1.4.3 Resolving Inefficiencies

Inefficiency reduction happens seamlessly when there is a culture that encourages continuous optimization, rewards incremental innovations, and promotes lean thinking. Initiatives like *Enterprise FinOps* and technologies like Robotic Process Automation (RPA) and automation can reduce inefficiencies considerably and unlock substantial benefits. As you will read further in the chapter on Enterprise FinOps levers, there are structured activities that can work in tandem to eliminate inefficiencies.

1.4.3.1 Leveraging the Power of Behavioral Science

Many operational inefficiencies persist despite process improvements and system upgrades because they are driven by ingrained behaviors. Behavioral science helps explain why and how to change them. Behavioral science is increasingly being used in marketing campaigns and product design and development, especially in mass-consumer-facing products and services that seek to increase stickiness and purchase conversion rates. Applying behavioral science enables more disciplined, value-driven use of

IT resources. Analyzing how people think, feel, and behave is one of the first steps in a design thinking approach to develop empathy with the user or consumer, understanding their roles and behaviors.

We will explore three key behavioral science concepts in this section.

- In "Loss Aversion," people tend to fear losses more than they value gains. People will expend greater efforts to avoid even small losses of established systems or entrenched processes, even though they may be slow and cumbersome. Applying this to IT costs, people may be more motivated to avoid expenses such as spending on an automation initiative or migration, even when it can result in lower operational expenses and productivity boosts. To combat this bias, cost-saving initiatives must have a clear rationale for the business gain.
- In "the Power of Defaults," people tend to follow the path of least resistance when faced with choices. In IT or Enterprise Architectural reviews, establishing default policies for IT spend or technology configurations for new projects or services can minimize costs without sacrificing functionality. For example, implementing a mandate to allow contingent workers only for a predefined period, without automatic extension unless approved, or a policy for avoiding over-provisioning can help reduce unnecessary spend on contingent resources.
- The "Social Norms Theory" can play an influential role. When people see others following practices that get rewarded (through recognition or other rewards), they are more likely to adopt similar behaviors. In IT cost optimization, leaders can sponsor and promote best practices for cost-saving initiatives as part of the organization's culture, and this can create a sense of social responsibility among employees to contribute to the cost optimization efforts.

Some of these behavioral science concepts are naturally implemented through initiatives like Enterprise FinOps that encourage a mindset of responsible technology adoption and shared accountability. Chapter 9 on "Mental Models" further elaborates this topic.

1.5 Business Value of IT

In a typical enterprise company, IT has few opportunities to directly generate revenue. Measuring and connecting IT spend to tangible business value, even if indirectly generated, is an extremely important activity for validating IT investment. Modern IT landscapes are a myriad and complex mix of heterogeneous systems and applications. You likely have data centers and have already moved away from maintaining your own data centers to co-located ones. Virtualization and automation have enabled private-cloud features for many of your on-premises hosted applications.

A major chunk of your enterprise systems has likely been migrated to SaaS platforms. Teams are migrating more applications to the cloud and are starting to develop cloud-native solutions. You also have legacy systems that will need to be modernized or phased out in the future.

Once considered a cost center within enterprise companies, business leaders today consider IT to be a strategic enabler of revenue growth. IT has demonstrated continuous improvement over the decades. Lean and agile methodologies, automation, virtualization, and cloud infrastructure have improved agility and speed. Monitoring and structured methodologies like IT Service Management (ITSM/ITIL) have improved operational efficiency. SaaS platforms have introduced rich feature sets that align with business processes. IT teams are shifting from being reactive to proactive incident resolution through techniques like AIOps and predictive maintenance.

But something is still lacking. There is a concerted effort needed to measure and communicate tangible IT value to the business. Business value addition from IT can be built around three core pillars. Your enterprise may have additional or other relevant top-level business objectives that could replace the core pillars that are shown here. We will elaborate on this further in later chapters by proposing a Business Value Framework that aims to measure both direct and indirect IT business value.

Let's look at three common drivers of business value, as shown in Figure 1.12. IT must contribute to the business's ability to win, compete, grow,

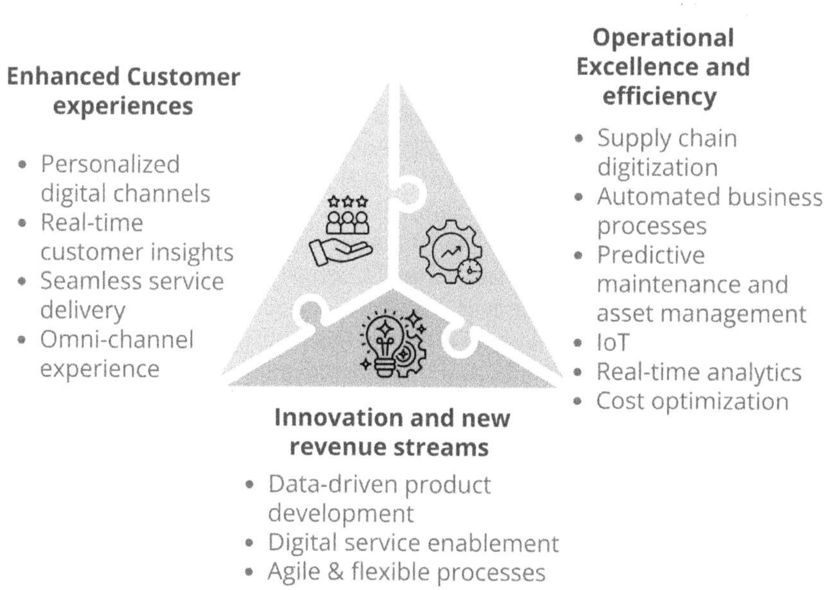

Figure 1.12 Typical pillars of business value addition

and change as needed in response to multiple internal and external factors. An enterprise thrives on its customers. Customer demands inform and shape business strategy, and customer experiences drive the ability to capture and grow market share from competitors and grow revenue. IT plays a critical role in influencing every touchpoint that a customer has with the company. From e-commerce platforms in the 2000s to omnichannel platforms today, AI, analytics, and machine learning enable personalized marketing campaigns, targeted product recommendations, and customer services that anticipate needs. Analytics platforms provide real-time data on customer interactions, preferences, and behavior. IT supports customer service teams with sophisticated call center and ticketing systems, chat and feedback platforms, and remote support tools to diagnose and resolve issues and boost satisfaction.

Operational excellence drives benefits across the entire business. Quality and lean methodologies like IT service management are in place at most IT organizations. We had instituted a Kaizen system, where any improvement, incremental or big, was recognized and tracked based on its impact on reducing costs, improving efficiency or productivity, or enhancing agility, with a leaderboard system to encourage and motivate contributors. Any migration of enterprise and business-critical systems, such as supply chain management or ERP systems, can potentially reduce inventory holding costs, minimize stockout situations, and enable real-time visibility across the entire supply chain. This not only improves your ability to meet customer demand efficiently but also reduces costs. Technologies such as Robotic Process Automation (RPA) can be applied to processes across any business line or enterprise function. In sales, it can speed up order processing; in HR, it can expedite talent hiring; and in Finance, it accelerates invoice management and improves cash flow, just a few of the examples. Agentic AI is another recent automation technology that can further eliminate manual tasks, reduce errors, and accelerate business processes. Another positive impact of automation is that it frees up employees so they can focus on other value-added activities.

IT can be a driver of business value. IT actively contributes to the creation of new value, whether it is products, services, or business models. Data analytics can provide valuable insights to help identify unmet customer needs, emerging trends, and opportunities for innovation. Working closely with business product teams, IT can be a partner in releasing new product offerings that embed technologies like AI and IoT and are born in the cloud for automatic scaling based on business demand. Virtualization and cloud services maintained by IT can unleash enhanced business models through subscription-based offerings, personalized digital experiences, and value-added services.

In the cost-center model, IT was responsible for delivering technology. In today's business value model, IT can deliver business value. As we will further elaborate in the Business Value Framework section in the chapter on Measuring and Monitoring Enterprise FinOps, for this to happen, IT must collaborate with the business to establish Key Performance Indicators (KPIs) that track all IT initiatives, providing clear accountability and demonstrating the ROI of IT investments.

1.5.1 Delivering Business Value through Enterprise FinOps

Enterprise FinOps is a cultural and operational shift that can empower the CIO to resolve many of these dilemmas listed in this chapter. It provides a balanced approach for operational efficiency and to drive strategic transformation and innovation. Enterprise FinOps brings a structured approach to the entire IT spend. Our focus shifts from just managing what is consumed to managing how and why it's consumed. This is an important mindset change in our journey from transforming IT from being a cost center to being business drivers.

Organizations can reap several benefits from Enterprise FinOps, as shown in Figure 1.13.

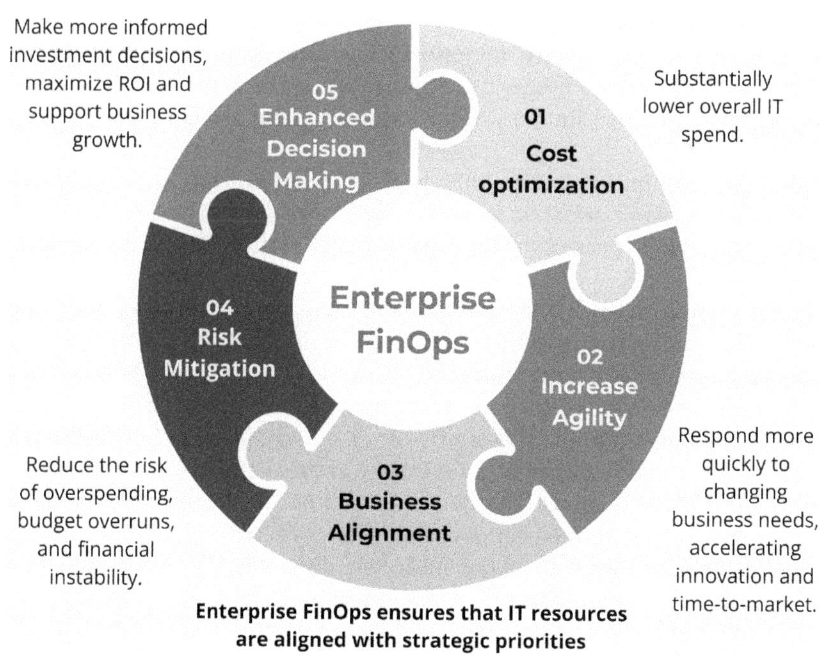

Figure 1.13 Benefits of Enterprise FinOps

- **Improved business alignment:** By linking IT investments directly to business outcomes, Enterprise FinOps ensures that IT resources are aligned with strategic priorities. Your business stakeholders know that IT is proactively and continuously optimizing costs and maximizing the return on every dollar.
- **Cost optimization:** Through optimized resource allocation and efficient operational practices, businesses can substantially lower their overall IT spending.
- **Increased agility:** With improved visibility and business alignment, IT teams can respond more quickly to changing business needs. This accelerates innovation and speeds up time to market.
- **Risk mitigation:** By proactively managing IT costs and measures such as scenario planning, organizations reduce the risk of overspending and budget overruns. Predictive techniques embedded into FinOps let you manage potential financial instability.
- **Enhanced decision-making:** With accurate cost data and financial insights, IT leaders can make more informed investment decisions, maximize ROI, and support business growth. Enhanced decision-making follows. A consolidated view into IT spend that lets you make informed IT decisions on project funding, budgeting, and determining which initiatives support business goals. You can predict and simulate scenarios to proactively manage IT risks.
- **Responsible technology adoption:** Through data transparency and access, Enterprise FinOps develops a culture of shared accountability and responsible technology adoption throughout the company.

Enterprise FinOps applies to the entire IT environment, from hardware and software to IT services, as shown in Figure 1.14. The principles and framework yield results through close coordination across multiple IT roles, from finance, operations, development teams, procurement, and vendor management. It extends traditional solutions such as IT budgeting or IT Financial Management (ITFM) and binds together engineering and operational improvement efforts.

Enterprise FinOps is not a short-term project or a single discrete initiative. It can transform all aspects of your IT culture in every portfolio area. You are creating a culture of financial awareness and business alignment within IT. While slashing costs is one goal, smarter investments fuel business value. Empowerment and visibility into IT costs give everyone the information they need to make informed decisions. I've witnessed how profoundly that can transform an organization. In Part III of this book, we will explore a complete implementation roadmap for assessing and implementing an Enterprise FinOps program across your IT organization.

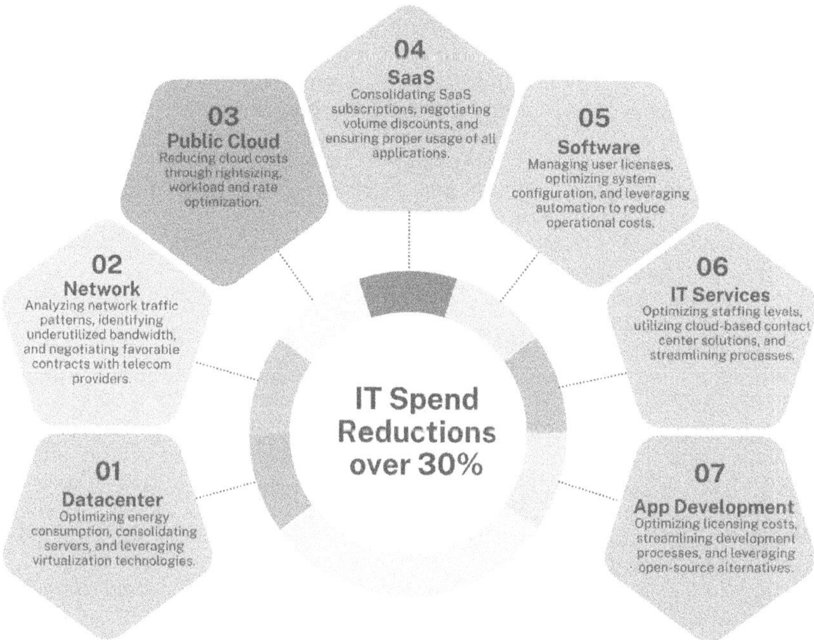

Figure 1.14 Enterprise FinOps applies across all IT spend areas

Newton's First Law of Motion states that "an object at rest stays at rest, and an object in motion stays in motion unless acted upon by an external force." This is an apt reflection of the inertia that often plagues IT. Organizations tend to resist change in legacy systems and entrenched processes until a compelling external force, such as cost overruns, business challenges, compliance risks, or competitive pressures, compels action. For CIOs, this law highlights the challenge of overcoming organizational resistance to transformation and innovation. Legacy systems may persist for years until a critical event, like a data breach or a significant outage, forces a reassessment of the IT landscape. The CIO's dilemma lies in identifying these external forces early and leveraging them to drive change, rather than waiting for crises to act as the catalyst. The law of inertia also highlights the importance of momentum once a change initiative is set in motion. Maintaining its trajectory requires sustained effort and alignment across departments, as there are significant forces acting to stop the momentum. Enterprise FinOps is that engine that lets you drive change and sustain the momentum.

References

Aberdeen, S. (n.d.). State of IT (2026). Retrieved from https://www.spiceworks.com/research/it-report/

BCG. (n.d.). IT spending pulse. Retrieved from https://www.bcg.com/publications/2025/it-spending-pulse-optimism-investment-and-priorities

Brian Christian, T. G. (2016). *Algorithms to live by- the computer science of human decisions*. New York, NY: Henry Holt & Company.

Carr, G. N. (2003). IT doesn't matter. *Harvard Business Review*, *5*, 41–49. Retrieved from https://hbr.org/2003/05/it-doesnt-matter

Heller, M. (2012). *The CIO paradox: Battling the contradictions of IT leadership*. New Delhi: Biblomania-Routledge.

History of the Internet. (n.d.). Retrieved from https://en.wikipedia.org/wiki/History_of_the_Internet

Ives, B., & Olson, M. H. (1981). Manager or technician? The nature of the information systems manager's job. *MIS Quarterly*, 49–63. https://doi.org/10.2307/249327

Jöhnk, J., Oesterle, S., Winkler, T., & Nørbjerg, J. (2019). Juggling the paradoxes - Governance mechanisms in bimodal IT organizations. Retrieved from https://www.researchgate.net/publication/332472162_Juggling_the_Paradoxes_-_Governance_Mechanisms_in_Bimodal_IT_Organizations

Langer, A., & Yorks, L. (2010). *Strategic information technology* (2nd ed.). Hoboken, NJ: Wiley.

Schein, H. E., & Schein, A. P. (2010). *Organizational culture and leadership*. San Francisco, CA: Jossey-Bass.

Synnott, W. R., & Gruber, W. H. (1981). *Information resource management: Opportunities and strategies for the 1980s*. New York, NY: John Wiley & Sons.

Zutshi, N. (2025). From IT to influence: How CIOs have evolved to business and boardroom leaders. *Forbes Technology Council*. Retrieved from https://www.forbes.com/councils/forbestechcouncil/2025/09/04/from-it-to-influence-how-cios-have-evolved-to-business-and-boardroom-leaders/

Part II

Enterprise FinOps Provides a Framework for Resolving the CIO's Dilemmas

How Does Enterprise FinOps Resolve the Challenges?

The next three chapters dive deeper into how Enterprise FinOps can address the challenges outlined in Part I. It describes the philosophy behind Enterprise FinOps and lays out a foundational framework, and then looks at technology debt reduction, a key priority that underlies any transformation efforts. Finally, we look at how Enterprise FinOps can be a catalyst to bootstrap transformation and innovation efforts.

DOI: 10.4324/9781003682196-4

Chapter 2

Enterprise FinOps

DOI: 10.4324/9781003682196-5

Enterprise FinOps is a holistic approach to cost optimization and business value alignment that extends to the entire IT spend, including hardware, software, cloud, and IT services.

- Enterprise FinOps reduces overall costs: A significant portion of your total IT spend is locked up as underutilized resources. A core mechanism of Enterprise FinOps is demand-based optimization, where resource allocation is dynamically adjusted based on actual consumption. Techniques like automatically scaling down resources during periods of low demand eliminate wasted spending. Visibility tools provide near real-time insights, allowing you to identify inefficiencies and take targeted actions.
- Enterprise FinOps increases operational efficiency: It establishes clear ownership and accountability for IT costs. Through automation, standardized processes are established for provisioning, managing, and decommissioning resources like virtual machines and software licenses. This reduces manual effort and improves resource utilization.
- Enterprise FinOps improves business alignment: By optimizing IT spend, we free up capital for strategic investments such as transformation and innovation pilots and new product development. Optimized infrastructure provides a foundation for faster application delivery and innovation, accelerating time to market and directly supporting revenue growth.

2.1 Understanding Enterprise FinOps

Organizations agonize over their IT spending, tangled in a maze of operational costs, cloud bills, services contracts, and forgotten SaaS subscriptions. Enterprise FinOps is a lifeline for companies to untangle that mess. It's not about cloud costs alone, though that's where many start. Here we look at every dollar tied to IT, from the server racks in your data center to the ERP system your finance and supply chain business relies on.

Enterprise FinOps can reshape how we think about IT costs. If implemented right, you could achieve over *30% savings* on your IT spend. These are strategic savings that give you the assurance that you are maximizing the value derived from technology investments. It's a shift in mindset from simply controlling costs to strategically managing the overall ecosystem. Tie this to the RTI360 model that was introduced in Chapter 1. The "Run" phase becomes a chance to trim fat from everyday activities. That leads you to the "Transform" phase, where you inject some part of those savings into modernizing infrastructure, improving processes, or reducing technology debt. Enterprise FinOps gives you visibility and business value alignment to embark confidently into "Innovate" journeys.

2.1.1 Strategic Importance of Cost Optimization

Cost optimization is one of the primary goals of Enterprise FinOps. It drives business agility by freeing up capital that has been locked up in IT inefficiencies. This increased visibility strengthens your business case for future technology projects. Without proactive cost control, your investments in digital transformation and modernization can quickly spiral out of control. The benefits continue in other ways. Detailed cost data provides invaluable insights for strategic decision-making. It lets you make informed choices about resource allocation and mitigates IT risk by providing visibility and control over technology costs.

Enterprise FinOps establishes a centralized view of all IT spending. A team deploys a new SaaS tool, but it might sit unused, eating up licenses and cash. With FinOps, you can see exactly how that investment is letting you reduce incident resolution time and speed up service delivery. FinOps creates standardized processes for cost tracking, analysis, reporting, and optimization, regardless of the application or service. Collaboration between IT, Finance, DevOps, and business units in a shared FinOps initiative breaks down silos and promotes shared responsibility for cost management. Mechanisms for predicting and controlling demand for IT resources prevent over-provisioning and over-designing. Guardrails such as automated alerts let you detect when costs exceed thresholds, and anomaly detection can alert you to sudden cost spikes. FinOps connects cost data to SLAs, letting you connect your investment in external service providers and SaaS systems based on the actual value you are receiving. Automation streamlines cost monitoring and reporting, reducing manual effort and improving accuracy. Cost policies such as spending limits ensure compliance and prevent overspending.

2.1.2 What Is Enterprise FinOps

Enterprise FinOps is built on the five pillars of Principles, Portfolio, Personas, Phases, and Processes, as shown in Figure 2.1. The Enterprise FinOps framework expands the scope of financial optimization to the entire IT spend, across cloud, hardware, SaaS software as well as outsourced services. The FinOps Foundation framework has been elaborated in Appendix 1 (FinOps Framework, 2025).

2.1.2.1 Portfolio

Portfolio represents your entire IT landscape. It's where your FinOps[1] strategy lives and breathes. You may have mapped your portfolio to data

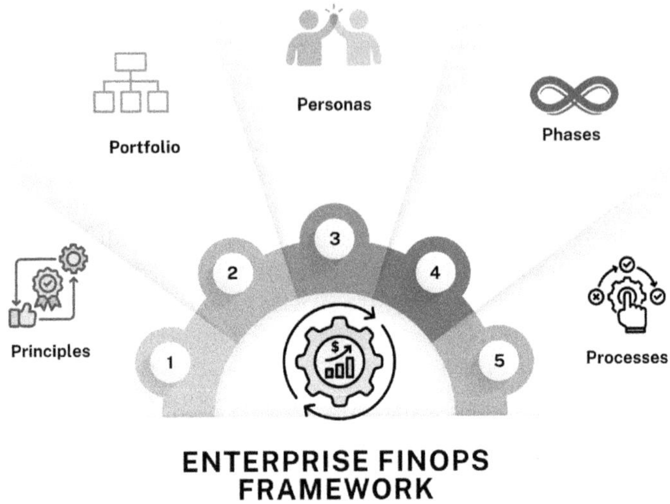

Figure 2.1 The Enterprise FinOps framework

centers, private clouds, or services such as the operations helpdesk. Each of these areas has its own unique characteristics.

2.1.2.2 *Principles*

Principles are the rules you live by, the compass that keeps you from drifting. Transparency gives everyone a clear view of where money goes. Accountability determines who takes ownership and action when server costs are rising. Efficiency cuts waste without sacrificing performance. Effectiveness aligns IT spending with business goals.

The key principles of Enterprise FinOps are illustrated in Figure 2.2. They comprise of the following:

1. Business value drives technology decisions. Business goals and objectives should guide technology investments and decisions.
2. Enterprise FinOps applies to all IT spend, whether hardware, software, services, or functions, not just the cloud.

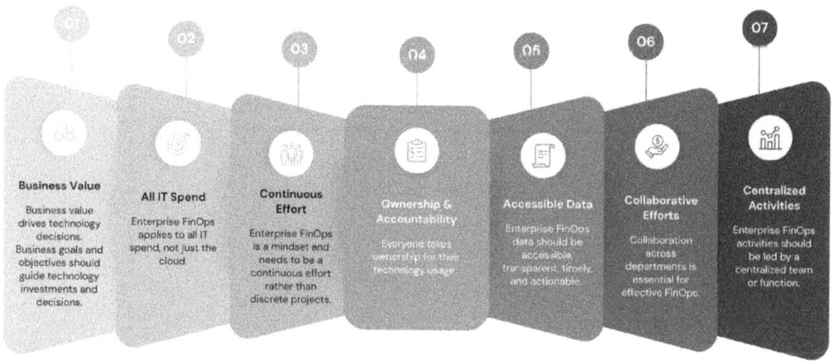

Figure 2.2 Enterprise FinOps principles

3. Enterprise FinOps is a mindset and needs to be a continuous effort rather than a discrete one-time project.
4. Everyone takes ownership of their technology usage. All users, regardless of individual organizational alignment, need to take accountability in managing IT resources and costs.
5. Enterprise FinOps data should be accessible, transparent, timely, and accurate. Actionable financial information informs decision-making.
6. Collaboration across departments is essential for effective FinOps, ensuring that all stakeholders are aligned with business goals and objectives. It is important that Finance, IT operations, product/engineering, vendor management, and business teams work in synchronization.
7. Enterprise FinOps activities should be led by a centralized team or function.

2.1.2.3 *Personas*

Personas are the people who make this all work. As illustrated in Figure 2.3, the core team is the FinOps team comprised of FinOps analysts and practitioners who provide strategic advice on Enterprise FinOps techniques, processes, and best practices to different IT teams. Financial analysts collaborate on IT billing and budgeting. IT managers are responsible for taking action on operations and engineering initiatives, department metrics, and costs. Business stakeholders lean on IT teams for services that keep them productive. Operations teams keep the lights on, and procurement teams work on rate optimization, benchmarking, and negotiating contracts that optimize quality and value. These roles are the human engine behind FinOps.

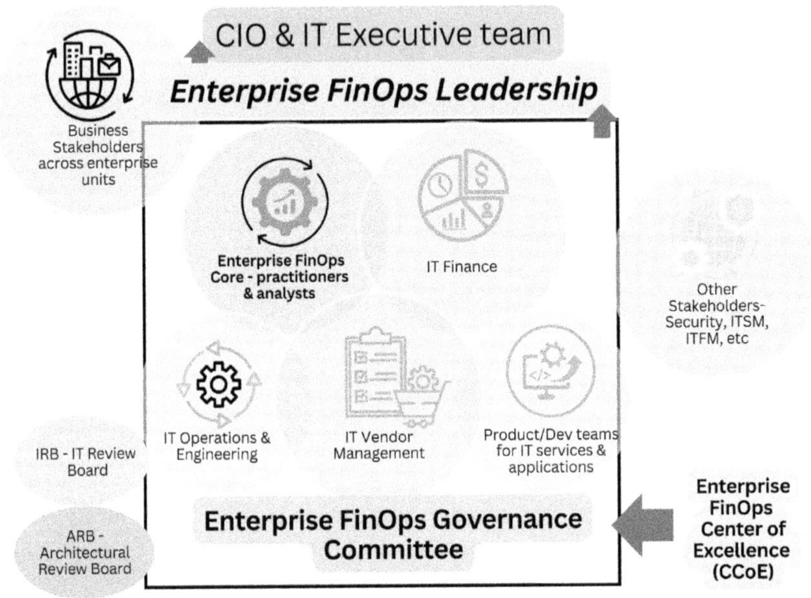

Figure 2.3 Enterprise FinOps personas

The Enterprise FinOps leader is usually a part of the CIO's IT executive team. The Governance Committee team is composed of representatives across IT Operations, Engineering, Finance, Vendor Management, and other stakeholders and is responsible for the governance of FinOps programs. The Architectural Review Board (ARB) ensures FinOps compliance is one of the design and architecture dimensions reviewed at architecture meetings, and similarly, the Investment Review Board (IRB) ensures that IT initiatives are in alignment with business objectives. The core team, along with its activities, methodologies, and processes, can be thought of as an *Enterprise FinOps Center of Excellence.*

2.1.2.4 Phases

Phases provide a roadmap for implementing Enterprise FinOps. Each portfolio in your IT organization may move at its own pace. Some might be stuck in the early stages of FinOps, still stuck in spreadsheets and manual cost reports. Others could be sprinting toward optimization, already reaping the rewards of smarter spending, tool integration, and some automation. Phases provide an iterative way for each team to move ahead in the Enterprise FinOps journey toward a common goal. The chapter on "Implementing FinOps" provides more details on activities and actions in each phase.

- In the "*Strategize*" phase, you establish a clear strategy for Enterprise FinOps that aligns with your overall IT strategy. This defines a vision and long-term goals.
- In the "*Assess*" phase, you map the terrain. This phase identifies opportunities by analyzing the IT landscape. You begin by auditing, not just financial audits, but also operational ones that seek to find the inefficiencies in IT systems. Assess also uncovers what's buried and comes before the hunt for value. A CRM system might be eating up budget without delivering the promised ROI. A public cloud might be underutilized. This phase is where you dig hard and where you ask, "What if we reallocated this?" or "What if we stopped paying for something we don't need or that is not being used?"
- The next phase, "*Optimize*," is where you roll up your sleeves and start cutting IT waste. Maybe the operations team shrinks a server from 24 cores to eight, or they decommission a redundant tool.
- "*Manage & Govern*" keeps the train on the tracks. Policies, procedures, controls, tracking KPIs, and metrics are the guardrails that prevent chaos. Reporting financial insights and FinOps gains builds trust. Chargeback and Showback reports provide transparency to business stakeholders.
- "*Expand*" is where you roll out Enterprise FinOps to cover every part of your IT organization.

This isn't a one-time project but a continuous endeavor. The moment you think you've got it all figured out, the world changes. It's a cycle. You strategize, assess, and find value. You optimize and manage goals and actions and make them part of your IT governance. Then you start again in the next iteration, for every part of your portfolio.

2.1.2.5 Processes

Processes are the tools you use in each phase. An Enterprise FinOps assessment provides a deep dive into where money is flowing. Rightsizing aligns workloads with the correct resources. License harvesting is the art of finding unused licenses buried in a corner of the network and repurposing them. It's not glamorous, but it's how you avoid wasting $100k on software no one uses. The chapters on Enterprise FinOps levers elaborate various processes and techniques for cost optimization and business alignment.

2.1.3 A System View of Enterprise FinOps

The Enterprise FinOps system view, depicted in Figure 2.4, originates from a vision and a strategy to gain a shared understanding of IT expenditure across the entire portfolio. Silos have traditionally choked this. Finance sees costs, engineering sees resources, and neither truly grasps the other's world. FinOps dismantles these barriers.

With an Enterprise FinOps strategy and vision in place, you can create the center of excellence. It starts with the Assess phase, and then Optimize and Manage/Govern. You gain visibility ideally through a single, unified FinOps platform, drawing data from everything, whether cloud, data centers, subscriptions, or even legacy systems. This gives you a holistic view where, before, there was only fragmented data. Teams use a mixture of disparate tools and methods to report back on their share of IT spend, but this fragmentation leads to a lack of true visibility. Integrating information from individual billing, manual, and cost monitoring systems into a single consolidated tool gives you a view of your entire IT spend and opens doors to continuous optimization on an organizational scale. This lets you understand IT spend and see exactly where, how, and why money is being

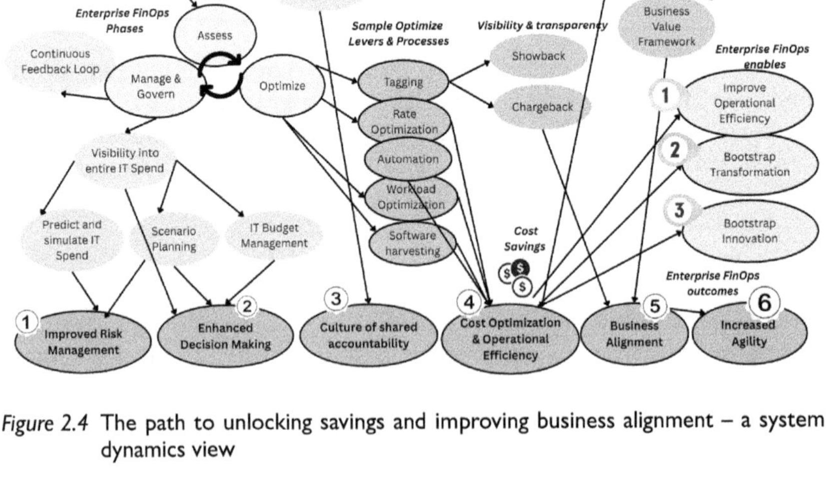

Figure 2.4 The path to unlocking savings and improving business alignment – a system dynamics view

spent by any part of your portfolio, whether applications, services, users, or environments.

Visibility and assessment let you identify optimization opportunities. It exposes underutilized resources, duplicate spending across business units or even "shadow" groups within IT itself. Techniques like application rationalization let you discover applications that no one or very few users use, which sip away infrastructure and costs needlessly.

But data alone isn't enough. Standardized tagging gives you a window and a granular view of where money is being spent. Assigning clear labels (such as project, department, unit) to every resource ensures accountability and allows for detailed analysis. It seems basic, but strong governance to maintain those tags is the often-forgotten key. Beyond tracking mere cost, we need shared metrics and KPIs that resonate with business as well as IT.

Optimizing the IT spend may involve discrete projects as well as continuous activities. Discrete projects may include activities like rightsizing environments, automated scaling, and migrations, while continuous activities include benchmarking, license harvesting, workload optimization, rate negotiation, and optimization. The chapters on Cost Optimization and Technical Levers describe these activities in more detail.

Businesses often complain about not understanding IT costs. Optimizing IT costs has traditionally been the responsibility of IT. With FinOps, business units are encouraged to be accountable for their IT consumption. Providing them transparency and visibility through clear "Showback" and "Chargeback" reporting lets business consumers understand how IT costs are being spent on services that they use and collaborate on cost optimization activities.

A Business Value Framework aligns IT spend with business goals and tracks ROI, providing visibility into projects and initiatives. Aligning IT investments with business priorities lets you provide a strong rationale and justification for strategic investments. Visibility into legacy costs can provide a data-driven approach to make decisions on transformations, becoming a data-driven process, not a gut-feeling decision. This strong business alignment provides confidence and trust to the business that IT is continuously optimizing spend and that IT resources are focused on initiatives that deliver the greatest value.

Once you have visibility into the IT spend, you can develop cost models and simulations to predict future IT expenses. Trend analysis, planned investments, ROI calculations, and usage patterns help in enhanced decision-making. It not only gives you a window into predicted IT spend, but also into avoiding overspending and simulating changes in business and their impact on IT, for example, growth in the manufacturing capability of the enterprise that may add workforce in factories. This improves IT risk management by giving you a proactive way to measure and manage risks to IT spend.

Managing FinOps effectively depends on regular reviews, data analysis, and collaboration with IT teams to implement optimization and cost savings measures that were identified. This cycle of "Assess-Optimize-Manage" unlocks a continuous feedback cycle. An added bonus is the culture of cost-consciousness and business stewardship that starts developing across all levels of the IT organization.

To make this work, you need cross-functional teams such as finance, procurement, operations, and engineering working together, under the sponsorship of IT leadership. When these teams collaborate, they unlock collective buying power. Finance needs to provide strategic oversight, establish cost models, and drive accountability. Procurement must negotiate contracts and manage vendor relationships. Operations monitor resource utilization and identify inefficiencies. Engineering acts on the optimization recommendations, but also makes cost-conscious design decisions when building products, applications, or services.

Finally, these outcomes of cost optimization, business alignment, enhanced decision-making, and others let you further improve operational efficiency through targeted initiatives, as well as bootstrap transformations and innovations.

2.1.4 Cloud FinOps vs. Enterprise FinOps

You may have already started a Cloud FinOps journey. As shown in Figure 2.5, Cloud FinOps can be considered a subset of Enterprise FinOps. Using Cloud FinOps, teams develop insights into cloud consumption, such as what's being used, by whom, and at what cost. You mostly use cloud provider tooling and integrations, although several independent tools are also available in the market for providing real-time cost visibility across multiple cloud platforms. Enterprise FinOps aims for a more ambitious and strategic approach to build a cost-aware culture across your entire IT landscape. Enterprise FinOps considers *all* IT assets, platforms, and services in its scope. This includes on-premises infrastructure, software licenses, network services, and even legacy systems that may be hosted on mainframes, or an application that may be lying in the dusty corner of one of your factories. Enterprise FinOps can steadily drive a cultural change across the organization by encouraging teams to consistently think about the value they are delivering to the business from IT and to proactively manage costs.

Figure 2.5 Cloud FinOps is a subset of Enterprise FinOps

2.1.4.1 Key Differences between Enterprise FinOps and Cloud FinOps

Table 2.1 highlights the key differences between Enterprise FinOps and Cloud FinOps. FinOps, you're tracking instance types, storage tiers, and usage with tools mostly provided by your cloud vendor. It's tactical, focused, and precise. Enterprise FinOps expands its scope to all of IT. Your costs could be in the cloud, on-premises data centers, or buried in a services or software licensing contract. Your IT spend could be in hardware, licenses, support fees, downtime, or even the costs of an ongoing project. In Enterprise FinOps, you need a unified platform that pulls data from everywhere to manage the entire IT budget as a single entity.

Accountability in Cloud FinOps is usually local. It's who's responsible for that SaaS tool or the redundant server that's eating up budget. But Enterprise FinOps defines ownership for every IT investment, aligning every decision with business goals. Cloud FinOps uses tactical moves like shrinking an instance, optimizing storage tiers, or cutting unused resources.

Table 2.1 Key differences between Cloud FinOps and Enterprise FinOps

Feature	*Cloud FinOps*	*Enterprise FinOps*
Scope	Primarily cloud services	All IT assets and services, including infrastructure, data centers, cloud and on-premises hosted applications, edge-hosted applications, and SaaS.
Time horizon	Short-term, tactical	Long-term, strategic.
Focus	Optimize cloud consumption	TCO, cost optimization, and strategic alignment to business.
Tooling	Cloud provider tooling	Broader range of tools and processes.
Collaboration	Cloud and DevOps teams	Cross-functional (finance, IT engineering, IT operations, development, IT procurement).
Governance	Lightweight, focused on consumption	Robust, multilevel accountability.
Measurement	Cloud consumption metrics	Business value, ROI, TCO.
Cultural change	Encourages cost awareness in cloud assets	Drives a cost-aware culture across all of IT.

It's like trimming a tree with small, precise cuts. Enterprise FinOps uses both tactical moves and big-picture decisions: where to invest, what to cut, and how to align IT with strategy. You can even pivot from cloud-only to hybrid models, saving by shifting workloads to on-premises hardware where it makes sense.

Automation in Cloud FinOps sets up alerts for unexpected costs or auto-scaling instances. Enterprise FinOps aims to roll out automation everywhere. You automate policies, governance, and even incident management and create a system that evolves with your business.

2.1.5 Role of Enterprise FinOps in IT Financial Management and Budgeting

Traditional IT Financial Management (ITFM) relied on forecasts, chargeback models, and variance analysis that often felt like walking in the dark across a crowded room. Enterprise FinOps redefines ITFM. It asks, "How does this service actually help the business?" It brings cost intelligence into the room where decisions are made. It helps you turn vague assumptions into actions. Budgets now become a conversation about outcomes. When you see exactly how much that failed project cost, or why that server is running 20% over budget, accountability becomes a shared responsibility. FinOps doesn't just highlight issues like overspending, security gaps, or inefficient resources. It gives your teams a structure to act quickly and decisively.

Total Cost of Ownership (TCO) analysis used to feel like an unnecessary chore whose results nobody used in any way. But with FinOps, you're mapping every hidden cost, from licenses to downtime. Variance analysis shows you when costs went over and also why they did. The data about sudden spikes in storage or failed upgrades explains the past and goes further. It allows you to shape the future. Capex vs. Opex decisions are no longer guesses. You can look at the ongoing costs of every asset, and suddenly, that $500K server on a tool that's hardly ever used shows up as a risk, not an investment. Enterprise FinOps transforms how the entire organization thinks about IT costs. You stop managing costs and start building value.

2.2 Typical Cost Drivers and Cost Factors in IT

Your IT organization is tuned to the distinct needs of your enterprise business and users. It conforms to the processes for your unique industry sector, products, and services. However, there are several common types of IT spend. The enterprise's users who are involved in creating the products, services, or value depend upon IT for essential services. These could be platforms for productivity, email, and team collaboration or customer-facing services such as websites. They could be employee services such as payroll systems, manufacturing systems that manage the company's factories, and many more. Figure 2.6 illustrates common cost drivers and their typical percentages. Here, we further analyze the drivers behind the spending.

Hardware and Infrastructure: Hardware and infrastructure costs are typically 30–40% of the overall Run spend (excluding major projects and transformations, which could involve significant initial investment). This includes IT spend on components such as laptops and end-user workstations, monitors, servers (on-premises and cloud-based), network and Wi-Fi routers, storage systems, mobile devices, etc. Recent spend also includes cloud services such as Infrastructure-as-a-Service (IaaS) and Platform-as-a-Service (PaaS). You may have potentially specialized hardware for IoT, although extensive automation (robotics, sensors) in manufacturing may go under the business unit rather than direct IT spend.

Important business drivers are ensuring reliable, scalable processes and equipment. The main cost drivers are the number of employees (especially for PCs, telephones, and mobile devices), operational requirements,

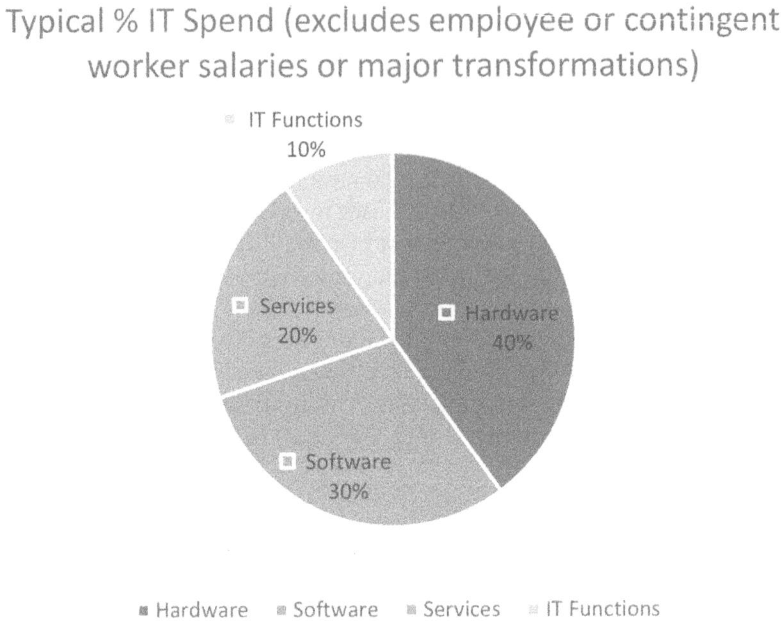

Figure 2.6 Typical IT spend percentage by portfolio

scale of production (production or customer applications), and number of sites (for network bandwidth and communications). FinOps' ability to track infrastructure consumption and identify underutilized resources can dramatically reduce costs. It focuses on workload optimization and *rightsizing*, ensuring the correct amount of capacity is provisioned without overspending. Automation is key for automating provisioning, scaling, and decommissioning processes.

Software: The next category is software, typically about 20–30% of IT Spend. Here, the focus is on licensing the software and its underlying development or operational platforms from external product vendors. Software costs also include developing or maintaining homegrown software. Examples include licensing enterprise systems for ERP, CRM, MES (Manufacturing Execution Systems), service management platforms, productivity and collaboration suites, HR systems, web applications and e-commerce platforms, etc. There may be thousands of enterprise-level software products in a company's portfolio, maintained directly by IT as well as commissioned by business units for specialized purposes such as simulation or lab testing. Software licenses may also be requested by individual users based on specialized roles, such as marketing content creators needing design software, engineers requesting simulation tools, or CAD/CAM software, or technical architects using diagramming or modeling software.

Here, the business drivers are focused on maintaining core business processes like sales, marketing, or manufacturing, supporting user productivity, and facilitating digital customer interactions. Cost drivers include the number of users using the software, the individual modules licensed from the vendor, application development and testing software used to create, manage, or deploy the applications, the number of developers and testers, licensing models, terms and service levels, etc. SaaS models are increasingly being used across the enterprise, especially for CRM, HR, collaboration, and ERP systems. FinOps' role is to ensure optimal licensing, consolidating licenses, renegotiating contracts, evaluating subscription-based models (SaaS) when necessary, and tracking actual usage. It also considers software retirement to identify and decommission outdated or unused software.

Services: The next major category is services, which could take up between 15 and 25% of IT Spend. Services could be outsourced or provided by in-house personnel. Typical services include helpdesk support, IT infrastructure management, cybersecurity, application development, employee and customer helpdesks/call centers, vendor management, and procurement. Services could be outsourced or use consulting services or contingent staffing. Services also include specialized support services from niche vendors.

Here, the drivers are to leverage specialized expertise. You reduce operational overhead and optimize support costs. FinOps can drive cost optimization through strategic sourcing, vendor consolidation, and performance-based pricing arrangements. It helps negotiate better rates and holds service providers accountable for performance.

IT Functions: Other IT functions that could take up between 10 and 20% of IT Spend include cybersecurity solutions (firewalls, intrusion detection systems, vendor management, security information and event management), employee and customer onboarding and recruitment and training, and legal services for contracts, intellectual property, or regulatory compliance. You may have unique functions and services that provide and augment the value provided by your IT teams.

The business drivers are to drive employee productivity and support regulatory requirements. FinOps also informs decisions around IT talent investment, justifying training or talent management programs based on quantifiable benefits and ensuring a rational allocation of resources.

Rather than just cost reduction, which implies a one-time activity, Enterprise FinOps seeks to achieve continuous cost optimization, or *strategic orchestration*. By providing visibility into IT spend, promoting a consumption-based mindset, and empowering teams to make informed decisions, FinOps enables the business to align IT investments with strategic objectives on a continuous basis.

2.2.1 IT Cost Factors

Let's define a cost factor as "the underlying core fixed or variable metric behind the total cost of ownership of the asset or service." This includes initial as well as operational costs of any asset across its intended audience and users, over its usage lifetime. Let's take a simple example of a laptop. Assuming a specific performance configuration, cost factors for a laptop would be the cost of the device, the cost of licensing the OS, and standard productivity and security software such as antivirus and network authentication. A key factor would be the number of units needed based on the number of your enterprise users. Other factors would be the operational support costs for maintenance and deploying image upgrades and patches, as well as the cost of maintaining an IT helpdesk for laptop repairs, software deployment, and user services.

Table 2.2 lists 15 cost factors and the potential savings that implementing FinOps could provide on ongoing costs, and Table 2.3 dives into fixed versus variable cost factors for typical IT assets

Actual cost factors will vary significantly based on the specific implementation, vendor or product brand, negotiated contracts, and operational practices across business and IT.

Also consider fixed and variable factors. For example, for laptops and workstations, the fixed costs are determined based on the device cost and the costs to maintain an IT helpdesk team to support users, and an IT imaging team to deploy patches. The variable costs would be determined by repair and replacement costs for damaged or lost devices. Cost Factors lets you develop a predictable model for budgeting and scenario planning.

2.2.2 SaaS and Software Cost Factors

SaaS simplifies the IT landscape considerably, albeit at a cost. From 1999, when one of the first SaaS platforms, Salesforce, was launched, to today, the SaaS landscape has changed considerably. (Fryer, n.d.). Today, CIOs have considerable SaaS choices for almost all of their application portfolios. The advantage is that the underlying infrastructure, as well as the application tiers, are completely managed by the SaaS provider. Often these are offered as multi-tenant offerings, where other companies' data

Table 2.2 IT cost factors and FinOps savings potential

Rank	*Cost factor*	*Category*	*Potential savings from FinOps (%)*	*Typical cost optimization techniques*
1	Server procurement costs	Hardware	15–30	Optimize sizing, explore cloud instances, consolidate workloads.
2	Software licensing costs	Software	20–40	Software harvesting, rightsizing licenses, cloud-based SaaS, exploring open-source alternatives.
3	Maintenance support costs	Services	10–25	Negotiate SLAs, self-service support, automation.
4	Leasing costs (data centers)	Infrastructure	10–20	Cloud migration, reduced footprint, co-location efficiency.
5	Cloud compute costs (VMs)	Cloud services	15–30	Optimize instance types, rightsizing, auto-scaling.
6	Storage costs (block/object)	Cloud services	10–25	Data tiering, data lifecycle management, data compression, data storage policies.
7	Network bandwidth costs	Network	10–15	Optimize traffic, compression, caching.
8	Database licensing costs	Software	15–30	Software harvesting, cloud databases (serverless, managed), rightsizing.
9	Backup and disaster recovery	Services	10–20	Cloud-based solutions, automated backups, efficient recovery.
10	Monitoring and logging	Services	10–25	Automation, cost alerts, intelligent monitoring.
11	Container orchestration	Software	10–20	Managed Kubernetes services.
12	Serverless computing costs	Cloud services	20–40	Event-driven architectures, pay-per-use.
13	User licensing costs	Software	10–25	Software harvesting, cloud-based alternatives, user management.
14	Managed services fees	Services	10–25	Optimize service level agreements.
15	Staffing costs (IT professionals)	Operations	10–25	Automation, optimized staffing models.

Table 2.3 Variable and fixed cost factors for some IT assets

Asset category	*Asset area*	*Fixed cost factors*	*Variable cost factors*
Hardware	Servers (on-premises)	Hardware cost, power consumption, room rent/utilities, server management staff salaries.	Maintenance contracts, power surges, downtime costs, storage expansion costs.
	Network infrastructure (routers, switches)	Hardware cost, network cabling, network security software licensing, network monitoring tools.	Bandwidth costs, internet service provider (ISP) fees, router firmware updates, security breach costs.
	PCs/laptops	Device cost, OS and software licensing, IT helpdesk support, IT management staff, training, asset tracking.	Repair costs, upgrades (RAM, Storage), repair costs, warranty extensions, device theft/loss costs.
Software	Business enterprise Systems (SAP, Oracle)	Initial license fees, implementation costs, ongoing maintenance fees, training costs, IT support costs.	System updates and patches, data storage costs, system configuration costs, business process optimization costs.
	Office productivity suites	Licenses, training, IT support, system integration costs.	User additions/removals, storage costs, helpdesk support costs.
Services	Cloud infrastructure (IaaS, PaaS)	Subscription fees, storage costs, data transfer costs, compute resources.	Usage-based charges, storage expansion costs, data transfer costs.
	Managed services (IT support, security)	Hourly rates, monthly retainers, service level agreements (SLAs).	Overtime costs, SLA penalties, incident response costs, transition and knowledge transfer costs.
	Helpdesk/call center services	Hourly rates, monthly retainers, staffing costs, software licenses.	Overtime costs, agent training costs, call volume increases.
IT functions	IT management and IT talent	Salaries, benefits, training costs, recruitment costs.	Leadership training costs, succession planning costs, employee turnover costs.
	Employee and customer training	Training materials, instructor fees, facility rental, IT support costs.	Training program updates, certification costs, employee turnover costs.

may reside on the same infrastructure foundation; however, providers offer comprehensive solutions to ensure privacy, security, and separation of data. Some also offer single-tenant solutions, where your organization's data and infrastructure are kept completely separated and isolated. For your IT department, this means that they do not need to worry about the maintenance aspects as they would with cloud-hosted or on-premises applications. Application maintenance and upgrades are handled completely by the vendors at scheduled intervals. While many organizations extensively customize SaaS platforms to conform to their business processes, core upgrades and maintenance can still take place seamlessly.

SaaS platforms are significantly more expensive than maintaining and running similar applications on your own infrastructure. You are also tied to the vendor, and migrating between platforms is not a trivial task, making SaaS renewals a major event for procurement organizations. Let us dive deeper into the cost factors for a typical SaaS software like Salesforce CRM.

2.2.2.1 *Recurring Subscription Costs*

- Subscription and licensing fees are the major components, taking up approximately 60% to 80% of the total cost. This also depends on what modules or editions are licensed on the platform. Core license fees are usually based on the user count and editions. While their licensing models may be subject to change, a typical SaaS CRM may have a fixed base subscription fee per user per month or year. To allow for user growth, SaaS vendors allow a limited number of downgrades in license numbers at fixed periods throughout the contract. Contracts are usually multi-year, with larger discounts for multiple years. Variable charges would be based on user growth or reduction and directly tied to user count changes.
- Most SaaS vendors also offer add-ons specific to the edition or module. Salesforce, for example, has licenses for Service Cloud, Marketing Cloud, Sales Cloud Einstein, etc. There could be transaction or volume-specific add-ons; for example, Marketing Cloud allows you to send emails, with each email incurring a usage charge.
- Another component is vendor support services. Generally, the premier level of support has the highest charge. Availability of training material may incur additional charges.

2.2.2.2 *Implementation Costs*

- Implementation and setup of the platform could incur significant upfront costs. Most SaaS vendors have consulting organizations that charge fees for implementation, training, and onboarding users, and for customization. Several third-party companies have built up niche services around SaaS platforms offering project-based services such as configuration, customization, data migration, and user training.

- Your business users will invariably ask for customizations. This could be custom forms suited to your business processes, or integrations with other enterprise systems. Variable costs could be caused by scope creep related to unexpected requirements or changes during implementation. Data migration may be a high cost as data cleansing and transformation could be extensive, depending on the quality and format of existing data, and the volume of data being migrated. Development may be needed for integration with other systems (e.g., ERP, marketing automation).

2.2.2.3 *Ongoing Operational Costs*

- The last category is ongoing operational costs. While the SaaS provider manages the underlying infrastructure, you will still need your own team to manage the environment and develop customizations specific to your business needs. This could take up around 20–30% of the total cost in annual operating expenses. For a CRM team, this cost would be in salaries or contractor fees for developers and administrators for maintaining the system, managing users, and configuring settings. Key activities include ongoing system monitoring, troubleshooting, and resolving issues.
- Indirect costs are often hidden. Considerable time is spent by internal teams (IT, sales, marketing) on training. Another hidden cost is that of change management for adapting business processes to fit the tool.
- Most SaaS platforms have developed extensive marketplaces, where external vendors can develop add-ons and integrations and offer seamless deployment into your implementation using subscription models. Salesforce has its AppExchange, with apps available for everything from Slack and Team integration to specialized modules such as outbound marketing. Here, the costs are variable; the more users of the app utilize, the higher the overall cost.

2.2.2.4 *Optimizing SaaS Costs*

It is important to assess diligently whether users are actively using their subscription and services. You can optimize SaaS costs by actively managing the number of users licensed on the platform, signing up for the right level or edition of the platform, and actively managing the modules or features that are licensed. It is not uncommon to find that your business

Table 2.4 Typical Enterprise FinOps potential savings on SaaS platforms

Rank	*Cost factor*	*Description*	*FinOps value (potential savings %)*	*Optimization activities*
1	Subscription costs	Base license, module or edition licenses	15–40	Software harvesting, optimize license tiers, consolidate modules, reduce licenses, utilize tiers rather than overcommit.
2	Admin or contingent worker salaries	Salaries for resources needed to maintain the platform	10–20	Automation, knowledge base optimization, improved efficiency.
3	Implementation and configuration	Initial setup, configuration, custom workflows, integrations	10–30	Standardized configuration, leverage pre-built integrations, phased rollout.
4	Custom development and integrations	Developing custom workflows, integrating with other systems	15–30	Use platform extensions, low-code tools, minimize custom development.
5	Training and knowledge management	Training users, building the knowledge base	10–30	Self-service knowledge base, efficient training programs.
6	Ongoing support and maintenance	Support contracts, upgrades	10–20	Optimize support tiers, proactive monitoring, leverage included support from the vendor.
7	System admin costs	Maintaining the SaaS instance	10–30	Automation, efficient system administration.
8	Integration platform costs	Integration platform as a service cost, marketplace add-ons	5–10	Minimize custom integrations, leverage platform extensions.
9	Reporting and analytics costs	Reporting tools, dashboard creation	5–10	Utilize built-in reporting, automate report generation.
10	Data migration costs	Migrating data from legacy systems	5–10	Efficient data mapping, automated migration tools.

units have licensed modules anticipating future usage, but have never actively used these features in any business process. Highly customized SaaS implementations dramatically increase cost. Poor user adoption can negate the benefits of the SaaS tool and increase training costs. Continual optimization of processes and configurations is key to controlling costs. Especially at renewal events, vendor and procurement organizations need to diligently leverage FinOps to assess the correct requirements from their users, and to negotiate the best deal with the SaaS provider.

As shown in Table 2.4, let us look at an example of how Enterprise FinOps can be applied to SaaS platforms. Enterprise FinOps can drive cost savings of between 10% and 40% in many cases.

2.2.3 *Data Center Cost Factors*

You've likely already saved millions in operational costs by letting go of your expensive owned data center premises and moving to a co-located data center. But even this is littered with hidden costs. As shown in Table 2.5, the lion's share of your data center budget, 40–60%, is likely tied to the physical infrastructure. This is the cold, concrete reality of rack space, power, network connectivity, and cooling. Rack space and power are fixed monthly costs, often ranging from $100 to $500+ per server. But location, redundancy, and uptime guarantees can push these costs skyward. Power consumption is a variable cost that scales upwards with server utilization. The more you run, the more you pay.

Network connectivity, another fixed expense, can range from $50 to $500+ per month per server, depending on bandwidth needs. While cooling is often bundled into data center fees, it can be a silent cost driver in high-density environments. Then there's the software side of the equation, which eats up 20–30% of the budget. Hypervisor licenses and management tools are essential for virtualization. System vendors offer support and maintenance services when your operations team needs expert help.

Automation and management tools are the unsung heroes of efficiency and could take up 10–20% of the budget. Configuration management

Table 2.5 Data center cost categories

Cost category	*% of IT spend*	*FinOps potential savings (%)*
Physical infrastructure	40–60	10–30
Virtualization and management software	20–30	10–20
Automation platforms and scripting	10–20	20–40
Operational and admin	10–20	10–20

platforms such as Puppet, Chef, Ansible, monitoring systems such as Zabbix, Nagios, and orchestration tools such as Kubernetes and Docker can cost anywhere from $200–$5,000+ per server yearly. The complexity of your environment determines the price. Security tools like antivirus software and firewalls add further costs but are indispensable to keeping your infrastructure secure.

The human element could take up 10–20%. This is where Enterprise FinOps can make a real difference and optimize the entire ecosystem for scalability, efficiency, and long-term savings. System and database administrators, operations and DevOps engineers are the backbone keeping your infrastructure running and executing workload optimization activities. Automation can offset expenses by reducing manual labor.

2.2.4 IT Services Cost Factors

Outsourcing services to external vendors could save money in the long run; however, there are hidden cost factors that could derail your savings. The biggest factor is the set of services you are outsourcing. This could be ongoing operational services like system maintenance or help desk. One-time services may include a system transformation or migration, or you may have outsourced the development of an application. These services are driven mostly by the project scope and timeline. Service Level Agreements (SLAs) are also factors, where a more stringent SLA for, say, 99.5% uptime or 24x7 services could be significantly more expensive than, say, 95% uptime. Then again, it's your choice of provider. There is a wide variance between the costs charged by different vendors for similar services. A niche vendor or a vendor offering "implementation" expertise for its own products could be much more expensive than a general-purpose IT services vendor, especially someone who may be able to leverage resources in low-cost or nearshore locations. Vendor management is the invisible work of aligning your team's priorities with the vendor's processes. Running an efficient Request-for-Information (RFI) or Request for Proposal (RFP) process, selecting the right partner, mapping workflows, working with the legal teams on ensuring your contracts are right, and negotiating terms all take time. Your team's time here matters because if you don't get this right, the entire outsourcing effort could backfire.

Then there's the transition of services. A critical part is the knowledge transfer, where the real heavy lifting takes place. Mapping your existing support processes, workflows, and service level agreements is critical for the vendor to understand your world. You'll spend time migrating FAQs, troubleshooting guides, and even those weird edge cases only your team knows. Training materials for the vendor's team are part of the cost too. It's ensuring the vendor gets your culture and not just a playbook. They need to understand your pain points and your expectations. There may be numerous pilot runs as the vendor starts shadowing you and then gradually takes over the outsourced work from your current, incumbent teams. They'll stumble, you'll give feedback, and you'll refine processes. This phase is where you'll catch gaps in the vendor's understanding or your own misaligned expectations. Tools for reporting and communication may add up to 10% of the service spend.

Once the transition is done, operational expenses take over and may account for 70–80% of your total budget for such services. You're paying for the vendor's talent. The vendor's account manager is your dedicated liaison, monitoring performance, resolving issues, and keeping you in the loop. Systematic reports on SLA performance, ticket volume, resolution times, and customer satisfaction let you track progress. Quarterly business reviews give you the opportunity to synchronize leadership teams, ensure vendors are addressing pain points, and align with your IT strategy. Change management could be a variable cost depending on what needs to be added. Minor updates may not always be included in the contract. In general, ticket volume directly impacts costs as more tickets mean more support hours. Complex systems and niche products may require higher-tier and more expensive expertise. Stringent SLAs can load you down. Optimize on what your business absolutely needs rather than blindly following industry standards or what your vendor is recommending. Faster resolution timelines mean higher service-level expectations. Pricing models can be tricky. There can be so many quirky models, from per-agent or per-ticket pricing to flat rates.

Outsourcing services is a partnership that requires transparency, alignment, and a clear understanding of what you're paying for. The real value lies in how well the vendor fits your needs and how prepared you are to navigate the costs that come with it. And then there are levers, such as vendor consolidation, that we can execute to further save costs.

2.2.5 Opportunities for Savings

Sometimes you may feel that your IT budget is like a black hole, swallowing resources without giving you anything back. As depicted in Figure 2.7, over-provisioning and costly rates are the tip of the iceberg, but what's really draining your finances may be buried deep inside the iceberg, in places you might not even suspect. Let's touch on some hidden corners of your enterprise where savings could be waiting to be claimed.

Departments often sign up for tools that duplicate existing licenses, pile on redundant features, or simply sit unused. You may end up paying for premium SaaS tiers that your team never touches. Abandoned subscriptions may be a costly sink. That "innovative collaboration tool" your

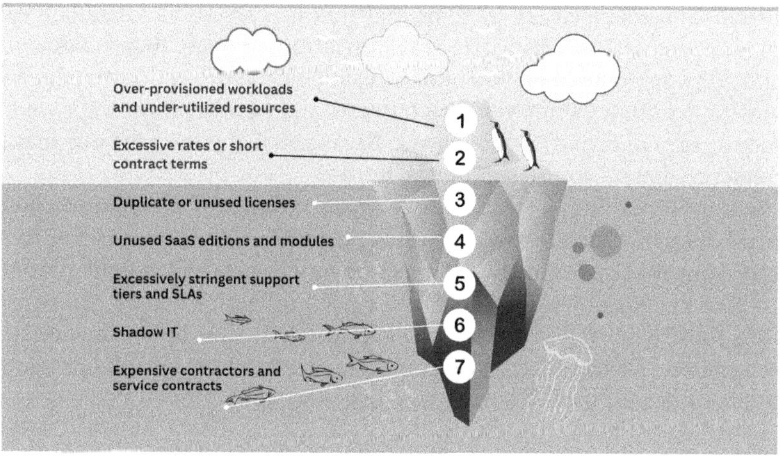

Figure 2.7 Savings can be hidden from obvious view

marketing team signed up for last year may still be on the bill, even though no one's logged in since Q3. Enterprise support contracts may be another minefield. You're likely paying for gold-tier support when bronze would do, or worse, paying for support you never actually use. Data transfer fees may be silently adding up. Whether you're moving files between clouds or backing up data from your cloud to on-premises storage, bandwidth charges can add up quickly. Storage is often over-provisioned by a factor of three or more, with data sitting idle while you pay for it. Networking costs are often underestimated but can be a shocker when you tally them up. If your servers are running at 10% utilization, you're leaking capital every single moment. Perpetual software licenses with annual maintenance fees or maintaining a sprawling fleet of desktop licenses could be another cash drain. Shadow IT is another silent load on your budget. You may be paying excessively for contractors and contingent workers who were onboarded at high rates and have been retained way past the original project timeline.

With Enterprise FinOps, savings are within reach. The next chapter outlines how you can implement Enterprise FinOps in your organization. Subsequent chapters talk about levers that elaborate on key techniques and processes in further detail. Optimizing SaaS subscriptions and eliminating Shadow IT could free up 10–30% of your budget. Renegotiating contracts and trimming third-party services could yield 15% more. Rightsizing infrastructure, shutting down idle resources, and streamlining storage could add another 10–30%. Application rationalization is another powerful tool. You retire legacy systems that no one uses and consolidate tools that duplicate effort. Prioritize modernization projects that reduce your technology debt and keep you nimble. Challenge your vendor management teams to negotiate better vendor contracts and build relationships that let you leverage collective buying power. Because when you're the one making the big purchases, you're setting the terms.

You need real, actionable data to make it happen. That means diving into IT analytics, third-party monitoring tools, and usage reports to see where your money is bleeding. Categorizing IT spending is your roadmap to where the biggest wins are. There's no "perfect" moment. Start now. Assess those SaaS subscriptions and applications. Shut down the ones that don't matter. Renegotiate those contracts. Turn off or consolidate servers that are under-utilized. Your bottom line will thank you.

2.3 Enterprise FinOps Aligns IT Spend with Business Goals

IT is the quiet enabler, the team that keeps the lights on, fixes broken systems, and avoids disasters, keeping your business running as expected. But the modern business environment needs more than a reactive model. Customers demand instant results, and technology evolves faster than ever. With ruthless competition perennially on your business horizon, IT needs to be more than a back-office function. It's time to be a strategic partner that drives innovation and aligns with the business's goals.

Enterprise FinOps offers an integrated way to make sure every dollar spent on technology actually does something useful, like accelerating product launches, improving customer experiences, or slashing waste. FinOps streamlines the whole process of getting things done. FinOps lets you approach automation with a steely but pragmatic determination, using the right level of automation for the task. Eliminating repetitive tasks and standardizing procedures, no matter where in the IT system, cuts delays, reduces errors, saves money, and lets teams focus on what matters. With FinOps, you can protect the business from security breaches, regulatory compliance issues, and disaster recovery nightmares. IT can predict what the business needs and act on it.

Enterprise FinOps lets you see the full picture, every expense, every team, every decision, and its potential impact, and align them all toward the same goal of a business that's agile, efficient, and future-ready. The appetite to strategically optimize will follow through naturally once people see the opportunities. Prioritization is important so you don't burn out your team. You link every cost-saving initiative to a business outcome.

Enterprise FinOps is working for many companies today. Fostering collaboration and adopting agile practices that keep everyone aligned with the business's priorities takes active efforts. Enterprise FinOps is a way to turn IT into a strategic force that drives value.

2.3.1 *Why Is Business Alignment Essential?*

If your IT investments aren't directly tied to the business's goals, it could stifle innovation and slow down progress. When IT spend isn't aligned with the core business, things fall apart as resources get funneled into projects that don't matter. You fund a new software tool that doesn't solve a real problem, while the team that actually needs support is left scrambling. Innovation becomes a guessing game as you pour time and money into technologies that don't address the business's pain points, and suddenly, the whole initiative feels like a waste. The business sees no return on investment, and the IT team feels like they're fighting a losing battle.

The chapter on "Measuring Enterprise FinOps" provides information on identifying metrics and KPIs for business alignment. You can start by understanding what the business really needs by looking for specific, actionable objectives. Once you've got that clarity, you can translate those goals into IT requirements. You can determine what systems, tools, or processes are needed to make those objectives happen and prioritize them based on impact. But alignment is a continuous process. You need feedback loops, such as regular check-ins between IT and the business, to ensure investments are still relevant and delivering value. Because just like technology, the business's needs change. If IT is operating in a vacuum, it's like building a bridge without knowing where it leads.

When done right, the benefits are huge. Aligned IT spending drives revenue. Think of the time that automation your team carried out shaved off hours off a process, freeing up teams to focus on higher-value work. Alignment breaks down silos and fosters collaboration. Mainly, it ensures everyone is working toward the same goals. When IT and the business are aligned, innovation changes from being possible to becoming inevitable. You're building the tools, systems, people, and processes that let the business move faster and adapt quicker. Treating IT like an expense is like buying a powerful engine for a car that only moves in reverse. It's wasted potential. But when you align IT spending with business goals, you're investing in the future of the company.

2.3.2 *Integrating Cost Optimization into IT Governance*

When you integrate cost optimization into your governance framework, you build a system that thinks about cost before it even spends. That's where formal reviews like the IT Investment Review Board (IRB) and the Architectural Review Board (ARB) come in (or whatever you have named these in your own organization). They're the brain trust that keeps your IT investments from going off the rails.

The IRB is your first line of defense against wasteful spending. It's your gatekeeper for every major IT investment across software, hardware, and services. You can set thresholds to determine which potential investments need to come to your table. Others can flow up to your IT executives on your team. Teams need to prove that their investments are worth it. A typical IRB is made up of people like the FinOps Lead, your IT Business Unit executives to keep the business goals in check, an IT operations lead to make sure it's technically feasible, an Architectural Lead to avoid reinventing the wheel, and a Vendor Management/Procurement lead to negotiate the best vendor contract. The process starts with a formal request. Whenever someone says they need something, it should be followed up with a Total Cost of Ownership (TCO) analysis, which includes everything from acquisition to training, maintenance, and operational costs. The IRB validates if this investment aligns with your business strategy. It explores alternatives, risks, and the business value.

The ARB focuses on architecture. It lets you determine if the investment or solution is in line with defined architectural principles. It opens the window by asking whether the solution reduces technology debt. The ARB is typically led by your Enterprise Architects, a FinOps Lead because cost still matters, and a Security Lead to avoid costly breaches. They challenge teams to consider if automation and right-sizing are already factored in, and if we are using Infrastructure-as-Code to automate deployments, ensuring consistency and reducing errors. They push teams to consider the plan to scale and how the solution maps into a Business Capability Model (BCM) if you have one. Architectural reviews determine if you are making the correct decisions on whether to deploy something to the cloud or on-premises, or if we are building for the future with cloud-native principles like microservices or serverless to cut infrastructure costs.

You'll soon develop a strong feedback loop between the IRB, ARB, and the FinOps team. The IRB looks at business value, ARB determines compliance with design and technology, and everyone thinks about cost and whether cost optimization is baked into the plan. Key KPIs like TCO, cost per user, and cost per transaction become tools that guide every decision. You've developed a system that thinks about cost before it even spends.

2.3.3 The State of FinOps Report

The latest "State of FinOps" (State of FinOps, 2025) report from the FinOps Foundation paints a picture of a rapidly evolving landscape, where the scope of FinOps is expanding to include AI, SaaS, and even data centers. With hundreds of respondents across diverse industries and sectors, this annual survey highlights several key trends and insights in cloud and SaaS spend. The report also emphasizes that FinOps isn't limited to the cloud anymore. Hybrid and multi-cloud environments are the new norm, and practitioners are being pushed to manage costs across diverse tech stacks, from SaaS subscriptions to on-premises data centers.

Despite the growing demand for FinOps expertise, many practitioners are feeling the pressure. The report highlights three major pain points: organizations are still grappling with unused and underused resources, with some reporting a huge percentage of their infrastructure going unused. That's a missed opportunity for cost savings. Without clear, application-specific cost data, forecasting and budgeting become a guessing game. Standardized processes for rate and usage optimization are still a work in progress. As enterprises grow, integrating FinOps into governance frameworks becomes a critical hurdle. It's not enough to have a FinOps team; they need to collaborate across departments, align with business strategies, and tailor practices to each technology scope. The report stresses that FinOps is a shared responsibility. That means working closely with collaborative groups such as the CCoE to ensure governance, compliance, and alignment with enterprise priorities.

The report outlines three major outcomes from robust FinOps practices:

- With granular, historical data, organizations can make timely decisions and assign clear cost ownership to individual applications or services.
- By optimizing rates and addressing underutilized resources, FinOps can cut costs and improve efficiency across all technology scopes.
- FinOps is described as "everyone's job," with cross-functional teams required to align on cost management strategies. That means integrating FinOps into product development, procurement, and operations and building a culture of accountability.

A few trends stand out.

- SaaS spend is on the rise, with more organizations moving to subscription-based models, forcing FinOps to adapt to new ways of tracking usage and managing costs.
- Hybrid and multi-cloud environments are reshaping the landscape, pushing FinOps to expand its scope to manage costs across diverse platforms. Consistency in governance and visibility will be key.
- The application of FinOps to AI is a hot topic, with practitioners asking for specialized tooling and workflows to manage AI-related spend, from training data to model inference costs.

The "State of FinOps" report reiterates that FinOps is letting organizations save money, drive innovation, sustainability, and alignment with business goals. The success of FinOps will depend on its ability to evolve with the pace of innovation.

2.3.4 *Industry FinOps Frameworks*

Before 2025, FinOps was like a narrow tunnel, focused on public cloud spend. Today it's a wide-open door. Teams are being asked to manage on-premises infrastructure, hybrid environments, SaaS and AI environments, and even legacy systems that haven't been touched in a decade. This is a recognition that FinOps techniques can be effective across all of IT. Today FinOps teams are a strategic partner, working with product teams to understand how a new on-premises data center impacts ROI, or helping engineering leaders evaluate whether a SaaS tool is worth the recurring cost. Your FinOps collaboration councils are the voices that look at systems that may cost $300,000 a year to maintain, but that we're only using 15% of their capacity. That's the kind of insight that only comes from visibility across all technology investments.

I introduced my Enterprise FinOps framework in this chapter. Let's explore how the industry has evolved other frameworks. Not surprisingly, there are robust frameworks from the major cloud providers such as AWS, Microsoft Azure, and Google that elaborate on Cloud FinOps. If you have a major spend with one of these players, there is detailed and ready guidance on how to optimize these environments, use tools embedded into the services, and save costs. Google Cloud FinOps (Google Cloud FinOps, n.d.) leans into a "Cost Accountability" model, pushing responsibility down to the team level. AWS FinOps (Lacarak & Raja, n.d.) talks about "Cost Ownership," and how to use tools like AWS Cost Explorer to let teams drill down into their own spending. Microsoft Azure FinOps (Microsoft Azure FinOps Toolkit, n.d.) emphasizes integration with tools that are baked into the Microsoft Azure platform. You can set up alerts in real time, automate budget thresholds, or even tie spending to performance metrics.

However, there's an even more compelling option, especially if you have multiple cloud vendors or want to apply FinOps across all of IT. The FinOps Foundation has developed a comprehensive FinOps framework (FinOps Framework, n.d.) that provides best practices and guidelines for implementing FinOps in your organization. With their 2025 iteration, this framework introduced "Scopes" that expand their concepts into other areas of IT. It aligns very well with the concept of Enterprise FinOps as outlined in this book. Appendix 1 in this book outlines this framework in further detail.

Whether you're starting with accountability, diving into visibility, or automating your way out of costs, the goal is the same: to control your spending, boost efficiency, align with business goals, and unlock value. The difference lies in how you get there. The next chapter discusses "Technology Debt Reduction," another key area for optimization as part of the Enterprise FinOps journey.

The Law of Conservation of Momentum states that the total momentum in a closed system remains constant unless acted upon by an external force. This law has similarities to the momentum that cost-saving initiatives establish through Enterprise FinOps. Once an initiative, such as cloud migration, software harvesting, SaaS adoption, or workload optimization, gains momentum, it will maintain its trajectory unless disrupted by factors like organizational resistance or politics, regulatory changes, budget cuts, or shifting business priorities. A company that successfully transitions to a hybrid cloud infrastructure may experience sustained cost savings and operational efficiency, but this momentum can be derailed if the organization fails to address emerging challenges, such as data security risks, exponential costs, or vendor lock-in. The CIO must act as a steward of momentum, ensuring that once Enterprise FinOps is set in motion, it is protected from disruptions that could reverse its progress. This requires strong executive support and a governance framework that anticipates potential roadblocks and adapts strategies to maintain the trajectory of value creation.

Note

1 FinOps specifies Enterprise FinOps throughout this book unless specifically referred to as the FinOps framework from the FinOps Foundation.

References

FinOps Framework. (2026). Retrieved from https://www.finops.org/framework/

Fryer, V. (2026). The history of SaaS: From emerging technology to ubiquity. Retrieved from https://www.bigcommerce.com/blog/history-of-saas/

Google Cloud FinOps. (2026). Retrieved from https://cloud.google.com/learn/what-is-finops?hl=en

Lacarak, M., & Raja, S. (2026). *FinOps-establishing-an-operating-model-for-the-cloud.* AWS. Retrieved from https://pages.awscloud.com/rs/112-TZM-766/images/FinOps-Establishing-an-Operating-Model-for-the-Cloud.pdf

Microsoft Azure FinOps Toolkit. (2026). Retrieved from https://learn.microsoft.com/en-us/cloud-computing/finops/toolkit/finops-toolkit-overview

State of FinOps 2025. (2026). FinOps Foundation. Retrieved from https://data.finops.org/

Chapter 3

Technology Debt Reduction

DOI: 10.4324/9781003682196-6

3.1 Understanding Technology Debt

Technology debt refers to the accumulated technical inefficiencies and outdated systems that organizations continue to use due to their critical role in business operations. It hinders an organization's ability to innovate, integrate, improve efficiency, or respond quickly to changing business needs. It often arises as a consequence of not addressing critical technical issues or design flaws over time. But it's not always due to human inaction. Technology, by nature, continues to age day after day. It has a shelf life that eventually expires. Vendors fade away into history. Even thriving product companies eventually stop supporting older versions of their technology due to the burden of maintaining older technology. While regular maintenance and upgrades can keep your systems humming for much more than the stated life, eventually, you need to consider upgrading the technology due to the accumulated risks and inefficiencies. Accenture defines "tech debt" as *"the cost in money and effort required for a company to keep its IT systems* up-to-date *and capable of meeting business needs"* (Accenture, 2025).

In the context of our RTI360 model, technology debt impacts and slows down Run, and reduction of debt is usually through Transform actions.

3.1.1 *What Is Technology Debt?*

The first use of the term "debt" in the context of IT is attributed to Ward Cunningham, who in a conference in 1992, remarked: "Shipping first-time code is like going into debt. A little debt speeds development so long as it is paid back promptly with refactoring. The danger occurs when the debt is not repaid" (Letouzey & Whelan, n.d.). Today, technology debt applies to every aspect of IT products, services, operations, and applications, not just software or code.

Technology debt can be seen in IT in various forms. Outdated technology is one of the most common. You will often hear end-users and system administrators complaining about slow or unresponsive systems. Outdated hardware, software, or systems that are no longer supported by vendors or have security vulnerabilities are one of the main causes of technology debt in IT. However, technical inefficiencies can also creep up over time through inefficient processes, manual workarounds, or poorly designed solutions that waste resources and slow down operations. Systems or applications that cannot handle increased traffic, data growth, or user demand lead to performance issues or crashes, clearly a problem when your business wants to scale up to meet increased demand or changes in demand. Even cybersecurity has its share of technology debt. Inadequate security practices such as weak passwords, unpatched vulnerabilities, or inadequate access controls put sensitive data at risk. The problem can also stem from poor design choices. Inefficient system architectures, monolithic designs, or a lack of modularity make it difficult to maintain, update, or scale systems.

You can manage and mitigate technology debt. As this chapter elaborates, there are several best practices and techniques that can help you reduce technology debt and keep it continuously down to manageable levels. Enterprise FinOps is a best practice that can be leveraged to manage and reduce your technology debt. As with most mitigation programs, it is important to first assess the situation to identify and prioritize the most critical issues. This can let you develop a plan to address these issues, justifying the allocation of resources and budgets to tackle the most pressing issues and implement changes to reduce technology debt over time.

3.1.2 How Does It Impact IT?

Technology debt has significant consequences for an organization's productivity, innovation, and competitiveness. It acts as a drag on your IT budget, increases costs that lead to increased maintenance, support, and upgrade expenses. Inefficient processes and outdated technologies slow down operations, leading to decreased productivity and revenue. Unpatched vulnerabilities or weak passwords put sensitive data at risk of being compromised. Ultimately, it is a barrier that limits innovation. Outdated technology inhibits your ability to innovate, respond quickly to changing market conditions, or adopt new business models.

The cost of addressing technology debt can vary widely depending on factors such as the scope and complexity, scale, and size of the IT landscape, regulatory or compliance pressures, such as in the healthcare or finance sectors. The more complex the technology debt issue is, the higher the costs will be. Larger organizations with more extensive IT infrastructure tend to have higher technology debt costs. A recent study from Pegasystems reflected the opinion from many of the survey participants that legacy systems and applications are preventing their organization from fully embracing more modern technologies such as AI (Technical Debt Stifling Path to AI Adoption for Global Enterprises, n.d.). Another major concern was the impact of technical debt on their ability to keep pace with more agile, innovative competitors. A study conducted by consulting firm Protiviti (The Innovation vs Technical Debt Tug of War, n.d.) indicated that organizations today spend a significant percentage of their IT budgets on technical debt management.

These estimates will vary based on your specific circumstances and scenarios. Technology debt incurs excessive costs in maintenance, and more so, it takes time and effort from your team to keep systems running and vulnerabilities fixed so that they do not break down operations. This is time and effort that could otherwise be spent on innovation. Legacy systems also prevent your IT landscape from being integrated into a seamless system, as they may not be amenable to sharing data with modern systems.

3.1.3 Technology Debt vs. Technical Debt

Let's dig down further into the nuances between "technical debt" and "technology debt." Today, we use these words interchangeably, and in general, technology debt can apply to any part of your IT landscape.

Technical Debt originated in the software world, primarily referring to the developer's decisions and choices that compromise code quality, design, or architecture. Quick decisions. Shortcuts in coding. Rushed timelines that led to incomplete testing. These are the ghosts that haunt IT departments long after the project is done. I've been in situations where the pressure to deliver forced teams to skip testing, write code with no comments, or pick a technology that sufficed for now. But those choices don't vanish; rather, they compound. A single missed step in documentation can turn a simple fix into a two-week nightmare. A convoluted algorithm, chosen to save time, becomes a bottleneck years later. Code is just the tip.

Technology debt applies to your entire IT landscape, whether hardware, software, or applications. Compromises across the entire stack can lead to technology debt. A poorly chosen database or an outdated server can slow down performance. How many "quick fixes" on your legacy system turned into long-term liabilities? Technology debt can increase maintenance costs by 30% or more. The real cost is harder to measure. It's in the lost opportunities, the team morale, and the risk of a single misstep derailing everything. Every time we rush, we're trading future clarity for present convenience. It can arise from decisions about the *technology platform*, such as the choice of programming languages, frameworks, databases, operating systems, or infrastructure. Examples include using a legacy database system that's nearing end-of-life, relying on an outdated library with known security vulnerabilities, or running applications on infrastructure that's no longer supported.

Table 3.1 summarizes the key differences between technical debt and technology debt. Recognizing this difference allows for more targeted remediation efforts. Technical debt mitigation focuses on the architects, developers, and programmers who code systems, with refactoring and code improvements. Technology debt requires a more strategic approach, potentially involving migrating to a new platform, upgrading to a supported version, or decommissioning outdated systems. In this chapter, technology debt focuses on the entire IT landscape, while we will use specific terms like Software Tech Debt, Cloud Tech Debt, or Hardware Tech Debt to refer to specific areas.

Table 3.1 Key differences between technical debt and technology debt

Feature	*Technical debt*	*Technology debt*
IT portfolio	Software and applications.	Any part of the IT landscape, including hardware, software, or services.
Potential causes	Developer decisions.	Technology platform choices.
Scope	Code quality, design.	Entire ecosystem.

3.1.4 Software Technology Debt

Software tech debt is the cost of rework. Coders choose an easy solution now instead of a better approach that would take longer. This is often subconscious. Compromises are made during software development to meet a deadline or address immediate needs. Project managers and sponsors push teams to address constraints in time or budget rather than investing in a more robust, maintainable, and scalable solution.

Software technology debt arises when developers make decisions that aren't ideal in the long run. This could be a hasty implementation, where developers rush to meet a deadline by using a quick-and-dirty solution instead of a well-designed one. Sometimes they make architectural decisions that aren't optimal for future growth or maintainability. It could be as seemingly minor as a lack of documentation, where developers and testers skip documentation to save time, which makes it harder to understand and modify the code later when new teams take over the code. Even when best practices, coding principles, and conventions are mandated, developers may ignore these mandates, resulting in code that is unpredictable.

As illustrated in Figure 3.1, there could be several sources in the IT lifecycle that leads to accumulation of software debt. One of the chief culprits is reduced or inadequate testing time, or a lack of structured testing. It is common knowledge that bugs in production systems cause more havoc and expense to fix than bugs detected before deployment. Some design choices stem from familiarity or lack of experience, as developers or architects choose to retain older technologies that are difficult to maintain or integrate with newer systems, or technical quick fixes, where they implement temporary fixes that do not address the root cause or underlying problem.

Software debt is a ticking clock. I've seen teams spend weeks untangling a single function because someone six months ago took a shortcut. Maintenance costs compound. A system built on shaky foundations requires constant patching. Every fix feels like a temporary bandage. Agility is a myth when you're drowning in debt. I remember a project where a client

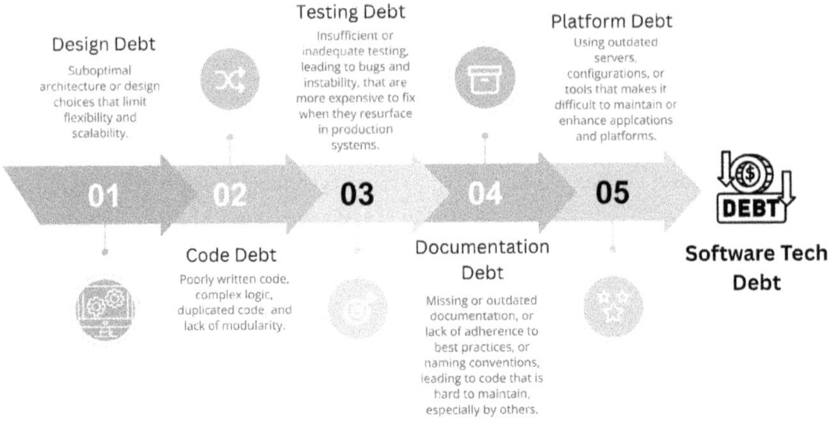

Figure 3.1 Software tech debt

needed a new feature in two weeks. The team had to pause everything to stabilize the existing system. That delay led to a missed opportunity, a lost revenue stream, and a frustrated leadership team. Thoughtworks has an excellent guide that provides various perspectives on identifying and managing technical debt (Thoughtworks, n.d.).

3.1.5 *Infrastructure Technology Debt*

Technology debt in infrastructure, such as in hardware systems, network devices, or PCs, is often overlooked because it's less visible than software debt, but it's a substantial contributor to operational costs, time spent on unplanned work, system downtime, and overall inefficiency.

As illustrated in Figure 3.2, maintaining legacy hardware and obsolescence are key contributors to infrastructure debt. Moore's law (Moore, n.d.), stated by Graham Moore, is the observation that the number of transistors in an Integrated Circuit (IC) doubles about every two years. Hardware devices have been fueled by a continuous release of even more powerful IC chips and other components almost every six months. This has resulted in vendors releasing upgraded iterations of devices in similar timeframes. However, every device has a generally reliable operational lifecycle, usually between five and ten years. However, operations teams continue to operate older servers, network devices, storage systems, and even workstations beyond their intended lifespan, often due to the high costs of modernization.

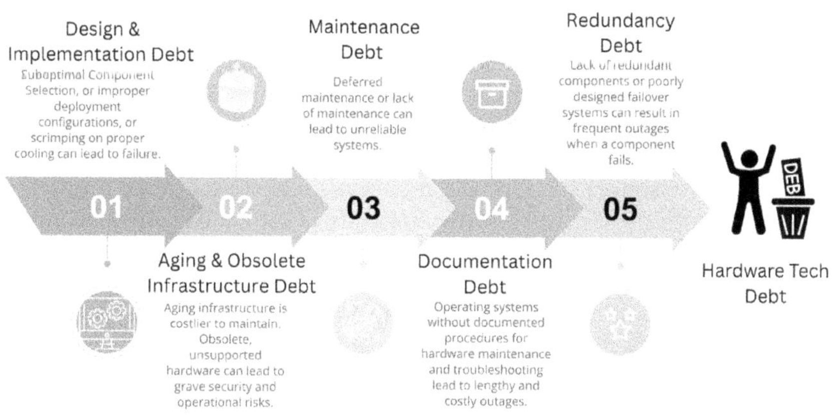

Figure 3.2 Infrastructure tech debt

There can be huge costs to this accumulated infrastructure debt. Delaying necessary upgrades due to budget constraints, perceived complexity, or a belief that the current system is still good enough can lead to unreliable, unmaintainable, and slow systems. Even more risky is obsolescence, where teams operate hardware that's no longer supported by the vendor. Even if you intended to maintain systems regularly, often the vendors have stopped releasing security patches or bug fixes. This results in costly unintended outages, or drives you to seek third-party support services that are niche and expensive.

Architects may pick the cheapest server just to save a few dollars, only to watch it choke under load. A bottleneck forms in the data center, where a single underperforming component slows everything down. Hardware compatibility is another trap. When you build a system with components from multiple vendors, you need thorough testing to ensure the whole system performs as intended. Network designs can be like highways with no traffic lights. Inefficient layouts create congestion. A single misconfigured router causes 30% higher latency. A poorly segmented network can become a backdoor for security breaches. A single missed or misconfigured firewall rule can lead to a data breach.

Then there's the physical side. Server racks are crammed into corners. Cables tangled like spaghetti. Cooling systems that barely function. I've had to recover painfully from mishaps where the rising temperature from a failed cooling system caused servers to overheat and shut down. A single failure brought the entire ERP system to a halt and took weeks to restore.

Operational debt is another killer. Teams defer maintenance because there's no window. Systems run on borrowed time. Delaying routine maintenance tasks such as cleaning up data from databases, patching, and firmware upgrades are common operational issues that arise from this technology debt. Operating systems without documented procedures for hardware maintenance and troubleshooting lead to lengthy outages. Relying on personnel without the proper training to maintain and troubleshoot complex hardware systems results in extended and frustrating resolution times.

Maintenance costs spiral. A server that's five years old will likely cost 30% more to repair than a new one. And that's before you factor in the downtime. Trying to get hold of compatible parts for older systems may become a nightmare unless you have an expensive service contract with the vendor, assuming they still support your version. Older hardware sucks up power. Overheating components can trigger cascading failures. Unsupported hardware is like leaving the front door unlocked. A server that can't handle a 10% increase in traffic becomes a bottleneck. Every shortcut and ignored warning adds to the debt. It's a domino effect. How many more compromises can you afford before the debt becomes a crisis?

3.1.6 *IT Services Technology Debt*

As shown in Figure 3.3, IT service technology debt stems from accumulated inefficiencies, workarounds, and suboptimal processes associated with the delivery of IT services like helpdesks, business or IT operations,

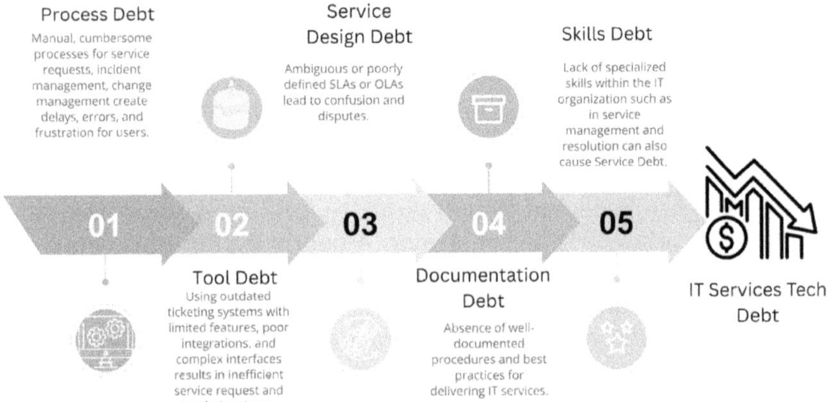

Figure 3.3 IT services tech debt

and projects. It's the invisible weight that slows down everything. I've seen it when working on optimizing our operations. A helpdesk team spends hours manually resetting passwords (until we replaced it with automation), and a project manager tracks tasks in spreadsheets. It even happens with related services when a new hire has to wait for three months to get a laptop and access to key systems fully working. It's a constant weight dragging down customer experience, employee morale, productivity, and business growth.

Lack of proper documentation also leads to service debt. I've worked at companies that had no case management systems until I set one up. When a server crashed, they had no idea what had happened before. No root cause analysis. Inefficient problem management procedures lead to the same problems repeating over and over again as the underlying root causes are never fixed, and temporary workarounds become permanent stop-gap arrangements.

Lack of skills increases service debt. Some teams lack the expertise in service management, SLAs, or automation. I've seen a helpdesk team struggle with SLAs that were vague or conflicting. Often, they resort to best efforts that simply end up with frustrated users.

Lack of specialized skills within the IT organization, such as in service management and resolution, can also cause service debt. Another overlooked area is poor service design. A company I worked with still relied on phone support for basic tasks. Users had no self-service options. Training was non-existent. The result was a helpdesk drowning in calls for things that could've been resolved in minutes. A single inefficient process can delay a project by weeks. A poorly designed SLA can spark a dispute with an outsourcing partner.

Ambiguous or poorly defined Service Level Agreements (SLAs) with outsourcing service providers, or Operational Level Agreements (OLAs for internal teams) lead to confusion and disputes. Reliance on outdated or inefficient service channels (e.g., phone support when self-service options exist) and poor user adoption or training increases service debt. Supply Chain, ERP, and CRM systems can suffer from excessively customized, poorly documented ERP integrations and a lack of automation for business processes.

3.1.7 Cloud Technology Debt

Given the premise of aging infrastructures and obsolete systems causing infrastructure debt buildup in traditional infrastructure, one would assume that IaaS and PaaS cloud services would always be free of any technology debt. Similarly, with SaaS providers offering services that keep their platforms relatively up-to-date, you could well assume that you could avoid

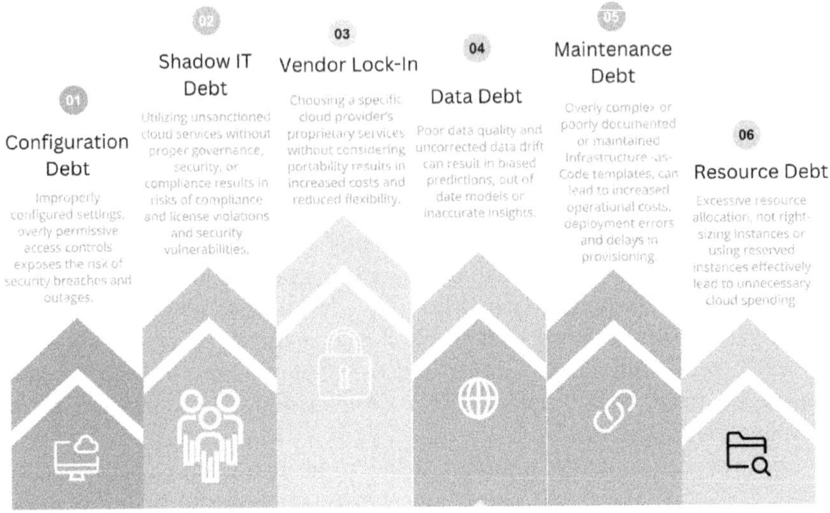

Figure 3.4 Cloud tech debt

software debt by moving to SaaS platforms. However, cloud services, SaaS platforms, and even modern technologies like AI/ML systems are impacted by technology debt, albeit in different ways. In fact, the agility and rapid deployment cycles of the cloud can *accelerate* the accumulation of debt if not managed carefully. Figure 3.4 summarizes some common sources of cloud debt.

Improperly configured security settings or overly permissive access controls expose the risk *of* security breaches and inflated cloud costs. Since cloud environments have been so easy to procure and provision, there is a risk of increased Shadow IT, where business units or even IT units outside the IT infrastructure group could utilize unsanctioned cloud services without proper governance, expertise, security, or compliance. This results in risks of compliance and license violations and security vulnerabilities.

A rather common form of cloud debt is vendor lock-in, where choosing a specific cloud provider's proprietary services without considering portability results in increased costs and reduced flexibility. This is especially true with SaaS systems, where portability of business applications among different SaaS platforms is especially limited, and users are reluctant to move to another system.

Even IaaS systems can accumulate cloud debt. Overly complex or poorly documented or maintained Infrastructure-as-Code templates, originally intended for automating manual tasks, can lead to management overhead resulting in increased operational costs and deployment errors. Over-provisioning or not using reserved instances effectively leads to unnecessary cloud spending.

Data-related debt even arises in AI/ML systems. Inaccurate, incomplete, or inconsistent data used to train models leads to biased predictions or inaccurate insights. Statistical properties of data change over time, causing model performance to degrade. If models are not retrained in timely intervals, this can cause decreased accuracy and unreliable predictions. You can't provide AI transparency and explainability if you are not tracking the origin and transformation of data. This can result in compliance issues when you cannot explain the behavior of a model. Overfitting models, where models are trained too closely to the training data, results in low accuracy in production.

As you can note from this section, the cloud and use of modern technology itself don't remove debt. It simply provides new environments and new ways to accrue it. Technology debt management and mitigation are equally important for cloud, SaaS, and AI/ML environments as they are for traditional systems. Enterprise FinOps can effectively and continuously reduce your cloud technology debt.

3.2 Technology Debt Management and Mitigation

Technology debt does not arise suddenly; it's a gradual, compounding process driven over time by a complex interplay of factors and events. But we can mitigate these using techniques that are an integral part of an Enterprise FinOps implementation.

3.2.1 Technology Debt Accumulates Over Time

The most common driver is short-term pressure, such as time constraints, aggressive deadlines, and pressure to deliver features "now" that invariably lead to compromises in quality, design, and documentation. It could arise in choosing and deploying hardware components or creating software applications. Developers often prioritize speed over best practices. As projects evolve, new features are added to the original requirements, often without sufficient consideration for their impact on the existing architecture. If you lack architectural governance, Shadow IT teams will find paths to provision resources. Without clear architectural guidelines, coding or hardware standards, teams can make inconsistent decisions, leading to a fragmented and poorly integrated system.

Central oversight is often lacking, and architectural consistency suffers. We already saw how documentation debt causes technology debt accumulation across the entire IT portfolio. When developers or system administrators leave, their knowledge and understanding of the system walk out with them unless the system or application and maintenance procedures have been documented properly. If the team isn't adequately trained on the current technologies, they're more likely to make mistakes and introduce new debt. As new technologies emerge, the team might lack the expertise to adopt them effectively, leading to the accumulation of outdated technologies.

Testing is usually your safety net, but unfortunately, it's the first that gets ignored when teams are in a rush. I've seen it often happen because the team prioritizes speed over security. A feature released without proper validation lets a vulnerability slip into production, which causes a 48-hour outage, a loss of customer trust, and thousands to clean up. Rushed releases are a recipe for disaster. But when teams skip best practices like regular refactoring, technology debt piles up like uncollected trash. One client had a legacy system that hadn't been refactored or optimized in five years. The code was a labyrinth of spaghetti logic. It was simply impossible to add any new features because it took months just to understand where to start. A development team once built a feature based on vague requirements from the business side. The operations team had no input, and the result was a system that was impossible to monitor or scale. The feature worked, but it was a nightmare to support. The cost of such issues is more than simply time or money. It erodes the trust between teams and triggers a slow decay of a system that was once functional.

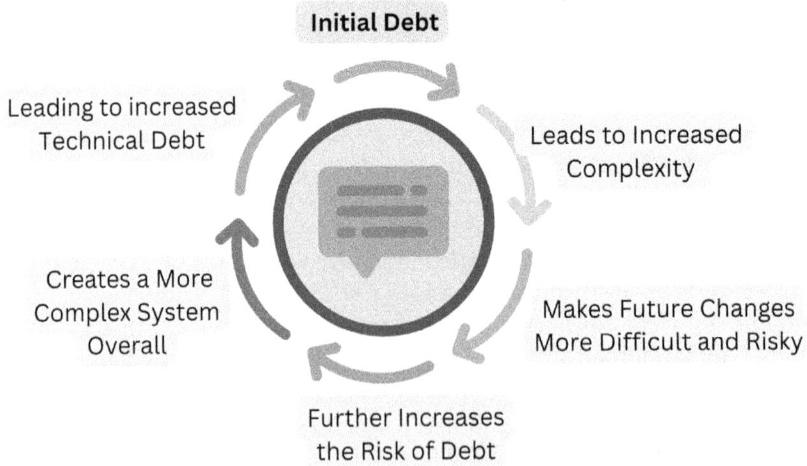

Figure 3.5 The compounding effect of tech debt

3.2.2 *Compounding Effect*

Technology debt doesn't work linearly. We've talked about the domino effect of debt. The debt keeps compounding in every iteration, as illustrated in Figure 3.5. Imagine a simple website built quickly to meet a deadline without proper documentation and a glorious lack of conventions, security checks, or coding standards. As the website grows and new features are added, the original code becomes increasingly convoluted. This creates technical debt. It makes it difficult to add new features or fix bugs. The more complex the system becomes, the more difficult it is to maintain, and the more debt accumulates. A complete refactoring of the code can solve this, but it will be an extensive effort.

3.2.3 *Application Rationalization*

Application rationalization (AppRat) is a foundational step in any serious effort to reduce technology debt. This is a strategic and systematic process of evaluating and prioritizing your portfolio of applications to identify redundancies, overlaps, and technical debt, directly informing the scope and direction of any future transformation plan. It involves analyzing the value, cost, risk, usage, and other factors associated with each application to determine the optimal course of action. The goal is to create a streamlined and efficient application landscape. It results in identifying which applications are aligned with your business goals and identifies opportunities for consolidation, retirement, and modernization, providing valuable direction for any debt reduction strategy. Surprisingly, even IT organizations within mature enterprises have not conducted a thorough application rationalization activity, leading to an accumulation of systems that slowly but surely drain away valuable IT budgets just to maintain and run, even if only a handful of business users were using such systems. I highly recommend launching an application rationalization program concurrently with any Enterprise FinOps program, and definitely prior to any major digital transformation initiative, if not already done.

3.2.3.1 *Benefits of Application Rationalization*

AppRat identifies redundancy. I've seen companies with five different tools for the same task, each one bloated, each one costing money, each one adding complexity. One client had three separate systems for customer data. The result was a team of ten people spending 20 hours a week reconciling conflicting records. Rationalization exposes these overlaps and also gives you the clarity to say which one to keep and which ones to let go.

AppRat lets you quantify complexity. Legacy systems are a classic example of tech debt in action. They're like old buildings with crumbling foundations. One company spent 20% of its IT budget just maintaining a 20-year-old ERP system. Rationalization highlights the problem and translates it into a tangible number. That 20% is money, and also time, resources, and opportunities lost. When you quantify the cost of complexity, you're making a business case for change.

AppRat clarifies business value. It lets you decide what's worth keeping and what's not. Some applications are like technology ghosts. They are invisible, still running, but delivering nothing. A finance team had a system that hadn't been used in three years. It was still on the books, still being maintained, still eating up resources. Rationalization gives you the data to ask whether the system is worth the effort. AppRat lets you prioritize modernization and focus on what matters. Not every system deserves a modernization overhaul. Rationalization helps you see the forest for the trees. One client during my modernization consulting days had 50 applications, of which only five were critical to their business. The rest were relics, holding the company back. By focusing on those five, they transformed their core systems while phasing out the rest.

Complex ecosystems are a nightmare. I've seen companies spend months trying to connect two systems because their APIs were incompatible. Rationalization helps you choose the right battles. Legacy systems increase security risks. AppRat identifies the biggest risk areas and helps you define a roadmap for mitigation.

People think that rationalization is mainly focused on cleaning up the past, but it's really about building a future that works. It helps you define the "future state" of your application landscape: which systems to keep, which to replace, and which to retire. I was part of a transformation team that used this process to migrate to the cloud, adopting SaaS solutions where it made sense. The result was a secure and scalable architecture that perfectly aligned with the company's business goals and gave them a solid foundation for projected growth and changes such as divestitures and acquisitions.

Technology debt doesn't disappear on its own. It grows, it festers, and eats away at your ability to innovate. But with the right strategy, you can turn the tide, reducing debt, streamlining operations, and paving the way for a digital transformation.

3.2.3.2 Process of Application Rationalization

The Rationalization Process typically includes the following:

- Discovery and inventory: this activity results in an Application Inventory that has a comprehensive list or catalog of all applications.
- Business process mapping: Linking applications to business processes.
- Application scoring: A technical assessment evaluates application quality, stability, and cost and assigns scores based on criteria such as business value, cost, risk, and technical feasibility. Financial Analysis involves assessing the Total Cost of Ownership (TCO).
- Application categorization: Grouping applications into categories (e.g., core, support, legacy).
- Planning for execution: Defining the appropriate technology debt reduction action for each application (e.g., retire, consolidate, modernize, or accept). The 7 Rs of legacy modernization, later in this chapter, elaborate further on this.

Many consulting companies have methodologies for AppRat. Gartner offers a comprehensive model called the Gartner® TIME framework (Gartner, n.d.). This is a method for evaluating and categorizing applications based on their technical and functional fit within an organization.

The TIME framework categorizes your applications into one of four quadrants:

- Tolerate – Accept the application in its current state for the time being.
- Invest – Prioritize gaining maximum value from this high-priority application.
- Migrate – Work on finding a better application to fulfill the business need(s).
- Eliminate – Remove the application, as it is not needed.

Several vendors, such as SAP (LeanIX) and ServiceNOW (ServiceNOW APM), offer specialized tools for Application Portfolio Management (APM). APM frameworks are also offered by many IT services vendors and provide a structured approach to managing the entire application portfolio. Invariably, the methodologies categorize applications based on their strategic value, risk, and cost, and help you determine an application rationalization roadmap for application changes.

3.2.4 *Big Bang Approaches to Mitigation*

A big bang approach to technology debt reduction uses a coordinated, simultaneous effort to tackle multiple initiatives across the entire IT landscape. The goal is to halt the accumulation of new debt while aggressively addressing existing issues and reducing accumulated debt. Before embarking on a big bang, a thorough assessment is critical. This involves mapping all forms of technology debt across software, infrastructure, cloud, SaaS, and service delivery, and prioritizing the targets based on business impact, risk, and feasibility. A big bang approach often introduces massive changes in the organization and is subject to several risks, such as significant disruption, cost overruns, failure to achieve desired outcomes, and potential user resistance. It often takes the form of legacy modernization and digital transformation programs. Big bang approaches allow you to implement standardized platforms and processes across all IT services, reducing complexity and dependencies. This involves the migration of critical applications and services to modern platforms, e.g., cloud, SaaS, and extensive process redesign to streamline workflows and eliminate manual tasks. The IT team needs to be upskilled to support new technologies and processes. Strong communication and management of the change plan lets you address potential disruption and secures buy-in from all stakeholders.

Such risks can be mitigated. Programs can be scaled and targeted to specific systems, or approached sequentially in a phased manner to reduce the risks and increase chances of success. Proof of Concepts (POC) let your teams test new solutions in a controlled environment before full-scale deployment. Big bang approaches need a lot of effort and coordination among multiple stakeholders, both IT and business, to succeed. Besides its impact on IT, business models are often being transformed through digital transformations; hence, it's important that business stakeholders collaborate in this effort. Any parallel execution needs to be carefully planned to avoid over-dependencies and conflicts, and to avoid over-committed, overworked teams. Typically, any digital transformation takes place over several years under a carefully coordinated plan.

3.2.5 Digital Transformation – a Holistic "Big Bang"

Digital transformation aims for a complete overhaul of the business, while legacy modernization often focuses on specific, core systems. Usually, legacy modernization is a *component* of a broader digital transformation strategy. This represents a broader "big bang" encompassing technology, business processes, customer experiences, and organizational culture. It's a holistic shift toward leveraging digital technologies to fundamentally change how an organization operates. From the IT perspective, it may involve a transformation of major IT systems that support business processes.

Omnichannel Customer Engagement would involve redesigning customer interactions across all channels – web, mobile, social media, etc. Transitioning to cloud-based services, including IaaS, PaaS, and SaaS, provides flexibility across the board. Digital transformation also involves cultural aspects, such as the adoption of agile methodologies to improve product time to market through iterative development, rapid prototyping, and continuous feedback, and DevOps practices for collaboration between development and operations teams to accelerate delivery. Change management is absolutely essential for communicating the vision, securing buy-in, and providing adequate training, which is crucial for user adoption of the new systems. You could even shift to a product-centric approach instead of your current platform or service-driven portfolio.

A genuine UX transformation forces you to confront the technology debt that's been making your systems frustrating to use. Bad or neglected user design has resulted in slow clients, outdated interfaces that look like they were from the 1980s, confusing workflows, and inaccessible features. It often happens when systems haven't been maintained in years. Fixing these problems addresses the root causes of technology debt.

When you automate testing, deployment, and operations, you're exposing and eliminating hidden technology debt. Manual processes can mask flaws for years. But automation will flag a broken dependency, a slow-performing database, or a security vulnerability in real time. Digital transformation does not aim to eliminate debt overnight. It shifts left, modernizes incrementally, and uses every opportunity to pay it down.

3.2.6 Legacy Modernization

Also termed as application or system modernization, this is a targeted "big bang" focused on completely replacing aging, monolithic legacy systems with modern alternatives. This is not simply patching old systems. It often involves a complete rebuild or migration of major systems to a modern infrastructure. Talking from the context of the applications that are hosted on legacy infrastructure, Application Modernization can take various shapes. I had written a paper several years back on how and why organizations should undertake legacy system modernization (Sawant, 2020).

Your legacy systems may have fueled your growth in the past, but they're reaching a maturity point. As you embark on new paths and strategies involving technologies such as social, mobile, analytics, and cloud strategies like AI and IoT, you'll likely end up, like most businesses, ignoring your old systems. There will be a phase when your legacy systems have reached a maturity point, while new technologies have already moved past the early adopter phase and are now in the growth phase. If you linger in this "stall" or "dilemma" zone, as shown in Figure 3.6, you risk missing out on the benefits and advantages offered by the new technology adoption, while competitors surge ahead. It's time to unlock the data and intelligence held in your legacy systems and include them in your digital transformation journey.

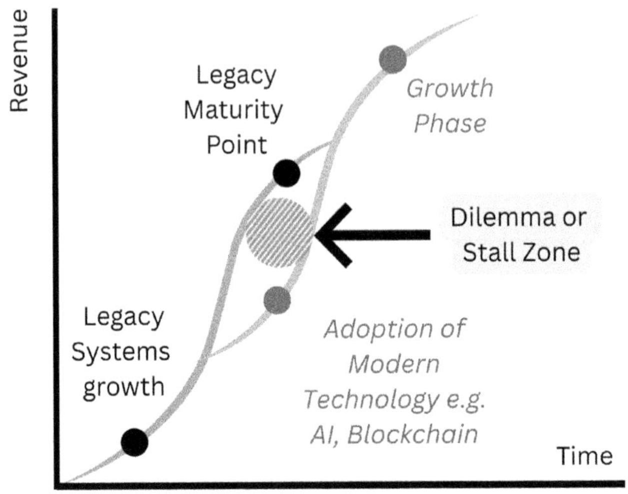

Figure 3.6 The dilemma or stall zone

3.2.6.1 The 7 R's

There are seven common approaches, often referred to as the "7 Rs," to legacy system modernization, each with its own degree of difficulty and payoff, as shown in Figure 3.7. The right option for your organization will help both reduce your costs and make your operations nimbler.

1. **Replace**

Completely decommission and replace existing legacy components.

The organization completely scraps the existing system and replaces it with a completely new system, taking into account new requirements and changed or optimized business processes. For example, replacing a legacy email system with cloud-based Microsoft 365, or your homegrown CRM system with Salesforce CRM.

Replacing with SaaS outright can be a faster route to the cloud, though it requires a significant amount of planning. You may also consider evaluating enterprise platforms or systems that meet the business need, and host them in a modern cloud environment.

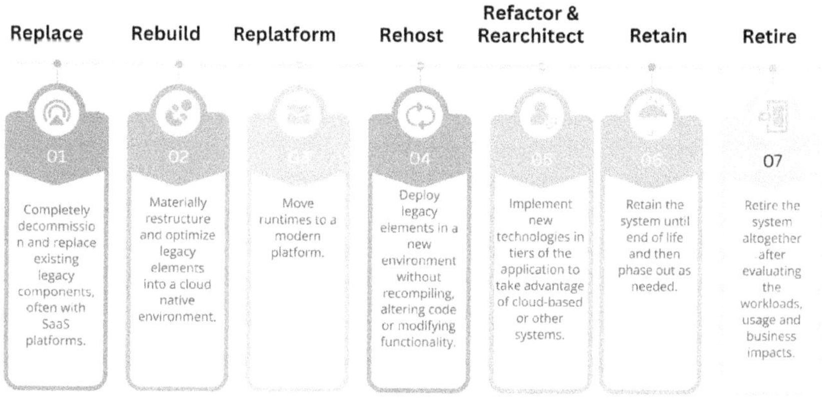

Figure 3.7 The 7 "R's" of modernization

2. **Rebuild**

Materially restructure and optimize legacy elements into a cloud-native environment.

A full rebuild is the longest, most expensive route, but it delivers the maximum benefits. For most businesses, this is the ideal end state, with many of these other options just serving as steps in the journey. A full rebuild rearchitects the legacy system into a fully modernized, cloud-native environment. This includes implementing DevOps methodologies and adopting technologies like containers, service meshes, microservices, immutable infrastructure, and declarative APIs. The combination of methodology and technology enables more flexibility, better performance, and lower operating costs in the long term.

3. **Replatform**

Move runtimes to a modern platform.

The replatform approach ports an application's components to a new runtime platform with minimal code changes and with the same features (e.g., moving a COBOL-based system from a UNIX or mainframe system to a LINUX or Windows environment).

Developers can make minimal changes to the code to adapt to the new platform without changing the code structure or the system's features and functions. An organization can take advantage of reduced infrastructure costs and improved performance, with minimal effort. Additionally, it's able to continue to derive value out of legacy investments.

4. **Rehost**

Deploy legacy elements in a new environment (physical, virtual, or cloud infrastructure) without recompiling, altering code, or modifying functionality.

By rehosting, organizations can maintain their investment in legacy systems, like ERP or databases, and take advantage of better performance and security from the underlying infrastructure of the cloud. Rehosting, also called the "lift and shift" migration approach, lets organizations get to the cloud faster without having to refactor or re-engineer existing systems. An enterprise takes its existing ERP system, database, or other workload and moves it into the cloud as is (e.g., moving an SAP system from an on-premises data center to AWS or GCP). Often, emulators are available that can perfectly run legacy systems in modern environments (e.g., COBOL mainframe emulator for Windows).

5. **Refactor and Rearchitect**

This involves implementing new technologies in tiers of the application to take advantage of cloud-based or other systems, with some code changes in selective tiers.

Usually seen in hybrid environments, this option leverages changing parts of the legacy component to optimize code for better performance. Often this involves changes on the backend without any major changes in the front end of legacy systems or to the functionality offered. This is less disruptive than a complete rewrite. In this scenario, an organization might move the database of a monolithic application to the cloud while still running the majority of the application on-site. As the term implies, the application architecture of the system is optimized, often with code changes.

6. **Retain**

Maintain the current environment with no changes or updates.

An upcoming merger, end-of-life announcement, or other consideration may mean that there isn't a compelling enough case for modernization. Even though the short-term decision is to retain, there should be a long-term strategy in place that ensures the sustainability of critical functions. Generally, retention is a temporary measure, not a long-term strategy. Organizations should be careful about adopting this "kick it down the road" approach. The longer inefficient, resource-heavy infrastructure sticks around, the less budget and resources are available to invest in innovation. Often, a retain approach may necessitate building "connectors" or "bridges" to interoperate with other modern elements in the organization.

7. **Retire**

Retire the system altogether after evaluating the workloads, usage, and business impacts.

After an assessment of the workload, you may determine that it is prudent to retire the application and move any remaining users to alternate systems that are already in place. Often, this may necessitate process redesign to make up for the gap in operational processes from the retired system, and may also offer an opportunity for improved and optimized business processes.

3.2.6.2 Legacy Modernization Is a Primary Technology Debt Reduction Engine

Modernization forces you to look under the hood. Take a monolithic application that's been cobbled together over decades. When you start breaking it into microservices, you're reorganizing code and potentially uncovering a minefield of hidden debt that you can safely address. It tells you where the pain points are, where the risks lie, and where your system is holding you back. Refactoring takes spaghetti code and turns it into something legible, maintainable, and scalable. Rewriting retains your logic and business expertise and replaces the parts of the system that are holding you back, like outdated modules and legacy databases that can't support modern workflows. Decoupling reduces complexity, minimizes dependencies, and creates a system that's resilient to change.

You've heard your architects and developer teams talk enthusiastically about design patterns. Refactoring gives them an opportunity to apply that to solve common coding and hardware challenges using proven methods. You're moving away from outdated architectures and embracing ones that support agility and innovation. You don't reach the summit of a mountain in one leap. You take one step at a time. And with each step, the path gets clearer, the air gets fresher, and the view gets better.

We talked about the cycle of compounding debt earlier. The longer you wait, the more it grows. The more systems you leave untouched, the more they become liabilities. But modernization breaks that cycle. Every system you modernize is creating a foundation for the next innovation. You're freeing up resources that were once tied up in painful and cumbersome maintenance and building a system that's future-ready.

3.2.7 The Myth of Zero Technology Debt

Zero technology debt is a mirage. It lures us into thinking our systems are forever. The truth is that business needs shift like the tide. You designed a state-of-the-art application that wowed business, but that became outdated the moment the market demanded something new. Technologies evolve, libraries deprecate, and what was cutting-edge yesterday is passe today, and needs constant hand-holding, maintenance, and enhancement. The pressure to deliver fast leads to shortcuts and half-baked solutions, and the inevitable accumulation of debt. Even the most disciplined and accomplished teams cannot escape the occasional typo or misconfigured server. A product management approach can minimize technology debt, but even that cannot eliminate it completely.

But you don't need to eliminate debt to succeed. You need to treat it like a living, breathing part of your system, one that you can't ignore but can guide. The goal isn't perfection but reducing the risks that debt introduces. Instead, let's focus on the issues with the highest impact and the greatest likelihood of causing pain. Let's refactor the code that's slowing down deployments. Let's find and fix the root cause behind the issues that cause outages. We'll scale the infrastructure that's crumbling under load, and create better training to onboard users and make them productive. Debt is not a burden, but a call to action. You aim for a system where debt is acknowledged, addressed, and kept under control on an ongoing basis. So, let's see how continuous debt management lets you do exactly that.

3.2.8 Continuous Technology Debt Management

Continuous technology debt management lets you manage technology debts to controllable levels. The key is shifting from needing reactive "big bang" approaches every few years to a proactive, iterative strategy. It involves embedding practices in everyday work such as design, development & operational maintenance. Enterprise FinOps is one such technique that leads to continuous tech debt management. The Enterprise FinOps principles of cost transparency, visibility, and accountability optimize IT spending, which is often a key driver of infrastructure and software debt.

3.2.8.1 Software Debt Reduction

Test-Driven Development (TDD), where developers, not testers, write tests before code, forces teams to design for maintainability and reduces the likelihood of introducing new debt. Agile practices like pair programming, which usually involve two developers working together where one writes code and the other reviews it, lead to better code quality and shared knowledge. Code reviews should focus on maintainability, design, and potential future debt. A crucial process is using automated testing for all stages of testing, including unit tests, integration tests, and end-to-end tests. Combined with test management and code repository platforms like GitHub, automated testing provides rapid feedback and catches regressions early. Adopting holistic processes like DevOps can generate complete toolchains that offer opportunities and hooks for embedding automation in the development and deployment process. Table 3.2 lists down potential mitigation strategies to reduce software debt.

You can introduce refactoring Sprints as small, focused but regularly scheduled efforts. Teams need to allocate a specific percentage of each sprint or as part of traditional waterfall or iterative projects solely to addressing technical debt. Periodization techniques can identify where to focus to reduce high-impact debt. A Boy Scout Rule, "Leave the code a little cleaner than you found it," encourages developers to make small improvements with every change.

Architectural debt management is important. Regular Architecture Reviews allow you to assess the overall system architecture to identify potential problems and areas for improvement. Microservices and containers, where applicable and feasible, can reduce architectural debt by promoting modularity and independent deployments. However, poorly designed microservices can *create* debt. Domain-Driven Design (DDD) can help you understand the complex relationships within your system and identify opportunities to simplify the architecture.

Monitoring and feedback loops are critical to ensure all roles in the team are aware of what is happening. Code Quality Metrics use tools to track code complexity, code duplication, and other metrics. Bug reports identify areas where code is prone to errors. Visibility tools like Zabbix work across your enterprise layers to identify bottlenecks and narrow down on areas where performance could be improved. Static Analysis Tools like SonarQube, Checkstyle, and PMD automatically detect code quality issues and can launch checks for security testing. The shift-left principle extends continuous debt management all the way back to developers writing the code. Integrated Development Environments (IDEs) have built-in tools that can automate common refactoring tasks or use AI-enabled coding suggestions. Integrate automated testing, refactoring, and code quality checks into your Continuous Integration/Continuous Deployment (CI/CD) pipeline or toolchain.

Table 3.2 Common software debt reduction categories and potential mitigation

Type	*Description*	*Risk*	*Mitigation task*
Hardcoded values	Applications where important configuration values (API keys, database passwords, thresholds) are directly embedded in the code rather than managed in a central configuration system.	Security vulnerabilities, inflexibility.	Code refactoring Code reviews for new development Coding standards.
Lack of logging or monitoring	Applications that don't adequately log errors or system events, making debugging and troubleshooting incredibly difficult.	Increased downtime, difficulty diagnosing performance issues.	Logging and monitoring tools or processes in the underlying platform.
Duplicate code	Sections of code that perform similar tasks but are repeated in multiple places.	Increased maintenance effort, higher risk of introducing bugs.	Code refactoring Code reviews for new development Coding standards.
Outdated libraries/frameworks	Using old versions of libraries or frameworks that haven't been updated for security patches or performance improvements.	Security vulnerabilities, performance limitations.	Code refactoring Code reviews for new development Coding standards.
Monolithic architecture	Applications built as a single, tightly-coupled codebase, making it difficult to change, scale, or deploy.	Slow development cycles, deployment bottlenecks, reduced agility.	Code refactoring Complete rewrites or replacements.

(*Continued*)

Table 3.2 (Continued)

Type	*Description*	*Risk*	*Mitigation task*
Poorly documented code	Code without clear explanations of its purpose, functionality, or dependencies.	Increased onboarding time for new developers, and difficulty understanding the codebase.	Coding standards Code reviews Update documentation.
Lack of automated tests	Absence of unit, integration, or end-to-end tests, making it harder to verify changes and prevent regressions.	Increased risk of introducing bugs during development.	Automation testing tool implementation.
Over-engineering	Adding unnecessary complexity to solutions to meet overly ambitious requirements.	Increased development time, higher maintenance costs, reduced usability.	Coding standards Code reviews and refactoring.
Complex inter-system integrations	Overly complex integrations with other systems, often built using outdated technologies.	Increased integration costs, potential points of failure.	Architectural reviews Legacy modernization.
Legacy hardware dependence	Reliance on outdated hardware that's nearing the end of its lifecycle.	Security vulnerabilities, increased maintenance costs, and limited scalability.	Legacy modernization.
Data silos	Data residing in disparate systems that can't be easily combined for analysis or reporting.	Missed business opportunities, poor decision-making.	Data management and governance.

3.2.8.2 *Infrastructure Debt Reduction*

There are several techniques for addressing infrastructure debt reduction continuously. Infrastructure-as-Code (IaC) is like a Swiss Army Knife, with tools for every IT job. When you automate provisioning and configuration, you're erasing the human error that turns a simple deployment into a disaster and setting the stage for future automation. CI/CD pipelines that kick off automated testing catch problems before they bite. You can slash deployment failures by over 60% just by integrating tests early. Configuration tools like Ansible, Puppet, or Chef let you avoid drift between your dev, staging, and production environments. These tools keep everything aligned. Real-time monitoring stops problems before they escalate. When you spot a slow-performing database or a memory leak and fix it, you're preventing a crisis. Aging hardware is a ticking time bomb. Regular audits save money in the long run by identifying unsupported servers before they fail.

Hardware doesn't simply die. It degrades over time. When you map out replacement timelines, upgrades, and decommissioning, you're building a roadmap. Finally, standardization: fewer models mean fewer support tickets, fewer training hours, and fewer sleepless nights. You can reduce support costs just by locking down hardware models. Infrastructure debt can be controlled through IaC, automation, audits, and smart planning.

3.2.8.3 *SaaS Debt Reduction*

SaaS works well when you want a high-performing platform that meets your business needs. With fast deployment and user onboarding, you can get started quickly. Maintenance is a breeze, and the Opex licensing suits your budget well, too, with no upfront costs. But it can become a minefield of unmanaged licenses, hidden costs, and compliance nightmares.

Your first line of defense is a solid governance framework. It starts with clear policies for license management and usage monitoring. Next is software harvesting. Our team used ServiceNow SAM (Software Asset Management) to harvest licenses from underutilized apps, freeing up over hundreds of thousands of dollars in annual spending by reassigning unused licenses to new users rather than buying new ones. In other cases, we ensured compliance by carefully tracking and demonstrating our usage that contested and corrected vendor records, avoiding any licensing overages. We saved over millions of dollars in another case by shedding unused modules.

Automated tools save money. They are the hidden but hardworking monitors of your SaaS ecosystem. They clean up unused licenses, track SaaS license limits, and make sure you're not paying for what you don't need. Agile isn't only for software development. When you build SaaS integrations with rapid iteration and feedback loops, you're preventing software debt. Every time you automate license harvesting or connect an API, you're building a SaaS ecosystem that's scalable, compliant, and ready for the next big thing.

3.2.8.4 IT Services Debt Reduction

You've faced the 3 a.m. panic when a critical system goes down and stops an entire factory, the spreadsheet hell of tracking SLAs manually, or the endless game of "who knows what" when a key team member leaves. Continuous debt reduction can be applied to IT service debt as well.

Imagine a world where SLAs are met consistently, complaints drop by 50%, and your team stops sweating over spreadsheets. Real-time SLA tracking and automation alert you to potential problems well before they cause an impact or an outage. Manual ITSM is a relic of the past. When you automate incident management, problem resolution, and change processes, you can reduce ticket resolution time. Service requests like user provisioning and access requests are administrative chores. They require extensive approval processes. Automating them cuts errors by 70% and reduces the admin burden that makes your team look like a glorified help desk. We saved 200+ hours a month by automating access workflows, freeing our Access Control team to focus on further optimization. The section on "Automation" in the "Future of Enterprise FinOps" chapter elaborates further on automation techniques that you can apply to services.

Every team likely has the "expert who knows everything," but it reflects a low degree of documentation and knowledge sharing. Automated documentation and knowledge sharing turn your team into a self-sustaining machine. A centralized knowledge hub makes the team productive and confident. No more "Did you talk to Bob?" redirections to find the person who may have answers in his head and scrambling around for the phone number at 3 a.m. Using 10 different tools to do 3 things is a recipe for disaster. Replacing fragmented solutions with integrated platforms reduces tooling complexity and cuts onboarding time. Regularly reviewing and refining your IT service workflows is how you stay ahead.

3.2.9 Enterprise FinOps Enables Continuous Debt Reduction

Enterprise FinOps brings financial accountability and visibility to IT spending with a data-driven approach focused on *value*. It has an added advantage – it lets you continuously manage and reduce your technology debt. It reduces and mitigates technology debt across the IT portfolio.

Technology debt doesn't suddenly appear out of nowhere. It's the accumulation of underutilized cloud instances, forgotten SaaS subscriptions, or outdated hardware that's still on the books. Enterprise FinOps cuts through that noise by giving you granular visibility across every corner of your IT ecosystem. Techniques embedded inside FinOps work continuously to reduce debt. Let's take a few common scenarios.

- Cloud over-provisioning: You've got a server that's running at 5% utilization? FinOps recommends rightsizing the workload.
- SaaS license waste: It was the next cool app, but the interest quickly faded. A 100-seat SaaS app now has only 20 active users! FinOps detects it. You stop paying for licenses that aren't even being used.
- Shadow IT debt: That "cool new tool" your marketing team signed up for without IT's approval? FinOps spots it. You can enforce policies without crushing innovation.
- Hardware debt: That server that's been sitting in a closet for two years, still on the lease? FinOps shows you the full cost of ownership – maintenance, upgrades, and disposal so you can make informed decisions on phasing it out.
- Software licensing: A software that's still being used by just a couple of users? FinOps asks you to move the users to other similar applications.

Feedback loops are the unsung heroes of continuous improvement. When teams regularly assess the impact of changes, they prevent them. We reduced recurring problems by 30% by implementing bi-weekly problem management retrospectives that turned lessons into action items. When we augment Enterprise FinOps with technologies like AIOps, it transforms reactive firefighting into predictive prevention. When machine learning models analyze patterns, predict outages, and auto-remediate issues before they escalate, you're saving the business. By making every cost visible, measurable, and actionable, you stop treating technology debt as a liability and start using it as a roadmap for smarter decisions. Before FinOps, you were guessing where money is going, fixing problems after they've already blown up. After you implement FinOps, you're aligning IT with business goals and building a system that thinks ahead.

3.3 Prioritizing Critical Issues and Measuring Technology Debt

3.3.1 *Prioritizing Technology Debt*

You do not always need an organizational debt score to get started on reducing technology debt. Prioritization is needed, as you can't tackle *all* the debt at once, or else you run into the risks mentioned in the Big Bang approaches. A Risk-Based Approach is the most common and also familiar to most IT professionals, where you categorize debt based on how severely it's impacting the project (Impact) and the probability of its occurrence (Probability). First, identify the top sources of technology debt, down to discrete, actionable items. Then use these two dimensions to calculate an

Table 3.3 Risk scoring and mitigation

Risk score	*Description*	*Mitigation*
Critical	Code is failing, systems are causing major outages, security vulnerabilities, or fundamentally preventing new features from being built.	*Fix this immediately.*
High	Significant performance issues, major scalability limitations, or creates major maintenance headaches	*Address at the earliest opportunity.*
Medium	Impacts some functionality, causes occasional bugs, or makes future changes difficult.	*Schedule for a later sprint or phase.*
Low	Minor inconveniences, inconsistencies, or areas that are unlikely to cause problems.	*May be deferred until refactoring is a larger initiative.*

overall priority score. Evaluate if the debt is going to cause a problem. Table 3.3 illustrates the urgency and priority that could be associated with the mitigation, based on the risk score. A minor inconsistency might rarely cause an issue, while a poorly designed piece of code could fail repeatedly under load.

3.3.2 *What Needs Immediate Attention?*

Sometimes, common sense and experience can indicate high-severity issues. As shown in Table 3.4, Tier 1 issues need immediate remediation.

3.3.3 *Risks of Under-investing in Modernization*

Remember our discussion on exploit vs. explore? There's a time to dig your heels in and recoup the investments that you've made. But systems age. Things break to the point where your operations team is constantly fixing issues. Technology moves ahead. Vendors keep tempting you with better and faster versions of everything. Technology debt is inevitable, but you can manage it. But when you wait, competitors sprint ahead. They're automating entire processes that your team still does manually. They are deploying systems that have made changing business models a breeze, while you're left playing catch-up. Compounding this is your rising operational costs. Maintenance bills balloon, and every patch applied becomes a potential mini-disaster.

But the real danger isn't in the price tags, it's in the invisible losses and in the revenue you're missing because your systems can't scale. It's like the eight hours of factory downtime while a critical system was being fixed.

Table 3.4 Prioritizing technology debt

Type	*Description*	*Action needed*
Tier 1 – Immediate attention – Red flag debt		
Security vulnerabilities	*Any* identified vulnerability (especially those publicly disclosed) is a top priority. This includes outdated libraries, unpatched systems, and insecure coding practices.	Immediately patch, upgrade, or fix the vulnerability.
Production outages	Code that's consistently causing outages, performance degradation, or system instability.	Stop further development; investigate the root cause and fix it immediately.
Critical business function impact	Debt directly impacting core business processes, revenue, or customer experience.	High priority – needs rapid resolution.
Compliance issues	Code that violates regulatory requirements or industry standards.	Requires immediate attention to avoid legal and financial consequences.
Tier 2: High priority – "Yellow flag" debt		
Significant performance bottlenecks	Code causing noticeable slowdowns, latency, or excessive resource consumption. *If* it's not directly impacting users, it's lower priority than Tier 1, but still needs investigation	Schedule for the next sprint, but monitor closely.
Code duplication	Large blocks of code are repeated across multiple modules. Can lead to maintenance headaches.	Refactor during a sprint, but monitor.
Complex and unreadable code	Code with excessive nesting, convoluted logic, or poor naming conventions. Difficult to understand and maintain	Refactor during a sprint, with a focus on improving readability.
Outdated libraries/ frameworks	While not always a security risk, using outdated versions can lead to compatibility issues and missed security patches	Plan for an upgrade during the next sprint

(*Continued*)

Table 3.4 (Continued)

Type	*Description*	*Action needed*
Tier 3: Medium priority – "Amber flag" debt		
Architectural concerns	Areas where the system architecture is becoming a bottleneck or limiting future growth	Assess and plan for architectural changes during a phased approach.
Lack of documentation	Missing or outdated documentation makes it harder to understand and maintain the system	Documenting should be part of a regular maintenance sprint.
Tier 4: Low priority – "Green flag" debt		
	Lack of test coverage	Areas where test coverage is low. Improve test coverage during a maintenance sprint.

It's in the customer trust you're losing because your data isn't secure, or the fines that could hit millions if you're found noncompliant with regulations. Companies can collapse under the weight of a single breach, and reputations can be shattered by a single oversight.

Modernization is a necessity and needs to be prioritized. You can do it prudently by managing risk. Every delay and every scenario that ends up in "we'll get to it later" can be a gamble. But you also need to be realistic. The systems you're clinging to are outdated, and they are potential liabilities. They're the reason your integration efforts hit roadblocks. They're the reason your data silos refuse to talk to each other, and your teams spend more time patching than innovating. You shouldn't have to choose between stability and growth, but build a future that doesn't require you to choose. But you need to act now because the cost of inaction is already too high. Your leadership keeps the lights on and is also lighting the way forward.

3.3.4 Measuring Technology Debt

Measuring technology debt is like putting together a complicated puzzle to arrive at the big picture. Let's start with the qualitative side. Code reviews find bugs, but the intent is to read between the lines. A trained reviewer can spot the telltale signs of software debt, such as code that's bloated with redundant logic, a design that feels like a patchwork quilt, or a function that's so convoluted it makes heads spin. These are roadblocks that will slow down every developer who touches the codebase.

Application rationalization can give you the broad picture. An assessment indicates areas of risk where unsupported systems are likely to cause issues. Architecture assessments don't just look at individual components but how they all fit together. A poorly designed API? A database schema that's a maze? These are red flags that scream, "We need to rethink this." And when you talk to people – developers, testers, even business stakeholders – you're gathering firsthand accounts of how messy the system feels to work with. That's where the real story lives.

Now, let's get quantitative. Cyclomatic complexity measures how tangled a code module is. The higher the number, the more likely it is to break, and the harder it is to test. Tools like SonarQube or CodeClimate show you where the pain points are. High duplication in code is a red flag for unnecessary complexity. A bloated line might not directly measure debt, but it often correlates with it. And if your defect rate is spiking, it's a sure sign that something is seriously wrong with your system.

Then there's infrastructure debt. Long bug-fixing times are a symptom of a system that's hard to understand. If it takes forever to resolve an infrastructure issue, it might be a document debt problem: missing diagrams, outdated architecture docs, or hardware that's been repurposed without anyone updating the records.

Metrics like cycle time or resolution time for service requests tell you how well your team is set up to handle problems. A helpdesk that can't fix issues on the first call is a customer experience disaster. Recurring problems are the worst – they indicate you're simply not paying attention to digging out root causes.

But the most powerful metrics are the ones that tell you how people feel. Customer satisfaction scores (like NPS - Net Promoter Score) show you where users are suffering. Organizations often struggle to manage tech debt due to a lack of measurement. I've proposed a customizable framework here that you can use to gauge your organizational tech debt that further extends the prioritization techniques. The metrics you ultimately use will depend on the nature of your IT landscape, the technology stack, and your organization's priorities. Tracking trends over time can identify patterns and areas where debt is accumulating.

3.3.4.1 RWTDS – A Framework for Evaluating Your Technology Debt Score

1. Assessment

Run an assessment using the techniques listed in this chapter to identify the top sources of technology debt. Prioritize them using the risk scoring method shown earlier. Now let's add other dimensions to develop the "Risk-Weighted Technology Debt Score" (RWTDS) framework, as illustrated in Figure 3.8

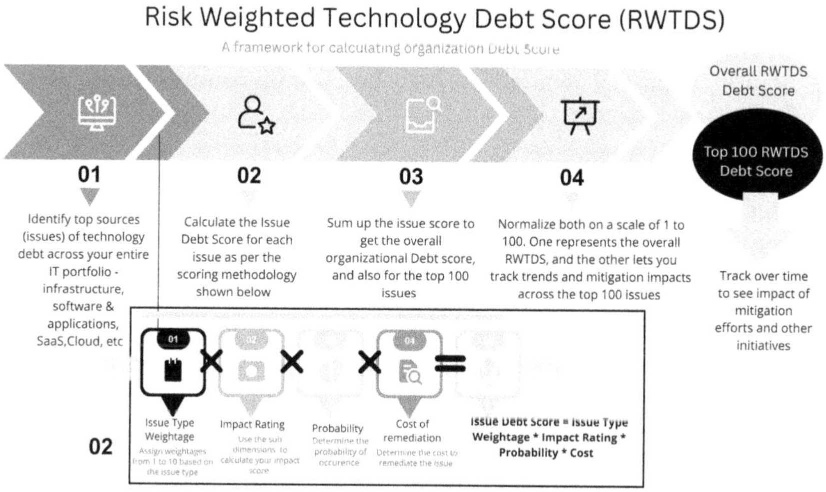

Figure 3.8 Calculating the risk-weighted technology debt score,

2. **Issue debt score for each issue**

Dimension 1 – Issue Type

Customize and assign issue types and assign appropriate weightages from 1 to 10; sample values are indicated below.

1. Security: (Vulnerabilities, insecure coding practices) e.g., weightage 8.
2. Performance: (Slow queries, inefficient algorithms) e.g., weightage 2.
3. Maintainability: (Complex code, lack of documentation) e.g., weightage 5.
4. Scalability: (Architecture constraints or bottlenecks) e.g., weightage 3.
5. Regulatory/compliance: (Non-compliance with standards) e.g., weightage 6.

Customize the issue types as per your unique business and IT landscape and assign weightages.

Dimension 2 – Impact score rating

This dimension reflects *what can happen* if the debt isn't addressed. Score each issue on each of the following:

- Business impact: (Financial cost, revenue loss, customer dissatisfaction) – Rated 1–5, with a score of 5 indicating high impact.
- Operational impact: (System downtime, support costs) – Rated 1–5.
- Security impact: (Potential data breaches, loss in customer trust) – Rated 1–5.

Sum up your scores on each of these 3 areas to calculate your overall Impact score.

Dimension 3 – Probability (Likelihood): How likely is the issue to escalate into a problem? Score on a scale of 1 to 5.

- **1 – Low:** Rarely occurs, easily detected.
- **3 – Medium:** Could occur under specific conditions.
- **5 – High:** Likely to occur frequently or under certain circumstances.

Dimension 4 – Cost of remediation

Consider the cost of remediation (time or effort). Get a realistic estimate from developers on how long it will take to fix the debt. This helps you compare it to the potential benefit. Consider the cost of the problem and the business impact if the problem *doesn't* get fixed. If it results in lost revenue, customer dissatisfaction, or security breaches, it deserves a higher impact rating. Estimate the resources required to fix the issue. Rate this on a scale of 1 to 5.

- **1 – Low:** Quick and simple fix (e.g., 1–8 hours).
- **3 – Medium:** Requires moderate effort (e.g., 8–32 hours).
- **5 – High:** Complex and time-consuming (e.g., >32 hours).

> *Issue Debt Score = Weightage from issue type * Impact Score * Probability Score * Effort Score*

3. **Organizational debt score for all issues**

- **Organizational RWTDS Debt Score** = Sum of all issue debt scores, normalized on a scale of 1 to 100.
- **Top 100 RWTDS Debt Score** = Sum of top 100 issue debt scores, normalized on a scale of 1 to 100.

A score calculated using the framework above not only illustrates the technology debt that is resident across your IT landscape, but also the risk that it represents, and the cost and efforts needed to fix it. Tracking this consistently over time, and after carrying out mitigation and reduction efforts, can give you a measurable and actionable way to gauge if your Technology Debt Reduction efforts are working. Since new issues could be added over time, it is important not just to calculate the overall organizational RWTDS Debt Score, but also the Top 100 RWTDS, which gives you an indicator of the most critical technology debt.

Ken Knapton, a former Forbes Councils Member, has proposed another data-driven approach to debt score measurement. The article mentions that proactively measuring and managing tech debt is essential for competitive advantage, especially for heavily leveraged organizations (Knapton, n.d.). Companies such as McKinsey and Gartner have published several articles on technical debt (McKinsey, 2022) (Williams, n.d.).

You can use KPIs such as Technology Debt Velocity (TDV) to measure the *effectiveness* of legacy modernization efforts. This is a metric that quantifies *how quickly* you're able to reduce technology debt during a modernization project. Rather than simply measuring *how much* debt you're addressing, it looks at *how fast* that reduction happens. A simple measure for TDV is offered below.

TDV = (Amount of Tech Debt Reduced)/(Time Period)

Amount of Tech Debt Reduced can be measured in various ways through the RWTDS assessment outlined in the earlier section, or through lines of code refactored, bugs resolved, improved code complexity metrics, reduction in system response time, etc. Specific metrics depend on how you're tracking your debt. Time period is measured in sprints, iterations, or weeks. TDV sets realistic expectations by establishing a baseline expectation for the speed of debt reduction. A high TDV demonstrates to stakeholders that your modernization efforts are actually having a tangible impact. TDV is a lagging indicator. It reflects the *outcome* of your efforts, not the *actions* you're taking. You still need to thoroughly assess the debt, prioritize, and design your modernization strategy.

The Second Law of Thermodynamics states that entropy in a closed system tends to increase over time. It provides a stark warning about the consequences of neglecting technology debt. Just as entropy represents the natural tendency of systems to move toward disorder, unmanaged technology debt, such as outdated code, fragmented infrastructure, unsupported hardware, or unpatched systems leads to increasing complexity, inefficiency, and risk. Without active management, this entropy can spiral out of control, resulting in higher maintenance costs, security vulnerabilities, and missed opportunities for innovation. The CIO must act as a channel directing resources toward reducing entropy by modernizing systems, refactoring code, phasing out systems, and adopting agile and continuous debt management practices like Enterprise FinOps. This requires a long-term perspective, where technology debt is not viewed as a one-time cost but as an ongoing investment in the organization's resilience and competitiveness. Proactive governance and practices like continuous debt reduction ensure that the system does not drift toward disorder through neglect or misalignment.

References

Accenture. (2025). What is tech debt. Retrieved from https://www.accenture.com/us-en/insights/what-is-tech-debt

Gartner. (n.d.). Gartner time framework. Retrieved from https://www.leanix.net/en/wiki/apm/gartner-time-model

Knapton, K. (n.d.). Measuring and managing technical debt. Retrieved from https://www.forbes.com/councils/forbestechcouncil/2022/08/10/

Letouzey, J.-L., & Whelan, D. (n.d.). Introduction to the technical debt concept. Retrieved from https://www.agilealliance.org/wp-content/uploads/2016/05/IntroductiontotheTechnicalDebtConcept-V-02.pdf

McKinsey. (2022). *Demystifying digital dark matter - a new standard to tame technical debt.* Retrieved from https://www.mckinsey.com/capabilities/tech-and-ai/our-insights/demystifying-digital-dark-matter-a-new-standard-to-tame-technical-debt

Moore, G. (n.d.). *Moore's law.* Retrieved from Wikipedia: https://en.wikipedia.org/wiki/Moore%27s_law

Sawant, V. (2020). A brief guide to legacy system modernization. Retrieved from A brief guide to legacy system modernization

Technical Debt Stifling Path to AI Adoption for Global Enterprises. (n.d.). Retrieved from https://www.pega.com/about/news/press-releases/technical-debt-stifling-path-ai-adoption-global-enterprises-says-research

The Innovation vs Technical Debt Tug of War. (n.d.). Retrieved from https://www.protiviti.com/us-en/global-technology-executive-survey

Thoughtworks. (n.d.). Identify, manage and overcome: A Guide to Technical Debt. Retrieved from https://na.thoughtworks.com/tech-debt-guide/

Williams, R. (n.d.). *Reduce and manage technical debt.* Retrieved from Gartner: https://www.gartner.com/en/infrastructure-and-it-operations-leaders/topics/technical-debt

Chapter 4

Bootstrapping Transformations and Innovations

DOI: 10.4324/9781003682196-7

4.1 Bootstrapping Transformation and Innovation

Besides being a strategic lever for cost optimization and business alignment, Enterprise FinOps has another benefit; the foundation it builds for future moves. It's a strategic bridge between what you're spending now and what you can achieve tomorrow.

4.1.1 Leveraging Savings for Strategic Initiatives

Operational savings sit like a forgotten relic, untouched and unspoken about, as illustrated in Figure 4.1. This is where Enterprise FinOps comes in. It treats inefficiencies as opportunities and unlocks these savings. It transforms them into fuel for growth, innovation, and the kind of transformation that turns IT from a cost center into a strategic powerhouse. Many savings inevitably go back into incremental improvements in your Run[1] operations. Now you have additional funds to reinvest back into the basics. Upgrade clunky software, improve your service management processes, deploy a case management tool, automate the mundane tasks that eat up hours, or consolidate redundant services. Cybersecurity and disaster recovery are other areas for prioritizing investment. They are insurance against chaos. Improving system reliability earns trust with the business.

But then you begin to consider bigger steps to unlock even bigger savings through Transform. This is where savings become a strategic lever. As we talked about in the "Technology Debt Reduction" chapter, application

Figure 4.1 Uncovering hidden opportunities

rationalization can identify opportunities for bigger savings by mapping your entire application portfolio. It lets you define a transformation roadmap to phase out legacy applications. You can make decisions on how to tap into the power and flexibility of SaaS, serverless, and PaaS platforms. Modernize and migrate on-premises virtual infrastructure with containers to provide cloud-like environments. Migrate critical workloads to the cloud for scalability and agility. Streamline processes and create capabilities that power your business.

Innovate is where you redefine what's possible. Set aside a chunk of savings as an "Innovation Seed Fund," giving teams a dedicated funding source for experimentation. Create innovation teams with the mandate to research and deploy AI-based systems, test IoT integrations, or experiment with blockchain. Smaller strategic initiatives can be funded entirely by the efficiencies you've unlocked. This fund should be prioritized based on potential impact and risk. Failure in innovation pilots is part of the equation. Lessons from prior iterations help you build a stronger and more resilient product. The only thing worse than a failed experiment is doing nothing. You are planting seeds for the future.

4.1.2 A Catalyst for Change

CIOs may feel as if they are stuck in a loop. You are constantly asked to justify IT investments, prove value, and deliver results, but reactive measures like constant cost-cutting keep your attention on the rearview mirror instead of the way ahead. You need to break this cycle. Enterprise FinOps can function as the catalyst for change, as depicted in Figure 4.2.

CIOs need to push boundaries as well as hold the line. It's like being on a tightrope. On one side, there is relentless pressure to innovate. Investors want disruption, and they have seen other companies transform themselves into nimble growth machines through judicious use of technology. On the other hand, your legacy systems are straining under the weight of outdated code and aging systems. Your business peers expect IT to be the engine of growth, not a bottleneck that's stuck in the past. The most powerful tool you have is your leadership. You're managing the status quo, but you're also shaping the future. It's an intricate balance, just like the first time you tried to ride a bike or a skateboard. You have to push forward, but don't forget to anchor yourself first.

Potential savings hidden in your Run are your most underutilized asset. Operational inefficiencies are like potential energy waiting to be converted into dynamic actions and motion. Enterprise FinOps is the engine. It converts the energy into momentum that drives your business forward through carefully prioritized transform and innovation initiatives. When you treat Run as strategic potential capital, you're shaping the trajectory of your

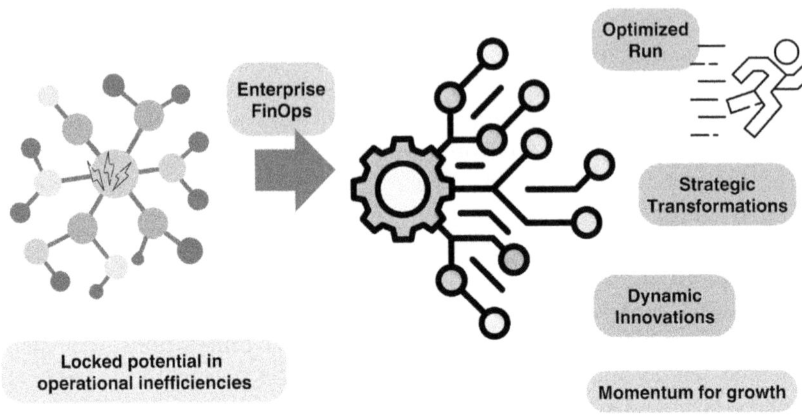

Figure 4.2 Enterprise FinOps[2] is a catalyst for change

entire organization. You're turning cost-cutting into a catalyst for growth and stability into a springboard for innovation.

Operational efficiencies and the resulting savings build a pipeline, a steady flow of capital that can be redirected toward innovation and strategic growth. Every time you automate a repetitive task, every time you upgrade a clunky system that sucks up unplanned effort from your team, you are freeing up resources that can be used in next-generation technologies. When you eliminate the drudgery of outdated systems and unplanned work that sucks up your team's time in fixing constant outages, your team can focus on higher-value work, such as training and problem-solving. You are maximizing the value of your current workforce. The authors of *The Phoenix Project* articulated this well (Kim, Behr, & Spafford, 2013).

The smallest wins can be the ones that trigger the change. A 10% reduction in cloud spend may feel like a drop in the ocean, but it can actually be the spark that ignites a firestorm of change. It's a shift in how people start thinking. Those early wins start breaking down silos and building momentum. Every process change opens the door for the next. When operational efficiencies feed modernization and innovation, and innovation fuels more efficiencies, you're building a flywheel that keeps spinning, driving growth, reducing risk, and positioning IT as the engine of your business.

4.1.3 Avoiding the Traps of "Quick Fix" IT Decisions

It's difficult to avoid the temptation to cut corners for a quick fix. It's okay to do so when you're dealing with a major system that's brought manufacturing to a halt. That's what operations teams do when they are resolving an incident by coming up with a quick resolution to get the system running as soon as possible. But if you ignore the root cause and the issue crops up again, it's a failure in your problem management process. Going further, if a root cause analysis points to a much-needed fix, and you ignore it, it's like a ticking time bomb. The "quick fix" mentality is not a lasting solution but a trap. Every time you sacrifice a strategic initiative to save money, you leave it up to chance because you know that fix is not going to last. You are driving yourself deeper into technology debt.

A hiring freeze is a classic move when budgets tighten. How often have you told your team, "Let's hold off on new hires for now?" But your team is already stretched thin. The skills gap widens and morale plummets. Productivity drops even more. And when that experienced engineer or analyst leaves for a better opportunity elsewhere, you're losing a person and also institutional knowledge, and the kind of expertise that can't be replaced overnight. Then there's the contractor shortcut. "We'll bring someone on for some time and move on." It can save you money, but the reality is that contractors aren't always aligned with your long-term goals. When the money runs out, you could be left with half-baked solutions and a pile of work that's going to cost you more in the long run.

Every time we choose the quick-fix path, it's a message that we're not ready to invest in the future. But the future doesn't wait. Competitors who are building AI platforms or securing their infrastructure are racing ahead. You need a smarter and more sustainable way to manage IT. Relentlessly pursuing operational excellence requires tough choices. It gets you a resilient organization that's surviving today and thriving tomorrow.

Your legacy isn't defined by how much you saved in a quarter, but by how much you built for the next decade. So, the next time you're faced with a decision for a quick fix, ask yourself whether you are fixing the symptom or solving the problem. The difference between those two choices is the gap between survival and transformation. Enterprise FinOps can be a game-changer for you. Rather than looking only at how much we are spending, it sees whether your investments are delivering value that matches their cost. It's unlocking value.

4.2 Balancing Short-Term Needs with Long-Term Investments

You need a strategy that thrives in the chaos. The RTI 360 framework that was introduced in previous chapters offers a solid foundation to launch your Enterprise FinOps strategy. Your "Run" is likely 40–50% of your budget. The core focus is on keeping the lights on. Without this foundation, everything else crumbles. You can't cut corners here, as your systems could buckle under pressure and erode the trust that you have with the business. Transform is likely taking up 20–30% of your budget. This is where you dig out of the technology debt hole. The aim is to modernize. Get rid of inefficient and unused applications. Integrate data silos. Refactor legacy code. Automate manual processes. It's the bridge between today and tomorrow. Teams that ignore this only find themselves stuck in a loop of reactive fixes. You're preparing for the next wave. The chapter on Technology Debt Reduction has more detailed techniques.

Then there's "Innovate," maybe 10–20% for pilots and to kick-start strategic projects. This is where you are betting on the future. High risk can result in high rewards. You are not throwing money at experiments, but planting seeds that might grow into something revolutionary. There's a risk that this may not give you the rewards that you anticipated. But the companies that thrive with innovation are the ones that take calculated risks.

Enterprise FinOps that provides proven methods for unlocking value that can be redirected elsewhere. Even small opportunities in transformation and innovation build a layer of trust and alignment with the business. You're building a partnership.

4.2.1 The ROI in Transformations

The upfront cost always feels like a mountain. Let's take a typical case, migrating from an on-premises legacy ERP system to SaaS. Convincing business is like painting a picture of what comes after the mountain.

Your business case will likely include the projected ROI. The TCO is not only the price tag on the SaaS invoice, but the entire lifecycle. As we talked about in prior chapters, consider the hidden cost factors like the hours spent on server maintenance, the data migration nightmares, and the training that's never-ending. Then contrast that with SaaS. You will likely have lower licensing fees and also operational savings. The way cloud systems can automate updates and reduce downtime can free up your team to do real work instead of reactively addressing patches and resolutions. That's a competitive advantage. When customers see their orders processed instantly, or their support tickets resolved before they even complain, loyalty becomes a habit.

A phased rollout reduces risk. Start small, pick one department, test the system, tweak the process. Let the team breathe. Let them see the benefits firsthand before scaling. Change management holds the whole thing together. Training and communication turn skeptics into advocates.

4.2.2 The Role of Innovation in Achieving Long-Term Goals

The real win is in building something that changes the game. Innovation creates the next big thing. You are spotting trends and testing ideas that don't fit into your current playbook. It lets you build capabilities that let you pivot when the world shifts. Companies that thrive during crises are experimenting, failing fast, pivoting, and learning even faster. They're the ones building safe spaces where teams can test wild ideas without fear of judgment. That's how you create resilience. You adapt, and you build something that others can't copy.

But you can't slap an "innovation" label on a side project and call it done. It means giving teams the freedom to explore, breaking down silos so engineers and marketers can collaborate on crazy ideas, and actually investing time, money, and talent in these initiatives. Let's face the reality that some innovations are going to fail. That's why you have small sandboxed pilots where you can fail without impacting business. When failure is off the table, learning stops. Trust people to navigate uncertainty. Innovation is not sustainable without freedom. When you let teams take risks, you unlock breakthroughs that redefine what's possible. Some will be game-changers for your business. Innovation fuels growth. It's the spark that can turn a small idea into a network effect that propels the entire company forward.

4.2.3 *Prioritizing Initiatives Based on Their Impact and Feasibility*

There's a simple template, as shown in Table 4.1, that you can use to create a standardized prioritization framework for innovation initiatives that's both rigorous and practical.

Strategic Alignment Score is a measure of how this initiative supports your organization's core strategic objectives, ranging from 1 (no alignment

Table 4.1 Impact and feasibility prioritization matrix

Initiative name	*Strategic alignment score (1–5)*	*Feasibility score (1–5)*	*Risk score (1–5)*	*Total score (1–15)*	*Priority level*	*Justification/notes*
AI chatbot for helpdesk (sample)	*4*	*5*	*3*	*12*	*HIGH*	*Commence pilot. Review through ARB for architectural guidance. Explore build vs buy. Ensure it integrates with existing helpdesk systems.*

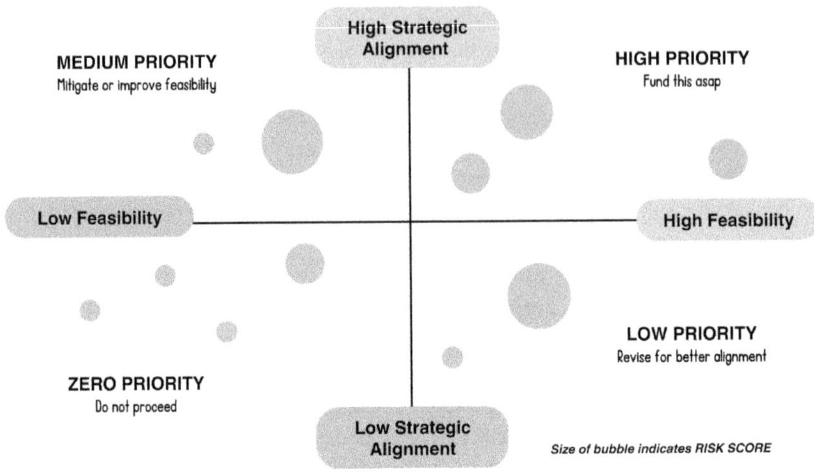

Figure 4.3 Decision matrix for innovation

and minimal impact) to 5 (perfect alignment, directly fuels a key strategic goal or has significant impact, such as substantial revenue increase or cost reduction).

Feasibility Score assesses how practical it is to implement, with 1 (very difficult with high technical complexity and significant resource constraints) to 5 (highly feasible with readily available resources).

Risk Score evaluates potential risks associated with the initiative, with 1 (high risk factors such as major technical challenges or significant cost overruns) to 5 (low risk).

The Total Score is the sum of the scores for a quick ranking. Assign **priority levels based on the** total score (e.g., High, Medium, Low). Rank initiatives based on their total score (high score = higher priority). You could optionally assign weights to each element (e.g., Strategic Alignment might have a higher weight than Feasibility).

You could extend this further into a decision matrix using the three dimensions as shown in Figure 4.3.

4.3 Making Changes

The tempo of keeping things running and pushing boundaries to innovate and modernize generates its own rhythm. Run is the heartbeat of your organization, keeping your systems humming in the background. Your eyes are on the metrics such as uptime, efficiency, compliance, and costs, always seeking to achieve optimized stability and ensure that the foundation doesn't crumble under the weight of neglect. But when the numbers start to tilt, when a core system shows cracks, or when regulations demand a rewrite, it's a signal to pivot. Optimized stability doesn't last forever. Complacency is the real danger.

Transform reimagines your landscape, one system at a time. You take the covers off the technology debt that's been piling up, align your systems with the business's evolving needs, and embrace the tools that redefine how you operate. It takes courage to acknowledge that "We've outgrown this." But Transform is a marathon, not a sprint. It's an ongoing journey that aims to future-proof your systems while still keeping the lights on.

Innovate is your wild card, the risks that could pay off in ways you've never imagined. It's the phase where you aim for disruptions, lean into risk, where you prototype, experiment, and chase the signals of the future. Some are gambles, and that's okay too. Maybe it's a technology or a new customer experience that's never been tried. This is where your organization bets on the unknown, where you say, "What if?" and then go build it. Innovate is the strategic investment in the next chapter of your business.

The real magic happens when these phases flow into each other. Sparks from innovate flow into and redefine Run. Run inspires strategic transformations. You dynamically shift resources, responding to signals. Your technology landscape is a moving target, and your strategy has to keep up. If you ignore the signals from your systems or the market, the danger is that the hole gets deeper with every passing day.

4.3.1 Managing Risk in Transformation Projects

Over 70% of digital transformation initiatives fail. It's rarely about the technology. It's the people and the processes. Thomas Davenport and George Westerman pointed out the dangers and risks of transformations in their HBR article, "Why so many high-profile transformations fail" (Davenport & Westerman, 2018). You can't digitize a business without a vision that's sharp enough to cut through the noise. Vague goals are a death sentence. They leave teams adrift, chasing trends instead of solving real problems. When innovation initiatives operate in silos, they sabotage each other. Without visible, sustained support from executive leadership, initiatives are like ships without a captain, drifting aimlessly. When end-users are excluded from the design process, you end up with systems that no one wants to use. Fear of job loss, resistance to change, and the sheer inertia of legacy systems all conspire to kill momentum.

Then there's executing the transformation. Overambitious timelines, bloated budgets, and the delusion that you can do it all at once are the kiss of death. Teams get overwhelmed, and projects stall. And when you cling to rigid waterfall methods, you're slowing down any remaining momentum. Silos that hoard knowledge like treasure keep ideas locked in fortresses. A focus on short-term wins over long-term bets is a recipe for mediocrity.

So how do you fix this? Start by redefining success. Transformation isn't just about deploying the latest AI tool or cloud platform. It's transforming the business, its people, its processes, its DNA, and where teams aren't handed a mandate but invited to co-create the future. Let's look at the inherent risks and mitigation strategies in Table 4.2.

4.3.2 *Management of Change*

Management of change (MoC) is often treated like a footnote in the transformation playbook. Often, it's a nice-to-have after the systems are deployed. That's a mistake. Because in the world of digital transformation, the people are the system. The MoC team is the architect of that system and needs to be fully involved in the design, planning, and execution of the transformation. A successful large-scale transformation requires a robust technical roadmap as well as an MoC roadmap. This team isn't here to run unimpactful training sessions. They're the ones who bridge the gap between "what we want" and "how we get there." They speak the language of the business. They translate jargon into impact and engage stakeholders. They listen to the concerns of the line of business, the fears of the HR team, the frustrations of the frontline workers, and turn those concerns into actionable insights.

Because if you don't address the "why" behind the change, you're just asking people to blindly jump off a cliff. They orchestrate communication. They craft a plan that's tailored to each group: a detailed email for the CFO, a live demo for the sales team, a training session for stakeholders, and Q&A sessions for the IT staff. They build feedback loops that let people voice their fears, their questions, their ideas and discuss ways to address this. Because if you silence them, you're losing trust and with it, potentially the whole project.

Management of change empowers your users. The team can design learning experiences through workshops and simulations, and then stay with the users long after the training ends. They measure what matters. They dig deeper into the root cause of the resistance, if any. For large-scale transformations, you need a dedicated team of MoC specialists, communication experts, and training developers. If you're investing millions in a digital transformation, also invest in the people who will make it work.

Table 4.2 Mitigating risks of transformation

Risk category	*Specific risk*	*Description*	*Potential mitigation strategies*
Strategic alignment	Lack of clear strategic direction	Transformations lack a clearly defined purpose, leading to disjointed efforts.	Establish a clear vision and strategic goals for the transformation. Align the transformation with the overall business strategy. Review and refine the strategy as needed.
	Unrealistic expectations	Overly optimistic forecasts of speed and outcomes.	Set realistic expectations based on thorough assessments. Develop a phased and modular approach with achievable milestones. Manage stakeholder expectations proactively.
People and culture	Resistance to change	Employees resist new processes, technologies, and ways of working.	Communicate the "why" behind the transformation clearly and repeatedly. Engage employees in the design and implementation process. Provide adequate training and support. Celebrate early successes.
	Lack of executive sponsorship	Without strong leadership support, the transformation loses momentum.	Secure visible and vocal support from senior executives. Hold executives accountable for driving the transformation.
	Lack of change management skills	Insufficient expertise in managing organizational change.	Invest in change management training for key personnel. Consider engaging a dedicated change management team.

(*Continued*)

Table 4.2 (Continued)

Risk category	*Specific risk*	*Description*	*Potential mitigation strategies*
Execution	Poor project management	Ineffective planning, execution, and control.	Utilize agile methodologies. Employ strong project management practices. Regularly monitor progress and address issues promptly.
	Siloed operations	Departments working in isolation, hindering collaboration.	Promote cross-functional collaboration. Establish shared goals and metrics. Break down silos through technology and processes.
	Overly complex projects	Trying to do too much at once.	Adopt a phased approach. Break up milestones into distinct modules. Prioritize initiatives. Focus on quick wins.
Technology	Inadequate technology infrastructure	Existing systems are not compatible with new technologies.	Assess current IT infrastructure. Invest in upgrades or replacements as needed. Ensure interoperability between systems.
	Data quality issues	Poor data quality leads to inaccurate insights.	Implement data governance policies. Invest in data cleansing and validation. Ensure data is accessible and reliable.
Measurement and monitoring	Lack of key performance indicators (KPIs)	Absence of metrics to track progress.	Establish clear KPIs aligned with strategic goals. Regularly monitor progress and report on results.

HBR's *On Change Management* features a thoughtfully compiled collection of essays and articles from leading thinkers, including "Leading Change: Why Transformation Efforts Fail" by John P. Kotter (HBR 10 Must Reads, 2011).

4.3.3 Organizational Structure

As you've probably heard often, the best technology strategies are built on the best people. But the structure of your organization, the way teams are divided, how decisions flow, and whether innovation is a shared priority or a priority only for selective corners dictates whether your resource flow even has a chance to work.

Functional silos exist in all organizations. These aren't just groups or departments with different KPIs. They're black holes where data is hoarded like treasure, and ideas wither in isolation. Innovation ideas stall and transform initiatives get stuck in red tape. There are other structural inefficiencies as well. Shadow IT is a drain on resources, costs, and efforts. Matrix structures could be a minefield of conflicting priorities. Imagine a team with two managers, each pulling in opposite directions. One wants to ship a product faster, the other wants to ensure compliance, and teams get torn between conflicting priorities. If project-based teams treat innovation like a one-off sprint and move on, they can end up leaving behind a trail of unshared learnings.

But the ideal isn't a perfect structure. It's a structure that's designed to be fluid. Think of self-organizing teams, where cross-functional collaboration is the default. This is the environment where resource flow works. But even here, challenges lurk. Executive sponsorship is critical to ensuring that teams don't lose steam. Your culture needs to embrace risk. Without incentives that reward collaboration, the best ideas will get buried. Start with cross-functional innovation councils that cut through the noise, identify bottlenecks, and ensure resources are moving where they're needed. Commission and empower a champion at the executive level who can say, "This is urgent," and take actions across IT portfolio lines to make things happen. Foster a culture where experimentation is encouraged, not punished. Invest in tools that break down barriers and platforms that let teams share data and align on goals.

The CIO is like the conductor of the entire orchestra. You are the one who ensures that Run keeps the lights on, Transform builds the future, and Innovate dares to dream. You're orchestrating the future of your organization, with one fluid, dynamic, and unstoppable step at a time.

4.3.4 The Pros and Cons of Different Organizational Approaches

The four organizational approaches below are only a few of the many lenses through which you can view your team. The right choice depends on your culture, your pain points, and where you want to go. Let's unpack them, but keep in mind that models aren't a magic wand. They're tools and only work if you use them with purpose.

1. The Bi-Modal Approach
   We've talked about this in the chapter on CIO dilemmas. Imagine dividing your IT team into two distinct worlds, one focused on speed, experimentation, and innovation, and the other on stability, reliability, and core infrastructure. It lets your team sprint ahead on new ideas while keeping the lights on for the rest of the business. But this model could be a breeding ground for silos. If you're not careful, the two groups will talk past each other, duplicate work, and lose sight of the bigger picture. You'll end up with a speed team that's disconnected from the stability team, each operating in a vacuum. To avoid this, you need effective governance that bridges the gap. The speed team needs to hand over operations to the stability team, or they will be in a mode of constant and endless experimentation.
2. Flattening the Hierarchy
   Flat hierarchies sound great on paper. There are fewer layers, faster decisions, more collaboration. But flattening without strategy is chaos. You'll end up with a team that's spread too thin, where individual contributors are juggling priorities they can't control. The empowerment of a flat structure only works if you've got leaders who can manage complexity rather than avoid it. You need people who can streamline without losing the map.
3. Outsourcing
   Outsourcing is a double-edged sword. It can be a lifeline if you're under-resourced or trying to cut costs. You're not handing off work and, more importantly, you're transferring responsibility. If your vendor doesn't align with your culture or your standards, you're risking quality and potentially your entire operation. The key here is effective control rather than cost. You can't pick the cheapest vendor and hope for the best. You need a governance and monitoring system that's as rigorous as your internal processes. SLAs give you a framework, but outcomes determine whether this is working for you. The outsourcing partnership requires trust, transparency, and a shared vision.
4. Building Products, Not Just Services
   Moving from a service-delivery-focused team to a product-oriented organization is a hard move. It's a shift that can unlock new revenue streams and uncover agility. Your team needs to change their entire mindset and think like product managers, not IT technicians. They need to understand customer needs and take ownership of outcomes.

4.3.5 Enterprise FinOps Is Technology-Driven Optimization

No matter which approaches you pick, culture is the glue. You can't outsource your values or flatten your hierarchy without trust. The right model will only work if your people believe in it. Enterprise FinOps provides a way to build and execute the strategy.

Reactive cost-cutting is a losing game. You are trimming budgets, but you're also slicing off the very tools that keep your business agile. But what if there's a better way? It starts with seeing IT spending as a lever. That means moving beyond the "turn off the tap" mentality and asking, "How can we do more with less without breaking the system?" Technology-driven optimization means you leverage what you already have to unlock hidden efficiencies. RPA is useful, but it's the beginning of your automation journey. Right-size your entire IT spend, monitoring usage, ensuring every dollar spent is tied to measurable outcomes. Data is your compass. The right tools and analytics can unearth inefficiencies you didn't even know existed. It can uncover processes that drag down productivity, resources that sit idle, or workflows begging to be automated. A value-based strategy that looks at the total cost of ownership pays off in the long term. Vendor consolidation lets you leverage your buying power to get better terms, better service, and better outcomes. Open-source software, PaaS, and SaaS are tools that embody service optimization principles and let you build agile, scalable infrastructure without the headache of legacy systems. The old way might give you quick wins, but a strategic mindset creates value.

Enterprise FinOps brings these and other techniques together in a seamless symphony. It blends accountability and transparency and brings a level of collaboration that's rarely seen in traditional IT environments. The first step is visibility. You can't optimize what you can't see. That means building a centralized, real-time view of your entire IT portfolio, down to the penny, by service, team, application, and, most importantly, business unit. Uncover hidden inefficiencies like applications and platforms that cost more than they're worth, resources that sit idle, or workflows that could be automated. Evaluate every technology investment through the lens of long-term value. That means asking hard questions like whether this aligns with our strategic goals, or whether it contributes to the bottom line. Enterprise FinOps lets you make sure every dollar spent is a vote for the future of your business. You need a dedicated FinOps team, armed with the right tools that connect data, people, and decisions. And you'll need to cultivate a culture where every stakeholder, from your IT decision makers to the frontline, understands their role in managing IT spend. Enterprise FinOps lets you build a smarter, more agile, and more innovative organization. You start moving from a reactive, panic-driven approach to a strategic, data-driven one.

4.3.5.1 Bi-Modal Teams

You've got that fast-moving, innovation-focused team. Speed, agility, and experimentation drive their actions. But without FinOps, they're like a racecar without brakes. They'll push boundaries, but if they're not mindful of cost, they'll burn through resources faster than they can prove ROI. Enterprise FinOps gives them the guardrails they need. It's the discipline that lets them innovate and deliver value.

4.3.5.2 *Flat Hierarchies*

In a flat structure, everyone's supposed to be empowered. But empowerment without accountability is a recipe for disaster. FinOps changes that. It gives your teams the tools to make informed, cost-conscious decisions. It turns responsiveness into responsibility.

4.3.5.3 *Outsourcing*

Enterprise FinOps ensures you're not paying for noise. You outsource to save time, reduce overhead, and focus on what matters. But if your vendor isn't aligned with your culture or your strategic vision, you're paying for a liability, not a service. FinOps is the lens that helps you see through the fog. It lets you track value. It's the difference between getting a vendor that does the work and a partner that understands your business and IT strategy and responds accordingly.

4.3.5.4 *Product-Led Innovation*

If you're building products, not simply delivering services, it's a visionary move. But without Enterprise FinOps, you're betting on a product that might not scale or a feature that might not resonate. The worst is ending up with a technology that might become obsolete before it's even launched. FinOps keeps you on track. It's the data-driven framework that guides your investments with business goals and lets you avoid overspending and Shadow IT.

FinOps creates communities that cut across silos, bringing together finance, IT, product, and operations. It fosters a culture where cost awareness is a shared responsibility. It's the way to align your investments with your goals, to turn chaos into clarity, and to make sure every dollar spent is a dollar that matters. As CIOs, you're shaping the future of your business. The time to embrace FinOps is now.

4.3.6 ***Role of FinOps in Transformation and Innovation***

Enterprise FinOps reshapes how your organization thinks about technology. It brings in a culture of accountability, visibility, business alignment,

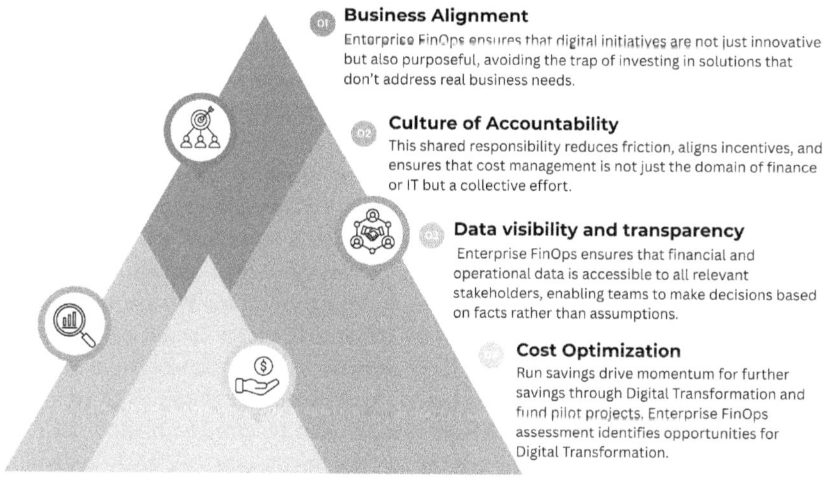

Figure 4.4 Enterprise FinOps provides a foundation for digital transformation

and shared values. It provides a foundation for digital transformation, as shown in Figure 4.4. Teams unlock savings in the RUN environment and uncover opportunities that can help you build a digital transformation roadmap and seed innovations. That discipline seeps into every layer of the business.

FinOps forces alignment early. When a team proposes a transformation task, the question is whether it moves the needle for the business. FinOps builds a shared map. Teams start collaborating. When finance, IT, and product teams all see the same data, priorities align, and that helps you build a stronger and sustainable digital transformation roadmap. Digital transformation is a marathon, not a sprint. FinOps keeps the pace steady. It's the compass that points toward value as well as efficiency. That's the kind of leverage that turns transformation from a risk into a competitive edge.

For Innovate, Enterprise FinOps brings visibility and business alignment. It lets you seed pilots and experiments that can demonstrate potential ROI and help build a business case that justifies further investment. FinOps brings a culture of accountability and responsible technology adoption that ensures that Innovate teams are experimenting within safe spaces, but also judiciously to ensure that they are heading toward realistic goals aligned with business.

Faraday's Law of Electromagnetic Induction states that "a changing magnetic field induces an electric current in a conductor." The magnitude of the induced current depends on the rate of change and the properties of the conductor, such as its material. This mirrors the dynamic interplay between operational efficiency, transformation, and innovation in Enterprise FinOps. Just as a changing magnetic field generates current, Run savings create momentum for Transform and Innovate initiatives. Enterprise FinOps is like the "conductor" that determines how effectively this momentum is harnessed, while management of change ensures that resistance is minimized. This analogy highlights the catalytic role of Enterprise FinOps in driving digital transformation.

The Law of Conservation of Energy states that energy cannot be created or destroyed, only transformed. This provides another compelling analogy for IT spend as a finite resource that must be allocated efficiently to generate value. Just as energy in a closed system must be directed toward useful work, IT budgets must be transformed into operational efficiency, innovation, or competitive advantage. Wasted spend, such as underutilized software licenses, over-provisioned servers, redundant infrastructure, or unproductive projects or talent, represents "lost energy" that fails to contribute to the organization's goals. The CIO can ensure that IT spend is not merely allocated but transformed into measurable outcomes. This requires rigorous prioritization, where the energy of the budget, IT systems, and workforce is directed toward initiatives that align with strategic priorities.

Note

1 Run, Transform, and Innovate are used throughout this chapter with context to the "Run," "Transformation," and "Innovation" pillars introduced in our RTI360 model in Chapter 1.

References

Davenport, T. H., & Westerman, G. (2018). Why so many high-profile transformations fail. *Harvard Business Review*. Retrieved from https://hbr.org/2018/03/why-so-many-high-profile-digital-transformations-fail

HBR 10 Must Reads. (2011). *On change management*. Harvard Business Review Press.

Kim, G. K., Behr, K., & Spafford, G. (2013). *The phoenix project: A novel about IT, devops, and helping your business win*. IT Revolution Press.

Part III

How Can You Implement Enterprise FinOps?

What Actions Are Needed to Implement and Sustain Enterprise FinOps?

Previous chapters outlined the philosophy and rationale behind Enterprise FinOps and introduced a robust framework that works across your entire IT portfolio. This part outlines a practical methodology and roadmap that you can customize as needed for your own Enterprise FinOps implementation. It describes the overall steps for implementing Enterprise FinOps through a phased approach. Cost optimization, business alignment, and technical levers are elaborated in subsequent chapters. The chapter on Monitoring and Measurements describes how you can arrive at Enterprise FinOps KPIs and metrics that are aligned with your IT strategy and business goals. Organizations often struggle with too many KPIs that lead to chaos and reporting inefficiencies. It shows how to derive a single KPI that represents the value provided by Enterprise FinOps. The chapter on mental models lets you create a culture of accountability and describes a few models that can play a big role in decision-making, prioritization, and lets you avoid common biases in IT decision-making.

DOI: 10.4324/9781003682196-8

Chapter 5

Implementing Enterprise FinOps

DOI: 10.4324/9781003682196-9

5.1 A Phased Approach

Using a phased approach works best for implementing Enterprise FinOps. As illustrated in Figure 5.1, the phases are the following:

- Strategize
- Assess
- Optimize, manage, and govern
- Expand

In the Strategize phase, you establish a clear strategy for Enterprise FinOps and define high-level goals on cost optimization, business alignment, and value realization. Although many of the activities are IT-led and IT-centric, this helps you build a business case for the program and ensure that your business peers are aware of a major initiative to bring about cost optimization and business alignment. In the Assess phase, you carry out a detailed Enterprise FinOps assessment among selected areas of your IT portfolio. Ideally, this needs to cover all IT spend; however, you may choose to select only a smaller portfolio area to begin with. You also carry out a Maturity Model assessment to determine how you are placed on various factors such as process, automation, and vendor performance. You identify the top opportunity areas that come out of your assessment. The next phase is Optimize, Manage and Govern, where the FinOps team works on different activities to optimize the environment. This is an iterative phase and is repeated continuously along with management and governance of FinOps

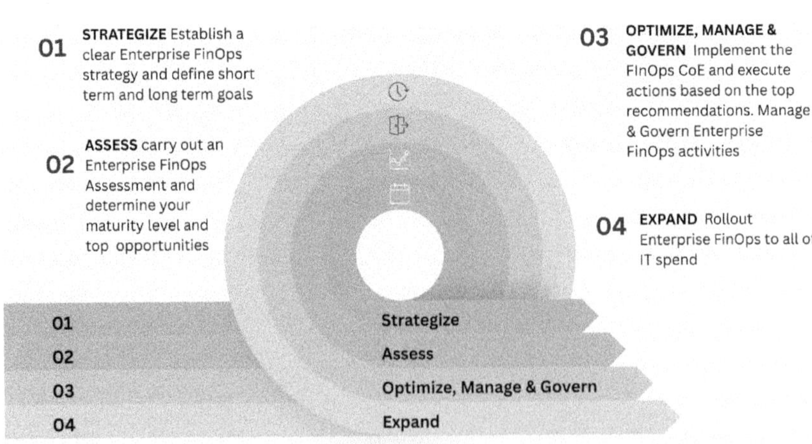

Figure 5.1 A phased approach for implementing Enterprise FinOps

activities. Governance policies and feedback loops are also established in this phase. The final phase is Expand, where the program is expanded to all parts of the IT portfolio and assumes a cycle of continuous review and optimization. You also spin off additional initiatives to further boost the impact of FinOps.[1]

Figure 5.2 shows some of the key tasks and activities associated with each phase.

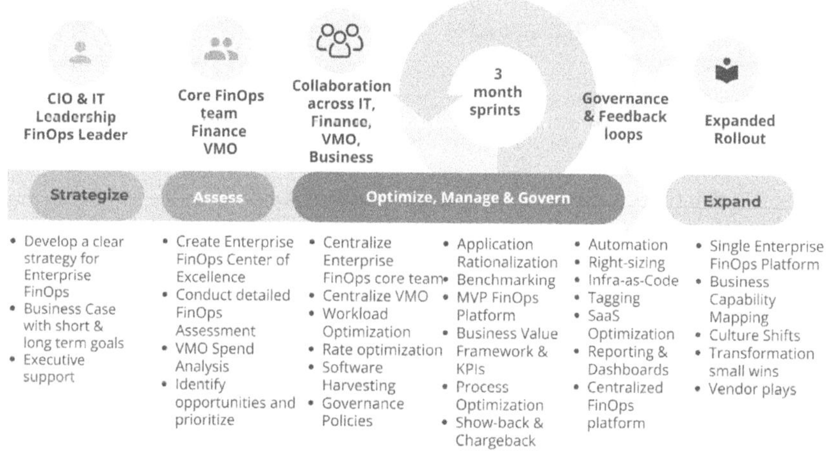

Figure 5.2 Activities and iterations in the phases

5.1.1 *Strategize*

The key steps are to define an overall Enterprise FinOps strategy for the organization, gain executive buy-in, and establish a core Enterprise FinOps leadership team. Figure 5.3 depicts key activities in this phase. You build a business case for Enterprise FinOps, as there will be some minimal initial investment needed (the savings from your first optimization cycle should let you fund any further investments).

5.1.1.1 *Defining Your Enterprise FinOps Strategy*

The Enterprise FinOps vision is to make IT a driver of business growth and a catalyst for innovation. We do this by transforming IT cost

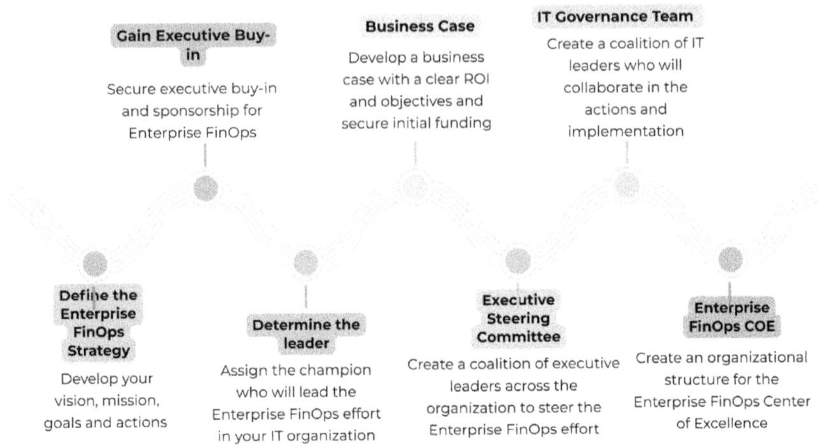

Figure 5.3 The strategy phase activities in Enterprise FinOps

management and aligning financial decisions with business goals. The four key goals are cost optimization, business alignment, value creation, and creating a culture of accountability, summarized in Figure 5.4. The Enterprise FinOps principles can help you define the high-level objectives and guiding practices. Actions are further outlined in this chapter. Your strategy will continue to evolve. The main goals are the following:

- **Cost optimization:** You want to save costs from your IT spend, but it's not simply a scavenger hunt. Let's first see what cost optimization is not. You're not just trying to get the cheapest vendor or product. You don't need to cut projects arbitrarily or reduce your workforce. If this is rolled out simply as a cost-cutting exercise without informed data, and you cut budgets that impact the applications and services driving stability or innovation, you'll be scrambling to fix broken workflows and long outages. What it is, is making sure you are getting the most value from your assets. Eliminate waste, reduce unnecessary spending, optimize processes, and maximize efficiency. You first understand where your money is going and why and then optimize with informed intelligence. Set a realistic target for cost optimization within a reasonable

Figure 5.4 Defining your vision and goals

duration, something like 20% to 30% cost savings in two years. And yes, this is totally realistic and feasible.

- **Business alignment:** The goal is to ensure that IT decisions are aligned with business goals. Every server upgrade, every SaaS tool, every IT service and project needs to be firmly linked to your key drivers. Ensure every IT expenditure directly supports organizational priorities, such as digital transformation, increasing efficiency, customer experience, market expansion, or competitive differentiation.
- **Value creation:** Cost savings are great, but there's more you can do with that. Invest it back into value creation. FinOps can be the engine that fuels innovation. It's a catalyst. Every dollar saved can be a dollar reinvested in quality and improve your competitive edge. Move beyond cost savings to drive innovation and enable new business opportunities through strategic resource allocation.
- **Culture of accountability:** IT is pervasive across the enterprise. Shared ownership means that everyone makes responsible use of technology, from the developer to the business user. Real-time dashboards show

everyone how their decisions impact the bottom line. Feedback loops let teams adjust without waiting for quarterly reviews.
- **Continuous improvement:** Embed a feedback-driven, adaptive approach to refine strategies and processes over time to stay agile and responsive to changing business needs. Provide real-time, actionable financial data to inform decisions.

5.1.1.2 *Executive Buy-In*

Enterprise FinOps aims for a significant transformation of the way your IT team operates. You're not doing a single discrete project, but executing multiple and continuous initiatives, especially in the Optimize phase. Collaboration across multiple teams is needed to synchronize in a common cause. A mindset shift is the ultimate goal. Executive support and sponsorship are essential to make this a success.

5.1.1.3 *Identifying the Enterprise FinOps Leader*

Identify an experienced and capable leader who will be your champion for Enterprise FinOps. Since Enterprise FinOps covers all IT spend, ideally, this role reports directly to the CIO and ideally would be a peer to your IT leaders, leading other portfolio segments such as infrastructure, cloud, ERP, business systems, AI and data, etc. Direct responsibilities should include core IT run and business operations, IT helpdesk, vendor management, IT service management, and platforms for cost, service, visibility, and asset management. Enterprise FinOps is a logical role extension as it uses the foundation provided by these services and platforms.

5.1.1.4 *Business Case for Enterprise FinOps*

Develop a business case for Enterprise FinOps that outlines your strategy and expected ROI. Remember that savings will follow through and eventually make this self-funded, but this will take time. You will need an initial investment to secure a strong core Enterprise FinOps team. You want to establish momentum as soon as possible. Consider hiring experts trained in Enterprise FinOps techniques and frameworks to help you assess FinOps opportunities, develop benchmarks and other services, and guide your team on Optimize tasks as your own team is coming up to speed.

5.1.1.5 *Enterprise FinOps Center of Excellence (CoE)*

A FinOps CoE is the glue that holds everything together. The principles, vision, and mission of Enterprise FinOps come together under one roof, led by your FinOps leader, and provide a foundation for implementation. The centralized FinOps team is typically a part of the CoE. The CoE's job starts with standardization. Define FinOps principles that match your strategy. Build or refine processes that elaborate on how budgets are set, how costs are reported and charged to business stakeholders, and how optimizations are prioritized. A governance framework is critical here. Develop a simple RACI at the team level that tells everyone who handles what. Engineers handle rightsizing, finance oversees budgets, and the CoE acts as the collaboration space. The CoE needs to be a knowledge hub. It develops a centralized repository of tools, best practices, policies, and training. The CoE builds momentum. It evaluates tools and automates reporting. It sets KPIs and metrics. Showback and chargeback policies get refined too. A CoE shifts how your organization thinks about IT spend.

5.1.2 Assess

This phase aims to get a baseline on your Enterprise FinOps roadmap. Key activities in the Assess phase are shown in Figure 5.5. The scope defines which parts of your IT portfolio are assessed. You get a handle on your current cost management approach, policies, and business reporting for IT spending, typically your "showback" and "chargeback" methods. You conduct an Enterprise FinOps assessment for your selected scope. A Vendor Spend Analysis determines how and what you are spending with external vendors on products, hardware and software, and services. A maturity assessment determines your maturity levels on various factors. Finally, you determine the top opportunities for optimization. To keep

Figure 5.5 Key activities in the assess phase

things manageable, I recommend focusing on the top 20 over the first year of Enterprise FinOps implementation.

5.1.2.1 *Enterprise FinOps Scope*

I recommend including your entire IT spend in scope for the initial assessment. Assessment itself does not risk business disruption. While it does take up efforts on the part of the assessment team and IT users who are involved, it is non-invasive and non-destructive. It's the optimization activities that follow in the next phase that may necessitate system downtime or involve re-prioritization of activities for engineering and development teams. However, if you do decide to go with a partial scope, I recommend starting with the infrastructure and cloud teams, and also include a major business system such as an ERP, HR, or CRM system, so you get a sense of how FinOps works across both infrastructure, software, IT services, and application layers. This also requires identifying the relevant stakeholders who will have a primary impact on the outcome, as well as those who may benefit from participating in future assessments. Establishing a clear understanding of the target group and their roles ensures that everyone involved is aware of what to expect during the assessment process.

5.1.2.2 *Current Cost Management Approach*

Evaluate how you measure IT spend. What tools do you use? How do you attribute costs to business units? This activity lets you determine if your current showback and chargeback methods use precise targeting of IT spend, or simply allocate spend based on other factors like the number of users or size of the business. Also, look at your current budgeting and forecasting approach within your IT portfolio units. This also gives you an idea of what tool improvements are needed. Is your data mostly stuck in spreadsheets, or do you have a cost management tool in place already? A key concept in FinOps assessments is the use of lenses, which refer to different functional perspectives used to inspect and analyze IT spend. These lenses provide a structured approach to evaluating various aspects of an organization's capabilities, such as cost optimization, resource allocation, and billing processes. One lens might be cost optimization that looks at how we are spending money. Another could be resource allocation, where we look at whether we are using the right tools for the right tasks.

5.1.2.3 *Enterprise FinOps Assessment*

A FinOps assessment, as illustrated in Figure 5.6, is a comprehensive evaluation of your organization's IT spend activities, conducted by your core

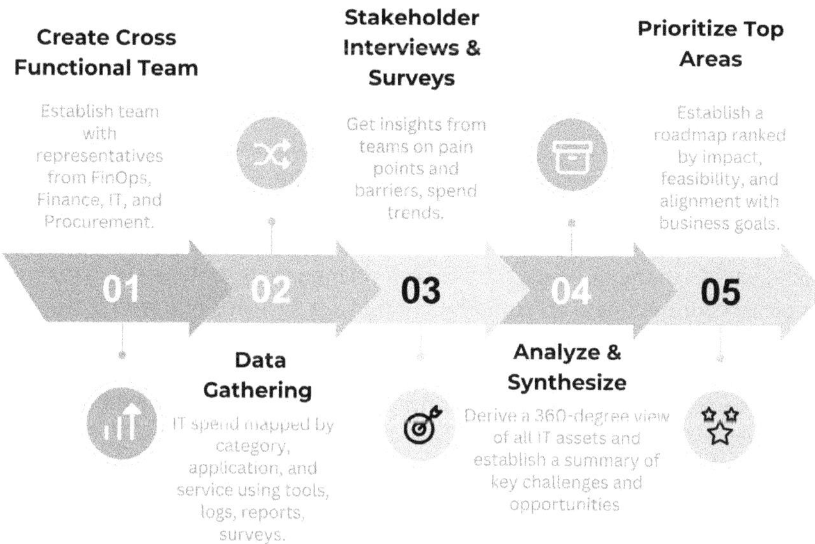

Figure 5.6 Enterprise FinOps assessment

Enterprise FinOps team, if already onboarded, or using external expertise unless available internally. They collaborate with IT finance, cost management teams, vendor management, service management, and asset teams, and IT engineers and developers relevant to the scope and IT portfolios being assessed. It identifies areas for improving and optimizing resource allocation. You gather evidence related to each lens through detailed analysis of IT financial data that shows where the money is being spent. You augment the process through stakeholder surveys and conduct interviews with portfolio operations and engineering teams. You are collecting data, documentation, and expert insights that provide a comprehensive understanding of the current state. You look at logs, talk to teams, and find the gaps.

An Enterprise FinOps assessment is like a flashlight that cuts through the fog surrounding your IT assets. It reveals where every dollar is going, whether it's delivering value, and what's bleeding your budget dry. Think of it as a 360-degree view – on-premises servers, software licenses, training, even the internal hours your team spends on maintenance and support. You need a single source of truth. No more silos hiding costs in the shadows. Maybe a team spent $50,000 last quarter on unused storage that could simply be decommissioned or phased out.

The assessment should result in a detailed breakdown of IT spend. It should list prioritized recommendations on optimizing the spend. After completing the assessment, assessors analyze the results and develop recommendations for improvement based on the findings. What are your top spending areas? Are you paying for unused licenses? Are your cloud instances underutilized? How is IT spend driving business outcomes? Do you have risks such as compliance gaps or vendor lock-in?

Then comes the analysis and recommendations. You identify the biggest risks and the biggest opportunities. The goal is to provide actionable insights that can be used by stakeholders across various departments. Typical recommendations could be saving 15% by using reserved instances. Using containers for on-premises applications to cut off 20% from maintenance and backups. Software harvesting could save 20% on your collaboration suite licenses, and renegotiating that SaaS CRM renewal, cutting out unnecessary modules, will yield another 20%.

Overall, a FinOps assessment requires diligent planning, execution, and collaboration among stakeholders. By following these steps, you can gain valuable insights into your organization's IT spend, enabling targeted improvements that optimize resource allocation and drive business value. Ideally, this should provide you with an approximate idea of how much optimization can save on your current IT spend. Thirty percent savings is not idealistic but a totally realistic target.

The FinOps framework from the FinOps Foundation has a comprehensive guide on conducting a FinOps assessment that can be modified as per your Enterprise FinOps scope (FinOps Assessment guide, 2025).

5.1.2.4 Enterprise FinOps Maturity Level

Enterprise FinOps is a journey, and like any interesting journey, it's nonlinear and full of surprises and detours. The Maturity Model, illustrated in Figure 5.7, is like a compass pointing toward where you could be, even if the path isn't well defined.

- At Level 1 – Initial – you're probably in a phase where you're completely consumed in managing IT costs. It's reactive, chaotic, and often feels like you were not even aware you were bleeding money. Cost is an afterthought. You're scrambling to fix problems as they pop up, like a fire drill with no fire alarm. Basic reporting exists, but it's fragmented, and rarely aligned with anything meaningful. Unplanned spending is the norm. You're hoping you don't get caught in a downturn that forces your hand on cutting costs through short-term quick fixes.
- In Level 2 – Emerging – you start to see the cracks in the foundation. Some rudimentary reporting is in place. You're tagging resources, but

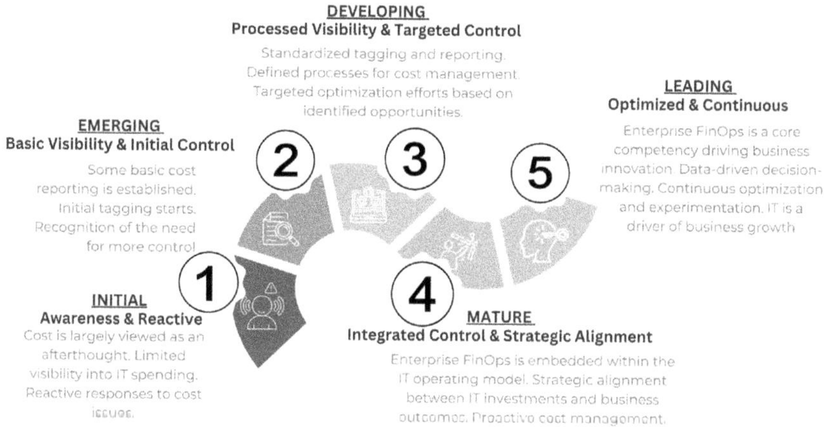

Figure 5.7 Enterprise FinOps maturity model

it's half-baked. You're not optimizing yet, just trying to get a handle on where the money is going. There's a fragile but emerging flicker of control. You're still reacting, but now you're reacting with a slightly better playbook.

- Level 3 – Developing. You've got standardized tagging and reporting. Processes are defined, and for the first time, you're actually doing something about real cost optimization. Rightsizing, automated shutdowns, and workload optimization are familiar activities for the team. You're having regular reviews with stakeholders. A structured Enterprise FinOps program can bring you from Level 1 to Level 3, and you can actually start benefiting from the savings here. There's still chaos, but you're building guardrails, and you can see the shrinkage in unplanned or waste spending.
- Level 4 – Mature – is where you're not just managing costs but also aligning them with the business. Enterprise FinOps is embedded in the IT operating model now. Cross-functional teams and portfolio reviews let you prioritize investments based on ROI. Your vendor management is negotiating and partnering with vendors as if they were an integral part of the team. Cost reductions are real and visible. You're making smarter decisions in every area of your IT spend. And even better, your investments in the program are paying off as you see these savings start to make a difference in your Transform and Innovate areas.
- Level 5 – Leading – is the hum of continuous and constant optimization. Your business knows and recognizes that IT is optimizing at every

single layer. Enterprise FinOps is a core competency across every pillar and practice within IT. Data-driven decisions, predictive modeling, and automation are the new normal. You're experimenting, innovating, and pushing boundaries. Cost efficiency is a baseline.

Your journey will look different from everyone else's. You'll have to tailor the metrics, the activities, the focus areas, and the outcomes. Some organizations might skip a level. Others might stumble. That's okay. The point isn't to reach Level 5 in a quarter but to keep moving forward, even if the path isn't perfectly clear. Don't seek perfection but aim for progress. Every step forward, no matter how small, is a win. Note that the FinOps Foundation proposes a different approach of Walk-Run-Crawl for their recommended Maturity model (FinOps Maturity Model, 2025).

5.1.2.5 Vendor Spend Analysis

Vendor Spend Analysis lets you optimize your spending with all external vendors. The first step is to analyze your spend by using procurement data to determine how your IT spend is spread. It addresses questions like:

- Who are my top vendors?
- What is the SLA performance on outsourced services?
- How much am I spending on cloud?
- Do I have multiple cloud vendors?
- Where do I buy my hardware and laptops from?
- Do we have channel suppliers and consolidators?
- Who provides my staff augmentation resources?
- Which portfolios have the most staff augmentation spend?
- Who are my top SaaS vendors?

Identify cost-saving opportunities and align spending with business goals. The analysis results in giving visibility on spend by vendor, product, IT portfolio department, and supplier type. If you have benchmarking data, it lets you compare costs against industry standards or historical data. It lets you detect trends such as increases or decreases in spend by vendor. Dashboards and reports can highlight trends and anomalies. This analysis helps uncover inefficiencies, such as overpaying for services, redundant contracts, excessive and underutilized features, and underutilized vendor capabilities. By consolidating spend, renegotiating contracts, or shifting to more cost-effective suppliers, organizations can reduce costs and enhance supplier accountability.

Vendor Spend Analysis also supports strategic sourcing by identifying high-impact vendors and opportunities for long-term partnerships.

Aggregate data from procurement systems, ERP platforms, billing systems, and contracts to maximize your buying power. Vendor Spend Analysis is a powerful assessment tool that provides you with insights on optimizing vendor spend, understanding the risk in your current contracts, assessing vendor performance, and renewal timings. It's also a foundational activity to develop expanded opportunities like vendor consolidation, staff augmentation reduction, and building strategic partnerships.

5.1.2.6 Top Optimization and Alignment Opportunities

The biggest outcome from the assessment is a list of cost optimization opportunities. Use a prioritization framework to determine the top (ideally 20) areas, including early wins, to boost the Enterprise FinOps program into the next phase of continuous optimization. Remember, you may still be at an early maturity level. Some of the core activities and structures for continuous optimization may not yet be in place. Focusing on early wins that are feasible lets you drive quick savings and provide a business case for further transformation. It lets you bootstrap innovation pilots. These early savings can also be used to further optimize Run^2 operations through workflow and process optimization and set you firmly on the roadmap for value creation.

5.1.3 Optimize, Manage, and Govern – Core Activities

So, you've identified millions of potential savings through a comprehensive Enterprise FinOps assessment. In the words of a famous TV sci-fi series captain steering another "Enterprise," albeit in the far reaches of a futuristic universe, you tell your team to "make it so." But you need a strong foundation to make that happen. Figure 5.8 explores core activities to commence optimization.

5.1.3.1 Centralized FinOps Team

If you haven't already established a FinOps CoE and started hiring core team members, it's time to do so. You will need people with backgrounds in cost optimization and a background in FinOps techniques. This team will serve as the guiding force leading your Enterprise FinOps implementation and working with the rest of the organization.

5.1.3.2 FinOps Leadership Group

This will be your working leadership group with representatives from each of your major IT portfolios, like infrastructure and business systems, IT

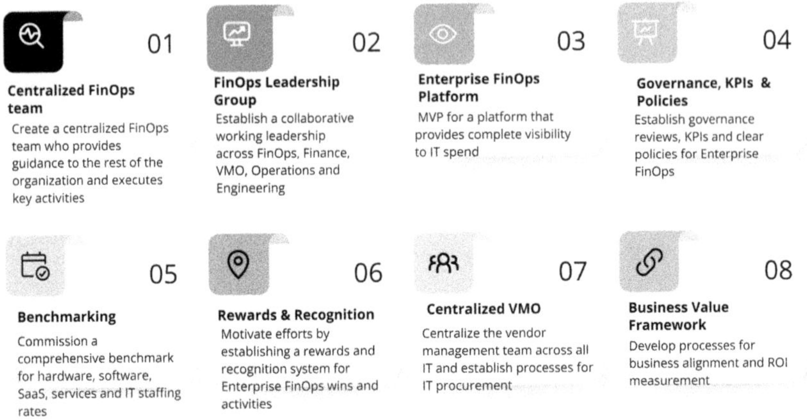

Figure 5.8 Core activities in the optimize phase

finance, operations, vendor management, and engineering. This team will be responsible for ensuring individual teams prioritize and execute the identified optimization activities.

Embedding FinOps into approval workflows forces you to ask the hard questions, like:

- Is this investment driving value?
- Is it optimized?
- Does it align with our priorities?

You're slicing expenses as well as evaluating whether a service is worth the price. That means digging into the total cost of ownership and cost factors like setup fees, recurring charges, and hidden costs like training or support. And yes, decommissioning may be a far-off goal, but if you don't plan for the end of a service's lifecycle, you're just setting yourself up for a surprise bill later.

You need to tie investments to KPIs, evaluate vendor lock-in, and assess security risks. Because if you're not considering these factors, you're exposing yourself to risk. Every investment needs a clear, data-backed rationale. You need to show how it ties to revenue, efficiency, or customer experience. When you are ready to stop treating IT spend like a routine and start making it a strategy, that's where the real change begins.

5.1.3.3 *Enterprise FinOps Platform*

A centralized platform for all IT spends is essential for FinOps. Determine the approach that works best for you. You may already have a service management platform like ServiceNow that may offer additional modules for cost management, or you may already have implemented a centralized ITFM or cost management platform like Apptio. Your cloud teams may be using native tools such as AWS Cost Explorer. The idea is to get started. Aim for centralized visibility where you aggregate and analyze data from across your IT portfolio. Include cloud, on-premises, and vendor spend. Connect with ERP systems, procurement platforms, and cloud providers to ensure holistic cost management. Once you have a centralized platform, you can expand it through automation. Automate tagging and cost allocation. In a further iteration, introduce anomaly detection to detect unexpected spikes in spending. Your analytics team can further enhance this with dashboards and analytics to prioritize optimization opportunities.

The FinOps Foundation maintains a list of vendors providing services and tools for FinOps as part of its FinOps Landscape section (FinOps Landscape, 2025).

5.1.3.4 *Rewards and Recognition*

Building a culture of accountability is reinforced through a rewards and recognition program that motivates and incentivizes teams. Encourage teams to adopt cost-conscious behaviors by rewarding cost-saving initiatives. Promote collaboration by acknowledging and rewarding cross-functional efforts.

5.1.3.5 *Centralized VMO*

Centralizing your procurement team has several benefits. You get a single picture of vendor contracts and performance data that lets you identify cost-saving opportunities. These will lead to further opportunities for cost optimization, such as renegotiating rates or switching to more cost-effective suppliers. It reinforces compliance and governance by ensuring that vendor spend aligns with enterprise policies. Any procurement-related policies can be driven through the centralized The Vendor Management Office (VMO) processes. Consolidating visibility on vendor spend gives you negotiation leverage. Aggregated spend data lets you bargain for better terms with vendors on volume discounts and SLA improvements.

5.1.3.6 *Business Value Framework*

A Business Value Framework (BVF) framework lets you align IT decisions with business objectives. It lets you focus on quantifying the business value of IT spend. Metrics like ROI and cost-benefit analysis help you prioritize where to invest. For instance, if a new AI tool is driving a 30% increase in customer retention, it's worth putting your efforts behind it. By mapping every dollar spent to business outcomes, the framework shines a light on areas you might have overlooked and uncovers hidden opportunities. The framework shows you where to invest in ways that directly impact revenue, efficiency, growth, or customer experience.

5.1.3.7 Benchmarking

Benchmarking gives you an anchor in turbulent seas. By comparing current IT spend and performance against industry benchmarks or internal targets, you can cut through years of blind contracts. Now you can set optimization goals with a valid reference. It becomes a critical data point when renewals are coming. You can track improvements over time to see the impact of other initiatives. Benchmarking might reveal that the organization's CRM costs per user are 20% higher than industry averages, prompting a review of resource allocation or renegotiation with the vendor, or even a switch to a different provider.

5.1.3.8 Governance, KPIs, and Policies

The FinOps team works with leadership and the CoE members to determine governance policies for Enterprise FinOps. Governance sets boundaries that protect the team from itself. Budgets, spending policies, and approval workflows are guardrails. Audits uncover where the gaps are before they become disasters. Metrics are proof that your culture is working. Start with a core set of principles. Don't try to do everything at once. Let automation handle the repetitive stuff. Let people focus on the big picture.

Policies aren't simply paperwork. Make every team responsible for its own spend. Use chargeback models that show exactly how much a team's usage costs. But ownership alone isn't enough. You need clear, simple rules. Let teams justify their spend, but force them to think critically about every dollar. Recognizing costs as they're incurred, not after and when the bill arrives, gives you a clearer picture of where money is going. Companies can reduce waste just by switching to accruals, as it gives them a proactive approach to optimizing costs. Risk should be baked into the policies. Set limits on instance sizes. Enforce usage thresholds. Formalize compliance checks. Many teams try to build a comprehensive 100-page policy document, but that can have the opposite effect of "too-much" and restrictive governance that slows down the entire organization. Instead, you can begin with clear, easy-to-understand guidelines. Let the program evolve as your business does. Table 5.1 lists down a few key policies that can be adaptedand customized as needed for your Enterprise FinOps program.

Table 5.1 Typical Enterprise FinOps policies

Category	*Policy title*	*Description*	*Key points*
Core accountability and ownership	Application cost ownership	All application teams are ultimately responsible for the total cost of their applications, including cloud infrastructure, services, and support.	Clearly assigns accountability.
Core accountability and ownership	Budget allocation and approval	All IT budgets are allocated based on demonstrated business value and require approval at the IT leadership level before expenditure.	Controls spending and promotes justification.
Core accountability and ownership	Cost monitoring responsibility	Each IT unit will designate a "FinOps Champion" to actively monitor their team's cloud spending, identify optimization opportunities, and report on progress.	Creates proactive cost management.
Core accountability and ownership	Change management and cost impact assessment	All proposed changes to infrastructure, applications, or services must include a documented cost impact assessment to be reviewed and approved.	Prevents uncontrolled spending.
Cost management and optimization	Reserved instance policy	All workloads exceeding defined criteria must demonstrate a workload optimization analysis.	Focuses on predictable, high-volume usage.

(*Continued*)

Table 5.1 (Continued)

Category	*Policy title*	*Description*	*Key points*
Cost management and optimization	Rightsizing policy	All virtual machines and other compute instances must be regularly reviewed and adjusted to match actual utilization levels; the ideal size should be no larger than the minimum required to meet performance demands.	Addresses over-provisioning.
Cost management and optimization	Spend limits and alerts	Spending limits are established for all cloud services and automatically trigger alerts when spending approaches predefined thresholds. These thresholds will be reviewed quarterly.	Provides automated controls and proactive monitoring.
Governance and reporting	Standardized cost reporting	All IT units must generate and submit monthly cost reports, broken down by service, application, and user, following a standardized template.	Ensures consistent data collection and analysis.
Governance and reporting	Budget variance review	Monthly budget variance reviews will be conducted to identify significant deviations and their root causes.	Promotes learning and corrective action.

The FinOps Foundation has listed a comprehensive list of KPIs as part of their FinOps framework. You can reference it here (FinOps KPIs, 2025).

5.1.4 Optimize – Ongoing Activities

These activities occur continuously as part of continuous optimization. Figure 5.9 demonstrates ongoing activities in this phase. They create a powerful framework for reducing costs, improving efficiency, optimizing processes, and aligning IT with business goals. Each step contributes to a more agile, cost-effective operation. When done holistically, these practices can lead to savings of 20 to 50% on your Run spend. Every step promotes stronger alignment between technology and the organization's broader objectives. The chapters on "Cost Optimization Levers" and "Technical Levers" provide a broader explanation of many of these activities.

5.1.4.1 Workload Optimization

The idea is simple. You ensure that your tool matches what you're trying to do. Workload optimization ensures that your computing resources, such as servers, virtual machines, storage, and networking, are used as efficiently as possible. A key technique is rightsizing. This adjusts the power of your servers to match the actual demands of the workloads they're handling. If a server isn't being used much, you might scale it down or even

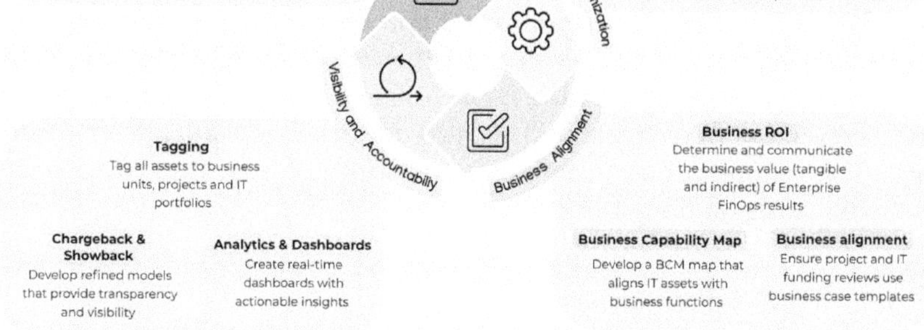

Figure 5.9 Ongoing activities in the optimize phase

shut it off when it's not needed. With the tools available today, this can be done quickly without impacting business operations. You can even automate this.

Consolidation combines underutilized systems into more efficient combinations. If you are still using physical servers, you can move workloads into virtual machines or containers to save space and reduce complexity. If you are already using virtual machines, use management consoles to monitor and optimize them. Migration shifts workloads from on-premises servers to the cloud, or vice versa, if you have excess capacity.

5.1.4.2 Rate Optimization

Your team keeps an eye out for vendor rates and services that offer lower costs for your demands. Lock-in long-term commitments for discounted rates. Reserved instances offer huge discounts for long-term commitment. If you forecast that your software utilization on a particular SaaS product is going to increase over time, negotiate bulk pricing with software companies. For workloads that are intermittent, you can use spot instances for workloads that don't need constant availability, like data or image processing or batch jobs. Regularly reviewing contracts ensures that pricing terms stay up-to-date with current usage patterns. Companies that do this well can cut cloud and software costs by 15 to 30%.

5.1.4.3 Software Harvesting

Software harvesting is a simple strategy that has a big payoff. It makes sure you're not paying for licenses or subscriptions you don't actually need. You can get started with simple user surveys or use tools like ServiceNow SAM (Software Asset Management) to scan your systems to find unused or redundant software. These are a drain on your budget. These can be decommissioned or reallocated to other teams that need them. This is indispensable during renewals to ensure that you are renewing only the number of licenses and modules that you actually need. Centralized SAM systems are like a silent monitor working in the background to track licenses in real time, preventing overpayment. This also ensures compliance with vendor rules. This optimization can eliminate up to 50% of wasted software spend and avoid costs on fines and audits.

5.1.4.4 Workflow Optimization

Workflow optimization streamlines internal processes. It reduces the time and resources spent on repetitive or inefficient tasks. Automation tools like Robotic Process Automation (RPA) bring in sophisticated techniques like screen-scraping, OCR processing (extracting digital values from scanned physical paperwork), and rules processing. You can automate business processes like quotes, invoice processing, and expense reconciliation. Anything that leaves a paper trail can be automated. You've heard of companies deploying features multiple times a day. You can speed up code deployment with CI/CD pipelines. Further accelerate your deployment by using automated testing and security and policy checks. Map entire workflows to identify bottlenecks and uncover areas for improvement. Often, a single bottleneck creates chaos in the overall workflow. Integrating systems, such as connecting ERP and CRM platforms, can eliminate the need for manual data transfers. The result is often a 10 to 30% reduction in labor costs and faster product launches.

5.1.4.5 Automation

Automation is a cornerstone of Enterprise FinOps. Tools like Puppet can enforce FinOps policies automatically, ensuring that resources are tagged correctly and cost limits are respected. You can use automation to scale systems up or down based on demand, preventing over-provisioning. Real-time monitoring tools alert teams to unexpected spikes in spending. This kind of automation can reduce manual effort drastically. Fifty to seventy percent reductions are realistic.

5.1.4.6 Value Stream Mapping (VSM)

Value Stream Mapping (VSM) (Manos, 2025) is a lean technique that helps identify where time and money are being wasted in IT processes and goes hand-in-hand with automation. You can map your workflow using established models and calculations that calculate the time it takes for the outcome between steps. VSM lets you spot inefficiencies such as redundant steps or bottlenecks. By tracing how IT investments contribute to business outcomes, you can also prioritize work to align with high-impact goals, like improving customer service. Companies often eliminate 20 to 30% of non-value-adding steps, speeding up time to market for new products or services.

5.1.4.7 Business Capability Mapping (BCM)

Business Capability Mapping (BCM) lets you align IT investments, such as your application portfolio and services, with the company's strategic goals. Start by defining which systems support key business functions. Cover areas like marketing, supply chain management, customer support, and sales and map IT tools and services to these functions. A BCM model or map is like reading invisible ink. You can now see where gaps exist and where resources should be focused. You can standardize on tools and eliminate redundant systems. Prioritize investments in high-impact areas, such as AI or cloud infrastructure, to ensure that money is spent on things that drive revenue or efficiency (Scott, Jeff, Forrester Research, 2009).

5.1.4.8 Tagging

Tagging assigns labels or metadata to data, systems, resources, or transactions to categorize, track, and manage them. Typical metadata is the project, business unit, department, or cost center. It enables cost allocation, resource tracking, and billing accuracy, especially in multi-tenant or shared environments. It is a common practice in cloud usage where providers like AWS or Azure use tags to help organizations monitor spending and apply cost controls. In finance and procurement, tagging helps classify vendor spend by category (e.g., "software," "hardware," "services") or business unit, enabling spend analysis and budget forecasting. Tagging enables visibility at a precise level. It's like using a laser versus a broad beam flashlight. Most organizations are flying blind. They know their IT costs are high, but they can't trace them back to specific projects, departments, teams, or outcomes.

Business units often complain about high IT costs and the lack of transparency. IT costs are often "peanut-buttered" across business units based on outdated factors like business revenue, or worse, just evenly spread across the major units. There is often no visibility on exactly how much the business is consuming and getting charged for their usage. With tags, you see the connection, such as that $5,000 a month for the SaaS platform is enabling the business to drive 300 leads into their sales system every month, and a potential revenue of $2M for the quarter.

But tagging takes discipline. A good tagging strategy is like a well-organized filing cabinet. Every tag has a purpose. A "Marketing" tag is generic. A "Marketing_Campaign_Xmas_GoogleAnalytics" tag is actionable. You can narrow down spend to specific activities being conducted by the marketing department and tie it to increased sales resulting from that campaign. You know exactly what your IT spend has resulted in. Tagging needs consistency. A tagging system that's a patchwork of ad-hoc labels is worse than none at all. You need a carefully designed schema that aligns with how your business operates. If finance uses "Department" and engineering uses "Team," you're speaking two dialects. Standardization is the glue that holds it all together.

Automation is the next step. You simply cannot tag manually over the long term. It's slow, error-prone, costly, and simply unsustainable. Use tools that enforce tagging policies at the point of creation, like when a new server spins up, ensuring compliance from the very start. With tagging, you can allocate costs precisely. HR knows how much their onboarding tools are costing, and leadership gets a clear view of where money is flowing.

5.1.4.9 *Chargeback and Showback*

Chargeback and showback create clarity and transparency. It is the essential step in building trust with the business. Business units often complain about not knowing where their funding goes. In chargeback, you allocate IT expenses to specific business units based on their actual consumption. A cost factor analysis can let you build accurate models for allocating everything from helpdesk costs to SaaS software. Showback is similar, except rather than charging the business unit, you are providing visibility into these costs. It is often used to educate or raise awareness on spending patterns. Together, they help departments see where their IT dollars are going and encourage smarter and more efficient use of resources.

5.1.4.10 *Analytics and Dashboards*

You have data, but unless you put this into an easily digestible format and provide the right insights to your stakeholders, the data is useless. Creating the right dashboards lets you transform raw data into actionable insights. These tools gather and analyze information on IT spending and resource utilization. They present it in visual formats that make anomalies and cost drivers easy to spot. Dashboards track progress on optimization efforts in real time, showing how efforts are paying off. While Chargeback and showback provide detailed visibility into who is spending what, dashboards turn that information into strategic guidance. Teams get motivated to make smarter decisions and continuously seek ways to reduce waste. The result is lower IT costs and better alignment between spending and strategic priorities.

5.1.5 *Expand*

5.1.5.1 *Vendor Consolidation*

Vendor consolidation simplifies operations by eliminating multiple vendors into a few chosen partners. There are two plays here. You save operational costs by consolidating services across vendors and use the larger volume to get better rates. In the second, you also open a door to innovation by selecting vendors who have expertise in the direction that you want to take forward. The cost savings come from reduced rates and from reducing inefficiencies in vendor management. You can also merge overlapping services and reduce the complexity of your IT landscape. Consolidating vendors fosters better relationships and quality. This approach strengthens negotiation power with vendors, as consolidated spending allows for bulk discounts and more favorable terms. Companies can save over 30% of their entire current spend on external services. But this is not an easy task and requires strong project management and execution to avoid business disruption.

5.1.5.2 *Shadow IT Reduction*

Shadow IT is notoriously difficult to eliminate. Duplicate services, products, and systems exist in corners of your enterprise, causing a drain on overall IT costs. You launch a sophisticated system for virtual collaboration, and you find that some customer helpdesk teams are still hanging on to alternate systems. You modernize a major ERP upgrade and discover that one of the mergers that your company did some years back is on a totally different ERP system. Shadow IT reduction uncovers and addresses unapproved software or tools that slip through the cracks of formal IT processes. This is also fraught with political risks. Businesses may have commissioned systems because IT simply was not performing or addressing their needs, and now these systems have become entrenched in their business workflows. Any change will lead to complaints about business disruption unless tactfully addressed. Cloud is often an area where Shadow IT thrives. The ability to commission entire production systems at the click of a button leads to disparate cloud technologies that now get firmly embedded in your IT environment.

These hidden systems often come with unexpected costs and security risks that can go unnoticed until they cause problems. Shadow IT reduction lets you gain a clearer picture of inefficiencies in your IT spend. One of the biggest drivers is compliance and security. It strengthens security by eliminating vulnerabilities from untrusted platforms and reduces the chance of data breaches or regulatory fines. You're removing the proverbial Trojan horses from your ecosystem before they cause the system to crash. Tools like IT asset discovery and network analyzers help identify shadow systems. It needs to be enforced through clear governance policies and approval workflows to prevent unauthorized tools from being used in the first place.

5.1.5.3 *Staff Augmentation Reduction*

Hiring external contractors is easy. Your IT leaders are bombarded with numerous calls every day from services firms looking to gain a foothold in your company. A contractor gives your teams flexibility and brings talent on board that would take months to develop otherwise. But it also comes at a cost. Contractors could be as much as 3X the costs of

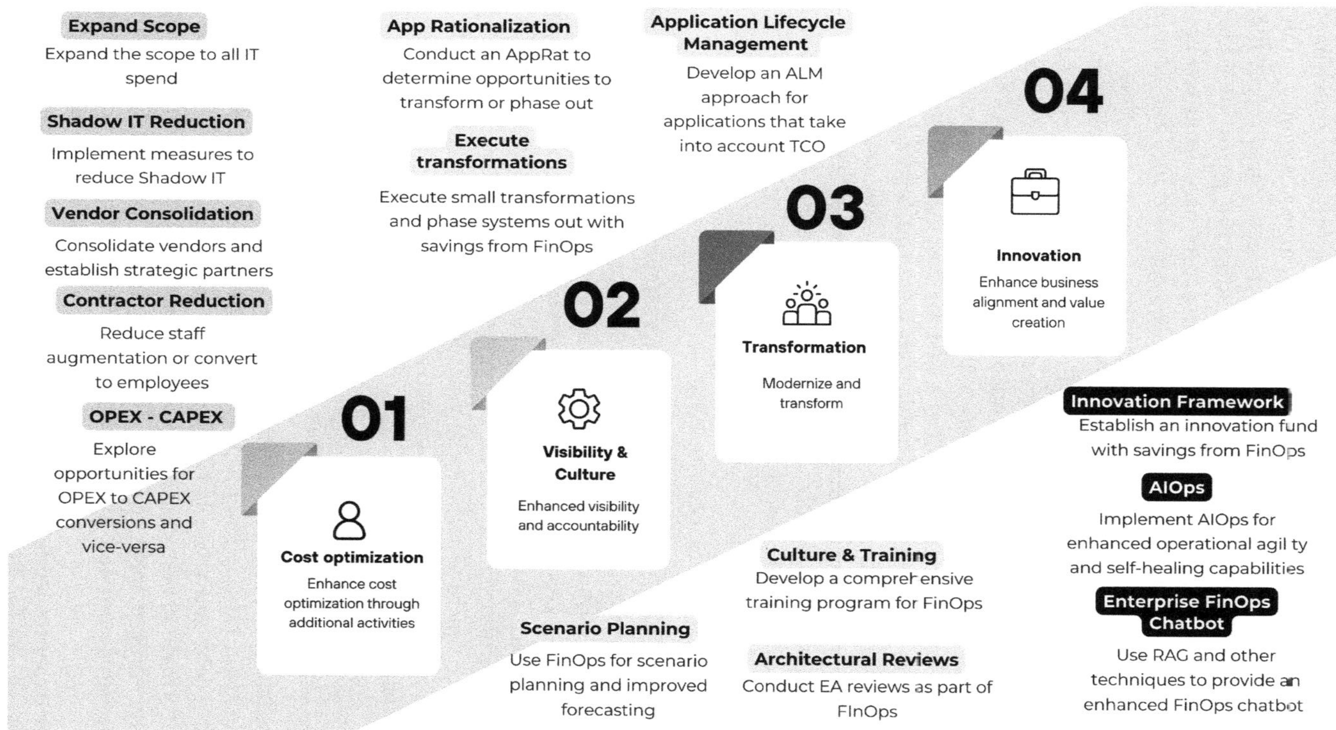

Figure 5.10 Expanding the scope of FinOps beyond the initial phase

employees. But it's not just that. When contractors leave, you invariably lose knowledge, even when you try to address it through knowledge transition and documentation. Running a contractor-vs-employee analysis is relatively easy. Most HR systems can quickly give you a report that lets you categorize your IT spend on contractors. But go in for additional detail and find out how long these contractors have been working for you. If you find that contractors have been retained for over 12 months, long after their initial project or consulting services, it's time to take a deeper look at your strategy. Use contractor-conversion plays to convert valued contractors to employees. Enforce policies that mandate going through an approval process for repeated renewals after a certain period of time, or after the project has ended. Another strategy may be to simply let them go. Your own IT teams will cite risks like business disruption. You may have to manage that on a case-by-case basis. Building in-house teams gives you more predictable expenses and better alignment with organizational goals. It also gives the company more control over quality and outcomes, ensuring that projects are handled by people who understand the business deeply. Invest in internal talent to develop a more resilient and capable workforce.

5.1.5.4 Opex to Capex, and Vice Versa

Shifting between operational expenses (Opex) and capital expenses (Capex) allows you to fine-tune and align financial strategies with long-term goals. With cloud models evolving every month, you have several opportunities to convert from Capex to Opex. SaaS is a classic example. This approach provides stability by predicting monthly costs and avoiding long-term commitments. The reverse is also possible. You can spread costs over time and reduce the volatility of recurring expenses. A company might reclassify cloud infrastructure as Capex to fund a five-year AI transformation plan.

5.1.5.5 Application Rationalization (AppRat)

We talked about AppRat in the chapter on "Technology Debt Reduction." Application rationalization pays off in multiple ways: it identifies technology debt and risks. It paves the way for selective as well as holistic transformation that can drastically reduce costs and improve business agility. AppRat seeks to eliminate redundant or underutilized software. By retiring outdated applications and consolidating functionality into fewer, more strategic tools, organizations can lower license and maintenance expenses while improving workflow efficiency. AppRat also results in a roadmap for your IT portfolio that ensures that the remaining applications align with current business needs. You create a transformation plan to maximize the value of your IT portfolio and also create opportunities for cost savings.

5.1.5.6 *Opportunistic Transformations*

Modernizations can offer quick wins for cost savings. If your AppRat identifies systems that are unused, you can phase them out quickly, retaining data as needed for compliance or regulatory purposes. If systems are being used by just a few users, transition them to alternate platforms. Migrate legacy systems to the cloud using tools. It builds momentum for broader FinOps adoption. These incremental changes also reduce technology debt.

5.1.5.7 *Application Lifecycle Management (ALM)*

ALM looks at the entire life of an application, from deployment to retirement. It continuously monitors the value of the application in meeting business goals. By monitoring expenses like licensing fees, support contracts, maintenance costs, and decommissioning costs, organizations can identify inefficiencies and prevent overspending. You can assess where the application is in the technology cycle and retire outdated or non-strategic tools. Upgrade tools as needed to extend their usefulness. ALM platforms can integrate with FinOps dashboards, enabling teams to make data-driven decisions that support continuous improvement and cost-effective maintenance (RedHat, 2025).

5.1.5.8 *Scenario Planning*

Scenario planning gives you a crystal ball to predict the future. It uses predictive analytics to model potential financial outcomes, from future growth to economic disruptions. Identify risks and develop mitigation strategies by simulating scenarios like SaaS license increases or regulatory changes that mandate data retention and increased storage costs. FinOps becomes the partner to business continuity. It may not be perfect, but it gives you a way to keep your budgets flexible in the face of uncertainty. A company might model the impact of a 20% cloud cost increase and take steps now to recover $5 million in savings through automation and renegotiation.

5.1.5.9 *Culture and Training*

FinOps cannot be done solely by the centralized FinOps team. They can identify optimization and alignment opportunities, but it needs to be implemented by engineering and operations teams. Conducting training workshops is one of the key roles for the Enterprise FinOps CoE. Knowledge breaks down silos and fosters shared accountability. Training equips employees to use FinOps tools and metrics effectively. This develops a culture of innovation and financial responsibility and ensures that cost optimization becomes a core part of operational activities.

5.1.5.10 Architectural Reviews

Architectural reviews let you align IT initiatives with strategic goals. By reviewing proposals for new projects and modernizations, you can identify inefficiencies, such as outdated infrastructure or redundant components. The EA team can suggest adjustments that reduce costs and improve performance. You can eliminate Shadow IT by identifying duplicate systems. If you have developed a standard IT application list, you can question why teams need an exception to the policies. Architectural reviews are positive governance. They provide the guardrails to ensure that teams are using their funds to align with business priorities.

5.1.5.11 Innovation Framework

Enterprise FinOps unlocks savings. While these savings may not be enough to fund a full-fledged innovation project, they allow you to pilot innovations. For that, you need an innovation framework. You are balancing experimentation with financial viability. By allocating resources to pilot projects, such as AI prototypes or IoT initiatives, you can test new ideas without overextending budgets. You do not need to go to business to seek funding until you have validated it through a pilot or POC and demonstrated a clear business case and potential ROI. This approach ensures that only initiatives with clear ROI and alignment with business goals make the route for seeking additional funding.

5.1.5.12 AIOps and Enterprise FinOps Chatbots

These are the future directions of FinOps, but quite feasible to implement today. AIOps uses artificial intelligence to detect anomalies, heal systems, identify operational issues, and optimize resource allocation. AIOps tools can identify unusual spending patterns, such as unexpected spikes in cloud compute costs, and recommend or conduct corrective actions like rightsizing instances. Enterprise FinOps chatbots let non-technical users analyze opportunities through natural language queries. These tools integrate with ERP systems, cloud platforms, and FinOps dashboards, ensuring seamless data flow and enabling instant decision-making. By weaving these initiatives into a cohesive strategy, Enterprise FinOps evolves from a cost-control function to a driver of innovation, efficiency, and long-term value.

5.2 Potential Challenges with Implementing Enterprise FinOps

Some of the biggest roadblocks to FinOps success aren't the tools or the data; it is the resistance to change and other factors as shown in Figure 5.11. When you come across statements like, "IT costs are not my problem," you know there is a siloed atmosphere. FinOps struggles because of trust gaps and the fear of change. Teams don't resist cost optimization because they're lazy, but because they think it's a witch hunt. There is a natural fear of being held accountable for inefficient resource use, or worse, being made the scapegoat for budget overruns. That's why the first step is radical transparency. Show them the methodology. Explain how the data was collected. Demonstrate that the goal isn't to punish but to empower them. Rather than pointing fingers, Enterprise FinOps gives you smarter ways to spend your money.

Then there's the data-sharing dilemma. Teams hoard information like a treasure chest, fearing it'll expose weaknesses and decisions that backfired. When you frame it as a collective effort, not a solo performance, the resistance softens. "We're all in this together" becomes the mantra. Pair that with robust governance, and suddenly, sharing metrics feels less like a risk and more like a win.

Teams treat cost optimization as a side task, not a core responsibility. That's why integrating cost considerations into sprint planning and design reviews is important for the success of Enterprise FinOps. I've seen organizations with ten different platforms tracking the same metrics, each with its own version of the truth. That's chaos. A single, unified platform lets you start seeing the full picture, not fragmented pieces.

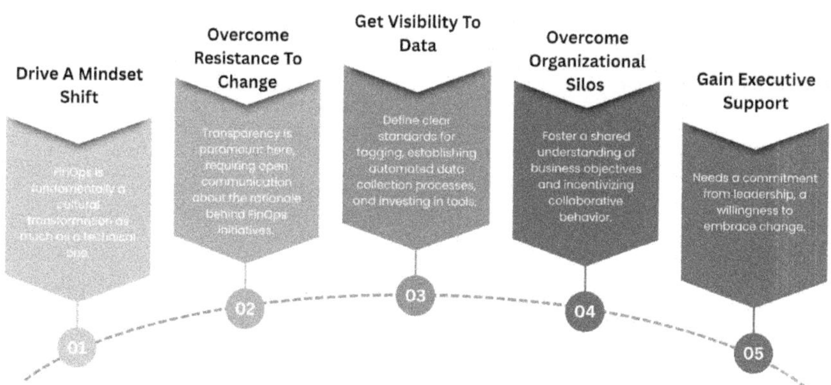

Figure 5.11 Potential challenges and mitigation

Without leadership backing, even the best strategies die on the vine. Teams think it'll slow them down. By eliminating waste and reducing redundant work, you're freeing up time for innovation. When teams see FinOps as a way to collaborate, innovate, and grow, FinOps becomes a game-changer. There is going to be resistance. IT teams have spent years defending their silos, their tools, and will defend their way of doing things. To them, FinOps may seem like an audit. Leaders need to stop talking about cost savings and start showing how smarter spending unlocks faster innovation. A 20% reduction in cloud waste might feel good, but a 30% increase in product delivery speed is where it stops being an audit. FinOps aims to equip IT leadership with the right tools and techniques and align technical capabilities with business outcomes.

5.3 Building a Continuous FinOps Culture

At its heart, Enterprise FinOps is a mindset shift. Building a continuous FinOps culture takes several steps, as shown in Figure 5.12. People don't change overnight. You can't just hand someone a FinOps dashboard and expect them to start optimizing costs. You have to rethink how decisions are made. You now ask, "What's the long-term cost of this decision? How does it align with the business's goals?" People are used to old ways. They're stuck in silos. You'll face pushback. You need to embed financial

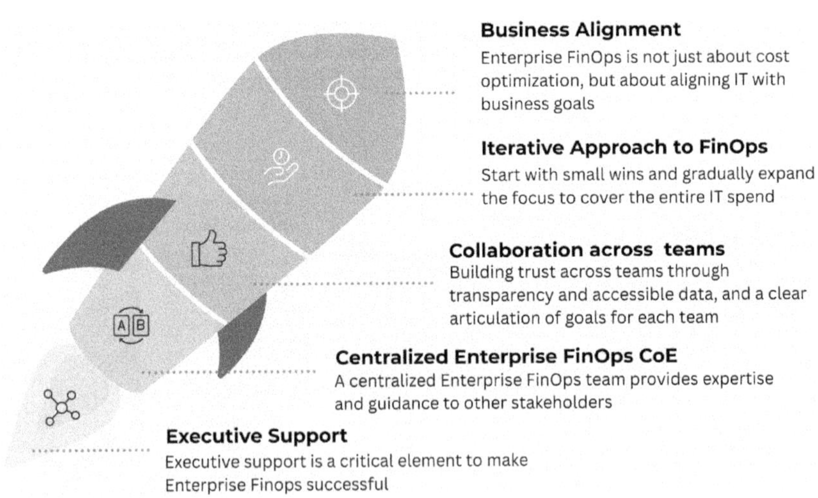

Figure 5.12 Building a continuous FinOps culture

accountability and collaboration into the fabric of your organization. It's not a one-time initiative. It's a long-term, iterative process. One goal is cost-cutting, and a bigger goal is cost optimization that ensures you're deriving the full value from your investment. A bigger goal is to drive value and innovation. IT decision makers should champion FinOps and show how it supports broader goals. Their support is also critical to securing and prioritizing resources for optimization actions. Cross-functional collaboration breaks down silos.

5.3.1 Enterprise FinOps Steering Committee

Establish a FinOps steering committee with representatives from finance, IT, operations, and business units to drive alignment and accountability. Collaborative workshops and regular sessions where teams co-create cost-saving strategies and share best practices strengthen this collaboration. Certifications from industry leaders, such as the FinOps Foundation, can help standardize knowledge, while internal knowledge-sharing platforms let teams learn at their own pace. Rewarding and recognizing continuous improvement motivates teams. Tools such as self-service dashboards give teams the power to analyze costs independently, reducing reliance on Enterprise FinOps teams. Soliciting feedback from teams and modeling future scenarios ensures the culture remains dynamic. A sustainable FinOps culture needs leadership support, cross-functional collaboration, education, and technology.

> The Law of Synergy states that the combined effect of two or more systems can exceed the sum of their individual effects. This highlights the importance of collaboration between IT and finance teams in implementing Enterprise FinOps and the compounding effect of all the activities described in this chapter in the various phases. When departments work in isolation, their efforts may be fragmented, leading to inefficiencies, misaligned priorities, and missed opportunities for cost savings. However, when teams collaborate through shared dashboards, cross-functional reviews, a common goal, and joint planning sessions, they can unlock synergies that neither department could achieve alone. The CIO must foster a culture of collaboration, ensuring that these synergies are not only possible but actively pursued. This requires breaking down silos, establishing common goals, and creating mechanisms for continuous communication and alignment.

Notes

1 FinOps refers to Enterprise FinOps and applies to the entire IT spend unless specifically mentioned with reference to the FinOps framework from the FinOps Foundation.
2 "Run," "Transform," and "Innovate" refer to the run and maintenance operations, transformations, and innovation pillars described in the RTI360 model in Chapter 1.

References

FinOps Assessment guide. (2025). Retrieved from https://www.finops.org/wg/finops-assessment/

FinOps KPIs. (2025). Retrieved from https://www.finops.org/wg/finops-kpis/

FinOps Landscape. (2025). Retrieved from https://www.finops.org/landscape/

FinOps Maturity Model. (2025). Retrieved from https://www.finops.org/framework/maturity-model/

Manos, T. (2025). Lean lessons: Value stream mapping–an introduction. *Quality Progress*, *39*(6), 64–66. Retrieved from https://asq.org/quality-progress/articles/lean-lessons-value-stream-mapping-an-introduction?id=f7f918b0c03f4bd2a8f68b18755d7917

RedHat. (2025). *What is application lifecycle management*. RedHat. Retrieved from https://www.redhat.com/en/topics/devops/what-is-application-lifecycle-management-alm

Scott, Jeff, Forrester Research. (2009). Business capability maps: The missing link between business strategy and IT action. *Architecture & Governance*, *5*(9), 1–7. Retrieved from https://www.researchgate.net/publication/279951524_Enterprise_Architecture_Governance_A_Framework_Approach

Chapter 6

Cost Optimization Levers

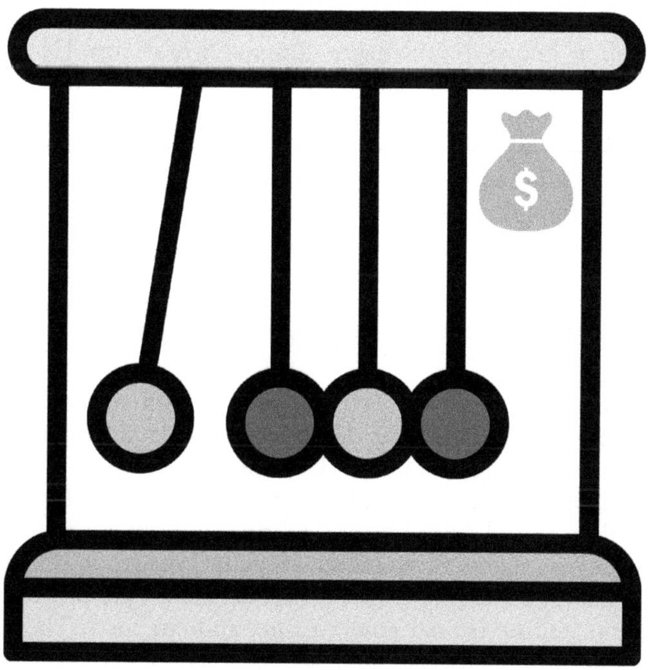

DOI: 10.4324/9781003682196-10

6.1 Analogies to Personal Finance

6.1.1 *A Cost Optimization Scenario at Home*

Let's use a simple analogy to illustrate the interwoven aspects of Enterprise FinOps by exploring a common household scenario of reducing energy costs in a typical American household. Mark, his wife Janet, and two kids live in a suburban single-family residence in Houston. He's never really paid too much attention to his energy bills, but this time, he gets sticker shock when his monthly electricity bill for August is over $600. He decides to investigate further.

The house is filled with smart devices, tablets, and laptops, as well as several kitchen gadgets, as both Mark and his wife are avid cooks. But he's concerned about appliances like washers, dryers, and air-conditioning units, which he knows are the major consumers of energy. He remembers that his energy provider had installed a smart meter some months ago that was supposed to provide detailed tracking of consumption. He looks at his bill closely and is surprised to find that, compared to other homes of a similar size, his house is consuming around 30% more electricity. It's right there in the bill, a benchmark that tells him something may be off. Details provided through the provider website and the electricity provider bill validate that his aging air-conditioning (HVAC) systems are the major consumers, with as much as 50% of power every day (measured in kilowatt hours or KWH) being drawn on hot summer days by the two HVAC systems alone.

Mark hasn't changed his electricity provider for many years, and a quick internet search comparing electricity providers in the area indicates that he is paying a higher rate per kWh on his month-to-month service plan. Switching to an annual plan itself would give him a better rate. He also finds that several providers are offering interesting options, such as free electricity on nights or weekends (Reliant Energy, 2025). Mark and Janet brainstorm further to explore how they can optimize their energy consumption, reduce overall power usage, and cut costs. They find that several rooms in their house, like the kids' playrooms and the laundry room, had lights on even when no one was using them. It's obvious that lights sip only a small percentage of overall power, but every bit helps. He's also heard that people who've installed solar panels on their roofs have cut down their energy costs drastically and even received a tax credit. Some are actually making money by selling back excess energy to the grid! They come up with a list of the actions they could take, segmenting these into two categories. The smart home levers are illustrated in Figure 6.1.

- Reduce costs (Table 6.1 highlights the actions they identified)
- Reduce energy consumption (Table 6.2 lists down actions identified).

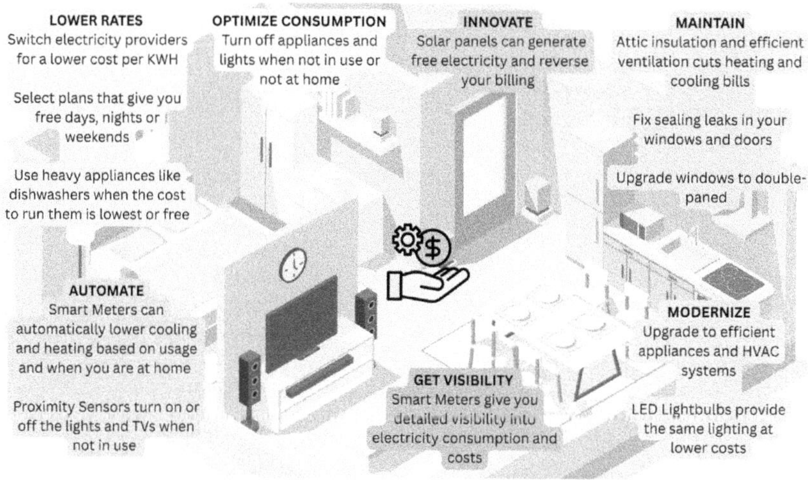

Figure 6.1 Smart home levers, optimizing your energy consumption and costs

They conclude that they could save *almost 30%* on current costs alone just by switching providers and also cut down energy consumption by over *20%* through small home upgrades that they could do quite quickly. This net impact is that their monthly electricity bill can potentially be lowered by around *30% to 50%*. In a few months, they will carry out the more expensive actions like installing attic insulation with these savings and also set aside some funds to save for their HVAC upgrade. What's more important is that every month keeps on adding to the energy savings pile.

6.1.2 Analogies to Enterprise FinOps Principles

Their actions have been very similar to the way Enterprise FinOps works in a typical IT environment. At its heart, it reduces IT costs, optimizes consumption, and drives a cost-conscious behavior across all stakeholders. Mark's electricity bill is similar to the total IT spend encompassing cloud costs, licensing fees, maintenance, and operational expenses. Lights, televisions, air conditioners, and other appliances, kitchen gadgets, etc., are like the infrastructure in a typical IT landscape. The smart meter and its digital home control are similar to monitoring and visibility software used in IT. Comparison with other similar homes is like benchmarking, where you get a sense of what your peers are paying for similar services. Just as he tracks electricity usage over time, seeing when he consumes more,

Table 6.1 Reduce energy costs

Action	*Potential cost savings (compared to current rates) (%)*	*Effort to implement*	*Cost to implement*	*Implement?*
Change service providers to get a better electricity rate.	10	Low	None, no annual contract. *Many providers also cover the service contract breakage fee if any.*	Yes
Choose a plan that offers a lower rate/ kWh and "free" electricity on nights and weekends.	10	Low	None	Yes
Install roof solar panels and batteries to generate his own electricity.	60	High	Very high – $50K+	No – maybe in some years.
Change in consumption behavior – Time washer and dryer to automatically run after 7 pm (new free nights start at this time).	10	Low	None	Yes

Enterprise FinOps provides a real-time, detailed view of IT spend. Usage patterns lead to visibility, one of the core Enterprise FinOps principles. Granular data allows you to track consumption by application, user, team, and project. Real-time monitoring and anomaly alerts identify spikes in usage and data to understand the drivers behind these jumps. Tagging lets you assign costs accurately to the business units consuming the services,

Table 6.2 Reduce energy consumption

Action	*Potential energy savings (%)*	*Effort to implement*	*Cost to implement*	*Implement?*
Upgrade the 15-year-old HVAC system to a more energy-efficient unit.	20	High	High – HVACs could range from $5K upwards.	Defer for later
Upgrade the home's heating/cooling control unit to a newer digital model that automatically adjusts the temperature based on usage patterns.	10	Low	Low – around $150 for a Google Nest meter	Yes
Install proximity sensors in all rooms to turn on and off lights only when it detects a person.	5	Low	Low – around $100	Yes
Upgrade bulbs to LED bulbs that use less energy for the same lighting level.	5	Low	Low – around $100	Yes
Install attic insulation.	10	Medium – need to hire a contractor	Medium – around $1,000 for the service	Defer
Check and fix window seals.	5	Low	Low – around $100	Yes
Install double-paned windows.	10	Medium – needs a contractor	Medium – around $5,000	Defer

which is necessary, similar to knowing which rooms in a house and which household appliances consume the most energy.

Some actions need to be prioritized as they have the biggest impact. Switching out electricity providers is similar to what your vendor management team does as it compares vendors, conducts rate optimization, and selects one that provides both the desired quality and rates, and also negotiates the exact services that you need. Longer-term contracts give Mark a better rate than month-to-month pricing.

Switching to more energy-efficient lighting like LED bulbs is like a minor migration to newer, more efficient services. Fixing the window seals and installing attic insulation is like IT maintenance. Upgrading the HVAC to a newer, more efficient model is like a small modernization project that requires investment, while installing roof solar panels is like a major program that creates substantial new value but needs extensive capital investment. Turning off lights when rooms are empty mirrors automation strategies in the cloud with automated instance shutdowns and reserved instances. Just as Mark regularly reviews his electricity bill and adjusts his consumption, Enterprise FinOps requires monitoring, analysis, and adjustment of IT spending, identifying inefficiencies and eliminating or reducing their impact. This is like understanding *why* certain appliances are running unnecessarily and taking steps to correct it. Mark has used optimization techniques similar to what Enterprise FinOps does continuously. Moreover, he and his family members have developed a cost optimization mindset that will remain and generate savings continuously.

Note that Mark and Janet take actions not just to reduce costs, but also to optimize their consumption and plan for future upgrades. Enterprise FinOps embodies *strategic investment*, *informed decision-making*, and builds a *culture of cost awareness*. Spending is not viewed as an expense, but as a critical component of the value equation.

6.1.3 Typical Situations in IT

IT spending can be chaotic. Everything from the software licenses on your developers' laptops to the printers in your office is waiting to be optimized. You have the obvious stuff like servers or cloud bills. And then it's the hidden spend that no one has thought about, like that SaaS tool your marketing team signed up for last year with varying individual editions, or the training program that went nowhere. Recurring spend is the blood in the veins of your IT budget. It's not the one-time purchase of a server; it's the monthly fee for that tool, the annual contract for software maintenance, and the support costs you forgot to track. I've seen companies spend over $2 million a year on premium support licenses that no one used.

Getting visibility is the first step. You can't optimize what you can't see. Resource utilization tracking isn't asking hard questions. Are those 100 software licenses actually being used? Is that $20,000-a-year cloud instance worth it if it's only running at 10% capacity? Are your employees using that fancy collaboration tool, or is it just another app collecting dust? One of our teams slashed software costs by 30% after auditing licenses. Another company reduced support costs by canceling redundant programs and aligning training with actual skill gaps. But it takes time and patience, and your executive sponsorship to make this happen, not just in an ad-hoc way, but in a systemic manner that revitalizes your organization. You'll need to involve everyone from the developers who think their tools are essential, the procurement team that signed the contracts, and the finance folks who just want to know where the money is. Visibility drives clarity.

Little things slip under the radar. Are your meeting rooms actually being used? So why would you allocate costly collaboration technology to retrofit those rooms with the latest in virtual meeting software? Could you replace that outdated printer with a newer model that cuts down on paper waste? Is that CRM software really being used to its full potential? The goal is to make sure every dollar you spend on IT is delivering value. If you're not asking these questions, you're wasting opportunities.

6.2 Vendor Management and Procurement

Vendor management and procurement is the process of systematically identifying, evaluating, selecting, contracting, and managing relationships with all external providers who supply goods and services to the IT organization. A key goal is to *control and optimize costs* while securing the best possible value. The Vendor Management Office (VMO) plays a key role in Enterprise FinOps and works best when centralized across all of IT. Typically, the VMO scope covers *everything* that the IT organization buys, from hardware such as servers, networking equipment, workstations, and laptops to software such as SaaS and software subscriptions. This also covers licensing fees for individual user subscriptions, open-source software, enterprise-wide collaboration, database, and OS licenses. They also procure services such as cloud services, managed services, and address maintenance and support contracts with hardware and software vendors. VMO also procures consulting, such as advisory services and external training programs for IT staff.

The VMO team works with other IT staff to identify IT requirements. A typical process involves market research to evaluate the landscape of potential vendors and understand their offerings, pricing, and quality and delivery reputation. They launch Request for Proposals (RFPs) and Request for Quotes (RFQs) outlining requirements and soliciting competitive bids. They assess vendors based on a combination of factors such as price, quality, Service Level Agreements (SLAs), security, and strategic alignment. They conduct contract negotiations to secure favorable terms such as pricing discounts, payment terms, SLAs, exit clauses, and intellectual property rights. Vendor performance tracking and relationship management are key functions for the VMO. It ensures compliance with SLAs and identifies cost reduction opportunities. But IT spending isn't a one-time purchase. If buying storage, look at the data access patterns and have the VMO question how often this data is used. Use cheaper storage for the stuff that's only accessed once a month, or maybe pull in your on-premises storage that was freed up from that migration last year. Soon, the VMO can build a list of custom cost factors for the different types of IT assets and patterns that will help them in negotiating the optimum deal.

Rate optimization and benchmarking are core tenets of Enterprise FinOps. Negotiate volume discounts, leveraging your entire enterprise's collective purchasing power to negotiate better rates. Conduct competitive bidding to solicit bids from multiple vendors and drive competition, or use volume contracts to lock-in prices ahead of time for regularly used services. Standardization and consolidation can reduce the number of different products and services used and drive cost savings. Lifecycle cost analysis determines the Total Cost of Ownership (TCO) through acquisition costs, maintenance, and disposal, giving you a view that can lead to predictive scenario modeling for future IT costs. Exit strategies are important but often neglected clauses in contracts. These let you avoid being locked into unfavorable terms, or if the vendor fails to perform or provide the contracted services (Gudmundsdottir, Hulda, 2025). Effective Vendor Management provides the *data* and *influence* needed to drive significant cost savings. By proactively managing relationships with vendors, the IT organization can reduce waste, optimize spending, and improve ROI on IT investments.

6.2.1 An Enterprise FinOps-Aligned VMO Strategy

With a strong Vendor Management Office (VMO), you're going beyond just managing vendors. You're turning them into allies in your cost optimization mission. Figure 6.2 illustrates the layers of activities that define a true Enterprise FinOps-aligned VMO strategy.

6.2.1.1 Process Optimization

- Conducting a strategic vendor landscape assessment is a deep dive into every vendor you work with, from the smallest volume resellers to the biggest cloud providers. It lets you list and categorize vendors, map their services, and attach clear cost tags to each through a vendor spend analysis. This is a map of your IT vendor ecosystem. It lets you see where your money is going. Every year, the VMO should do a periodic risk assessment, peeling back the layers on each vendor's financial health, security posture, and compliance readiness. It's like a health check for your vendor relationships. When I was in charge of the VMO team as part of leading the Technology Operations group, we even created a strategic vendor selection roadmap that provided guidance to my

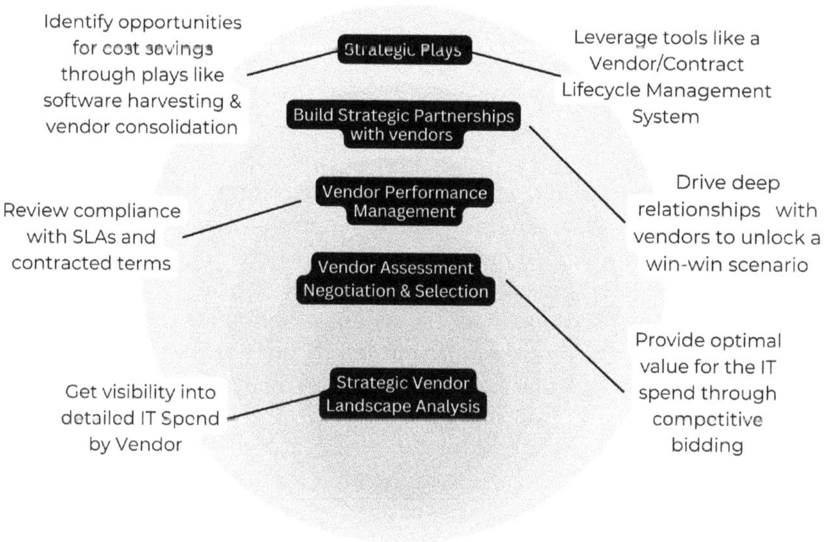

Figure 6.2 Enterprise FinOps-aligned vendor management strategy

IT peers on when to select strategic vendors and when to go in for niche providers or consultants.

- Contract Management is where the VMO usually gets buried under paperwork. Enterprise Contract Lifecycle Management (CLM) systems can help you automate the chaos. Contracts get reviewed, approved, and tracked in real time. No more missed renewals leading to a scramble against a deadline. All of it is monitored. If a vendor misses an SLA target, the VMO can act quickly.
- Software harvesting is the VMO's version of a digital spring clean. They audit licenses and hunt down the ones that are redundant, underutilized, or outright forgotten.
- Use a Vendor Scorecard to evaluate vendors on price, quality, service, and innovation. The ideal VMO goes beyond procurement. Vendor Relationship Management (VRM) builds relationships. You collaborate and align goals to create a win-win environment for both sides. And when a vendor sees that they're not just a vendor, but a strategic partner, they're more likely to invest in your success.

6.2.1.2 *Rate Optimization*

- Strategic negotiation based on lengthier terms is straightforward but may not be right all the time. A 3–5-year commitment can lock-in better pricing, but you don't want to commit to a usage level that's way above your needs just to get a discount. You end up paying for capacity you'll never use, and your teams lose the incentive to optimize. Tiered pricing offers a more flexible alternative. Pay for what you use, and you're not stuck with minimum spend commitments. And don't forget the total cost of ownership analysis. Don't simply look at the upfront price. Factor in maintenance, support, training, and even the cost of downtime. Because sometimes, the cheapest option isn't necessarily the best one. I've seen companies get burned by poor vendor management. We've had contracts that lock with cloud providers with capacity that went unused.
- Resellers could be goldmines for commodity items. They'll undercut the competition on servers, laptops, and even software licenses. The VMO's job is to leverage that network, not just for cost, but also for value.
- We'll talk more about vendor consolidation in a later section. By consolidating services with select vendors, you reduce complexity, boost your negotiating power, and unlock economies of scale.
- If you're not comparing your costs to industry standards, you're flying blind. Benchmarking comes to the rescue. You're measuring what you're paying and also how that stacks up against the competition. Outsourcing benchmarking to a specialist firm is a smart move. These consultants constantly monitor the market pulse and tailor benchmarks to your IT profile. They give you a snapshot of where you're overpaying, underperforming, or missing out on better deals. They have a wider lens on the overall industry to generate some fairly accurate numbers that align closely with what you are doing.
- Dynamic Bidding can be a game-changer for smaller, standardized items. Imagine an auction where vendors compete to offer the lowest price for a server, a software license, or even a cloud service. I've seen companies save 20–30% on services just by letting vendors bid against each other.

6.2.1.3 *Vendor Optimization*

- Service Level Agreements (SLAs) are your insurance policy. A strong SLA goes beyond setting expectations; it forces vendors to deliver. Uptime guarantees, response times, and penalties for non-compliance (and conversely, rewards for exceeding SLAs) are the difference between a vendor who just meets your needs and one who partners with you and your goals. Strategic partnerships can justify higher upfront costs. If you're a key client, vendors are more willing to invest in innovation, co development, or even throw in extra services or funds.

- Due diligence is essential. You don't just take a vendor's word for their financial stability or track record. You call other clients to check references, but not only the ones they hand you. Having multiple suppliers is good for competition, but too many is a nightmare. You typically want 3–5 strategic vendors who can cover your major IT needs. They're your go-to partners, not your backup plan. And don't forget the niche players who might offer specialized expertise or disruptive solutions. Test them with pilots or Proofs of Concept (PoCs). You want to see if they're a good fit for projects that are strategic.
- Outsourcing some of your VMO processes can be a lifeline to stretched teams. If your internal team is drowning in RFPs and RFIs, the VMO could hand that baton to a specialist firm. Think of it like building a coalition. You partner with a vendor for price, innovation, early access to tech, and maybe even co-development. You are partnering for value.

6.2.2 Hardware Procurement Strategies

The pendulum has swung away from spending Capex on buying servers and data centers. Today's focus is on operational flexibility over upfront capital investment. It has rewritten the rules for vendor procurement, especially when it comes to hardware and infrastructure. The big one is the flexibility offered by public cloud providers offering IaaS and PaaS services. You pay only for what you use. No more buying racks of servers that sit idle. The vendor handles the hardware, and you focus on your workloads and pay for what you consume. Agility meets scalability. Your critical systems can be configured to scale dynamically as per your requirements. And for non-critical workloads, spot instances let you use spare capacity at a discount. It's like getting a discount on a hotel room during off-peak hours. Platforms like AWS Lambda, Google Cloud Functions, or Azure Functions let you build apps without worrying about servers at all. You just write the code, and the cloud handles the rest. You pay only for the execution time or the API calls you use. Serverless computing is truly hands-off computing (GeeksforGeeks, 2025).

Your strategy may be leaning toward a hybrid cloud, with a balance between a private cloud-like environment and public cloud services (IBM, 2025a). As per IBM's hybrid cloud architecture, a hybrid cloud computing environment combines and unifies public cloud, private cloud, and on-premises infrastructure to create a single, flexible IT infrastructure. They define on-premises infrastructure as a traditional form of computing infrastructure that includes on-premises data centers and computing resources that a business owns and operates at its own physical location. Public cloud infrastructure refers to services provided by third-party cloud service providers such as AWS, Google Cloud Services, IBM Cloud, Oracle, or Microsoft Azure, and private cloud infrastructure is a dedicated cloud infrastructure operated solely for a single organization, either on-premises or hosted by a third party.

Co-location offers the middle ground between owning a data center and relying entirely on the cloud. Instead of building and maintaining expensive facilities, you rent space in a co-location center run by giants like Equinix, Digital Realty, or CoreSite. These providers manage the physical infrastructure (power, cooling, security), while you handle your servers. Want to upgrade your storage or swap out components? They'll do it for a fee, so you don't need to send out your team to remote locations for a 10-minute task. You avoid the capital hit of data center ownership, and they take care of simple maintenance tasks (TechTargets, n.d.).

Maybe you need a small but powerful mini-data center on the edge within the secure environment of a factory for resilience and 24x7 operations, even when the network goes out. Instead of locking your budget into purchasing servers, storage, or networking gear, you can lease them from industry giants like IBM, HPE, Dell, or Cisco (NextLevelTech, 2025). Think of it as a subscription model for your IT hardware. It saves upfront costs and also gives you predictable monthly expenses that align with your cash flow. The perks are rapid scaling, avoiding the risk of obsolescence, and bringing on add-on services like custom image deployment. Companies can also customize services like buy-back options and global support. Leasing often beats buying in the long run.

Vendors now offer pre-configured "in-a-box" servers with operating systems, middleware, and apps baked in as per your exact specifications. No more hours of setup or troubleshooting. You plug them in, and they're ready to go. Everything from storage provisioning, backup, and disaster recovery can be ready to go, so you can focus on your applications and data instead of the plumbing.

These models offer both financial and technological flexibility, but they also come with risks. Avoid vendor lock-in by choosing solutions and vendors that can adapt to your evolving needs. Sometimes, Capex could be advantageous from a tax perspective, especially for R&D or foundational systems. Your tax and finance professionals are your best partners in advising you on this. The days of Capex-dominated strategies are fading. Opex, flexibility, and partnerships that grow with your business are here to stay.

6.2.3 *SaaS and Software Licensing Strategies*

The premise is simple. If you commit to a longer term or a larger footprint, you get a bigger discount. Volume Licensing Models offer substantial discounts. Enterprise Agreements (EA) involve committing to a multi-year contract for a large number of licenses. This works well for predictable needs and can offer significant cost savings. But for organizations with a small to medium set of users, or with large fluctuations in user base, look at concurrent licensing models, where you can pay only for active users. Other models, such as per-active-user licensing, are similar to concurrent licensing, but with fixed monthly/annual fees based on the number of users.

Software Harvesting and Lifecycle Management is a critical Enterprise FinOps technique for managing software licenses actively, whether on-prem, individually purchased, or SaaS. It is important to ensure that your contract allows you to transfer licenses across users in your company. Software Asset Management (SAM) tools like ServiceNow SAM (IBM, 2025b) can discover all software installed on the network, identify unused licenses, and reclaim them. You can also reclaim unused licenses from terminated employees or inactive users. This needs to be supplemented through IT policies that establish what constitutes "unused." For example, someone could be an occasional user of Microsoft Visio, using it once every three months. License reclamation programs establish a formal process for identifying and reclaiming unused licenses.

Channel Procurement through resellers and third parties like IT services companies has become a popular alternative choice for buying or renewing software instead of directly from the product vendor. In some cases, this is true even for SaaS subscriptions for major enterprise platforms. Major IT services providers often strike global agreements with product vendors to provide a one-stop service to customers, with product licensing, upgrades, and maintenance bundled in. As of 2025, IT services firms like Wipro and Cognizant were offering competitive licensing rates on some SaaS software renewals, leveraging their global elite partnerships (Cognizant, 2024). Leverage Master Reseller Agreements (MRAs) for broad product coverage. Resellers often offer discounts for volume purchases and simplified management. Some Independent Software Vendors (ISVs) sell directly, cutting out the reseller markup. This can be advantageous for smaller deployments. Specialized SaaS Aggregators can consolidate discounts across multiple SaaS vendors, offering a single point of procurement, especially for niche SaaS products.

A centralized VMO can set up a formal process for buying any license, even those that normally would be purchased directly by individuals on a business card. For example, graphic design tools like Canva or Adobe Design that may cost less than $20 per month per user often slip through the cracks, but the collective usage across a large enterprise could be in the thousands of users. A formal process lets you track usage across the entire company, using volumes to negotiate better discounts, and also enables features like Single Sign-On (SSO) for easier and secure access to the applications. An additional risk mitigation is that a formal process ensures that the sharing and transmission of data across cloud platforms is in compliance with legal and security standards.

Strategic Agreements with product vendors can also yield substantial savings. Bundled software, where you purchase multiple software applications from the same vendor, can give additional discounts. Upsells of different extensions and modules from the same vendor are often negotiated with the original contract, offering as much as 70% off the retail price for such modules. Subscription bundles can combine multiple SaaS services into a single subscription, making it easier to manage the contract.

SaaS is often priced based on usage. Negotiation tactics like usage-based pricing, or on metrics like API calls consumed lets you fine-tune agreements based on predicted usage. As any finance professional will advise, payment terms are also negotiable. Vendors are often willing to extend favorable payment terms (e.g., Net 60 or Net 90). Multi-year subscriptions can be spread over months, subject to your local regulations. Often, the license terms allow a "true-up," allowing you to increase the number of licenses at tiered rates, or even "true-down," where you can decrease the committed number of licenses and pay only for what you have consumed. Most VMO teams have a specialized SAM team that handles compliance, software harvesting, and software procurement. Before any procurement, conduct a thorough SAM audit to identify existing licenses and usage patterns. As needs change, revisit contracts to ensure you're getting the best deal.

6.2.4 Cloud Provider Strategies – Model-Driven Approaches

VMO teams need to understand different models offered by public cloud providers and the models' implications. IaaS is best suited for organizations with strong IT expertise and a need for maximum flexibility. Platform-as-a-Service (PaaS) simplifies development and deployment by abstracting away the underlying infrastructure. The provider may offer a managed database platform, avoiding the need to have your own cloud database administrators. PaaS is ideal for developers focused on building and scaling applications, reducing operational overhead. API-driven models are becoming increasingly common, especially with serverless computing. Your developers build applications using APIs, and the cloud provider handles the infrastructure, scaling, and management. This is particularly well-suited for cloud-native applications like microservices and event-driven architectures.

As we'll talk further in the next chapter on technology levers, your cloud or IT operations teams need to regularly monitor CPU, memory, and network utilization to ensure instances are appropriately sized and avoid over-provisioning. A common breach is when developers provision highly responsive, high-performance environments for development and testing, and often promote them directly to work as production environments. High-performance models may be necessary when you are doing extensive data migrations or training AI models, but production needs may be less stringent. This also causes security risks as production environments may need tighter control over access, ports, and identity management, which may be overlooked when development environments are promoted to production at the click of a button.

Committing to using compute resources for a defined period (typically 1–3 years) can offer significant discounts. This is only effective if you can accurately predict your long-term usage. Providers term it differently. As of the moment, this model is termed as reserved instances in AWS (AWS, 2025), Committed Use Discounts in Azure, and Sustained Use Discounts in Google Cloud. Spot instances (AWS)/Preemptible VMs (Google Cloud) allow an interesting model. They are basically offering you excess capacity across their entire cloud at a substantial discount. You can utilize spare compute capacity for fault-tolerant workloads that can handle interruptions. Services like auto-scaling can automatically adjust compute resources based on demand and improve efficiency and responsiveness. Containerization (Docker, Kubernetes) is another engineering technique where you can deploy applications in isolated containers for portability, scalability, and resource utilization.

VMO teams need to be familiar with contractual considerations. Enterprise-Level Agreements (ELAs) or EAs provide predictable pricing, volume discounts, and service level commitments. This is best for organizations with consistent, high-volume usage. Pay-Per-Use maximizes cost efficiency when demand fluctuates but requires diligent monitoring and optimization. Consumption-based billing is shifting to a model where you only pay for what you actually consume, which can be very cost-effective for variable workloads.

A significant but hidden cost is data transfer. Migrating to a cloud-based database will often involve significant amounts of data to be transferred from your on-premises database to the cloud. Regular usage of cloud-based applications by users located in your office locations could involve substantial data transfer on every transaction or process. IT teams need to optimize data transfer patterns to minimize charges. A thumb rule is to store data closer to where it's used. Utilize different storage tiers (e.g., infrequent access, cold storage) to optimize costs based on data access frequency. The cost for the same terabyte of data can be drastically lower for cold storage as opposed to fast-performing memory (think of archived reports or data that may need to be retained only for compliance purposes rather than for active analytics).

Enterprise FinOps cloud operations practices include cost monitoring through tools that track cloud spending and identify areas for optimization. Tagging is essential to allocate costs properly to your internal business consumers.

6.2.5 Outsourcing Models and Strategies

Outsourcing services to external vendors usually involves long-term contracts. A typical term that makes financial sense would be 3 to 5 years. Master Service Agreements (MSAs) cover all services provided, establishing clear SLAs, governance, and escalation procedures. They're the foundation for a stable, cost-effective relationship. A Statement of Work (SOW) lets you define and change specific services under the umbrella of the MSA. For well-defined projects, fixed-price contracts offer predictable costs. It is key to consider outsourcing providers as fully qualified extensions of your IT team and as strategic partners rather than just as vendors; however, your legal team also needs to ensure that there are exit clauses in case of nonperformance by the vendor.

Volume staffing strategies include staff augmentation, usually by hiring contractors to supplement existing teams on specific projects, with the work being managed by the IT employees and managers. This offers flexibility and reduces overhead. The Time and Material (T&M) model is suitable for evolving projects, or for maintaining a flexible workforce in situations where you need to scale up and down frequently in response to changing business conditions. Many companies have a volume staffing partner who manages staff augmentation under their umbrella and maintains compliance with local labor laws. Although their fees may range from between 5% and 25% over hiring contingent workers directly, they often provide a fast and streamlined model to procure contingent workers quickly and onboard them on projects. In addition, we have seen a rise in the "Employer of Record" (EoR) models, where companies can onboard people on your behalf as contingent workers in specified countries without needing you to establish legal entities or manage payroll complexities, and transition them over to you after a period once you establish the legal and HR structure (ADP, 2025). This is especially useful when you are trying to rapidly set up a nearshore or remote center. VMO needs to keep track of all such contingent resources as well.

An issue that we often see in large enterprises is where contingent worker contracts get renewed for multiple years. Since contingent workers usually cost up to 3X the cost of an employee, this represents a significant strain on the IT budget. One response to prevent this is to provide strict governance policies when renewing contingent worker contracts, or even providing defined guidelines on how long a contingent worker can be brought onboard for. Another play, usually run by the VMO, is to run a contractor-conversion activity, subject to compliance with contractual agreements with the vendors providing these resources, and contingent on the staffing resources accepting the offers.

Dedicated teams, where entire teams are outsourced for multiple years, provide a more integrated approach. IT services vendors often provide flex models where they maintain a core baseline team and additional resources can be ramped up or down quickly within the existing contract without needing amendments. Some vendors also offer contract-to-hire models, where the outsourcing provider provides resources that can be hired as employees after a defined period, usually between 6 and 12 months. Build-Operate-Transfer (BOT) models, the vendor staffs an entire team based on your requirements, usually for a complete portfolio such as Helpdesk or CRM, and the team can be transitioned to your IT team after a defined period, usually one to three years. This is particularly common in support.

Companies often take advantage of offshore low-cost locations to build Centers of Excellence (COEs) or Development Centers, establishing shared services centers with standardized processes, reducing duplication, and improving efficiency. Offshoring to Low-Cost Locations (India, Philippines, Eastern Europe for the USA and Europe) offers significant cost savings but require careful consideration of communication and cultural differences. Nearshoring, which involves outsourcing to countries geographically closer (Mexico, Brazil, Canada for the USA), reduces time zone differences and improves communication. Usually, IT teams work in a hybrid model combining onshore and offshore teams for 24x7 support operations as well as follow-the-sun for development teams, speeding up product and application development (Zinnov, 2024).

IT service providers provide niche services in several areas, such as Application Development and Maintenance (ADM), where the entire lifecycle of a software application is outsourced, Managed Services (MS) where the provider manages and operates a specific IT service (e.g., servers, databases, security), and Business Process Outsourcing (BPO) where non-core business functions (e.g., customer service, finance, HR) are outsourced in their entirety.

Key strategies are to clearly define KPIs and SLAs and establish measurable goals and service level agreements to track performance, conduct regular governance meetings with the outsourcing provider to review progress, address issues, and adjust plans, and develop a detailed plan for transitioning projects and knowledge to the outsourcing provider.

6.2.6 *Counteracting Vendor Influence*

Vendors aren't always clear with you on the risks of runaway costs, and their priorities can clash with yours. Sales teams have major incentives to push more, not just keep what you've got. A major part of their commissions is tied to upsells on additional modules or licenses, rather than simply renewals. So, while they are happy to keep your business, their real goal is to expand it by selling you more licenses, bigger instances, or premium services like support, even if you don't really need them. It's the system they're working within.

Vendors have aggressive revenue targets. They're selling products that add value to your teams, but they're also selling growth. Their pricing models extol the benefits of higher tiers. "Why pay for the basic plan when you can get the premium one for just a bit more?" they'll ask. But that "bit more" can add up, especially if you're not using all the features. And sales teams are usually rewarded based on volume, not value. The more licenses they push, the higher their commission. They might even downplay costs such as data transfer fees, API call charges, or the true price of premium support. These costs aren't always obvious, and if they're not in your usage reports, it's easy to miss them. Some vendors don't even provide detailed usage breakdowns, making it hard to spot inefficiencies or track where your money is going.

Then there's the "always on" mindset – a concept I've seen in action time and again. Vendors, especially those in the IaaS space, love to tell you to "keep your instances running 24/7," even if your workload doesn't demand it. "Anticipate future growth," they'll say. But what if that growth never comes? You're still paying for capacity you're not using. It's like buying a car and leaving the engine idling all day. It's inefficient, but somehow justified by the vendor's pitch to be always ready. Then there's the default settings trap. Vendors often configure systems to automatically scale instances or apply the highest-tier settings by default. Of course, this costs you more, but you may not really need this. You think you're in control, but the system is quietly working in the vendor's favor.

The bottom line here is that vendors are skilled at promoting overconsumption. It's a systemic issue in how their business models are structured. But a strong Enterprise FinOps program and collaboration from the VMO can counteract this. The key is to ask the hard questions and demand transparency. Because if you don't, you'll end up paying for features you don't need, capacity you're not using, and services you can't justify. So, the next time a vendor pushes an upsell, pause and ask whether your team really needs this. You're not being distrustful; you're simply making sure your spending aligns with your goals, not the vendors.

6.2.6.1 *Enterprise FinOps Is a Strategy to Guard against Oversells*

Vendors are experts at selling, but they're not always experts at aligning their incentives with your bottom line. That's where a strong Enterprise FinOps program comes in. It ensures that every renewal, acquisition, upgrade, or new module aligns with your business goals. Without it, you're handing over the keys to your budget to someone else's playbook. An Enterprise FinOps program provides built-in mechanisms to counter vendor influence on unnecessary spend. *Before* any discussion, conduct a detailed needs assessment and due diligence. Document precisely what your organization *actually* needs, not what you *think* you need. Your requesting organization, an IT or business unit, needs to substantiate what they need. You can always grow and add on needed features at a later stage.

Pilots and free trials allow you to test the software and determine if the features are truly what your business needs. Quantify requirements (e.g., number of users, specific features, integrations). If the vendor or your business requestor is asking for expensive features and module additions, ask why this additional feature will directly benefit your organization and justify the increased cost.

Push back on inflated SaaS usage estimates. Ask for a baseline usage assessment before committing. Understand how usage is tracked because if it's based on metrics you don't control, you're signing up for surprises. For traditional software licenses, avoid perpetual models unless there is a strong case. It locks you into paying for extended services like maintenance or support contracts, and you pay more upfront. A subscription model can be more flexible and often cheaper, and avoids lock-in. Negotiate shorter contract terms. The longer the contract, the harder it is to pivot if things change. Scrutinize the contract by paying attention to renewal clauses, volume discounts, and termination rights.

Be transparent with vendors. A partner is better aligned with your goals and your objectives and has long-term investment. Share your cost goals upfront. Demand detailed usage reports so you can identify optimization opportunities. And challenge their recommendations. Just because a vendor says, "You need this," doesn't mean it's the right move for your business. But involve them early. Instead of treating them like a transactional partner, shift left by bringing them into the cost modeling process from the start. Work with them to find cost-saving opportunities. It's a win-win where your business gets what it needs, and the vendor earns your trust. Don't treat your vendors as adversaries. They're part of your ecosystem. The goal isn't to fight them or mistrust them at every move, but it's to build a strategic partnership. Proactive governance, robust monitoring, and clear communication are your tools. That's Enterprise FinOps at work. The best FinOps programs protect your business from the unintended consequences of vendor-driven campaigns.

6.2.6.2 *Strategies to Drive Down Costs*

Negotiating any IT costs is a strategic positioning. Start by researching the market. Use online comparison tools, industry reports, and even competitor websites to understand what's standard. You'd be surprised how often vendors assume you're unaware of their own pricing. Ask for discounts upfront, especially if you're a non-profit, government entity, or early adopter. These categories often unlock hidden deals, and vendors rarely advertise them. Use the power of mental models in your strategies. State your desired range early. It sets the tone. Then, start low, and offer a price lower than what you're willing to pay. It creates room for negotiation. You don't want to give them the first move.

Volume discounts are powerful, even if your initial purchase is small. Express intent to scale. Vendors love the idea of future growth. It's what makes their sales teams tick. You get a better deal; they get a long-term commitment. But don't overcommit. If you don't need a feature, say so. Every unnecessary module adds cost. Support tiers matter too. Lower-tier packages are cheaper, but they might leave you hanging. Weigh the trade-off. Value matters more than price alone. A tool that integrates seamlessly with your systems might cost more, but it saves time and headaches.

Be ready to walk away. If a vendor isn't flexible, let them know you're not the only option. Be aware of promotions. Vendors often run deals around product launches or renewals. A bundled offer or a limited-time discount can save you thousands. You're protecting your organization from being played by vendors who think you'll never say no.

6.2.7 *Mitigating Vendor Lock-in Risks*

Long-term commitments unlock big discounts, but those same commitments can lock you into a vendor's roadmap, pricing, and even their technology stack. You're buying a product, but also could be signing a contract that might outlive your current needs. Modular procurement can be an option. Instead of bundling everything with one vendor, break your needs into pieces, where each piece of the puzzle can be swapped out without dismantling the whole thing. This gives you more leverage. If one part of the puzzle isn't working, you can replace it without throwing the entire system into chaos.

Standardized services also matter. If your cloud provider uses a proprietary format, you are stuck. If their APIs are compatible with others, the risk and barrier to switch become less daunting. Push for exit clauses that let you migrate data and apps without paying a ransom. Ensure you are aware of data portability fees upfront.

Leverage phased rollouts and trials to start small and actually test and experience the vendor's service or products. You also get user feedback directly from the field. Scale only if it meets your requirements. Annual renewals let you reassess every year instead of being stuck for years. A booming industry has risen in cloud and software aggregators who will shop around for you, cutting costs without forcing you to pick one vendor's entire ecosystem.

There are sophisticated tools that simplify migration between providers. The easier it is to move data and apps, the less scary vendor lock-in feels. Conduct quarterly contract reviews to assess vendor performance, pricing, and market shifts. Understand the ripple effects and cost of switching providers with a dependency map of your services. Retraining, the migration itself, and lost productivity are costs to consider. Knowing the numbers helps you make informed decisions. And don't forget to check if the vendor's roadmap aligns with your goals. A provider that's moving in the opposite direction is a liability, no matter how low the price. A discount today might cost you a competitive edge tomorrow. It's necessary.

6.2.8 Vendor Consolidation

As shown in Figure 6.3, reducing the number of vendors you work with dramatically reduces overhead, streamlines processes, and unlocks significant cost savings. This strategy can result in substantial cost optimization. As the VP for Technology Operations with vendor management as one of my responsibilities, I recently led a vendor consolidation initiative that consolidated our vendors into a few strategic partners, resulting in millions of projected savings. Besides the cost savings, we had several other benefits in reduced operational overhead, more focused and strategic relationships with our selected partners, and the ability to leverage partner expertise in our innovation roadmap. The consolidation was carefully planned and executed to avoid any business disruption. There was an upfront cost, as some existing vendors had contract termination fees and some had transition fees. Some retooling and integrations had to be recreated. A strong project management team ensured a successful and smooth transition of services.

Vendor consolidation can reduce operational overhead with fewer contracts to manage. It frees up your VMO team for other strategic activities. Consolidated purchasing volume leads to better pricing and negotiated

Figure 6.3 Benefits from vendor consolidation

discounts. A single point of contact reduces administrative burden and communication complexity, resulting in streamlined vendor management. Consolidating services across vendors leverages economies of scale, as the more you use a service, the lower the unit cost.

It allows for the implementation of standardized processes, reducing duplication and rework. A single vendor can often deliver services more efficiently due to shared best practices and a focus on a common platform. Consolidating around a smaller number of vendors can facilitate the implementation of automation and deep integration with vendor ticketing systems, further reducing operational costs.

Quantifying the ROI of vendor consolidation can be challenging. At the low end, small to medium businesses can expect a 5–15% reduction in overall IT spending. This typically involves consolidating a few key services (e.g., managed services, security, SaaS) and standardizing processes. Complex enterprises can get over 30% reduction in IT spending. This demands a strategic, transformative approach, often involving significant organizational changes and a focus on achieving operational excellence (Linsley, Rod; GatekeeperHQ, 2025).

The rationale is clear. The more services consolidated, the higher the potential ROI. The more fragmented your existing vendor landscape, the greater the potential savings. However, a poorly executed consolidation can actually *increase* costs and result in business disruption, so a phased and carefully risk-managed approach is essential. Successful implementation requires strong change management to address resistance and ensure adoption. Consolidating around a single vendor can increase risk, so it is recommended to go with a few strategic partners rather than just a single partner. You might lose access to specialized expertise that was provided by multiple vendors.

Traditional outsourcing is often a transactional exchange of services. A strategic partnership shifts the focus to mutual success where the vendor's success is tied to your business goals, and vice versa. A strong partnership provides access to the vendor's specialized knowledge, best practices, and potentially, new technologies. Vendor consolidation expands and complements your Enterprise FinOps play. The partnership fosters a culture of data-driven decision-making, with both organizations sharing data and insights. The collaboration drives continuous improvement, with both organizations actively seeking ways to optimize the service delivery. The partnership enables proactive cost management, with both organizations working together to identify and mitigate potential cost risks. Invest in relationship building as strong relationships foster trust, collaboration, and open communication.

6.2.9 Centralized Vendor Management

Centralizing vendor management is a strategic shift. Instead of having application teams, infrastructure teams, and security teams each juggling their own vendor relationships, you have a single VMO team steering the ship. Avoid duplicated contracts, hidden costs, and a lack of oversight. When you centralize, you could aim for over 15% savings on total IT spend. Administrative costs drop by 20–40%. You get a boost in vendor performance.

A centralized team can eliminate redundant services, cut out unnecessary features, and negotiate better terms. They also eliminate Shadow IT that is sapping spend. When you consolidate all IT spending into one view, ELAs, volume discounts, and strategic partnerships become possible. Your VMO team becomes a force multiplier for the best rates. All IT teams now interact with the VMO team. No more finger-pointing. No more delays. Issues get resolved faster, and performance metrics become non-negotiable. Vendors know they're being monitored for quality and performance.

Your centralized team can now generate comprehensive reports on spending, performance, and risk. You can spot underutilized services, renegotiate contracts, or pivot to better solutions. Without executive buy-in, you'll face resistance. And invest in tools like vendor management software and contract lifecycle systems that will feed and become part of your holistic Enterprise FinOps platform.

6.2.10 Outsourcing Negotiations to a Third-Party Specialist

Many niche companies and advisory firms offer services to conduct vendor negotiations on your behalf. Leveraging a third-party specialist to handle vendor negotiations sounds counterintuitive; however, let's consider the advantages and also the setbacks. This can dramatically shift the risk/reward dynamic and can deliver substantial cost savings. These companies usually operate on a fee-based reduction model, which means that if you don't get any savings over your initial offer, you do not have to pay anything for these services. Let's dive into a scenario. You receive a $3 million quote from your CRM SaaS vendor for a three-year contract. You engage a specialized negotiation firm to negotiate on your behalf. They manage to bring the price down to $2.4 million without any reduction in scope. Their fee is usually a percentage of the total cost savings they achieve, usually 10–20% of the annual savings as compared. With 20%, they would charge you $40K per year as a fee, totaling $120K overall, and you have saved almost $500K.

Negotiation firms possess specialized knowledge and have experience in squeezing out favorable terms with a wide range of vendors. There is a purely objective focus on cost reduction and value, removing potential biases that might exist within your own team. They free up your IT team to focus on strategic initiatives, rather than getting bogged down in the time-consuming process of negotiations. If negotiations fail, you only pay for the savings they achieve. There are other variations of this model, in which you engage such companies early on in the sales cycle and pay them a retainer fee for their services, along with a smaller percentage of the overall transaction, say 2%. I personally recommend the fee-based model, as it is outcome-based, and clearly has a strong motivation for the negotiation provider to squeeze out the best savings possible for you.

Some Managed Service Providers (MSPs) offer a full suite of services, including vendor management, contract administration, and ongoing performance monitoring. An Enterprise FinOps consultant can conduct a deep dive into your contracts, identify opportunities for optimization, and even execute the negotiations themselves. Online auction platforms can help you secure competitive bids from vendors, particularly useful for smaller, less strategic services such as fixed bids on projects with well-defined scope and requirements, or staffing rates. Joining a collective purchasing group allows you to leverage the combined buying power of multiple organizations. You can always hire an independent procurement advisor who specializes in your industry or service category. To use any of these models, it is important to conduct thorough due diligence on the negotiation vendor; else you risk wasting your time and potentially ending up with a bad deal. Include contractual safeguards to protect your interests, such as a "no savings, no pay" clause.

Deloitte publishes a survey on global outsourcing trends (Deloitte, Coronado, & Stoler, 2024) that contains rich insights into multidimensional sourcing.

6.2.11 *Outsourcing the RFI/RFP Process*

For larger services initiatives, you can outsource the entire Request-for-Information (RFI) and Request for Proposal (RFP) process. This can improve your vendor selection, drive down rates, and significantly reduce the time and effort involved. Sometimes, this approach may be better than using internal teams, especially if your VMO teams are understaffed or overwhelmed with other activities. Other advantages are reduced bias, as external firms are not biased toward any particular vendor (Deloitte, 2025).

Managing the RFP process is a resource and time-intensive undertaking. It needs rigor and expertise on the underlying service area and industry context. Typically, such services are offered by niche firms. A key activity is to work with your teams to structure the RFP. This means understanding your business and IT requirements, technical needs, and budget constraints, and crafting this into an RFP with rigorous scoring criteria and relevant technical specifications. Often, there is a short RFI phase to shortlist potential vendors. Next, vendors submit proposals that are competitively evaluated. The firm conducts vendor demonstrations and presentations, facilitates reference checks and validations, and can even negotiate the contract terms on your behalf, working with your legal team. Outsourcing the RFP process can stimulate competitive bidding, drive down rates, and result in a faster selection of a qualified vendor. The cost to you can vary significantly depending on the scope of the project and the firm you choose. Generally, you'll pay a project-based fee, with a not-to-exceed commission.

6.2.12 *The Power of Benchmarking*

There's nothing like market intelligence to give you a leg up when you're negotiating something. It establishes a baseline based on information from companies like yours. Once you receive your initial quote from the product or service vendor, you get a sense and the knowledge to know whether you're getting ripped off or getting a good deal already. You can then apply your own cards to sweeten the deal further. Benchmarking lets you wield that knowledge strategically to drive down renewal or new licensing rates and optimize your overall IT spend. Without a clear understanding of what your peers are paying for similar services, you're essentially negotiating blind. Benchmarking provides you with the data you need to confidently challenge inflated rates and demonstrate that you're not overpaying.

There are many specialist and advisory firms like Gartner and Everest that focus on providing benchmarks (Everest Group, 2025). These are typically for outsourcing services, staffing rates, or could be for product licenses, or even infrastructure elements. Typically, these firms are engaged on a retainer basis and provide customized benchmarks as well as periodic industry-wide updates. These specialized benchmarking firms continuously collect and maintain cost data for a wide range of IT services across cloud infrastructure, SaaS applications, managed services, and more, often segmented by company size and industry. The data is analyzed to identify average, median, and percentile rates. This provides a clear picture of what's considered "normal" pricing.

When it's time to renew or commission services or a product, you leverage this benchmarking data to challenge inflated rates. If your current rate is significantly higher than the industry average, you have a compelling argument for a lower rate. You'll know what a fair rate is, which helps you set realistic expectations with your vendors. Knowing that your rate is in line with industry standards can strengthen your position for negotiating volume discounts.

Benchmarking gives you confidence to determine the *value* you're receiving for your money. It helps you assess whether you are getting the level of service that you're paying for. As IT has become more complex and fragmented, it's harder than ever for individual organizations to keep track of the latest rates and best practices. Benchmarking provides a crucial way to stay informed and competitive.

6.3 Consumption Patterns

Analyzing consumption patterns across the company provides you with insights into predicting future IT usage across business units. You can build this up to further improve the customer experience of IT and to optimize systems to address peak workloads and seasonal demands from your systems.

6.3.1 *User Personas*

User personas are often overlooked outside product development teams. But they could play an important role in Enterprise FinOps. Think about how you procure and assign laptops. Executives get sleek, mobile machines that last a day on the road. Developers prefer workstations with GPUs and processing power that could crunch numbers and test programs all night. Different personas have widely varying expectations from IT that can help them become more productive. User personas match tools to the needs of the people using them. Instead of forcing everyone into a one-size-fits-all framework, we start by asking who's using this system, and what they actually need. We're aligning IT with real human behaviors.

A business manager or budget owner's world revolves around high-level dashboards, variance reports, and ROI calculations. They're looking at financial and production targets. A developer or engineer is in the weeds, designing infrastructure, optimizing resources, and automating workflows. Integration with Infrastructure-as-Code tools and the ability to automate repetitive tasks are what they ask for. An Operations team member is focused on staying ahead of problems. They need real-time alerts for anomalies, performance dashboards, and visibility into resource usage and metrics. A financial analyst is all about precision. They're not interested in vague metrics but want detailed breakdowns, reconciliation reports, and seamless integration with financial systems. The security engineer needs to spot anomalous patterns that might indicate vulnerabilities or misconfigurations.

Engage your user design team to come up with user personas across the company. But personas aren't just labels. Once you have personas, the next step is critical for Enterprise FinOps, where you identify consumption patterns for these personas. You begin by identifying your key user groups, such as business managers, technical architects, ops teams, financial analysts, and security engineers. Each one has a distinct role, a unique set of priorities, and a different way of interacting with data and systems.

FinOps dashboards become personalized. A business manager gets a clean, high-level view. A DevOps engineer gets a deep dive into resource allocation. An ops team member gets alerts and real-time metrics. Automated workflows follow the same logic. If a cost spike hits, the ops team gets an alert. If a budget is off by 10%, the business manager gets a report. You make the system work for the people using it. User surveys should be a regular part of the process. Usage analytics track how people are actually interacting with the system.

Don Norman's book *The Design of Everyday Things* (Norman, 2013) is a treasure house of concepts on user-centered design and design thinking approaches and can help you design user personas in the context of Enterprise FinOps.

6.3.2 *Opex vs Capex*

The distinction between Capital Expenditure (Capex) and Operating Expenditure (Opex) is central to the successful adoption of Enterprise FinOps. Table 6.3 provides a comparative overview of these financial models. A purely Opex or Capex model is rarely optimal. Combining elements of both, you can make decisions based on *what* you get, not just *how much* you pay, and prioritize investments that drive the greatest value.

Table 6.3 Opex vs. Capex: A comparative overview

Feature	*Opex (operating expenditure)*	*Capex (capital expenditure)*
Definition	Costs incurred over a period (typically annually). Recurring, predictable expenses.	Costs incurred upfront to acquire an asset. A major, initial investment.
Assets covered	Services (SaaS, managed services, MSPs), software licenses, cloud consumption, short-term projects.	Servers, data centers, networking equipment, software development, major infrastructure projects.
Advantages	Flexibility and agility: Easily scaled up or down based on need. Lower initial investment: Reduces upfront capital outlay. Predictable costs: Easier to budget and forecast expenses. Focus on outcomes: Prioritizes value delivered, not asset ownership. Reduced risk: Shifting operational risk to the provider. Consistent cash outflow: Predictable monthly/annual expenses No large upfront investment.	Long-term cost certainty: Predictable costs over asset's lifetime Ownership and control: Greater control over the asset. Potential for higher returns: Especially with depreciating assets (e.g., servers). Strategic asset control: Aligning IT investments with long-term business strategy. Large upfront investment: Significant initial cash outlay. Delayed cash flow: Cash flow isn't affected until the asset is fully depreciated.
Disadvantages	Less predictable long-term: Can be challenging to forecast over extended periods. May mask true asset costs: Over time, the total cost can exceed initial expense. Reduced incentive for long-term investment: Focus on short-term operational efficiency. No tax benefits: No depreciation benefits.	High initial investment: Requires significant upfront capital Long-term commitment: Lock-in to the asset. Risk of obsolescence: Technology evolves rapidly; assets can become outdated. Depreciation tax shield: Reduces taxable income

The traditional IT budgeting process used Capex. It required substantial initial expenses for hardware purchases, software licenses, and major infrastructure improvements. These were often viewed as "investments" with a long-term payoff. The unfortunate part was that it was frequently justified without a strong connection to specific business outcomes. Incorrect classification creates visibility problems with costs, which spiral into inaccurate budgeting. Total Cost of Ownership (TCO) optimization through FinOps extends its focus to include all costs. A thorough TCO analysis of all major assets must be performed to find potential efficiency improvements and determine which model is appropriate for a given IT asset or service. The IT asset lifecycle management process is a key component of FinOps. The classification needs to be reviewed at different stages of an asset's lifecycle because a Capex asset can potentially transform into an Opex asset when it undergoes a refresh process. CloudEagle.ai sums up the topic succinctly in their blog (Srinivas, 2025).

6.3.3 Capital Allocation Strategies

Enterprise FinOps fundamentally shifts the focus of IT spending from simply managing costs to optimizing them, driving value. The optimization of expenses needs a conscious and strategic method to distribute resources in the most efficient way. The main issue now is to determine which resources should receive funding for the best possible return on investment, rather than following a simple cost reduction strategy to cut expenses. The previous method of IT capital allocation depended on departmental requests, perceived needs, and technical justifications, which did not link directly to business results. FinOps principles propose a different operational model where IT is perfectly aligned with business. The framework provides organizations with a method to make investment decisions through a comprehensive evaluation of business value, risk assessment, and cost analysis.

IT capital allocation refers to the strategic process that determines how organizations distribute their financial resources (money, time, and personnel) to IT-related assets, services, and projects. The process of IT expense tracking serves as a foundation for strategic investment decisions that help organizations achieve maximum return on investment (ROI) and support their business objectives. The IT asset lifecycle includes all stages from purchasing new assets to their maintenance needs and eventual disposal.

Capital allocation in IT applies to a wide range of IT offerings. Figure 6.4 depicts typical Opex and Capex spends in IT environments. Hardware such as servers, networking equipment, workstations, or laptops are typically considered capital assets because they have a useful life of several years. Extended enterprise software solutions, including ERP and CRM systems, require their software licensing expenses to be classified as capital

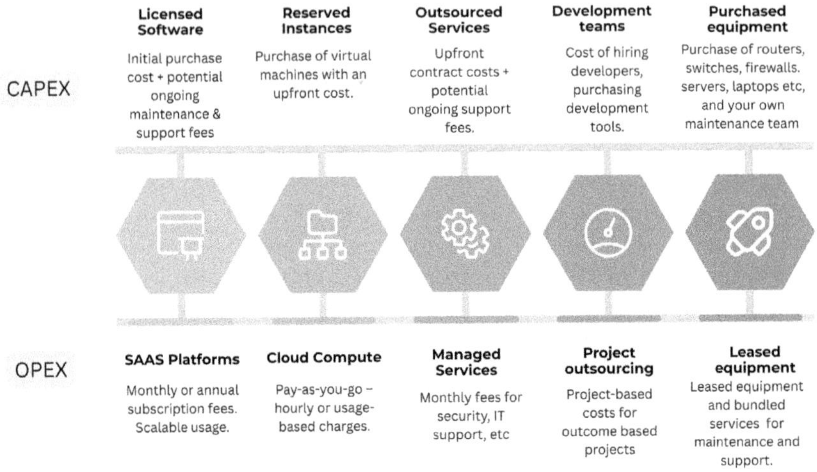

Figure 6.4 Opex vs Capex in IT systems

expenditures. Cloud-based SaaS subscriptions qualify as capital expenses because they need long-term commitments and produce non-physical assets. IT services such as cloud services (IaaS, PaaS, SaaS) can be treated as either capital expense (Capex) or operating expense (Opex). If the contract is for several years, the investment is considered a long-term asset, and the cost is depreciated over the asset's useful life as Capex. However, short-term SaaS subscriptions, where the cost is expensed as incurred, are often treated as Opex. The development of new IT products and services through hardware and software investments and asset purchases constitutes a direct capital allocation choice.

6.3.3.1 The "Invest" Approach vs the "Run" Approach

Capex in IT represents a long-term investment. The process requires companies to acquire assets that will create value throughout three or more accounting annual periods. This commonly includes tangible assets such as hardware as well as long-term *software licenses*. While SaaS subscriptions can seem like Opex, multi-year enterprise software licenses (e.g., SAP, Oracle, major ERP systems) can often be treated as Capex because of the significant investment and long-term commitment. Normally, there is a *significant upfront investment*. *Since* Capex cost is *depreciated* over its useful life, only a portion of the cost is recognized as an expense on the income statement each year. In a way, the asset is declining in value over time.

Opex represents *ongoing expenses* necessary to maintain and utilize existing IT assets. It's the "run the business" expenditure. These include recurring services such as SaaS subscriptions (short-term agreements), cloud service fees (IaaS, PaaS), managed services, and cloud usage charges. Maintenance and Support fees such as software maintenance contracts, technical support fees, and IT Service Management (ITSM) tools are also often treated as Opex. Salaries and benefits for contracted IT staff who actively use and maintain IT systems are generally considered Opex; however, salaries and training for key IT professionals could be considered capital expenditures because they represent an investment in human capital. Normally, Opex is used for contracts that expire within one year.

Cloud computing has created a new reality. While cloud services are often billed on a recurring basis (like a subscription), many companies still treat them as Capex, especially for long-term commitments. This is often justified by the long-term benefit of the cloud investment.

The classification of IT costs depends on both the company's accounting rules and the characteristics of the contract and the anticipated advantages from the IT investment. The primary difference between these two concepts lies in the timing of content availability and the ownership rights of the content.

6.3.3.2 Tax Advantages of Capital Allocation

The allocation of strategic capital through investments generates superior tax advantages over the typical method of accounting for IT expenses as operating costs. The useful life of hardware and software assets allows businesses to depreciate them for tax purposes, which reduces their taxable income. This spreads the expense of an asset over the duration of its value. The depreciation process generates a tax shield that decreases taxable income and results in reduced tax obligations. In the USA, businesses can claim full deductions for qualifying capital assets under the Section 179 deduction when these assets enter service during the same year, which provides immediate tax relief. Similar to Section 179, bonus depreciation allows for accelerated depreciation deductions, further reducing taxes. Businesses can minimize their tax expenses by using tax-loss harvesting to time their capital asset sales for maximum offset of capital gains with capital losses. The rules for IT asset depreciation and expensing under tax law depend on asset type and location, as well as current tax regulations. Your IT finance and tax professionals are best qualified to ensure accurate accounting and tax planning.

6.3.4 *Why Capex and Opex Matter in FinOps*

Enterprise FinOps treats Capex and Opex as two sides of the same coin. They simply represent different forms of cost. By managing both effectively, or by adopting a hybrid approach, FinOps achieves a more holistic and optimized approach to IT spending, driving maximum business value.

Capex is the expensive servers, data centers, hardware where you pay upfront, and the costs are fixed, whether you use the asset 100% or 10%. Opex, on the other hand, is the day-to-day grind: cloud services, software licenses, and support contracts. It's variable and scales with usage. Enterprise FinOps is a natural fit for Opex assets because you can make decisions that reduce them. If you're running a cloud app that spikes traffic, your Opex goes up. If it's quiet, it goes down. Capex investments take time to pay off. If you pour millions into a data center but underutilize it, you're locking up capital that could be used elsewhere. That's where Enterprise FinOps steps in. You can't avoid Capex that's already been invested, but you can make sure every Capex dollar works as hard as possible.

FinOps also shines in Run, where the bulk of Opex lives. Through technical engineering, contract negotiation, and other levers that we have discussed in this chapter, FinOps turns Opex into a strategic tool. Use Capex for high-performance, mission-critical systems that need stability and control (like core enterprise platforms). Use Opex for scalable, demand-driven workloads (like seasonal e-commerce spikes). The result is a portfolio that's both stable and agile.

6.3.5 *Software License Optimization, or License Harvesting*

Software License Optimization is feasible and impactful almost immediately, and does not involve any engineering or development activities to get started. Identifying and decommissioning unused licenses within your organization can lead you to over 30% savings on annual license fees, for on-premises, SaaS, as well as individual user software. While there are sophisticated license management tools for Software Asset Management (SAM), it's often simply a matter of assembling a team to conduct a software audit and maintain a list of users. Automated solutions involve the integration of your SAM tool with other platforms so you can automatically track usage. While renewal events are the perfect opportunities for whittling down licenses only to what your users need, you can get started on this at any time, as new users can be granted existing licenses from what you've harvested. Often, a dedicated SAM team is given this responsibility across the enterprise. I've elaborated on this further in the section on Software Harvesting.

License harvesting is a multifaceted strategy that addresses cost reduction, risk management, and budgeting. It's a critical component of a well-rounded Enterprise FinOps approach. Many organizations over-purchase software licenses. This often stems from conservative estimates where initial forecasts are often overly cautious, a "Just in Case" mentality where licenses are acquired, anticipating future needs that don't materialize, or simply a lack of visibility with poor tracking of license usage. It involves systematically identifying and reclaiming unused licenses. User surveys would be the first step to gather information from users on their actual software needs. Usage Audits regularly monitor software usage and pinpoint inactive licenses. Software Asset Management or License Management (SAM or SLM) tools can automatically detect inactive licenses.

The savings can be significant – often 10–30% or more of total software spend. Most software vendors have strict terms of service that prohibit unlicensed usage. Vendors can levy hefty fines for unauthorized software usage. In severe cases, organizations could face lawsuits. Non-compliance can damage an organization's reputation and erode trust. Active harvesting mitigates risk by proactively identifying and removing unlicensed software; you ensure compliance with vendor terms, significantly reducing this risk. While saving money, you are also safeguarding your business.

License Harvesting is extremely useful as a budgeting tool to predict usage. Traditional budgeting often relies on historical data, which can be inaccurate or misleading. License harvesting forces you to base your forecasts on *actual* usage. Analyzing harvested license data reveals usage and consumption patterns such as peak usage times, specific features used, and user behavior. This provides a much more accurate basis for forecasting future license needs. By using actual usage data, you can avoid over-purchasing and make more informed decisions about license renewals. Harvested data allows you to model different usage scenarios and plan accordingly.

License harvesting requires strong collaboration between IT, VMO/procurement, and legal teams. Open communication with software vendors is essential. Establish a formal process for license harvesting, including regular audits and reporting. Develop a clear retention policy for harvested licenses.

6.3.6 Product Licensing Strategies

A traditional method is on-premises licensing. You purchase a perpetual or a term license. You own the software, and the vendor generally provides ongoing maintenance and support. This model is often favored for high-security or regulatory compliance needs. If this was a term license, usually one to three years, you renew the license based on your ongoing requirements, typically with a not-to-exceed price for renewals. In Software as a Service (SaaS), you pay a subscription fee to use the software. The vendor manages everything – infrastructure, maintenance, and updates. A hybrid model is BYOL (Bring Your Own License), where you purchase the license yourself and manage its deployment, maintenance, and updates, whether on-premises, in your private cloud in your datacenter, or on a public cloud instance. It's often seen with large enterprise systems like SAP, where you can deploy licenses on the cloud or in your datacenter, but can be subject to changing licensing policies from the vendors. AWS offered BYOL licenses for Windows Server and SQL Server in 2019 (AWS, 2019).

SaaS Licensing significantly reduces capital expenditure and can easily scale up or down based on usage. The vendor handles updates, security patches, and infrastructure. A subscription model provides budget certainty and can let you quickly get started with minimal IT overhead. However, multi-tenant environments and usage-based pricing increase complexity. On-Premises Licensing provides you greater control over the software, data, and security. It is easier to customize the software to meet specific business needs. On-premises licensing can actually result in a lower TCO than SaaS if usage is consistent. It requires significant IT resources for installation, maintenance, and security.

In BYOL, you avoid the upfront license cost. You maintain control over the license. You are responsible for all IT infrastructure costs, maintenance, and support. Ensure you have the internal expertise to manage the license effectively.

High-security environments often favor on-premises or carefully managed SaaS solutions. Certain industries have specific requirements that may

Table 6.4 Key Differences in licensing models

Feature	*SaaS*	*On-premises*	*BYOL (with SaaS)*
Cost structure	Subscription (recurring)	Perpetual + maintenance	Subscription (managed by you)
Management	Vendor-managed	Customer-managed	Customer-managed
Updates/patches	Vendor-provided	Customer-provided	Customer-provided
Scalability	Highly scalable	Limited by infrastructure	Limited by infrastructure
Security	Vendor-managed (shared responsibility)	Customer-responsible	Customer-responsible

influence licensing choices. Assess your internal IT skills and resources. Calculate the TCO over the expected lifespan of the software, including licensing, infrastructure, maintenance, and support. Table 6.4 lists down key differences between SaaS, on-premises and BYOL models.

6.3.7 Reducing Shadow IT

Shadow IT is a slow drain on your resources. The term comes from unmanaged and unapproved tools and services that users may deploy in the "shadows" of your organization. While it might seem like a quick fix for an immediate need, it's a major driver of technology debt and costs, creating security risks, compliance nightmares, and financial waste. Users feel that IT is slow, inflexible, or disconnected from their day-to-day needs and is unable to meet their requirements. They're frustrated by cumbersome processes, long approval cycles, and solutions that don't match their actual work. Meanwhile, cloud services and SaaS tools are just a click away, easy to sign up for, easy to use, and can be completely invisible to IT. But users don't realize the risks they're taking. It can lead to unpatched vulnerabilities, data leaks, and a lack of visibility into what's being used. Shadow IT is not just a problem with business units; even IT groups within your own organization may be duplicating systems due to a lack of sharing information.

Shadow IT introduces redundant systems, fragmented data, and a patchwork of tools that don't integrate. It creates a false economy with short-term gains in speed and flexibility, but long-term losses in security, compliance, and operational efficiency. A single unapproved app could expose your data to a breach. A poorly managed SaaS tool could lead to a compliance violation.

But Shadow IT doesn't have to be a losing battle. Managing it is a critical step in any Enterprise FinOps strategy. Start by mapping what's out there. Use discovery tools, network monitoring, and user surveys to uncover the tools, apps, and services your teams are using without its knowledge. Once you've got visibility, you can classify the risks, such as which tools are duplicated, which have potential risks, and which are just inefficient.

You can then bring Shadow IT into the fold. It needs a layered approach. Processes like Enterprise FinOps provide the foundation, technology provides *visibility* and *control*, while executive sponsorship provides the *authority* and support necessary to make the program sustainable.

Replace rogue tools with approved alternatives that meet both business needs and security standards. Consolidate redundant systems to eliminate waste. Rebuild trust by working with business units to understand their pain points and deliver solutions that are fast, flexible, and secure. A strong centralized vendor management process for any and all IT spend can enable checks and balances to prevent the licensing or purchase of duplicate assets, such as hardware or software. Another good governance practice is to implement Architectural Review Boards that review any technical projects and programs. Software licensing and audits ensure that license consumption across the organization is tracked and managed. Enterprise FinOps includes all these processes as part of its framework. Cybersecurity tools can identify unauthorized cloud apps. Cloud Access Security Brokers sit between users and cloud applications and can detect anomalous traffic. Network Traffic tools monitor network traffic patterns to identify unauthorized applications. Endpoint Detection and Response (EDR) solutions can detect malicious activity originating from unauthorized applications installed on endpoints. Identity and Access Management (IAM) solutions can identify users accessing cloud applications without proper authorization.

Executive sponsorship is the key to implementing policies, enforcing controls, and holding individuals accountable. A comprehensive Shadow IT policy should be outlined to define acceptable use, security requirements, and approval processes. This needs to be communicated clearly and enforced consistently. While some Shadow IT is inevitable, it is important to document the circumstances in which it can operate and also establish timelines for Shadow IT to be transitioned over to the assigned IT units. To prevent individual users from purchasing software or cloud services using "Procurement P-cards" or corporate business cards, establish policies at the financial level to govern such purchases through an appropriate approval process.

More importantly, remove the gaps that could lead to Shadow IT. Make it easier for users to request new software or services. A simplified, quick approval process reduces the temptation to go rogue. Provide users with approved, secure solutions that meet their needs. If a user needs a collaboration tool, offer a managed solution that's already been vetted by your team. Work with business units to understand their needs and provide support. This builds trust and reduces the likelihood of them going outside of IT's control. Educate users about the risks of Shadow IT, such as security vulnerabilities, compliance issues, and potential cost overruns. Continuously monitor network traffic and user activity to identify and address Shadow IT incidents.

If you are transparent about the true cost of unmanaged services and the financial impact of Shadow IT, and offer alternatives, you build trust with users. After all, while the goal of reducing Shadow IT is to stop users from using unauthorized systems, it's also to build a culture of responsible technology adoption.

The Law of Leverage states that a small force applied at a distance from a pivot can generate a large torque. This illustrates how cost optimization strategies, negotiation, governance frameworks, policies, and process improvements can act as "levers" to drive significant changes in IT spend behavior. Just as a small force applied at a strategic point can amplify its impact, even minor adjustments in FinOps practices, such as process improvements, industry best practices, clarifying roles and responsibilities, establishing a collaborative CoE, updating policies, or implementing cost-tracking tools, can lead to substantial reductions in waste and better alignment between IT and business goals. The CIO must identify and use these levers. These are the points of influence where small changes can yield outsized results and invest in them to maximize the return on IT spend.

References

ADP. (2025). *Employer of record*. Retrieved from https://www.adp.com/resources/articles-and-insights/articles/e/employer-of-record.aspx

AWS. (2019). *Bring your own licenses for microsoft windows server*. Retrieved from https://aws.amazon.com/blogs/aws/a-new-simplified-bring-your-own-license-experience-for-microsoft-windows-server/

AWS. (2025). *Reserved instances*. Retrieved from https://aws.amazon.com/aws-cost-management/aws-cost-optimization/reserved-instances/

Cognizant. (2024). *Cognizant elevated to global elite partner in service now partner ecosystem*. Retrieved from https://news.cognizant.com/2025-01-30-Cognizant-Elevated-to-Global-Elite-Partner-in-ServiceNow-Partner-Ecosystem

Deloitte. (2025). *Outsourcing advisory services*. Retrieved from https://www.deloitte.com/us/en/services/consulting/services/about-our-outsourcing-advisory-services.html

Deloitte, K. A., Coronado, J., & Stoler, M. (2024). *US global outsourcing survey*. Retrieved from https://www.deloitte.com/content/dam/assets-zone3/us/en/docs/services/consulting/2024/us-global-outsourcing-survey-2024-report.pdf

Everest Group. (2025). *Benchmarking services*. Retrieved from https://www.everestgrp.com/custom-decision-support/benchmarking/

GeeksforGeeks. (2025, August). *What is serverless computing*. Retrieved from https://www.geeksforgeeks.org/blogs/what-is-serverless-computing/

Gudmundsdottir, H. (2025). Retrieved from https://www.devoteam.com/expert-view/exit-clauses-in-it-contracts/

IBM. (2025a). *Hybrid cloud strategy*. Retrieved from https://www.ibm.com/think/insights/hybrid-cloud-strategy

IBM. (2025b). *Software asset management*. Retrieved from https://www.ibm.com/think/topics/software-asset-management

Linsley, Rod; GatekeeperHQ. (2025). *Vendor consolidation*. Retrieved from https://www.gatekeeperhq.com/blog/vendor-consolidation

NextLevelTech. (2025, April). *The pros and cons of hardware leasing*. Retrieved from https://www.nextleveltech.com/blog-post/computer-hardware-leasing

Norman, D. (2013). *The design of everyday things*. New York, NY: Basic Books.
Reliant Energy. (2025). *Truly free weekends plan*. Retrieved from https://www.reliant.com/en/residential/electricity/electricity-plans/plans/truly-free-weekends-plan-lf
Srinivas, M. (2025, August). *Capex vs opex*. Retrieved from https://www.cloudeagle.ai/blogs/capex-vs-opex
TechTargets. (n.d.). *How to build a successful co-location strategy* (J. Lulka, Ed.). Retrieved from https://www.techtarget.com/searchdatacenter/ehandbook/How-to-build-a-successful-colocation-strategy
Zinnov. (2024, April). *Global capability centers*. Retrieved from https://zinnov.com/offerings/gcc-setup-and-transformation/global-capability-center-setup/

Chapter 7

Technical Levers for Enterprise FinOps

DOI: 10.4324/9781003682196-11

7.1 Enterprise Architecture

7.1.1 Architectural Principles

Architectural principles guide how your IT systems are designed, built, maintained, and secured. I've stated some of the top architectural principles here that are aligned with Enterprise FinOps principles, as shown in Figure 7.1. This can be used as a blueprint and modified as needed by your EA team to align with your business's DNA. Organizations such as the Open Group publish standards as part of their TOGAF framework that include architectural principles (Hawley, Darren; on behalf of The Open Group Internal Architecture Board, 2008).

7.1.1.1 Embed Cost Optimization into Design

Cost optimization is the perfect collaboration between Enterprise FinOps and Enterprise Architecture. Every decision, from choosing cloud and SaaS providers to provisioning resources, should question the cost implications. Eliminate features that don't deliver value, retire legacy systems that are too expensive to maintain, modernize clunky systems, and automate wherever possible. For infrastructure, known platforms with consistent components let you predict costs and arrive at reliable TCO. It's like knowing the price of a car before you even start building it because you are estimating parts, labor, and time. Consistent design choices reduce spending variability. They help identify and eliminate redundant resources. If your architecture is built with standardization and automation in mind, it's easier to spot inefficiencies.

7.1.1.2 Automate Repetitive Tasks and Processes Where Feasible

Why spend hours manually adjusting settings or performing a database administration task when a script can do it in seconds? Automation saves time, reduces errors, and frees up human effort for higher-value work. Automate testing, deployment, and infrastructure provisioning. Manual processes are slow and expensive. Tools like Terraform, Ansible, or Puppet let you write Infrastructure-as-Code (IaC). Version control has been used for ages for software development. Using it for infrastructure is a safety net for your systems. If something breaks, you can roll back to a working state with a few keystrokes. But sometimes the effort of automation may be too significant. Beware of teams that try to automate everything without analyzing how frequently that task or process is used.

7.1.1.3 Security by Design – Embed Security at Every Stage of the SDLC

Security by design is a necessity in today's modern IT landscape. Rather than leaving security as an afterthought, waiting for the cybersecurity team to fix issues reactively, you can bake security into every stage of the

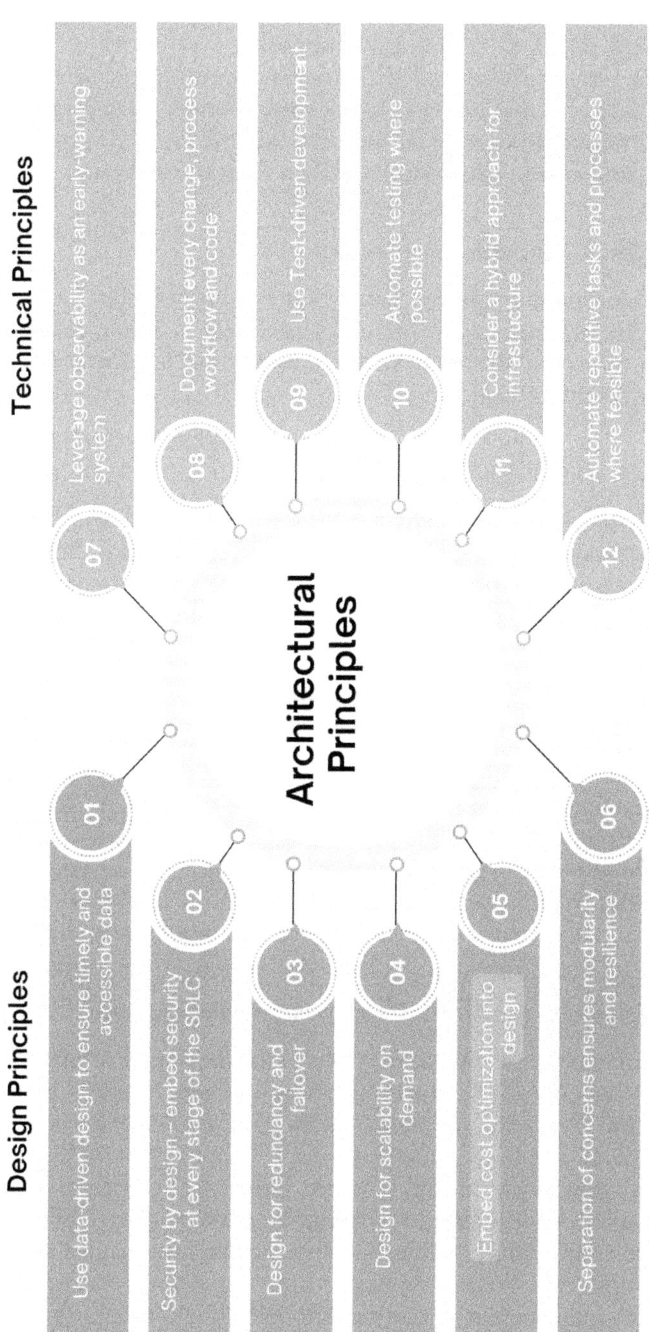

Figure 7.1 Architectural principles

software lifecycle. From the first line of code to deployment and maintenance, security needs to be a consideration for every layer of the application, from infrastructure and data to maintenance processes. Data is especially vulnerable and needs to be secured, whether by encrypting data at rest or in transit. If your organization is geared for it, design for zero-trust access, and ensure that compliance is a foundational pillar.

7.1.1.4 *Design for Redundancy and Failover*

It's designed for maintainability. Think of it as a backup plan for your systems. If one server crashes, another picks up the slack. While you certainly gain uptime, you avoid the hidden costs of downtime, like lost productivity or customer dissatisfaction.

7.1.1.5 *Design for Scalability on Demand*

Design systems to grow with demand. Whether you're expecting a surge in users or planning for a new product line, your architecture should adapt without breaking the bank. With modern architectures, you can use techniques like containers, microservices, and APIs. Public cloud services will offer PaaS and serverless platforms.

7.1.1.6 *Leverage Observability as an Early-Warning System*

Without robust monitoring, alerts, logging, and tracing, your systems are flying blind. Imagine a system that crashes at 3 a.m. on a Friday. Without visibility, you're guessing where the problem is. Tools that track performance and correlate issues across infrastructure and applications let you fix issues before they escalate into outages. An AIOps platform combines observability with advanced techniques like self-healing and predictive analysis.

7.1.1.7 *Separation of Concerns Ensures Modularity and Resilience*

Separation of concerns keeps your systems from becoming a tangled mess. Divide responsibilities into layers like data storage, business logic, user interfaces, and front-end scripting. Clean code makes systems easier to maintain, debug, and scale. If one layer fails, the others shouldn't collapse with it. Break down systems into reusable, independent modules. If a module fails, you can fix it without rewriting the entire system. Microservices and containers make this possible, but they require APIs that act as the glue between components. Loose coupling means your systems don't depend on each other in fragile ways. If one service goes down, others should keep running.

7.1.1.8 Use Data-Driven Design to Ensure Timely and Accessible Data

Data-driven design means you build systems around the data they need to function. Whether it's customer analytics, transaction logs, reporting, or user behavior, your architecture should prioritize data accessibility and integrity. Storing data is just the beginning. You should also optimize how it's retrieved, processed, and shared.

7.1.1.9 Document Every Change, Process Workflow, and Code

Documentation is like an insurance policy. If a developer or system admin leaves, or a system fails, it tells others what they need to know. Code commenting lets new developers carry on from where the previous one left off. It lets them refactor complex pieces of code. It helps your operations and engineering teams fix issues quickly, track changes, and ensure consistency.

7.1.1.10 Use Test-Driven Development

In Test-Driven Development (TDD), your team writes tests before code. It catches bugs before they result in costly production downtime. It forces them to think about edge cases and performance bottlenecks. Fewer bugs are released into production. The result is faster fixes and a system that's built to last.

7.1.1.11 Automate Testing Where Possible

Test automation takes the pain out of testing and ensures fewer errors for systems that frequently go through changes.

7.1.1.12 Consider a Hybrid Approach for Infrastructure

Hybrid models combine the benefits of the public cloud with a private cloud based on on-premises or co-located datacenters. Traditional datacenter infrastructure is adopting public cloud features at a rapid pace. Organizations blindly opt for a public cloud-first approach, but it isn't always the answer. Some businesses need on-premises for compliance, while others prefer hybrid models for flexibility. The key is to balance scalability and security. If you go all-in on public cloud, ensure your data is protected. If you're hybrid, define clear boundaries for what's on-prem and what's in the cloud.

These principles aren't set in stone. They're a starting point. Your EA team can add other principles like coding standards, standardized or reference architectures, as necessary. Review them quarterly and challenge them when they no longer fit your business. The goal is to build a system that's as adaptive and resilient as your organization.

7.1.2 Architectural Reviews

When you're knee-deep in running IT and trying to limit governance to the least necessary to maintain speed and agility, it's easy to see formal reviews as just another obstacle. But some reviews are not trying to slow you down. They are making sure you're not going to get bogged down in future escalations and cost overruns. Think of them as a sanity check for every major IT initiative. If you don't pause and ask the hard questions early, you're waiting for the bill and repercussions to arrive later.

The Architectural Review Board (ARB) is one of these reviews. Their job isn't to block progress but to spot the red flags before the money is even spent. They look for duplication with existing systems, compliance with EA principles like standardization and alignment with business goals, and cost factors that may be hidden. The ARB review prevents cost overruns, eliminates Shadow IT, and finds standardization opportunities. If every team could use the same tools and the same infrastructure, you would be eliminating duplicated efforts and mitigating IT risk. The ARB ensures that every project fits into the broader IT strategy. If the ARB is the gatekeeper, teams are less likely to spend on unapproved or duplicate tools that could blow the budget. AWS has a comprehensive article on the ARB (Weber & Richards, 2025).

Some of the key questions these reviews ask:

- Is this the most cost-effective solution? (The cheapest option isn't always the best.)
- Can we use something we already have? (Because reinventing the wheel is expensive.)
- What are the long-term costs or TCO? (Because a project might look cheap now, but it could be a money pit later.)
- Does this design promote standardization? (Because consistency is a cost-saver.)
- What automation are you planning to include? (Automation saves costs and reduces errors.)

Just like your EA principles, your EA team can customize these questions and come up with a template that can be reviewed at the ARB.

7.1.2.1 Approved Asset Lists

Pair the ARB with an "Approved Asset" list, spanning all of IT. It's a centralized, actively managed list of approved software, hardware, and services. It's evolving as your business needs change. Without it, you end up with a technology graveyard that hogs technology debt. Every team starts buying their own SaaS tools, their own software licenses, their own laptops and servers, and their own cloud services. But with an Approved Asset List, you promote standardization and lower costs. Everyone uses the same tools.

If you conduct a Business Capability Mapping (BCM) as described in the next section, you can also ensure that the Approved Asset List conforms to business processes. You can negotiate better pricing. When you're buying in volume, you get better discounts and fewer surprises.

You streamline procurement. Instead of juggling 25 different vendor contracts, you have a few strategic but deeper and more relevant relationships.

With the Approved Asset List, you can improve your chargeback and showback models. If a business group or department is using something only for themselves, they see the cost and may start thinking about efficiency. The list needs to be revisited periodically. If an asset isn't being used, it's time to decommission it or repurpose it. The ARB and the Approved Asset List make sure your IT investments are efficient and aligned with the business.

7.1.3 Business Capability Mapping

Business Capability Mapping (BCM) is a process of identifying and categorizing the *functional* areas of your business that IT supports. A partial view of a BCM map is shown in Figure 7.2. An Approved Asset List may merely list software applications. BCM focuses on what the business *does*, not just *what IT provides*.

The Open Group, an industry organization that publishes standards and guides on architecture, publishes a Business capability guide as part of its TOGAF architecture standards. As per this guide,

> Business capabilities provide an abstraction of the business reality in a way that helps to simplify conversations between interested stakeholders. Defining a business capability's supporting components (roles, processes, information, and tools) provides a business context for those supporting components. Creating a business capability model for the enterprise promotes more of a common understanding of the business.
>
> (The Open Group Architecture Forum Business Architecture Work Stream, 2018)

Mapping a Business Capability Model to enterprise applications and platforms promotes standardization and reduces duplication of systems for any given business process or capability. Instead of looking at individual applications, you map the business around capabilities that represent key

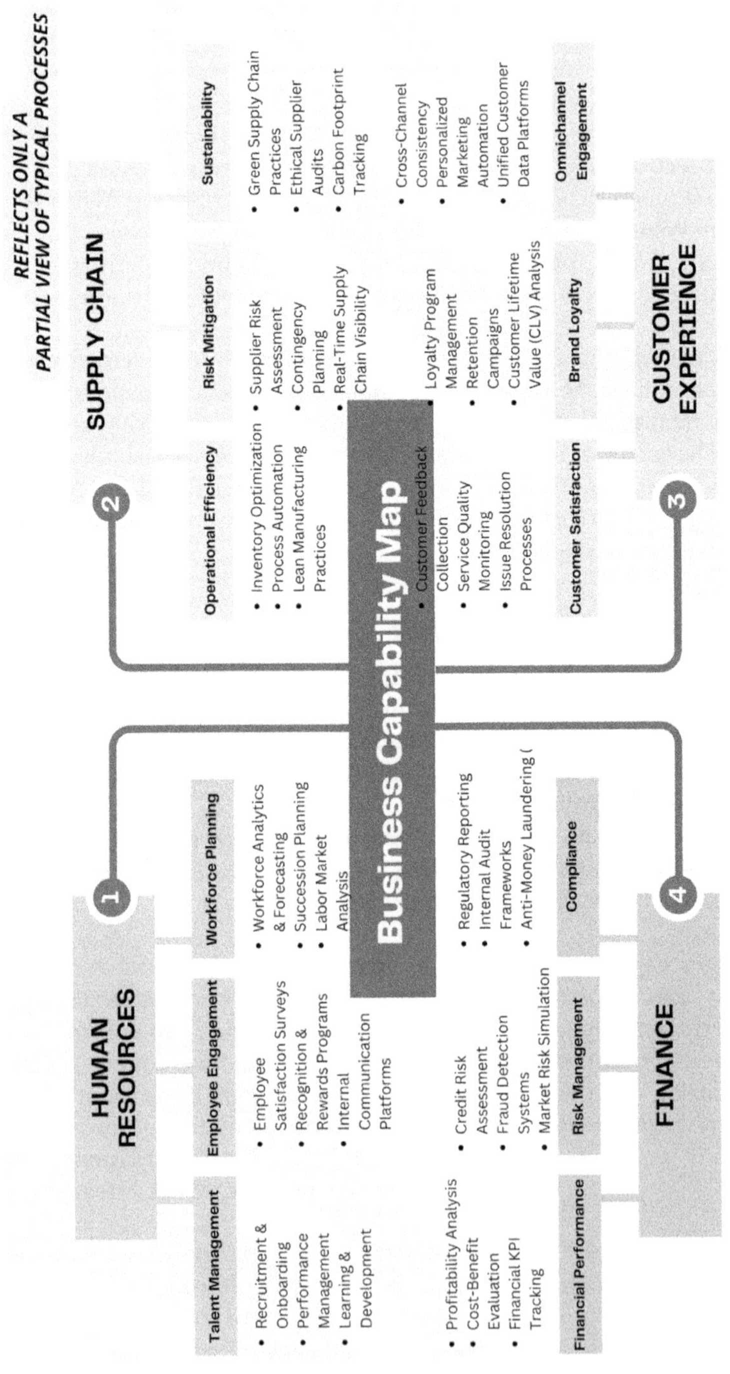

Figure 7.2 Sample partial business capability map showing four enterprise processes

business functions, such as customer order management, supply chain optimization, financial reporting, lead management, or resource onboarding. Capabilities are often organized hierarchically, with high-level capabilities such as customer experience being further categorized into more granular capabilities like customer support or customer onboarding, to the desired level, usually no more than three levels deep. The next step is to map IT capabilities, services, platforms, and processes to the business processes. BCM is represented visually to illustrate the relationships between capabilities and IT assets.

7.1.3.1 Benefits of BCM

- BCM is *always* a collaborative effort between IT and the business units. It needs to reflect a deep understanding of how the business actually operates and promotes business alignment for IT investments.
- It lets you trace exactly which IT capabilities are being used by which parts of the business. Chargeback models are improved when you use BCM to tag your business units accurately.
- BCM also tells you which capabilities are lifelines for the business. If your sales team relies on a specific CRM tool, you know to invest in keeping it running. If a capability is redundant, like two departments using separate but similar data platforms, you can make a powerful case for consolidation to save money and reduce complexity.
- BCM forces you to look at vendor relationships with fresh eyes. If three different teams are using five different vendors for similar services, you're paying more than you need to. With BCM, you can negotiate better deals, gain volume benefits, bundle contracts, and even consolidate to a single provider if it makes sense.
- BCM shows you how capabilities are connected. If one system fails, it can show you what business units or processes could be impacted.

There are several tools that let you implement a BCM map. You can also easily build one with tools that you likely already have, such as Excel or Visio. Enterprise tools, usually categorized as Enterprise Architecture (EA) or Application Portfolio Management (APM), let you maintain the BCM easily and integrate with other sources of IT data. ServiceNow APM lets you map capabilities and analyze costs – all in one place. Bloomfire is great if your teams need to collaborate on capability definitions and align IT with business goals. SAP LeanIX lets you visualize your architecture, supports chargeback models, and integrates very well with other tools. The reference section has links to sample BCM maps for your industry (SAP LeanIX, 2025).

7.1.4 *Reference Architectures*

Reference Architectures (RFAs) are like blueprints for IT systems. They are pre-designed frameworks that help you build, integrate, deploy, and manage infrastructure without reinventing the wheel. They are like proven recipes. They outline the ingredients like services, tools, actions, and strategies needed to create a stable, scalable IT environment. Examples include the VMWare Horizon 6 Reference Architecture (VMWare, 2014), Microsoft's Azure Well-Architected Framework (Microsoft Azure, 2025), AWS's Well-Architected Framework (Amazon AWS, 2025), Google Cloud's architecture model (Google Cloud, 2025), and TOGAF (The Open Group, 2025), which is more generic and industry-focused.

When you base your architecture on a recognized RFA, you're creating a map of how your IT systems support specific capabilities. For example, if your marketing team relies on a data analytics platform, an RFA can show you exactly which compute, storage, and networking resources are tied to that capability. RFAs are built with efficiency in mind. The Azure Well-Architected Framework explicitly tells you to right-size compute instances, avoid over-provisioning, and automate monitoring to lower your cloud bills. An RFA might highlight ways to avoid redundant storage setups or underutilized virtual machines and give you clear areas to cut costs. It's like having a financial auditor built into your architecture.

RFAs should be selected based on your infrastructure strategy – whether hybrid, on-premises, or public cloud. If you're on AWS, the AWS Well-Architected Framework is a natural fit. If your org is using Azure, it is practical to use their model. But they need to be adapted to the unique needs of your business. The RFA is just the starting point. Ideally, development teams should collaborate with infrastructure and EA teams at the design stage itself to understand how to develop and deploy applications as per RFA guidelines.

7.1.5 *Application Lifecycle Management (ALM)*

ALM orchestrates the entire life of an application, from the first requirement to the day it's retired. It includes the entire process of designing, developing, deploying, and maintaining software applications. You start by defining and documenting application needs and creating the application's architecture and code. The testing part ensures the application meets quality standards, and deployment covers rolling out the application to users. The operational part addresses monitoring, supporting, troubleshooting and updating the application, and tracking and managing application configurations.

It's like a symphony where every instrument (developer, tester, operations team) plays a part, but without a conductor, the music falls apart because it lacks synchronization. Requirements management is the first scribble that the composer makes on a notepad, inspired by some idea or thought. Design is the composition where it lays out what the experience is that the composer wants the audience to have, development is the practice sessions where individual performers practice their parts, testing is like the rehearsal, deployment is the performance where the audience actually hears the symphony, and operations are the encore.

ALM can let you predict how much software costs over its entire lifecycle. When you design with cost in mind, you are tuning the outcome to make sure it's not too big, too slow, too clunky, or too expensive to maintain. Early cost awareness stops you from building a bridge that's too long for the river it needs to cross. If requirements aren't documented, you may end up rebuilding the same feature three times. If version control is haphazard, you could lose track of what's working and what's broken. Robust ALM tools, like Git for version control or Ansible for configuration management, catch errors before they become disasters.

ALM reduces errors and also has extensive hooks for automation. CI/CD pipelines can automate testing and deployment. When developers check in code, and it starts the workflow of testing, security checks, integration build, and deployment to production, you can save hours off the process. Standardized environments such as development, testing, pre-production, and production cut the complexity of managing different setups that all look slightly different.

7.2 Technical Levers for Cost Optimization

7.2.1 Workload Optimization

In workload optimization, resources are efficiently allocated and utilized to meet the specific needs of services or workloads. This involves activities like rightsizing to maximize resource utilization (e.g., CPU, memory) for workloads, scaling resources in alignment with demand signals rather than over-provisioning resources and causing low utilization during non-peak hours, and conducting rightsizing analysis to eliminate idle or unused resources. Performance tuning uses deeper analysis to optimize the workload without consuming additional resources.

There are several techniques used in workload optimization. Figure 7.3 illustrates some common activities. Take that cloud app used by your sales team. It crashes during morning calls because the backend can't handle the traffic. Your teams may scale up the application during peak hours. But with workload optimization, you would dig into the root cause of the crash. While the instance may be under-provisioned, it could also be that the code is leaking memory and crashing, or caching isn't being used. Your development team could use a variety of techniques to fix it. They could refactor the code

Figure 7.3 Workload optimization activities

on their next sprint, or look up algorithms that are taking up lengthy processing times and optimize them with faster, more efficient algorithms, upgrade libraries to the latest versions, or rewrite the database queries. Implementing caching strategies that reduce the server load can speed up the data flow between client browsers and the server. They have a whole toolbox of things that could make the app run smoothly. See the guide from the FinOps framework for more specific examples (The FinOps Foundation, 2025).

When you pair rate optimization with workload optimization, you're creating a feedback loop that both slashes costs and boosts performance. Imagine a server running at 30% capacity because it's oversized, while inefficient queries are causing unnecessary strain. Fixing both by resizing the server and rewriting the queries creates a domino effect with lower costs, better performance, and a system that feels like it's been upgraded 3X. When workloads are optimized, IT spending drops, but the benefits go deeper when productivity rises, and customers stay happy. This combination ensures that every application runs at its peak. It consumes only the resources it needs, when it needs them. They're the twin engines of a smarter and more cost-effective IT future.

7.2.2 *Rightsizing*

Rightsizing uses detailed insights into actual resource utilization to eliminate waste and maximize the value derived from IT investments, whether in the cloud, data center, SaaS, or elsewhere in the IT portfolio. The actual work would depend on the unique technical characteristics of the environment. Many organizations have historically adopted a "better safe than sorry" mentality, often resulting in significantly oversized servers, virtual machines, SaaS environments, and cloud resources. Many resources remain largely idle during periods of low demand. This approach leads to substantial operational inefficiencies. It's like buying a mansion that you neither live in, lease, sell, nor rent out to the holiday seeker. Compute cycles, storage, memory, and network bandwidth keep costing you regardless of whether the resources are actively being used. A company could end up spending millions on servers that sit idle most of the time.

Over-provisioning is the old way of thinking. Rightsizing tunes what you need to what you're actually using, letting the whole system perform at its peak. Observability and monitoring tools can easily be deployed to detect over-provisioned systems. They can uncover patterns like a server that's 20% utilized during off-peak hours and reaching 60% in the five days of the month-end close. With the technology available today, you could downsize that server during the day, then scale up when the traffic hits. There's no waste or overspending. Just smart, real-time adjustments. It's a myth to think that rightsizing is not useful for on-premises systems. With virtualization technology, your on-premises infrastructure is functioning more like a private cloud. Rightsizing can ensure that you get a true sense of what capacity is available for future deployments. Cloud and virtualization software providers offer auto-scaling features that let you anticipate traffic based on patterns and real-time monitoring. With data-driven decisions, bottlenecks vanish and performance sharpens. Customer satisfaction boosts when users don't get frustrated with lagging systems.

But changing culture is hard. Rightsizing is an integral part of Enterprise FinOps. A holistic Enterprise Assessment will likely identify several opportunities through a rightsizing analysis where servers are over-provisioned, and utilization is way below thresholds. Start off with one underutilized server, measure and adjust. Bring in auto-scaling tools next. Every time you right-size, you're building a system that's more in tune with what your business actually needs.

7.2.2.1 Rightsizing Analysis

A rightsizing analysis gives your infrastructure a health check and a roadmap to do what it's supposed to do. The process looks at metrics like CPU utilization, memory spikes, disk I/O that's either too fast or too slow, and network traffic. It measures the application performance through response times and transaction rates. The financial cost analysis will let you know what the old configuration is costing you. Segmenting this data lets you see patterns such as a marketing app that's underpowered during a campaign or a development server that's running in production by accident.

It's not enough to know where the underutilized resources are. You have to know why they're underutilized. Sometimes the team may have provisioned a server for a peak event that never happened. Or the application is simply not used as much as it should be. This root cause analysis makes sure that rightsizing is a sustainable strategy. Once you've got these answers, your teams can make changes. A typical response would be to shrink a server to half the current provisioned cores. They might delete an entire environment that's been sitting idle for six months, or shift it to a spot instance. Native tools like AWS Cost Explorer can show you where your money is leaking. Observability tools like New Relic or Datadog can tell you if your apps are slow because of a database bottleneck or a misconfigured cache.

7.2.3 *Auto-Scaling*

With auto-scaling, the platform dynamically adjusts computing based on real-time demand. It ensures optimal performance for your workloads by scaling up the resources such as compute power, virtual machines, memory, or bandwidth during traffic spikes and scaling down during low usage. Auto-scaling automates manual scaling processes, improves cost efficiency, and also prevents errors. Many cloud platforms and data center virtualization tools use metrics to trigger scaling actions automatically. This eliminates manual resource provisioning and reduces downtime. Auto-scaling is critical for Infrastructure as a Service (IaaS) and leads to cost efficiency.

7.2.4 *Performance Optimization*

Performance tuning adjusts system configurations, resource allocations, and application behaviors to maximize the efficiency of the workload. There are multiple factors that can degrade performance, such as latency, bandwidth, memory, or even poorly written code. Multiple workloads conflict with each other for the same resources. You can minimize latency and ensure optimal utilization of computing resources. Typically, the characteristics of the workload are analyzed to understand specific demands, such as compute-intensive tasks, data processing, GPU-intensive actions, or real-time transaction processing. Technical actions can include optimizing hardware configurations, refactoring software algorithms, and adjusting parameters like thread pooling, caching mechanisms, and database indexing.

Auto-scaling, load balancing, and container orchestration tools can dynamically allocate resources based on workload patterns. Observability software usually identifies bottlenecks in metrics like CPU utilization, I/O latency, and memory usage that can trigger actions by the team to optimize and test the workload with revised parameters. Databases and web servers, for example, can show tremendous improvement in performance by tuning database queries or using caching mechanisms.

Performance tuning is critical in workload optimization to ensure that systems operate within desired performance thresholds without over-provisioning resources and is a critical task for engineering teams in the context of a well-implemented Enterprise FinOps program.

7.2.5 *Serverless Architectures*

Serverless architecture or computing is a risk-transfer mechanism. The operational burden of managing infrastructure shifts from your team to the cloud provider. It doesn't mean there are no servers; rather, it means your developer and operations team don't have to worry about provisioning, scaling, patching, or maintaining them.

If your team is stuck wrestling with servers that crash, scale, or demand updates on a regular basis, you need to think about redesigning that critical application with serverless computing. It's like you're hosting a party, and someone else handles the setup, the cleanup, even that broken chair. All you do is pour drinks and mingle with your guests. With serverless, there are no servers to manage, just code that runs when needed. You pay for what you use, and the cloud provider handles the rest. Servers fade away into the background, like a well-oiled machine you never need to see.

Function as a Service (FaaS) platforms like AWS Lambda and Azure Functions work like this. You write a snippet of code that runs when something happens. It uses API calls provided by the serverless platform. Let's assume you are processing a customer order. The cloud provider spins up compute power automatically and scales back down when the process ends. It's a dramatic difference with no idle costs or wasted resources. It consumes a fraction of what traditional setups demand, where you pay for the API's consumed.

This is a shift in how you think about budgeting. Developers don't need to juggle servers or containers. They write code and the cloud provider takes care of the rest, whether scaling, patching, logging, or security. It speeds up development and cuts out operational tasks. It lets your team innovate instead of firefighting.

For Enterprise FinOps, this is a significant point. You're not locked into fixed server costs that sit idle 90% of the time. You pay only for the milliseconds your code runs. A retail company that needs to adjust prices in real time designs a serverless function that runs only when inventory changes. A media company processing thousands of videos can break tasks into bite-sized functions for trimming, editing, adding subtitles, or encoding. Each fires up only when needed.

But writing serverless code needs expert talent, both at the design and development level. You need to design applications that know which APIs to consume. You still need to track costs meticulously. You need to know what drives your costs, whether execution time, memory, or how often functions are called. The real win is agility when you can deploy features in minutes, not weeks. You ship code as fast as your developers can write it. It gives you a competitive edge.

Serverless tools provide detailed visibility into resource consumption. You can track costs down to the millisecond, identifying areas for optimization with precision. Since they don't have to worry about infrastructure management, your IT team can focus on higher-value activities such as application development, business logic, and strategic initiatives. Serverless lets you prototype fast and deploy new features quickly. This agility allows you to quickly respond to changing business needs and market opportunities. Your applications can handle sudden spikes in traffic without requiring manual intervention.

7.2.6 *Rate Optimization*

In rate optimization, you minimize the cost per unit of resource usage (e.g., per hour, per transaction, per GB, per API call) and select optimum models like reserved instances or spot instances to reduce overall spending. You also negotiate with vendors for the best possible rates and volume discounts. The goal is to secure the lowest possible cost for resources and avoid overpaying for services with higher rates when alternatives exist.

Rate optimization aims to get you the most cost-effective rate for your assets. Just like rightsizing, this can apply across all your IT spend. Rate optimization constantly analyzes and refines how you're using your money. Figure 7.4 depicts typical rate optimization activities. The FinOps framework publishes more information, specifically on rate optimization techniques for cloud providers (FinOps Foundation, 2025).

For services, use benchmarking and your vendor management teams to look for the optimal vendors who can provide you with the service quality you need. For data centers, look at co-location vendors who have the right balance between cost, performance, responsiveness, and flexibility. Cloud introduces a whole new set of techniques. There are sophisticated tools that

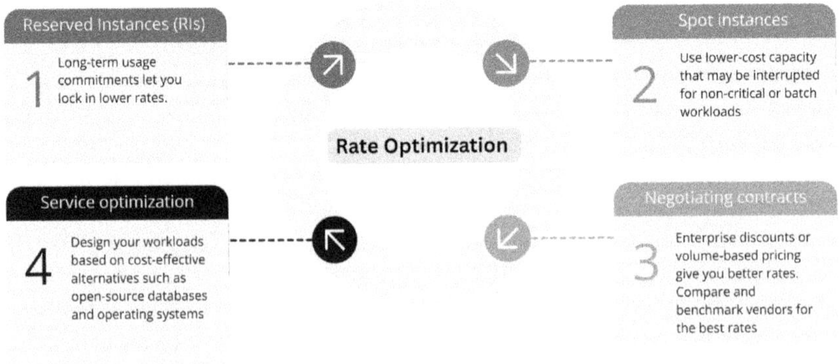

Figure 7.4 Typical rate optimization activities

help you with rate optimization, such as AWS Compute Optimizer, Azure Advisor, or Google Cloud Recommendation AI. They point out the obvious, such as a 10% utilization database instance or an over-provisioned development environment. Teams may be paying for a supercomputer to run a simple application.

Think of a growing e-commerce company. Every holiday season, they face the same problem a flood of traffic that could crash their site if they're not ready. The traditional way would be to provision a fleet of massive instances and hope you've covered the worst-case scenario. But using rate optimization to predict that surge, they could dynamically adjust resources in real time with just enough power to handle the rush and a lot less money spent on idle servers.

It's a continuous cycle that analyzes, adjusts, validates, and repeats. Maybe your development team is running oversized instances because they've got a habit of over-provisioning. Rate optimization spots that, and the team can start trimming those down by reducing sizes, simplifying configurations, and testing each change systematically to make sure performance doesn't take a hit.

Rate optimization is often the first step. It's like tightening the fuel cap to make sure you're not wasting gas on idle servers or overpaying for reserved instances. But if the engine's still burning oil, you're not fixing the real problem. That's where workload optimization comes in. Rate optimization can uncover hidden value. A data analytics team might be using a $500/hour instance to process datasets when a $50/hour instance, paired with smarter code, does the same job just as fast. You realize you've been paying for power you didn't need. With rate optimization, you can uncover savings and resources to invest in innovation and further optimization.

Workload optimization and rate optimization work effectively when combined together. Workload optimization ensures resources are used efficiently, while rate optimization ensures you pay the least possible for those resources. Together, they are critical levers to achieve cost-effective, scalable, optimized, and sustainable operations.

7.2.7 *Spot Instances (SI)*

Cloud providers have spare compute power lying around, and instead of letting it sit unused, they sell it at a discount through spot instances (SIs) (AWS Spot Instances, 2025) (Azure Spot VMs, 2025). Google too offers "Affordable compute instances suitable for batch jobs and fault-tolerant workloads. Spot VMs offer the same machine types, options, and performance as regular compute instances" (Google Spot VMs, 2025).

But there's a catch. If someone else outbids you, your instance goes to them before you've sealed the deal. It's like winning a bid on a used car, only to find out the seller changed their mind. You get a notice, but you have to make other plans for your daily commute. You can pair this with workloads that can handle a little chaos. Think of a media company that needs to transform video files. The load is not urgent, so they can do this during off-hours. They know their transcoding jobs could pause and resume. But the savings with SIs are enough to fund a new team member. A research lab runs simulations that could restart mid-process, turning a potential disaster into a minor hiccup. Systems that don't panic when the rug gets pulled do best on SIs.

You can't throw spot instances at every problem. They're not for mission-critical apps that can't afford any downtime. They're for the long tail of your operations, such as batch jobs, test or development environments, or data analysis that doesn't need to run 24/7. Enterprise FinOps forces you to think strategically and map your workloads to the right tool. It's clear that you are accepting some risk with SIs by trading stability for savings. That's a tough pill to swallow for some CIOs, but I've seen it work. It's another lever that can work in the right place. You stop treating cloud resources as a utility and can free up budget for other things.

7.2.7.1 Spot Utilization

You're at an exclusive concert, and the tickets are limited. If everyone wants in, prices go up. If no one cares, you might get a front-row seat for a ridiculously low price. That's Spot Utilization in a nutshell. It's the ratio of how many discounted compute resources are being used right now versus how many are sitting idle, waiting for someone to claim them. A 70% utilization means 70% of the available "tickets" are already taken. The higher the number, the harder it is to get a deal with that provider. It's classic supply and demand at work. Cloud providers are always scanning their systems for unused capacity. If utilization drops, maybe because a bunch of companies paused their workloads during a slow afternoon, they'll flood the market with cheap compute power. That's your cue to grab it before someone else does. But if utilization spikes, say, during a holiday sale or a global event, those same resources become scarce, and the price jumps.

Enterprise FinOps is also about the right timing. Take that e-commerce company I mentioned earlier. During the holidays, they need to scale up fast. If they wait until utilization is high, they'll pay a premium for spot instances. But if they bid when utilization is low, maybe late at night or midweek, they can lock-in rock-bottom prices.

You need tools to do this right, such as monitoring systems that can track trends and auto-scaling policies that adjust on the fly. Overall, you need a clear understanding of which of your workloads can afford to pause or restart. It's not right for every workload. With a hybrid cloud model and containers, you can diversify across providers to avoid getting stuck in a single market. You can build a buffer layer of on-demand instances or use RIs to fall back on when spot prices spike. Cloud and virtualization offer you many choices when it comes to workload optimization. You stop being a passive buyer and start being a strategic player. You learn to read the market, understand your workloads, predict utilization patterns, and make decisions that align with your business goals.

7.2.8 *Service Optimization*

Service optimization means that you are selecting cost-effective alternatives to reduce expenses while maintaining or improving service quality. This ideally is done during design time, prior to even a single line of code being written or resources being provisioned. Many cloud and virtualization providers offer open-source equivalents of typical server-grade software. For example, PostgreSQL is an enterprise-grade open-source software available on Microsoft Azure and other platforms, and can be deployed in your on-premises infrastructure as well. I executed a major implementation where we saved millions of dollars in annual costs just by migrating our enterprise real-time data processing platform to PostgreSQL on Azure. Open-source solutions eliminate licensing fees and often provide comparable or superior performance through community-driven innovation. This shift lowers upfront costs and lets you avoid vendor lock-in.

Service optimization can be embedded as an architectural principle and can also be reviewed through governance processes like the Architectural Review Board and other Enterprise FinOps collaborative sessions. This is a prime example of a deeper Enterprise FinOps assessment and analysis that can be conducted even on existing systems to uncover potential savings. Service optimization can also apply to SaaS platforms, infrastructure and monitoring tools, and cloud services. Organizations need to consider trade-offs to ensure that alternatives align with operational needs and long-term strategic goals.

7.2.9 *Reserved Instances*

Reserved Instances (RIs) are a pact with your cloud provider, locking in a fixed rate for a year or three, usually. The concept has trickled down from the leasing industry. It's like signing a lease on a penthouse or a car instead of paying rent-by-the-hour. You commit to a space, and in return, you get a price that's fixed for the duration. It's like getting your own on-premises server, but in the public cloud. See reference 'Reserved Instances 2025.'

On-demand pricing is a gamble. One day, your compute costs are stable. But when you commission those extra machines to deal with the spike in your quarterly reporting period or a holiday rush, the prices can change dramatically. RIs let you plan ahead. But RIs have double edges. They are great when you can predict long-term demand. But if you overbuy, that's like leasing ten penthouses when you only need one. You're just wasting cash. If you underbuy, you're left scrambling and need to resort to more expensive pay-per-use. The sweet spot is finding that balance by matching your workload's rhythm to the right RI type and quantity.

RIs are not the perfect antidote. Your workloads evolve. A server that's busy today might be idle tomorrow. Enterprise FinOps enforces teams to track utilization, performance, tweak configurations, and keep your cloud spending aligned with reality. With techniques like RI reselling, you can even sell RIs that you don't need. I had teams automate this, flagging underused RIs and selling them on a marketplace or through specialized tools to avoid the trap of sunk costs.

With RIs, you are also balancing risk. You're trading the provider's volatility for your own stability. They take on the burden of demand swings while you get a fixed cost. It lets you stop chasing fires and start building something without the risk of your cloud bill shooting up in the middle of a quarter. Keep in mind that RIs are for workloads that hum along predictably. If your business is all spikes and sprints, like a startup launching a viral app, you may need to look for other solutions.

See more details on the RI services available through AWS (Reserved Instances, 2025), similar offerings from Google Committed Use Discounts (Google Reservations, 2025) and Microsoft Azure Reserved VM Instances (Azure Reserved VM instances, 2025).

7.2.9.1 Reselling Reserved Instances

You lock in an RI for a development project that's now in production elsewhere in your infrastructure, or maybe the project was canceled because of changed business requirements. It's like buying an RV for a road trip you never took. It's still there, still costing you, but no longer useful. You can let it sit, or try to repurpose it for some other workload. Now you can also sell that unused capacity.

RI resale lets companies monetize their excess committed cloud capacity. This addresses the risk of over-provisioning when committing to long-term instances. There are dedicated resale platforms as well as cloud cost management providers with integrated resale features. Many cloud providers, such as AWS, offer marketplaces for reselling RIs (AWS EC2 Reserved Instances marketplace, 2025). Specialized Cloud Managed Service Providers (MSPs) also offer RI resales. However, cloud providers are changing the rules when it comes to resale of RIs, so do watch out for what works with your vendor. For example, only Amazon EC2 Standard regional and zonal reserved instances can be sold in the AWS Reserved Instance Marketplace, as of now.

Before AWS changed its terms on RI resales, you had platforms and tools where you could configure your excess RIs, and they would handle the rest. However, since the AWS changes in late 2024, resales need to be done through the AWS marketplace. You can always leverage specialists if your team lacks the in-house know-how or needs a custom plan. That's when Managed Service Providers or consultants step in to align that process with your long-term goals.

7.2.10 Containerization

Your teams are trying to deploy an application, but the dependencies are like mismatched puzzle pieces. It worked in development. But now some pieces work, some don't, and no one's sure why the application is crashing. Containerization changes that. It's like giving your technology stack a company bus to ensure everyone and everything moves together, no matter where you're headed. Containers guarantee your application runs the same way, regardless of where it's deployed.

Some popular tools for containerization are Docker and Kubernetes. Docker packages apps into containers. You can download and run containers in any environment, regardless of operating system or underlying hardware, as long as it supports Docker. Kubernetes acts like a traffic cop. It orchestrates the flow to make sure everything runs smoothly. Unlike virtual machines, which are like entire minicomputers with their own operating systems, containers share the host OS's kernel. It results in smaller image sizes and faster startup times. The system can be scaled to demand without missing a beat.

Let's consider an e-commerce company with a dozen microservices, each handling everything from personalization and inventory to payments. Traditionally, deploying these would mean dedicating servers for each microservice. A release would entail slow deployments, compatibility nightmares, and a system that struggles to keep up during Black Friday sales. Every change would mean a cumbersome testing cycle in the changed microservice and also in the overall system once the system has been deployed to production. With containers, you can package each microservice into a container and orchestrate it using Kubernetes. Now the system is resilient. If one service fails, Kubernetes reroutes traffic. During peak hours, it scales up automatically.

Containerization makes financial sense, too. You can cut down hardware costs and energy bills by sharing resources and reducing the number of servers. Using "just-in-time" lean concepts with dynamic scaling lets you ramp services up or down as needed. The business benefits are clear when you can deliver features to market more quickly with faster deployment cycles and reduced errors. Containers let you build modern systems that are resilient, agile, scalable, and aligned with Enterprise FinOps.

7.2.11 *Multi-tenancy Models*

In multi-tenancy, a single instance of an application, platform, or service and the infrastructure it runs on serves multiple, independent customers, termed as tenants. Each tenant's data, configurations, and usage are isolated and protected from others using a sophisticated combination of techniques such as virtualization, data segmentation, containerization, and robust security controls. The platform manages the shared resources, ensuring that one tenant's activity doesn't interfere with another's. Cloud providers utilize this model for their compute services, and SaaS providers do similarly for their platforms.

Imagine a single multi-rise complex where every apartment is unique inside, but the plumbing, electricity, and security are shared. You share the foundation while keeping everything else strictly private. Think of it as a luxury apartment complex where your neighbors can't see into your living room, even though they're using the same elevator as you. The cloud provider manages the shared resources while ensuring your data doesn't bleed into someone else's. Your providers make you feel like you've got your own dedicated server, even though you're sharing the same underlying hardware.

There are two main flavors of multi-tenancy: Shared Infrastructure and Shared Platform. Shared Infrastructure is the bare-bones version with multiple tenants on the same physical servers. It's the cheapest but also the riskiest if not managed carefully. A spike in one tenant's usage could slow things down for everyone else. Shared Platform, on the other hand, uses virtualization or containers to create software-level isolation. It's like having your own apartment with a private door, even though the building's systems are shared. This balance of cost and performance is why most cloud services lean into Shared Platform.

It's an effective technique for cost control. Instead of each tenant paying for their own server, they split the cost of a shared infrastructure. That's how cloud providers achieve economies of scale by turning a $10,000 server into a $100-per-month shared resource. For example, a SaaS CRM provider might host 100 companies on the same platform, each with their own data and settings. No one knows the others exist, but they're all using the same codebase.

This is perfect for Enterprise FinOps. Also, if you have multiple tenants for your business units, you can track which tenant is using the most resources, allocate charges fairly, and optimize spending. It's like having a dashboard that shows you exactly how much each apartment in the building is using the elevator.

But there is a security risk. A single breach in the building's system could compromise everyone. Regular audits and robust SLAs, firewalls, and security configurations are essential. If you're not monitoring performance, another tenant's workload could slow things down for you. Sharing and shielding are the two opposite ends of your balance. For your organization, embracing it unlocks cost savings and improves resource utilization. It aligns with FinOps principles. Get it right, and you'll feel like you've got the whole building to yourself. Get it wrong, and you'll be stuck sharing a broken elevator with everyone else.

7.2.12 *Capacity Exchange Programs*

Similar to the restrictions on RI resales, cloud providers have been tightening the rules around such transfers. As of June 2025, RIs and SPs may only be used by a single end customer. AWS partners are no longer allowed to buy discounted cloud capacity through these programs and resell or share it across customers. The key point is that AWS instances must be used by the buyer.

Capacity Exchange Programs (CEPs) were like a marketplace, facilitating the temporary borrowing or lending of unused compute capacity between organizations, driven by dynamic demand. On one end, there are the capacity providers. These were customers with excess supply of computing power, or Managed Services Providers who had purchased bulk instances, intending to carve them up across customers at discounted prices. On the other hand, there are the demand providers like startups scaling up or retailers prepping for Black Friday or someone who needed a temporary spike in computing power. The platform acted as the choreographer, ensuring the right resources met the right need at the right time.

While capacity exchange programs are not available at this time, this will continue to be an evolving space as both cloud providers evolve their technologies and MSPs and vendors evolve their services and tools. Continue to stay tuned for features or offerings that further benefit cost and rate optimization.

> The Law of Compounding states that small, consistent actions yield exponentially greater results over time. In Enterprise FinOps, this law reflects on how technical actions such as workload optimization, rightsizing, architectural reviews, or even automated cost tracking act as force multipliers. Just as compound interest amplifies savings over time, incremental technical improvements can result in exponential outcomes. A single 15% efficiency

gain in a critical enterprise system can unlock millions in savings and reduce technical debt over a period of time. The CIO can identify these compounding levers and embed them into the technical fabric of the organization through Enterprise FinOps, ensuring that each small action becomes a catalyst for sustained and exponential impact.

References

Amazon AWS. (2025). *AWS Well-Architected*. Retrieved from https://aws.amazon.com/architecture/well-architected/

AWS EC2 Reserved Instances marketplace. (2025). Retrieved from https://aws.amazon.com/ec2/pricing/reserved-instances/marketplace/

AWS Spot Instances. (2025). Retrieved from https://aws.amazon.com/ec2/spot/

Azure Reserved VM instances. (2025). Retrieved from https://azure.microsoft.com/en-us/pricing/reserved-vm-instances/?msockid=2291cf6773506c4d0c97d93972026d2c

Azure Spot VMs. (2025). Retrieved from https://learn.microsoft.com/en-us/azure/virtual-machines/spot-vms

FinOps Foundation. (2025). *Rate optimization*. Retrieved from The FinOps Framework: https://www.finops.org/framework/capabilities/rate-optimization/

Google Cloud. (2025). *Google cloud well-architected*. Retrieved from https://docs.cloud.google.com/architecture

Google Reservations. (2025). Retrieved from https://docs.cloud.google.com/compute/docs/instances/reservations-view

Google Spot VMs. (2025). Retrieved from https://cloud.google.com/solutions/spot-vms?hl=en

Hawley, Darren; on behalf of The Open Group Internal Architecture Board. (2008). *Case study: The open group architecture principles*. The Open Group. Retrieved from https://pubs.opengroup.org/onlinepubs/7499919799/toc.pdf

Microsoft Azure. (2025). *Well-architected framework*. Retrieved from https://azure.microsoft.com/en-us/solutions/cloud-enablement/well-architected/

Reserved Instances. (2025). Retrieved from https://aws.amazon.com/aws-cost-management/aws-cost-optimization/reserved-instances/

SAP LeanIX. (2025). *Business capability map templates*. Retrieved from https://www.leanix.net/en/wiki/ea/business-capability-map-examples-and-templates

The FinOps Foundation. (2025). *Workload optimization*. Retrieved from https://www.finops.org/framework/capabilities/workload-optimization/

The Open Group. (2025, May). *The TOGAF standard v10*. Retrieved from https://publications.opengroup.org/c220

The Open Group Architecture Forum Business Architecture Work Stream. (2018). *Business capabilities*. The Open Group Series Guide. Retrieved from https://publications.opengroup.org/

VMWare. (2014). *VMWare horizon reference architecture*. Retrieved from https://vmware360.com/files/pdf/products/horizon/VMware-Horizon-6-Reference-Architecture.pdf

Weber, D., & Richards, M. (2025, April). *Build and operate an effective architecture review board*. Retrieved from https://aws.amazon.com/blogs/architecture/build-and-operate-an-effective-architecture-review-board/

Chapter 8

Measuring and Monitoring Success

DOI: 10.4324/9781003682196-12

8.1 Defining KPIs for Financial Optimization

Key Performance Indicators (KPIs) and metrics let you measure your IT environment and services, and manage the progress of technology initiatives to drive demonstrable business value. They are frequently used interchangeably, but there are subtle distinctions between the two, as listed in Table 8.1. It's a difference that profoundly impacts how you assess your IT performance and strategically align your technology investments with overarching business goals. You can harness the power of both metrics and KPIs to transform your IT organization into a truly strategic driver of success.

Table 8.1 Key differences between metrics and KPIs

Feature	*Metrics*	*KPIs*
Definition	Raw data measurement	Specific, targeted measurements aligned with business context.
Purpose	Record information	Track progress toward goals.
Focus	What *is* happening	What *should* be happening.
Number	Often many	Typically, a few (5–10).
Example	Website traffic Number of product views Number of abandoned carts	Conversion rate (percentage of visitors who make a purchase) may indicate if your marketing efforts and website design are effective, while Average order value lets you know if upsell campaigns are working and customers are buying more per transaction.

8.1.1 *Metrics*

A metric is simply raw data. It's a simple measurement of some aspect of your business, process, talent, or performance. Examples could be website traffic, measured by the sheer number of visitors, offering an idea of online engagement, or sales revenue as a direct indication of commercial activity. Customer satisfaction scores are an indicator of what your customers feel about the overall experience and quality of your services. System uptimes, average resolution times, or the number of tickets point toward operational stability and dependability. These metrics, on their own, merely present a quantitative observation that you can further track as highs or lows, increases or decreases as compared to previous values. They give you a sense of how you are progressing and let you establish baselines and targets.

But you need to tie them with a strategic business context in order to determine the direction and priority of your initiatives, to understand when you need to step in with an intervention, or when to let things run as usual. A high number of support tickets could mean a transformation go-live or a marketing campaign gone wrong. It could indicate a failing system. Metrics alone may not let you understand if the support team is effectively addressing customer needs, resolving issues efficiently, or if the transformation requires more user training.

8.1.2 *Key Performance Indicators (KPIs)*

This is where Key Performance Indicators (KPIs) step in. KPIs are specifically chosen metrics or aggregated combinations that directly align with and measure progress toward achieving your most important business goals. The difference between metrics and KPIs is like the difference between a map and a compass. Metrics show you where you are. KPIs tell you if you're heading the right way. If your goal is to boost customer loyalty, your KPIs might be Net Promoter Score, average retention, churn rate, or average lifetime value.

KPIs don't work unless you pick them carefully. I've seen IT teams drown in 30 KPIs, each one vying for attention. It's chaotic and confusing. Limit yourself to 5–10 at the top level. Pick the ones that matter. If your goal is faster product launches, track deployment time, defect rates, and stakeholder feedback. If deployment time is rising, it's a signal that your automation tools are outdated or your team is overworked. KPIs force you to dig deeper. You need to ask yourself what's the one thing you need to measure to know if you're doing things right in IT, and then build a KPI around that. Metrics will naturally follow.

Also, refer to the article at ITChronicles on "Metrics vs KPIs" (Horowitz, 2022).

8.1.3 Backward vs Forward-Looking KPIs

Backward-looking KPIs are like a rearview mirror. They show you where you've been, but they don't tell you how to get where you're going. It's a lagging indicator. Quarterly sales revenue is a snapshot of what happened last quarter, but it doesn't explain why customers left or why a product launch failed. Someone needs to connect the dots. But those numbers can be powerful if you use them right. We once tracked customer churn rate over six months and found a 12% spike after a major product update. We dug into the root cause and discovered a flaw in the customer onboarding process. Backward-looking KPIs let you dig into the past to fix the future. They're the breadcrumbs that lead you to the problem.

Table 8.2 Backward vs forward-looking KPIs

Feature	*Backward-looking KPIs*	*Forward-looking KPIs*
Data source	Past performance	Current data and trends
Focus	What *has* happened (lagging)	What *will* happen (leading)
Purpose	Analyze and understand	Predict and plan
Action	Reactive (respond)	Proactive (prevent, guide)

Then there's the other side of the coin. Forward-looking KPIs tell you where you're headed. That's a leading indicator. If you're planning a new marketing campaign, a predicted lead conversion rate can be derived from historical data and current market trends. This gives you a roadmap to decide how much to spend on ads and which channels to prioritize. Website traffic forecasts can anticipate seasonal spikes and allocate resources before the rush hits, triggering actions to scale servers in time.

The real synergy happens when you blend both. Backward-looking KPIs give you the history, while forward-looking ones show you the path. Inventory turnover projections can help you cut excess stock, while customer lifetime value forecasts guide retention strategies. A KPI is a decision. If you're tracking the wrong thing, you're making the wrong choices. Use both to create a feedback loop. Let the past guide you, but let the future drive you. Table 8.2 lists down key differences between backward-looking and forward-looking KPIs.

The article "KPIs: What Are Key Performance Indicators?" has more information on leading vs. lagging indicators (Twin, 2025).

8.1.4 Calculating Return on Investment (ROI)

ROI helps to quantify the value of IT investments in financial terms. It is a key KPI that IT can use to prioritize initiatives that align with strategic goals and demonstrate business impact. A positive ROI proves that your IT spend matters. Cost savings are obvious calculations. If automation cuts order processing time by 20%, that's a clear win. But what about revenue growth from a new CRM system? What if you were able to track how many more deals close because sales teams have better data? Indirect non-financial metrics like productivity gains also need to be quantified and included in the ROI calculation. Measure how much faster a team finishes tasks after adopting a new platform. Measure the increase in NPS scores from your IT upgrades. Measure how many security breaches your firewall blocked last quarter, and what was the cost avoidance from not having to respond to potential breaches. Refer to Figure 8.1 and the example

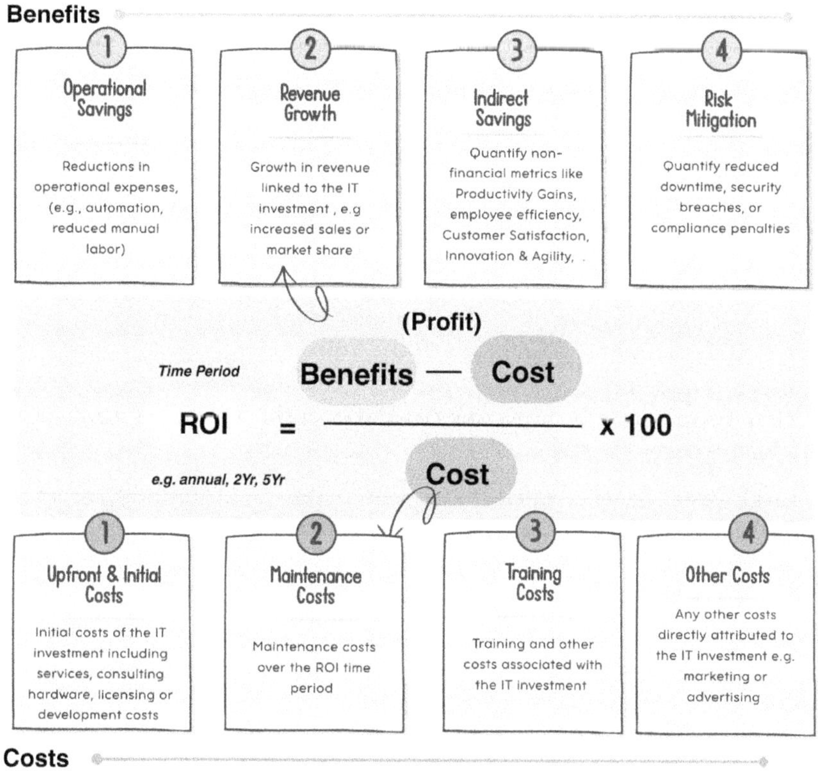

Figure 8.1 Calculation of ROI with both tangible and intangible business benefits

calculation for a simplified and practical view of the process to calculate ROI across both tangible and intangible business benefits.

Payback periods are a part of the business case, too. A cloud migration that costs $2 million could pay for itself in 24 months. That's a talking point at the next executive meeting. It is important to put the ROI and payback period in the context of the time horizon. When you have multiple IT investments competing for priority, all other things being equal, one with a faster payback would tend to have a higher priority. Compare your IT team's performance to industry averages. Model what happens if a project fails and build a plan to avoid that. Align everything to business goals. If your company's priority is customer retention, your ROI metrics should reflect that.

Joe Knight has published an excellent guide on measuring ROI, available through HBR Tools (Knight, 2015).

8.1.5 Defining and Measuring ROI for IT Projects

EXAMPLE:

- Total investment Cost: $50,000
- Annual Benefits: $120,000 (e.g., reduced downtime, productivity gains) or $20K/month
- Net Profit: $120,000 – $50,000 = $70,000
- ROI: ($70,000 / $50,000) × 100 = 140%

Time Horizon: ROI can be calculated over a short-term (~1 year) or a long-term (~5 years)

Break-Even: Benefits equal investment at this point, resulting in an ROI of 0%. If benefits continue to accrue over the time horizon, ROI will be positive. Hundred percent ROI is when the benefits are 2X the investment.

Payback period: Time required for the investment to recoup its cost through savings or gains, i.e., reach 0% ROI, here <2.5 months to reach $50K in savings at $20K/month

Net Present Value (NPV): Discounts future cash flows to evaluate long-term profitability

ROI opens deeper conversations with the business. If your business leader peers ask you why you are spending $50k on a new analytics tool, one way to respond would be to extol far and wide about the features and potential benefits of the tool. Or you could pull out the math. One hundred twenty thousand dollars in annual projected benefits from productivity gains and operational cost savings from phasing out the older system that no one liked, and not renewing the license for that. Minus the $50k cost gives you $70k net profit. Calculate the ROI, and you get 140% over just a year. In fact, the tool pays off its investment with the break-even in less than three months after it goes live.

ROI isn't always about cash. What if the tool reduces errors by 40%? That's a cost savings you can't quantify in a spreadsheet. Or maybe it cuts training time in half, freeing up your team to focus on innovation. The difficult part is quantifying non-financial metrics like these and include

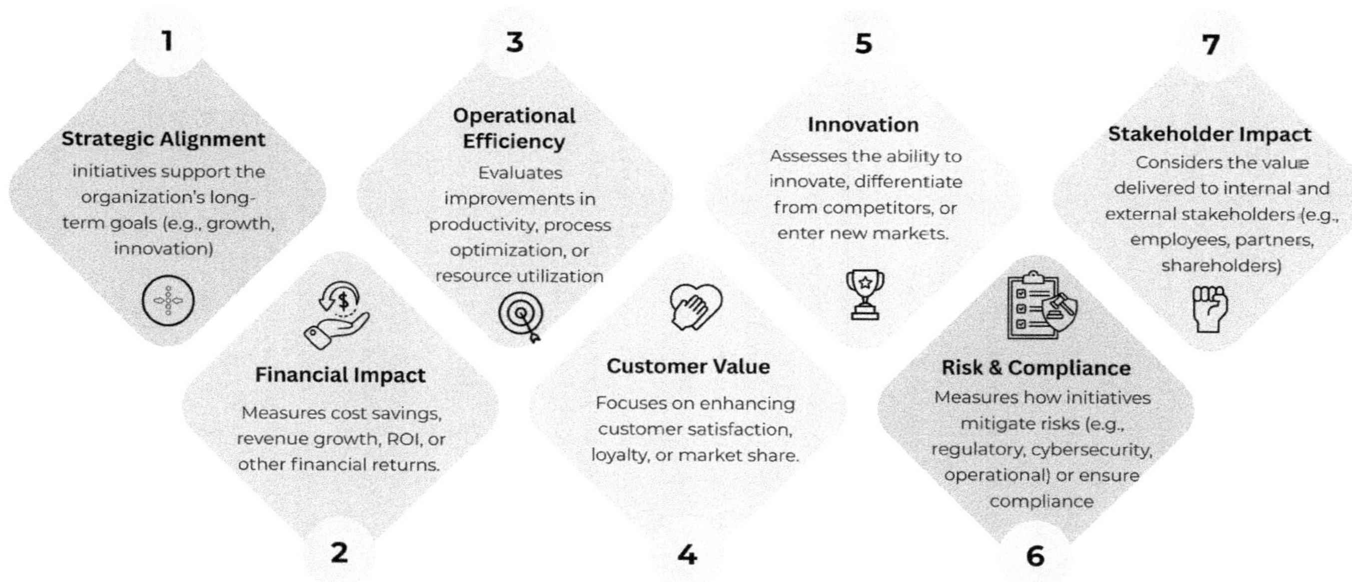

Figure 8.2 Dimensions of the business value framework

these in the ROI calculation. The challenge is to attribute business gains in intangible areas to a specific IT investment, when there are so many other factors at play in the enterprise.

A five-year payback period may feel long, but if that tool is in alignment with your long-term strategy, and it prevents a $1 million security breach down the line, the math changes. Don't let ROI discussions get stuck on short-term wins, only to miss the long-term value. A tool that improves customer satisfaction by 10% might not show up in the ROI formula, but it could boost retention rates. The best ROI calculations mix cold, hard facts with the intangible stuff that keeps your business moving forward.

8.1.6 The Business Value Framework

You may already have an IT strategy that is firmly aligned with your business strategy. The *Business Value Framework (BVF)* is a conceptual model, illustrated in Figure 8.2, to evaluate how business and IT investments contribute to organizational goals and outcomes. It helps organizations align strategic objectives with operational initiatives and measure the impact of investments. You can use the BVF to prioritize projects that deliver the most significant returns and to determine the right KPIs and metrics that work for your organization. The framework typically includes the following seven dimensions to assess value.

1. **Strategic Alignment** ensures that your IT initiatives support the organization's long-term goals such as growth, innovation, sustainability, or stakeholder value. KPIs here would focus on measuring alignment with corporate strategy and strategic objectives delivered through IT.
2. **Financial Impact** is very number-centric. It measures cost savings, revenue growth, ROI, and other financial returns across both tangible and direct contributions, and also quantifies intangible, non-financial value from efficiency, productivity, and customer satisfaction. KPIs would be ROI, NPV, cost savings, revenue increase, and payback period.
3. **Operational Efficiency** is a foundational IT role. This dimension measures improvements in productivity, process optimization, or resource utilization. Typical metrics are uptime, system reliability, error reduction, cost per unit, IT cost by revenue, and IT cost per user. You could bundle metrics into KPIs such as a weighted SLA for uptime across all business systems supported by IT.

4. **Customer Value** enhances customer satisfaction, loyalty, or market share. KPIs commonly used to measure customer value are Net Promoter Score (NPS), customer retention, customer lifetime value (CLV), and customer experience score.
5. **Innovation** illustrates your ability to create new value, innovate, differentiate from competitors, or enter new markets. It can be measured through metrics such as the number of patents, product launches, business value delivered and innovation index.
6. **Risk Reduction and Compliance** is a measure of how initiatives mitigate regulatory, cybersecurity, operational, or geo-dimensional risks and ensure compliance. Typical metrics would be a Risk Score, risk reduction percentage, compliance rate, and incident reduction.
7. **Stakeholder Impact** reflects the value delivered to internal and external stakeholders such as your employees, partners, customers, and shareholders. KPIs would be employee satisfaction, partner satisfaction, shareholder returns, and customer satisfaction.

The BVF can help you prioritize IT projects. You can assign weightages to different dimensions or the KPIs within them and use them to calculate a prioritization score. The BVF quantifies the benefits of investments with a 360-degree view across financial, operational, and strategic outcomes. Using the BVF ensures that IT investments are aligned with organizational goals and stakeholder needs. You can use it to communicate value to your stakeholders, whether your own IT teams, your peers in the executive leadership team, or board members and investors. It helps you translate technical or operational achievements into business terms for non-technical stakeholders. It enhances your decision-making by giving you a structured approach to evaluate trade-offs. You can develop your own model based on this conceptual BVF model, align to something that's already adopted by the larger enterprise, or you can adapt models offered by consulting companies and industry groups.

Industry groups and consulting companies have developed several models as shown in Figure 8.3 that can give you an established method to realize BVF rather than developing your own model. This section highlights three of these models that I feel are well-suited for IT organizations to implement their own BVF. You can adopt one of these as a foundation and further customize it to your own requirements, or customize the conceptual BVF model directly.

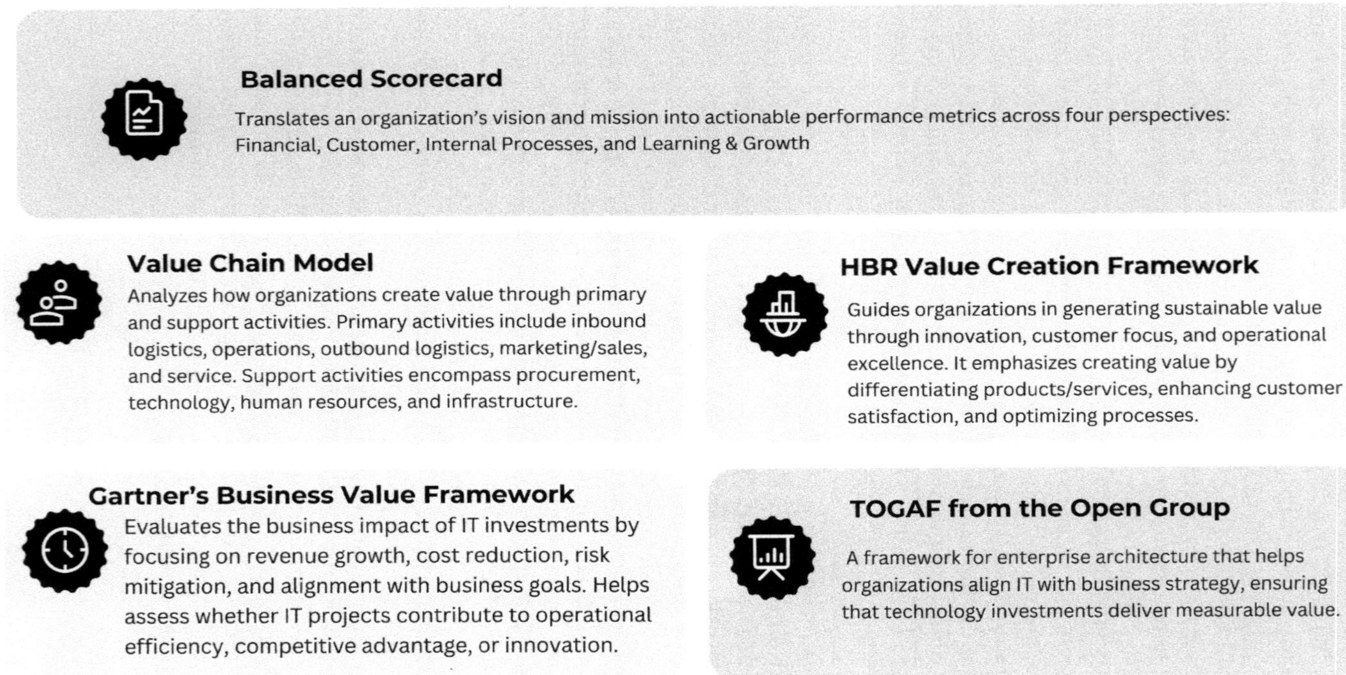

Figure 8.3 Industry frameworks for business value

- The Balanced Scorecard (BSC) was developed by Robert Kaplan and David Norton (Kaplan & Norton, 1996). It has four perspectives: Financial, Customer, Internal Processes, and Learning and Growth. These perspectives translate the organization's vision and mission into actionable performance metrics. The Financial perspective looks at profitability and cost management. The Customer perspective focuses on satisfaction and loyalty. Internal Processes address operational efficiency and innovation, and the Learning and Growth perspective puts a focus on the human angle through employee development, and also knowledge retention and management. Organizations that want to balance short-term financial goals with long-term strategic objectives would be interested in BSC.
- The Value Chain Model was introduced by management consultant Michael Porter in his book *Competitive Advantage* (Porter, 1998). This model looks at value creation through a two-dimensional model of primary and support activities. In the vertical set are primary activities that directly create value for the company, such as inbound logistics, operations, outbound logistics, marketing/sales, and service. The horizontal tier has support activities for each of the primary functions, such as procurement, technology, human resources, and infrastructure. The model lets you identify sources of competitive advantage by evaluating factors such as cost leadership and differentiation in each activity. Use it for strategic analysis and competitive positioning as well as cost optimization. The process lets you identify value-adding activities. You can locate areas for improvement in each of the primary activities, such as reducing waste or enhancing customer experience. The model is best suited for businesses aiming to optimize internal processes and gain a competitive edge through strategic resource allocation. This is well-suited for IT organizations for enterprises in the manufacturing sector.
- Gartner's Business Value model (Smith & Proctor, 2013) emphasizes a very strong IT perspective. It looks at the business impact of IT investments through factors such as revenue growth, cost reduction, risk mitigation, and alignment with business goals. The framework is ideal for IT governance as well as ROI analysis. Use the framework to assess whether IT projects are adding value, whether it's operational efficiency, competitive advantage, innovation, or a combination of these. The model gives you several metrics for evaluating IT investments. It is ideal for enterprises prioritizing technology-driven value creation. You may need to enhance it further to support cross-functional initiatives.

Table 8.3 provides a comparison of some of these industry BVF models. Our goal is to leverage BVF to derive KPIs and metrics for the IT organization. It‘s likely that your enterprise has already adopted a framework such

Table 8.3 Comparison of popular industry business value framework models

Framework	*Purpose*	*Key components*	*Focus areas*	*Advantages*
Balanced Scorecard	Align business activities with strategic goals and measure performance.	Four perspectives: financial, customer, internal processes, learning and growth.	Strategic alignment, performance measurement, and long-term goals.	Holistic view of organizational performance; integrates financial and non-financial metrics.
Value Chain Model	Analyze internal activities to identify sources of competitive advantage.	Primary activities (inbound logistics, operations, outbound logistics, marketing, sales, service) and support activities (procurement, technology, HR, infrastructure).	Operational efficiency, cost leadership, differentiation.	Helps identify value-adding activities; useful for operational improvements.
Gartner's Business Value Framework	Evaluate the business impact of IT investments.	Revenue growth, cost reduction, risk mitigation, and alignment with business goals.	IT governance, value measurement, and alignment of IT with business outcomes.	Tailored for IT; provides clear metrics for evaluating technology investments.

as Balanced Scorecard for its overall business strategy. If so, it would make sense to align your framework to the same. You can also consider the Gartner BVF framework, as it is very IT-centric and supported by detailed guidance from Gartner on how to implement it.

8.1.7 Typical IT KPIs and Metrics at the CIO Level

We'll use the seven dimensions outlined in our conceptual BVF framework to arrive at typical IT KPIs and metrics. Remember, these are just samplers. Please customize them as per your own distinct and unique perspectives and to keep KPIs at the CIO level to the top five or ten. The next challenge is to ensure that KPIs and metrics at lower levels flow into the top-level KPIs. When you cascade KPIs from the CIO down to individual teams, you're asking everyone to speak the same language.

1. Strategic Alignment

Weighted Uptime is the average and aggregated uptime of all critical systems. Assign weights based on their impact on business operations. This KPI shows how IT supports mission-critical systems. You could extend this similarly to other critical SLAs.

- Total IT Spend vs. Business Value Delivered compares overall IT investments and their impact on business metrics like revenue and cost savings in business units. It demonstrates the ROI across all IT initiatives and activities, but it could take significant efforts to track.
- IT Debt Score summarizes technology debt. This KPI highlights risks such as legacy and out-of-support systems that may hinder long-term goals for innovation and operational agility.
- IT Contribution to Strategic Goals measures IT support for business objectives, such as revenue growth. It can also apply to business events such as opening a new factory or the launch of a new product. This is useful in validating IT's role in achieving strategic milestones.

2. Financial Impact

IT Cost as a Percentage of Revenue measures IT spending relative to total company revenue. This tracks IT's financial burden on the organization and can be benchmarked with organizations of similar size and in the same industry sector.

- IT Capex-Opex ratio balances capital investments such as hardware and datacenters with operational expenses. This is a great KPI to track for sustainable IT financial planning.
- Return on Investment (ROI) measures the return from IT projects. This can be used to justify IT spending to stakeholders and seek support for further investments.

- IT Spend Forecast Accuracy measures how well IT budgets predict actual costs. This improves financial planning, keeps your team on budget, and reduces overspending.
- IT Cost Savings from Optimization tracks savings from all cost optimization activities. This can be a guide for cost-efficiency improvements.
- IT Spend per User measures IT costs per employee. It can identify disparity in IT spend across business units.

3. Operational Efficiency

System Uptime and Availability (Weighted) monitors system reliability, weighted by impact on business. This metric ensures critical systems remain operational and is critical to ensure trust in IT services.

- Business Process Improvement (BPI) measures efficiency gains from process optimization. It tracks progress in reducing operational waste.
- IT Asset Utilization Rate tracks how effectively hardware, software, or cloud resources are used and ensures optimal use of IT infrastructure.
- Automation Rate measures the proportion of workflows automated. This is a powerful KPI if you want to reduce manual effort.
- System Performance Metrics (e.g., server or API response times) measure technical performance and ensure systems meet performance expectations.
- Mean Time to Resolve (MTTR) measures incident resolution speed. It reduces downtime and operational disruptions. It also reflects the stability of systems.

4. Customer Value

Net Promoter Score (NPS) for IT Services tracks customer sentiment toward IT services.

You can also use similar scores for individual IT services like software installs, end-user services, CRM, or help desk. This ensures IT meets end-user needs.

- Revenue Impact of IT Initiatives links IT projects to customer-facing outcomes, such as an e-commerce platform driving sales. It demonstrates IT's role in revenue generation.
- Customer Retention Rate Due to IT Services tracks how IT impacts customer loyalty. It validates IT's contribution to customer retention.
- Customer Support Ticket Resolution Rate measures the percentage of tickets resolved within SLAs. It ensures the timely resolution of customer issues.

5. Innovation
Innovation Velocity measures the speed of feature rollout. It tracks the pace of product development.

- The number of Completed Innovation Projects tracks the quantity of new initiatives delivered. It measures innovation output and scalability.
- Percentage of Features Delivered on Time measures adherence to project timelines.
- IT R&D Investment as a Percentage of Revenue measures commitment to innovation and tracks long-term IT investment in research and development.

6. Risk Reduction and Compliance
IT Security Incident Frequency and Impact tracks the frequency and financial/reputational impact of security breaches. It boosts proactive risk management.

- Vendor Performance Score ensures contracts align with compliance standards and vendors are delivering as expected. It mitigates risks from third-party dependencies.
- Compliance Audit Pass Rate measures adherence to regulatory standards. It ensures legal and regulatory compliance.
- Data Breach Response Time tracks the speed of incident resolution. It minimizes damage from security incidents.
- Number of Compliance Violations is a standard metric that tracks deviations from regulatory requirements. It identifies gaps in compliance frameworks.
- Percentage of Systems with Up-to-Date Patches measures cybersecurity hygiene. It reduces vulnerabilities in the IT infrastructure.

7. Stakeholder Impact
Employee IT Support Satisfaction measures satisfaction with internal IT services. It improves employee morale and productivity.

- The number of Stakeholder Complaints Related to IT measures dissatisfaction with IT services. It identifies pain points in stakeholder engagement.
  - Employee Productivity Index quantifies improvements in productivity due to IT tools. It demonstrates IT's contribution to operational efficiency.

8.1.8 Enterprise FinOps KPIs

We'll build Enterprise FinOps KPIs that are aligned with the top-level CIO metrics and KPIs provided in the earlier section. This ensures that you can measure the effectiveness of Enterprise FinOps as you continue to march toward your goal of reducing IT costs, optimizing the IT environment, improving business alignment for IT initiatives, providing visibility to accurate cost data, reducing technology debt, and developing a mindset of financial accountability.

Consider the following KPIs specifically to guide your Enterprise FinOps progress.

1. **Percentage of IT Spend Aligned with Strategic Business Goals**
   This measures how well IT investments align with organizational priorities and ensures resources are directed toward initiatives that drive business value. The target is 100%.

$$\frac{\text{IT Spend Aligned with Strategic Goals}}{\text{Total IT Spend}} \times 100$$

2. **Return on IT Investment (ROI) for Strategic Initiatives**
   This evaluates the financial impact of IT investments and validates that IT spending delivers measurable business value.

$$\frac{\text{Net Business Value Generated by IT Initiative} - \text{Cost of Initiative}}{\text{Cost of Initiative}} \times 100$$

3. **Total IT Spend Optimization Rate**
   This measures *progress in cost optimization*. It looks at the percentage of IT spend (hardware, software, cloud, services) that has been reduced or optimized. This can be a guide for cost-efficiency improvements. E.g., \$20 million saved on a \$500 million baseline budget would be 4%. Target 20% in the first two years of an Enterprise FinOps program launch.

$$\frac{\text{Reduction in IT Spend (vs. baseline)}}{\text{Original IT Spend}} \times 100$$

4. **Cost per Unit of Service (e.g., per User, per Transaction, per GB of Storage)**
   This measures efficiency in delivering IT services and highlights areas where costs can be optimized without sacrificing service quality.

$$\frac{\text{Total IT Spend}}{\text{Units of Service Delivered}}$$

5. **Cost per User of Service (e.g., IT Helpdesk Cost per User, Total CRM Cost per User)**
   This measures efficiency in delivering IT business services and highlights areas where costs can be optimized without sacrificing service quality. This is useful to drive activities such as renewals, software harvesting, and service optimization. However, balance this appropriately based on upgrades and new features delivered by the service.

$$\frac{\text{Total IT Spend}}{\text{Number of Users}}$$

6. **Percentage of IT Spend with Accurate Cost Allocation**
   This ensures transparency and traceability of IT costs and enables informed decision-making and accountability. It boosts the effort to gain real-time cost visibility through tools and tagging.

$$\frac{\text{IT Spend with Accurate Cost Tags}}{\text{Total IT Spend}} \times 100$$

7. **Percentage of Users with FinOps Awareness**
   This encourages a cost-conscious mindset and promotes accountability through training and collaboration.

$$\frac{\text{IT Users Trained on FinOps Principles}}{\text{Total IT Users}} \times 100$$

8. **Technology Debt Reduction Rate (Year-over-Year)**
   This measures progress in eliminating outdated or inefficient IT infrastructure. It reduces long-term costs and improves system performance. This assumes you have adopted a metric such as the one outlined in the chapter on "Technology Debt Reduction" to calculate a Technology Debt Score.

$$\frac{\text{Technology Debt Resolved}}{\text{Initial Technology Debt}} \times 100$$

Tracking these KPIs can provide a *comprehensive view of Enterprise FinOps maturity*, enabling organizations to balance cost control, cultural awareness, technology debt reduction, innovation, and business alignment.

The FinOps Foundation publishes a comprehensive list of KPIs as part of the FinOps framework (FinOps KPIs, 2025).

8.1.9 *IT Value Delivered (IVD) – A Single KPI for Enterprise FinOps*

If you needed just one KPI to measure your Enterprise FinOps program, you could use IT Value Delivered (IVD). I've shown here how you can calculate this. IVD is a composite metric that bundles cost savings, operational efficiency, and strategic impact into one number. Think of it as a dashboard that tells a story, shifting the focus from merely costs to business value instead. Instead of saying that you saved $1.4 million on cloud cost optimization, you can say that the FinOps program delivered $3.5 million in total value this quarter, with $1.4 million from cost optimization, $1.05 million from faster project delivery, and $1.05 million from boosting revenue through digital tools. It's the kind of conversation that demonstrates the value of IT.

$$IVD = (Cost\,Savings \times 0.4) + (Efficiency\,Gains \times 0.3) + (Strategic\,Value \times 0.3)$$

Note – Adjust the weightages as needed.

- Cost optimization: This isn't simply slashing budgets. It's strategic savings that can be applied elsewhere where things are desperately needed. Did you negotiate better SaaS rates? Cut cloud waste by 20%? Renegotiate a licensing deal? Every dollar saved here is a win.
- Operational efficiency gains: If your team reduced deployment time by 30%, or cut manual processes by automating 50% of tasks, you are creating a lasting gain for your users. Track metrics like time to market, service-level improvements, or reduced downtime.
- Strategic value realization: Use measures like ROI to determine how your FinOps initiatives impacted revenue and other direct business metrics through IT investments in transformation and innovation. Did a new analytics platform unlock a 15% increase in customer retention? Did cloud migration free up resources for a new project?

Table 8.4 lists down a few practical examples of the components to measure IT value delivered. Adjust the weights (here, 40-30-30) as needed. If your company is pivoting toward AI, maybe strategic value gets a bigger cut. If cost discipline is the new priority, adjust the formula accordingly. IVD adapts to your needs. Start with a baseline. Before launching your FinOps program, document where you are. What's your current cost structure? How long does it take to deliver a project? What's your maturity

Table 8.4 Components of the IT value delivered KPI

Component	*Sub-component*	*Method*	*Metrics*
Cost optimization	Cloud cost reduction	Utilize cloud provider cost management tools (e.g., AWS Cost Explorer).	Track changes in cloud spending compared to a baseline period. Normalize by usage (e.g., / CPU hour, /GB storage).
	License optimization	Use license management tools to identify underutilized or redundant licenses.	Track reduction in license spends due to reclamation, downgrades, or consolidation.
	Hardware optimization	Conduct hardware audits and decommission unused servers and devices.	Track reduction in hardware spends.
Efficiency gains	Reduced project delivery time	Track project timelines from initiation to completion.	Calculate the percentage reduction in project delivery time.
	Increased service uptime	Use service monitoring tools to track service uptime.	Calculate the percentage increase in service uptime.
	Reduced incident resolution time	Track incident resolution times using ITSM tools.	Calculate the percentage reduction in incident resolution time.
	Improved throughput	Quantify improvements in processing speed or volume.	No specific metric provided.
Strategic value realization	Revenue attributed to IT initiatives	ROI calculations	Quantify the increase in revenue directly attributable to IT initiatives.
	Market share growth	Analyze market share data before and after IT-enabled product/service launch.	Track percentage change in market share.
	Successful digital transformation outcomes	Define metrics aligned to transformation goals.	No specific metric provided.

score? Monitor progress regularly, ideally quarterly or annually. Share IVD metrics with your teams and executive stakeholders. If strategic value is lagging, dig into why. Reflect, adjust, refine, and repeat.

8.2 Continuous Monitoring and Analysis

With traditional reporting, you're reacting to problems that already happened. Real-time analytics lets you stay ahead of the curve. It lets you spot trends as they form, predict where costs might spiral, and adjust before it's too late.

8.2.1 *Using Analytics to Drive Informed Decisions*

Data can tell a compelling story. Let's use a *layered analytical* approach to make this even better, as illustrated in Figure 8.4. Table 8.5 provides a high-level comparison of such analytical techniques and their implications on IT spend.

Eric Siegel, in his 2013 book *Predictive Analytics - The Power to Predict Who Will Click, Buy, Lie or Die*, offered an insightful journey into how it drives millions of decisions (Siegel, 2013). Also see the article "Predictive vs Prescriptive Analytics" (Tableau, 2024).

We'll look at other tools and techniques that extend this layered approach, as shown in Figure 8.5. Anomaly detection is like having a watchdog for your spending. It spots that $10,000 charge you didn't notice because it's buried in a 500-page invoice. Trend analysis helps you see the big picture. Maybe your storage costs are rising because of seasonal traffic, and it tells you there is an opportunity to optimize. Segmentation

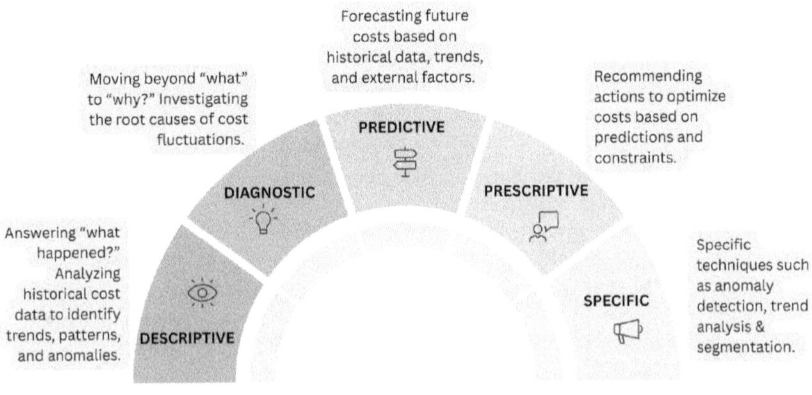

Figure 8.4 A layered analytical approach for Enterprise FinOps

Table 8.5 Comparison of analytical techniques

Analytic approach	*Description*	*Typical questions*
Descriptive analytics	This is the "what happened?" phase. You're looking at historical cost data, spotting trends. While you're seeing the numbers, you're trying to detect and understand the patterns.	"Why did cloud costs spike last quarter?"
Diagnostic analytics	This is the "why?" part. We start connecting dots and uncovering root causes.	Why did that spike happen? Was it a one-off event, or is it a recurring issue? Did your team forget to turn off a massively configured test or development environment after the project went live three months ago? Did your contract include a tiered clause that suddenly increased your rates?
Predictive analytics	"What-if," predicting what happens in the future. You can forecast spend based on current trends and historical data. You can move from mere cost management to strategic foresight.	Are we expecting a 15% spike in the next month as well? How can we adjust?
Prescriptive analytics	Going from "what if" to "what's next." It doesn't just tell you where you are headed but also how to get there. There are both manual (analyst and expert -driven) as well as tool-driven (e.g., AIOps) approaches for this. Analytics becomes a decision-making engine, not just a reporting tool.	"Shift to a reserved instance model," "automate resource scaling to prevent overprovisioning."

lets you slice and dice your cost data by different parts of your portfolio. Maybe your legacy systems are eating up 40% of your budget, while your new AI tools are barely sipping into it. Correlation analysis digs into why that cost exists. Did a recent merger cause a 25% increase in SaaS licenses? Or is your security tool flagging more threats because of a new compliance standard? This is where analytics starts to influence strategy.

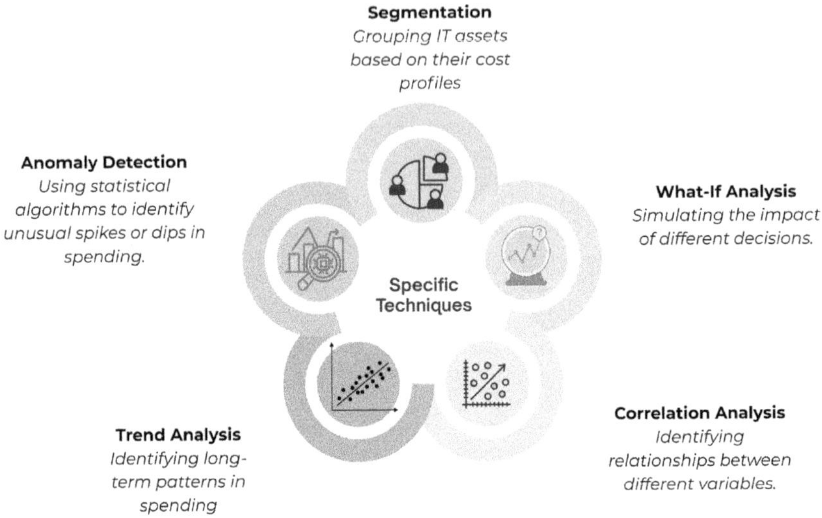

Figure 8.5 Specific analytic techniques for Enterprise FinOps

But data doesn't mean much if it's inaccurate and you can't trust it. You've got to clean it, transform it, and make sure it's consistent. Without data quality, your insights are only guesses. Once you've got clean data, it's time to visualize it. Charts, graphs, and dashboards are the language your stakeholders understand. Layering cost optimization information with business metrics demonstrates the value of your Enterprise FinOps program. Insights are only as good as the decisions they drive. If your analytics say, "We can cut costs by 20% by right-sizing," your teams need to plan to make that happen. A successful FinOps program is built on continuous refinement. You have to keep evolving, adapting, learning, and acting on insights. Tools like cost analytics software, FinOps platforms, and business intelligence platforms are your allies in turning data into a strategic asset.

Predictive analytics feeds off real-time alerts. Tools can flag anomalies before they become disasters. If a specific application is consistently maxing out its CPU resources, instead of waiting for a monthly report to show a 30% overspend, you get a real-time alert. Your team can scale the app, tweak the code, or reallocate resources before the bill hits. From cost control, you are going to cost intelligence.

Real-time data lets you track exactly how much each asset is consuming, down to the last CPU cycle and the last gigabyte of storage. That granularity means you can allocate costs with surgical accuracy. Developers need to see the cost impact of their code changes in real time. If a new feature is eating up 20% more compute resources than expected, they see it immediately.

They can optimize before it becomes a problem and accelerate development cycles while eliminating unnecessary spending at the source.

8.2.2 *Using Historical Trends to Inform Future Strategies*

The best FinOps strategies look at today's numbers but also dig into the past to uncover patterns. Many businesses experience predictable spikes in demand during certain times of the year. Black Friday is a shopping mega-event. It's also a predictable storm that hits your servers every year. You can time your provisioning to proactively scale resources to meet peak demand, avoiding over-provisioning and wasted costs through the rest of the year. People often treat daily or weekly usage like noise. But if it's not random, then there's an underlying cause. Analyzing when specific applications or services are most heavily used can inform decisions about resource allocation and scheduling. If you notice your analytics dashboard spiking every Monday morning at 9 a.m., it could be that your user base is concentrated in a region that starts work early.

Gradual increases or decreases in usage over time can be a clue. It highlights areas where you need to investigate and potentially adjust your strategies. A slow creep in database queries? That's not a problem yet. But if you spot this as a consistent increase, you know this will cause a 40% increase in costs next year unless you investigate and fix it now.

Predictive modeling goes beyond simple tracking. Your server and application logs and billing data contain a mine of information collected over months and years. Time Series Analysis looks up historical data points collected over time to forecast future values and anticipate future costs. Regression models let you detect links between seemingly disparate factors. You can correlate variables and see the invisible threads connecting application usage to infrastructure costs or other events. You can train ML models to automate predictive analysis and continuously improve forecasting accuracy. This technique can be of immense use in capacity planning, avoiding both over-provisioning (wasted costs) and under-provisioning (performance issues), or vendor negotiations to arrive at the optimum renewal numbers.

8.2.3 *A Centralized Enterprise FinOps System*

If you're trying to run an Enterprise FinOps program without a centralized system, you're flying blind. It's going to take your team a lot of manual effort and heavy lifting to put the complete picture together. You've got data everywhere, from cloud costs, on-premises expenses, SaaS subscriptions, call center charges, service contracts, the list goes on. But it's all over the place, and no one's looking at the same numbers. You can't optimize what you can't see.

If you can get cost and spend information from all your IT environments feeding into one platform, you get a single source of truth. Once you have a handle on collecting data, it's time to make it actionable. A centralized system gives you the power to drill down into spending by project, team, or even individual user. You can trace costs back to a specific application or team. You can adjust budgets before it becomes a problem. Real-time dashboards give you visibility into the future, letting you spot issues before they blow up. Chargeback and showback mechanisms become a click of a button rather than a complicated exercise in Excel. Your business gets the transparency and visibility that it has long desired, and you can make sure that business units fairly pay for what they use rather than peanut-butter spreading costs due to lack of data. You create accountability and smarter spending habits.

Manual data collection is a time sink. A centralized system, integration with source systems, and automation take that burden off your team, freeing them up to focus on what matters. You can start with the right platform that integrates seamlessly with your IT environments. You also need robust governance policies to keep data consistent and a change management plan to drive adoption.

8.2.4 *Integrated Tools for FinOps*

Building a centralized FinOps system will take a conscious effort. There are many tools in the market today, but your IT environment is unique. Any platform will inevitably need integration and some customization. Native cloud tools are good for starters, but if you have a multi-cloud strategy, the billing data is going to be quite different for each provider. You need a layered strategy.

At the core, you need a dedicated FinOps platform, something like CloudHealth by VMware, Flexera One, Apptio Cloudability, or one of the other tools in the marketplace. These tools are built for cost management, with deep integrations into cloud providers and on-premises systems. They give you that centralized foundation you need for true visibility.

Enterprise FinOps addresses your entire IT spend. Your IT environment is a mosaic of systems, hosted both in the cloud and in on-premises data centers, and may also be on edge systems like remote offices or manufacturing plants. IT management platforms like ServiceNow ITOM tie into the bigger picture of IT operations. ETL tools like Informatica PowerCenter or MuleSoft let you integrate cost data across your enterprise systems. ServiceNow Software Asset Management (SAM) lets you optimize licenses.

Automation is the backbone of modern IT. Infrastructure automation gives you a foundation. Configuration management tools like Ansible or Terraform ensure consistency. And when you treat infrastructure as code, it's creating a playbook that scales with your needs. Scheduling and orchestration engines let you automate batch jobs, maintenance windows, and updates. Cloud providers sell spare capacity at a discount, but if the price jumps, you lose money. Tools that automate bidding and switching between on-demand and spot instances are your hedge against unexpected cost charges. Governance and policy automation can be embedded into your IT workflows.

8.3 Financial Modeling for Scenario Planning

Spreadsheets are static, brittle, and utterly unprepared for the chaos of real-world variables. It takes extensive analysis to address scenarios like what happens to your IT spend if your user base doubles next year or if that SaaS contract were to renew at 20% higher rates. There are many more variables that could be at play. Your services contracts may have a 5% increase in expense, or you may need to factor in an increase in employee salaries due to inflation. That's where financial modeling for scenario planning comes in to help you.

Financial modeling for scenario planning constructs a comprehensive, quantitative model that depicts the intricacies of your IT environment's costs and resource consumption. It's a living, breathing representation of your IT environment, mapping every dollar spent on compute, storage, SaaS, personnel, and the invisible levers that pull those numbers. Think of it as a digital twin of your financial health, complete with formulas that model how variables interact. Assumptions about expected future values, such as growth rates, inflation, and discount rates, are also explicitly defined within the model.

Such models are a playground for "what-ifs." They simulate business growth and global risk scenarios as well. You could simulate how your infrastructure would hold up if a new product line launches or the financial impact of a spike in tariffs. Financial modeling offers a stress test for your assumptions. Sensitivity analysis lets you uncover which variables are pulling the strings. Maybe it's the cost of data transfer, or the rate at which your team scales up during peak seasons. Whatever it is, you'll know where to focus your energy. You're no longer guessing but running simulations with stakeholders, aligning IT with finance, and turning what-if scenarios into a strategy that tells everyone how you'll win. You are building a strategy that bends but doesn't break.

8.3.1 Mitigating Economy Fluctuations

IT spending has a stark reality in today's world. Your technology investments are dancing to a much bigger tune, that of geopolitical changes. Whether it's a booming economy or a recession, interest rates spiking or inflation creeping up or tariffs hiking customs duties, every economic shift can send ripples through your IT budget. The economy is similar to a pendulum. When it swings toward growth, expanding GDP, low unemployment, and easy credit can make companies feel flush with cash. Suddenly, that long-ignored ERP migration project gets the go-ahead. New applications, AI tools, and infrastructure upgrades get greenlighted. But when the pendulum swings the other way, companies tighten their belts. That SaaS subscription is now a "must cut." Even your team's salaries might come under scrutiny.

When interest rates rise, borrowing gets pricier. The series of server upgrades that your data center teams have been asking for so long needs a change from Capex to Opex. Leasing feels like the smarter move. Inflation eats into company margins, forcing you to dig deeper for cost savings. A strong labor market means higher salaries, but it also means more pressure to justify every dollar spent on IT. Businesses don't just sit back and wait for the economy to dictate their moves. During downturns, you'll likely see a rush of Capex to Opex moves with pay-as-you-go and no upfront costs.

You can extend your scenario planning to simulate economic scenarios like recession, inflation spike, interest rate crashes, as well as risks like natural weather disruptions. You stress test your budget against the worst-case scenarios and anticipate how they'll shape your IT spend. The economy doesn't care about your IT goals. But you can't afford to let it dictate them.

8.3.2 Building the model

- If you have invested efforts in Enterprise FinOps and scenario planning, you may already have a robust core financial model that tracks IT spend by category (cloud, SaaS, hardware, personnel, etc.).
- Identify key drivers and pinpoint the variables within your model that are most sensitive to economic conditions, such as the number of users, application usage, cloud, and SaaS subscription costs.
- Next, identify scenarios such as:
    - The baseline case assumes a reasonable growth rate, stable market rates, and a steady economic environment.
    - Optimistic growth with strong demand for IT services. This would result in increased user counts, application usage, and cloud spend.
    - A pessimistic scenario assumes recession or economic slowdown, where your drivers reduce and vendor rates increase.
    - An extreme scenario would be like a supply chain disruption with supply chain issues affecting hardware costs and lead times.
- Next layer in the economic drivers such as GDP growth rate, inflation rate for hardware, software licenses, and cloud services, vendor pricing, and interest rates. Use formulas within your model to translate

the economic assumptions into changes in the key driver variables. For example:
  - Cloud Compute Costs = Base Cloud Compute Costs * (1 + Inflation Rate)
  - User Growth = Base User Growth * (1 + GDP Growth Rate)
- Using sensitivity analysis, create tables showing how changes in each economic driver impact the overall IT budget for each scenario.

Building that first model will take some time and expert work from your teams. But once you have it, you have a strategy that outmaneuvers economic uncertainty.

8.3.3 Building Resilience through Enterprise FinOps

Resilience is knowing your SaaS vendor might raise rates next quarter, and having a plan to absorb that without blinking. Visibility is your first line of defense. Stop relying on models that assume the future looks like the past. Stress test your costs under the scenarios mentioned earlier. Build dashboards that tie your spending to real-time economic signals like inflation rates or user behavior shifts.

Diversify your vendors. If every egg is in one basket, you're asking for trouble. Negotiate rate escalation clauses in contracts. When energy prices spike and your provider hikes fees, those clauses are a hedge. Shift to consumption-based models where possible. Paying only for what you use forces teams to think about efficiency, not just volume.

Set aside a contingency fund, but don't just tuck it away. Use scenario-based budgeting. And build budgets that reflect those outcomes. Regular risk assessments and insurance coverage let you further safeguard your IT spend from instability. An Enterprise FinOps program helps you develop resilience.

8.4 Reporting and Communication of Financial Insights

Financial insights can mean different things to different IT stakeholders.

- Business executives care about impact. They want summaries that cut through the noise and dashboards that highlight the ROI of your FinOps initiatives and connect them to their business drivers.
- Your IT leadership wants details that drill into every corner of their IT portfolio, such as costs, application spend, SaaS pricing, and KPIs.
- Application owners and IT portfolio leaders need actionable insights, not academic analysis, such as simplified dashboards that show cost per user, application performance, and risk hotspots. Recommendations on

how and where optimizations can happen empower them to fix problems before they blow up.
- Frontline users such as developers, analysts, and everyone who touches the system want self-service portals with real-time monitoring of their usage and costs. These tools shouldn't feel like an extra burden on their time.

Analytics and BI Tools like Tableau or Power BI let you provide this clarity. Most cost management platforms have rich analytics and reporting engines built in. But the best tool in the world is useless if no one gets it because you're just showing numbers without the insights and the connection to business impact. Enterprise FinOps is also about people. Use it to make sure executives, IT, business units, and even individual users see the value in what you're delivering.

8.4.1 Building Trust with Business through Consistent Reporting

Trust is built with consistency and transparency, as shown in Figure 8.6. Reciprocity is a two-way street. You give them information, and they give you their insights. People want to feel heard. Maintaining trust is a daily task. You have to define what every metric means. You have to open the door for questions. You have to explain why the numbers changed.

- Make it relevant. FinOps teams could fall into the trap of thinking that they have the data, so the job is done. But to build trust, you need to make those numbers meaningful to the people who need them most through, and with the data that matters to them, as mentioned in the previous section.
- Being predictable and consistent is important. When you report the same metrics every week, month, or quarter, you're creating a rhythm.
- Objectivity sustains trust. If your reports feel like a sales pitch or a plea for more budget, you've lost the battle. Trust dies when people think your data is biased.
- Be transparent. Every number has to be explainable. If you show a 10% drop in cloud costs, don't only say that you saved money, but show what your teams did through rightsizing or workload optimization. The transparency builds credibility.
- Know their goals. Trust is built on relationships that develop when you know the goals of your stakeholders. You have to understand their pain points and treat them like partners. And when they trust you, they start collaborating.

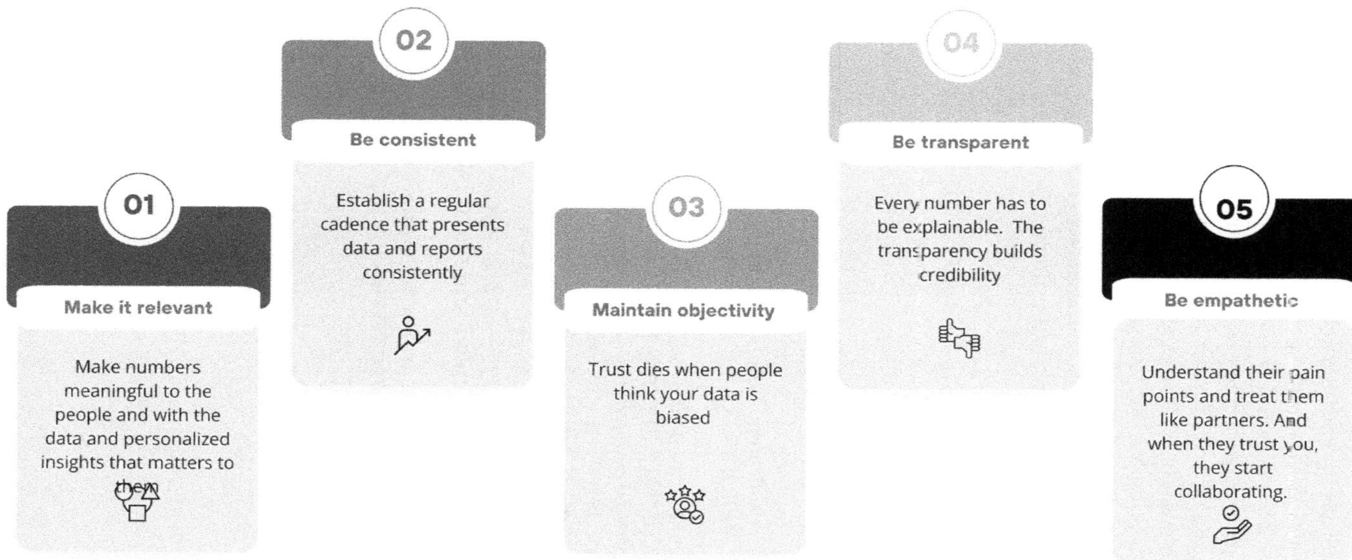

Figure 8.6 Building trust through consistent and objective reporting

The Law of Feedback states that systems adjust behavior based on input from their environment. This is central to the measurement of Enterprise FinOps. Just as feedback loops in biological systems allow organisms to adapt to their surroundings, measurement frameworks in FinOps, such as KPIs and real-time analytics, enable organizations to recalibrate strategies in response to changing conditions. The CIO must ensure that these feedback mechanisms are not only in place but also integrated into decision-making processes, allowing the organization to respond dynamically to data-driven insights. This requires a culture of continuous improvement, where feedback is not just collected but acted upon to drive better outcomes.

References

FinOps KPIs. (2025). (T. F. Foundation, Producer) Retrieved from https://www.finops.org/wg/finops-kpis/

Horowitz, J. (2022). *Metrics vs KPIs*. Retrieved from https://itchronicles.com/business-intelligence/metrics-vs-kpis/

Kaplan, R. S., & Norton, D. P. (1996). *The balanced scorecard: Translating strategy into action*. Boston, MA: Harvard Business School Press.

Knight, J. (2015). *HBR tools: Return on Investment (ROI)*. Cambridge: Harvard Business Review.

Porter, M. E. (1998). *Competitive advantage: Creating and sustaining superior performance*. New York, NY: Free Press.

Siegel, E. (2013). *Predictive analytics - The power to predict who will click, buy, lie or die*. Hoboken, NJ: Wiley and Sons.

Smith, M., & Proctor, P. (2013, March). The gartner business value model: A framework for measuring business performance. Retrieved from https://www.gartner.com/en/documents/2379317

Tableau. (2024). *Predictive analytics vs prescriptive analytics*. Retrieved from https://www.tableau.com/analytics/predictive-analytics-vs-prescriptive-analytics

Twin, A. (2025, June). *KPIs: What are key performance indicators?* Retrieved from https://www.investopedia.com/terms/k/kpi.asp

Chapter 9

Mental Models for Enterprise FinOps

DOI: 10.4324/9781003682196-13

An Enterprise FinOps implementation would be limited in its effectiveness if it doesn't result in a mindset shift. The entire IT team and their business stakeholders need to develop a culture of shared accountability and continuous improvement. It's a way of thinking that transforms how organizations perceive and interact with technology spending. Typically, IT spending has often been viewed as a back-office function, disconnected from business outcomes. CIOs have struggled to counter this. Frameworks like the Balanced Scorecard or COBIT result in IT strategy that aligns with business at the top levels but doesn't always reach the far corners of the field. That's where FinOps[1] comes in. At the heart of it is the notion that every dollar spent on technology should be evaluated through the lens of business value. This shift moves the conversation from "how much are we spending?" to "what value are we creating?"

This mindset also dismantles silos. In many organizations, finance, IT, vendor management, and business teams operate in isolation, each with its own priorities and metrics, interfacing only at intersection points on transactional processes. FinOps breaks this down. It fosters collaboration and shared ownership. When everyone understands that their collective actions impact the bottom line, they become more intentional about how they use resources. The cultural shift positively impacts another key principle, that of accuracy and transparency in data. Teams may resist sharing insights or may continue to make decisions based on intuition rather than evidence. The mindset shift ensures that data becomes a shared language. A FinOps program will fade away in a few months before it realizes its full potential if the mindset shift doesn't take place. A mindset rooted in adaptability and long-term thinking lets organizations pivot quickly and sustain momentum.

In this chapter, we explore mental models, algorithms, and management patterns that let us develop this culture of accountability and exploration that can be indispensable guides to a successful FinOps implementation.

9.1 What Are Mental Models

Mental models function as basic simplified explanations and guidelines to help people understand their environment and interact with it. Think of them as lenses through which we view and understand complex systems. They function as useful tools that help people develop their thinking process to reach decisions and execute actions. While they may not offer the perfect solution to every problem, they are useful constructs to assist us in shaping our own thoughts to arrive at a decision or action.

Mental models have guided human progress since ancient times by shaping the social, technological, and cultural evolution and spread of human civilization throughout the world. The development of tools and technological advancement during the early ages of human history depended on mental models such as cause and effect, which explained how different actions produced specific effects. People needed to develop a system for cyclical thinking because they required knowledge on planting sequences, seed selection, harvesting periods, and seasonal patterns. People developed calendars and religious festivals and built their worldview through their understanding of natural cycles. The Greeks and ancient Indians developed organized mathematical systems that became the foundation for engineering and architectural advancement and scientific exploration. Through his philosophical work, Aristotle developed mental frameworks on governance, justice, and ethics that continue to influence political theory and legal systems throughout the ages. It influenced the Romans in ancient times and also the leaders of the French and American revolutions in later times.

Basic mental frameworks that explained what defines right and wrong and how humans relate to divine power served as the foundation for building complex belief systems. Models such as the scientific method and hypothesis testing brought groundbreaking methods to learn through observation and experimentation. Recent centuries have developed new mental frameworks that explain globalization, democracy, creative thinking, human rights, and environmental sustainability that deeply affect our modern world.

This chapter outlines only a few of the hundreds of mental models and concepts that are available. Shane Parris has compiled an excellent library of mental models with examples from diverse fields including psychology, mathematics, history, and science (Parrish, 2025). The models in this chapter have been curated and selected based on what I believe is their contextual relevance to the RTI360 model and for Enterprise FinOps. As you build up an Enterprise FinOps program, encourage your teams to add to this and maintain a working list based on what works for your organization and goals. I highly recommend that all practitioners involved in your company's Enterprise FinOps implementation explore the models cited here and also introduce their own from other sources to serve as a decision-making repository and knowledge base for your organization.

9.1.1 Significance of Mental Models for Complex IT Initiatives

Think about the last time you had to justify an IT investment that felt like a gamble, and you had to make a decision with only limited information. You knew the numbers didn't add up, but you couldn't explain why. That's where models step in. They don't simplify complexity; instead, they force you to confront reality.

IT investments are rarely simple. They're tangled in workflows, buried in dependencies, dependent on talent, and shadowed by long-term risks.

How does this tie into our five-year plan? Who else does this impact? That's where models like lifecycle costing and total cost of ownership become your allies. Models help you bridge those gaps. They give everyone the same language and the same framework to talk about value, risk, alternatives, and impact.

Teams that share the same models don't just work better. They form and they norm together. You don't have to explain the same thing a dozen times. You don't waste hours debating the same problem from different angles. You're all looking at the same map, even if the terrain is rough. That's how you spot risks early and build trust. Some people think that strategy is about big ideas, but it's also about the tiny gears that keep the machine running. Mental models are those gears. You want to survive uncertainty, but going further, you want to thrive in it. And that starts with models that help you see the world as it is, not as you wish it were. This becomes a powerful and practical guide for your Enterprise FinOps journey and leads to a culture of collaboration and accountability.

9.1.2 Occam's Razor – The Principle of Parsimony

Occam's Razor, articulated by William of Ockham, states that "entities should not be multiplied beyond necessity." In other words, the simplest explanation or solution is usually the one that works best. Focus on robust, established solutions before jumping to complex or experimental ones. When deciding whether to upgrade a legacy system versus maintaining it, Occam's Razor suggests evaluating the operational risk and cost of disruption associated with transformation. If a reliable but dated solution still meets the business need, it's still the most rational choice. Ultimately, there has to be a clear business need or gain to justify the risk of disrupting stable operations. A server infrastructure that struggles with performance issues may be better off with a focused upgrade and optimization of current resources instead of a completely new platform replacement because this approach delivers the most affordable and dependable solution.

In Transform, if modernization is necessary, you could begin with smaller steps of architectural evolution instead of performing a complete overhaul of the system. For Innovate, Occam's Razor recommends prioritization. If multiple potential "disruptive" innovations are proposed but you can only focus your funds on one, the most straightforward, readily achievable one, and particularly one that can be validated quickly with a minimal investment, is the best. It prevents wasted resources and the risk of pursuing unrealistic ideas. Avoid throwing resources at unattainable concepts and prevent unnecessary resource waste.

Occam's Razor helps organizations identify and eliminate unnecessary layers of complexity. This directly results in cost reductions and performance enhancements.

9.1.3 *The Pareto Principle (80/20 Rule) – Focusing on Impact*

As shown in Figure 9.1, the Pareto principle generally states that 80% of some outcome is due to 20% of all possible causes. Let's see this in action. You are staring at a spreadsheet where someone used pivots on an analysis of IT support tickets, and you realize that 80% of your support cases come from 20% of your systems, or 20% of the same type of problem. That's the Pareto Principle in action.

I saw this in action recently when I asked my help desk team to analyze our top problem areas. It turned out that password reset requests from manufacturing sites were triggering 40% of the calls to our helpdesk, and 80% of the other calls were due to the top five issues. We ended up exploring a solution for self-service password resets that would work on a mobile phone. And then we went on to prioritize solutions for the remaining 20%. Apply that to other IT scenarios, such as your IT spend. You may well discover that 20% of your services are the ones bleeding (80%) of your money, or dragging down performance on the most frequent outages.

Conversely, 20% of something may be delivering 80% of the outcomes. In the Run^2 phase, survival is the game. You can't optimize everything all at once. You need to find the 20% of services that deliver 80% of your

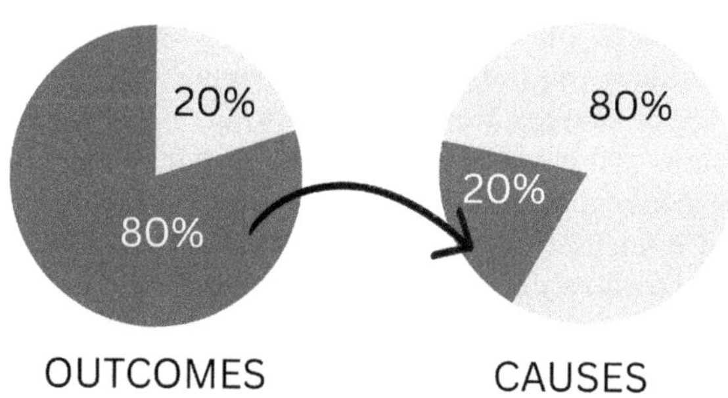

Figure 9.1 The Pareto Principle, or the 80/20 rule

value and lock in on them. That might be a single legacy app that's the backbone of your customer experience or a redundant platform eating up 30% of your budget. Focus there. Stabilize, streamline, and stop wasting time on the rest, at least for now. You don't mean to ignore the other 80% but are choosing where to fight your battles first. The same applies to transformation. When you're deciding which apps to modernize, don't spread yourself thin. Pick the 20% that will deliver the most strategic value and align with your business goals, those that are ripe for automation, and phase out those that are underperforming. This doesn't mean picking out the easiest wins but picking the ones that matter. When it comes to innovation, some companies chase every AI trend, thinking that something may pay off, only to end up with a cluttered portfolio of half-baked experiments. The Pareto Principle stops that madness. Focus on the 20% of ideas that will deliver 80% of your strategic impact. That could be a single AI tool that cuts costs by 40% or a new platform that unlocks a new revenue stream.

You don't need to be perfect. You need to make the best possible choices with the information you have. The 80/20 rule gives you super-vision that stops you from drowning in complexity and allows you to start swimming toward clarity.

9.1.4 System 1 and System 2 Thinking – Intuition vs. Deliberation

Daniel Kahneman, in *Thinking Fast and Slow* (Kahneman, 2013), talked about two systems of thinking that operate simultaneously but often at odds. System 1 is intuitive and fast, while System 2 is deliberative and slow. "The automatic operations of System 1 generate surprisingly complex patterns of ideas, but only the slower System 2 can construct thoughts in an orderly series of steps," said the author.

Some decisions just click. Your mind reacts in a sub-second. Just like a reflex, it's instinctive and almost effortless. That's System 1 in action. It's important and immensely useful in most areas of life. But in IT services, maybe you need to slow down a little. It's the part of your brain that says, "Hey, that server's crashing, get a team to patch it now!" without stopping to ask, "What else might break if we do this?" It's quick, but it's also prone to mistakes. You fix it, but hours later, your backup system fails, leaving you exposed to bigger problems. System 1 is like that friend who rushes down the stairway and jumps on the subway train without checking the destination. They're fast, but they're not always on the right track.

Then there's System 2. That's the part that says, "Wait. Let's map out the dependencies. What's the full cost of this change? What happens if we don't fix it?" It's slower, but it's also way more precise. It's the part that forces you to dig into data, ask hard questions, and not just react. Speed is important, but more important is making sure that while you're solving one problem, you are also avoiding a dozen others.

Systems thinking is like looking at your entire IT portfolio as a living, breathing thing. Not a bunch of silos, but a connected web of dependencies. If you shift to the cloud, don't just stress about the cost of the migration, or whether on-premises data centers get you better compute values. You also need to reflect on how that shift impacts your security, your compliance, your team's workflows, and your agility. There's always some ripple effect. Your IT ecosystem is more than a bunch of tools. It's a symphony. If you tweak one note, the whole song changes.

In Run, System 1 thinking is about speed and getting the broken system operational at the earliest possible time. You fix a vulnerability with a quick patch. But System 2 says, "Let's look at the full picture. What's the risk if we run the patch?" It's going to take some more time to do the Root Cause Analysis (RCA), but it's the difference between a temporary fix and a sustainable solution.

During Transform, System 1 might get you excited about a big modernization project. "We have to do this now!" But System 2 says, "Okay, let's plan this out. Let's talk with our business folks first. We'll break it into phases. We need to minimize the business disruption."

In Innovate, System 1 may trigger you to try a new AI trend without testing it first. System 2 would suggest starting with a proof of concept and validating that it aligns with outcomes that would be useful to the business. Sometimes, that's the difference between an experiment and a real win.

FinOps principles push you to move from quick fixes (System 1) to deliberate, data-driven decisions (System 2). The most powerful tool is the ability to see the whole system and to act with both speed and precision. The hard part is to use System 2 when the pressure is on. But that's where the real value resides. But if you want sustainable solutions, make a conscious effort to turn on your System 2 thinking.

9.1.5 First Principles Thinking

Sometimes you review a strategy or a plan for a major initiative and realize that it's built on a foundation of assumptions and best practices. You get that inner feeling that says, "This doesn't seem right to our situation." That's the danger of relying on industry norms or "this is how it's always been done." First principles thinking cuts through that noise. It's like rebuilding from the ground up, not based on what others did, but on what actually works for your business. Ayk Martirosyan has proposed a three-step framework to apply first principles thinking to any problem (Martirosyan, 2021).

Whether you're faced with a cloud migration, a legacy system upgrade, a services outsourcing, or an AI implementation, the default is to ask, "What did companies like ours do?" System integrators and partners may helpfully offer numerous case studies of customers who successfully did exactly that and thrived. But if you apply first principles, you need to dig deeper into the core requirement and strip away the fluff and the buzzwords and ask, "What's the simplest way to solve this problem?" In the Run phase, this mindset pays off in the long term. You patch a server because that's how you've always fixed outages.

But first principles urge you to explore more, maybe the next day, on finding the actual root cause of that downtime. During Transform, it tries to align decisions with the business's core goals. You're not modernizing for the sake of newer technology but to solve long-standing issues that constrained your business agility. In Innovate, instead of jumping on the next AI trend because everyone's doing it, you question what the true value it brings to your business. It forces you to ignore the noise and focus on the real question. And when you do that, you stop wasting money on solutions that don't align with your business's true needs. When you're making decisions based on foundational truths rather than assumptions, you're strategically aligning them.

9.1.6 *The Feedback Loop*

A feedback loop monitors the outcomes of decisions and actions and uses that information to adjust future decisions. This is a critical concept in IT decision-making, where the impact of changes is often uncertain. Implementing loops is the basis for continuous improvement and more informed decisions by compelling you to continue looking for the impact of your decisions. The implementation of this process enables organizations to enhance their operations through data-driven decision-making and collaborative discussions.

In the context of Run, the CIO can use KPIs and dashboards to conduct regular reviews that help identify necessary adjustments that might involve switching to different innovation paths or improving the transformation strategy. The feedback loop also enables the shared ownership principle by showing direct results of personal decisions, which promotes accountability throughout the organization. Organizations need to use real-time data for fast adjustments to achieve their best investment returns while reducing their exposure to risk.

In the context of Transform and Innovate, the implementation of pilot projects to modernize essential services will expose hidden technical problems and operational barriers. Shift your feedback loops to the left so that you gain useful information as early in the cycle as possible. This can be done using design thinking approaches such as focus groups, agile, or product-centric teams that involve business users as essential partners in IT processes. Without a robust feedback loop that tracks key metrics like cost, feature fit, performance, and user satisfaction, the CIO risks investing heavily in a solution that doesn't deliver.

The article, "What Is the Feedback Loops Mental Model?", explores the science behind positive and negative feedback loops (Feedback Loops, 2025).

9.1.7 *The Minimum Viable Product (MVP)*

The concept of Minimum Viable Product (MVP) is familiar in IT. The MVP term originated from lean, product management, and agile methodologies. The term was popularized by authors like Eric Ries (Ries, 2011).

You narrow down and prioritize the minimum features necessary to launch the first version of a product that is complete enough to meet the requirements of users and address a particular problem. In the context of Enterprise FinOps, apply it to strategy as well as software and services. Think of it as a way to test your assumptions without betting the farm. You shouldn't be spending six months designing a solution that might not even work. When you're trying to align cost management with business value, you need proof. Maybe you're considering automating cloud spend tracking. Instead of rolling it out across the entire company, start with one department. Give them a tool, track what happens, and see if it actually cuts waste. That's your MVP. It's not perfect, but it's enough to validate whether the tool gave them the desired outcomes.

Cross-functional collaboration is another hidden gem. Imagine a finance team, an IT lead, and a product manager sitting down to test a shared cost visibility dashboard. The truth is that they are here to work on breaking down silos. Roadblocks will crop up. Maybe the finance team doesn't trust the data. Maybe the IT team thinks it's too complicated. But those are the problems you need to solve before scaling. Your MVP isn't the end of the story. It's actually just the first chapter. You refine the tool, tweak the process, and repeat. I've worked with companies that ignored this step. They rolled out a full-scale solution, only to find out it didn't align with their actual needs. That's a costly lesson. If the tool reduces cloud costs by 15% in one department, that's a talking point. If it improves transparency by 30%, that's a big win. Stakeholders care more deeply about outcomes rather than theory. You can't wait for perfection. The goal is to create a culture where everyone feels responsible for how technology spends their budget.

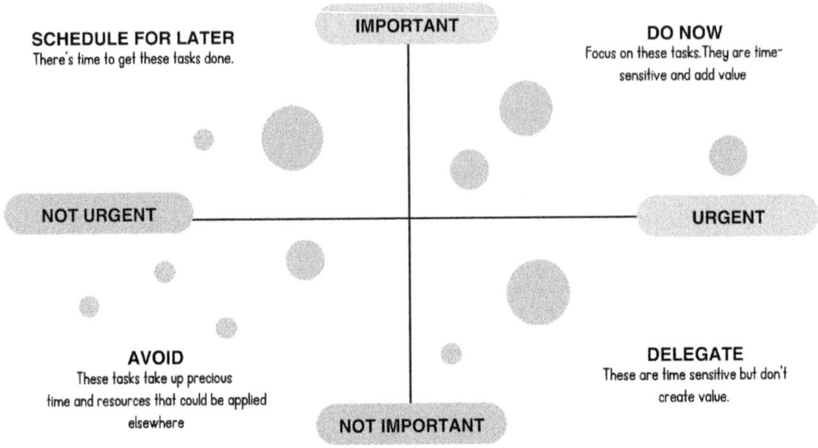

Figure 9.2 The Eisenhower Matrix, used here for prioritization

9.1.8 The Eisenhower Matrix

The Eisenhower Matrix, depicted in Figure 9.2, is a simple but effective time management framework. President Dwight D. Eisenhower quoted an unknown source during a speech, stating, "I have two kinds of problems: the urgent, and the unimportant. The urgent are not important, and the important are never urgent." The matrix was popularized as a time management tool by Stephen Covey, the author of *The 7 Habits of Highly Effective People* (Covey, 2004).

You can use this model for comparing any series of items along any two dimensions. You can also add a third dimension to it for added emphasis. While the 1st two dimensions determine the position of whatever is being measured on the X and Y axis, the size of the bubble could reflect the 3rd dimension. Years ago in my days of solution consulting while with Hewlett-Packard Enterprise Services, I created a model in Excel that ranked outsourcing opportunities along dimensions of win probability, customer confidence, and solution feasibility, to let us determine which opportunities to focus our teams on.

You've often seen similar charts and models from consulting companies comparing products or which companies are leaders or innovators in their segments. When used in a classic time management or prioritization use case, the Eisenhower Matrix categorizes tasks into four quadrants based on the two dimensions of urgency and importance. The goal is to focus on what truly matters while avoiding distractions.

The four quadrants are the following:

- Urgent and important (do immediately).
- Important but not urgent (schedule for later).
- Urgent but not important (delegate or minimize).
- Neither urgent nor important (eliminate or avoid).

In the context of Enterprise FinOps, it lets teams align cost management and optimization efforts with strategic business priorities while avoiding reactive, short-term decision-making. FinOps teams may try to juggle everything at once. The matrix gives you clarity. If a task is urgent and important, like addressing a cloud bill that's spiraling out of control, you act immediately. If it's important but not urgent, like planning a vendor contract renewal, you schedule it. If it's urgent but not important, like responding to a random upsell proposal from one of your IT vendors, you delegate or minimize it. And if it's neither, you cut it.

FinOps balances firefighting with strategy. I've seen teams waste months on tasks that don't move the needle. The Eisenhower Matrix puts things in the right context. It helps you determine whether this is a fire you need to put out now or a bridge that you need to build. Take vendor renegotiation, for example. It's important and critical, but it's rarely urgent. Teams often delay it, thinking they'll get to it later. Sometimes that later never comes. The matrix forces you to prioritize what truly drives value. Instead of getting bogged down in routine chores, focus on renegotiating contracts that could save millions.

Teams get buried under urgent but low-impact tasks like repetitive reports and a never-ending loop of crisis management meetings. With the matrix, you re-establish focus on the things that matter. You delegate, automate, or eliminate. Collaboration also gets messy when priorities clash. A finance leader might see cost optimization as urgent, while an IT manager sees it as a long-term project. The matrix creates a shared language. Now, vendor renegotiation becomes a joint priority, not a battle of whose turn it is. The matrix provides rationale for data-driven decisions. Instead of reacting to a sudden IT spend spike, you analyze trends, identify waste, and benchmark against industry standards.

Enterprise FinOps is a moving target. What was important but not urgent last quarter might be urgent and important next. A tool you ignored for years suddenly becomes critical as AI adoption ramps up. You need to revisit and reprioritize frequently.

9.2 Recognizing and Avoiding Cognitive Biases

People tend to make irrational judgments through established patterns that lead them to deviate from rational thinking during decision-making processes. Our brains employ mental shortcuts to handle complex information by simplifying it. Because our brains are wired to conserve energy, these shortcuts are often helpful, allowing us to make quick decisions. However, they can lead to systematic errors in judgment, especially when dealing with situations that you encounter in complex IT programs. Figure 9.3 illustrates various types of cognitive biases. The identification and active reduction of these biases is a fundamental requirement for successful and accurate IT decision-making.

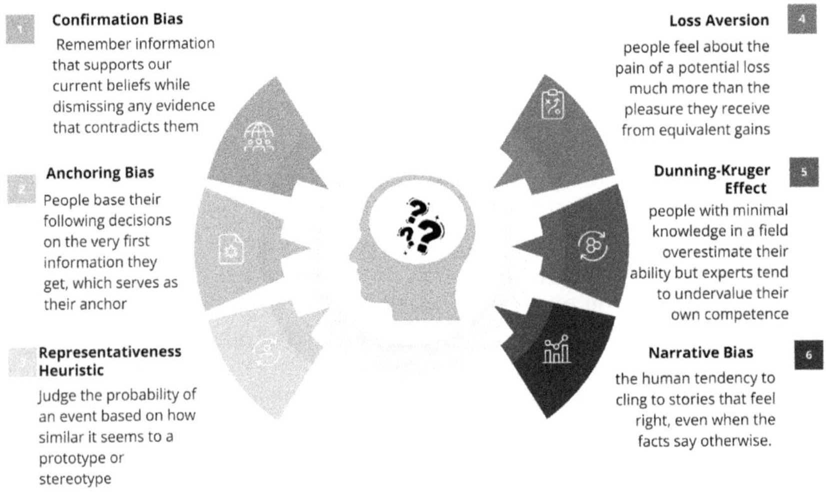

Figure 9.3 Various types of cognitive biases

9.2.1 *Avoiding Biases*

Our brains function with limited processing abilities. The human brain lacks the ability to quickly process all available information, so it depends on heuristics, or mental rules of thumb as shortcuts, especially when faced with limited information. Some biases are thought to have evolved as adaptive mechanisms in our ancestors, helpful for survival in a dangerous world, where we had to make fight-or-flight decisions. Our emotional states, including fear, hope, and optimism, tend to alter our decision-making abilities. But in IT decision-making, taking the time to analyze information and avoiding cognitive biases can lead to better decisions. It's a commonly seen bias where people tend to search for and understand information that supports their current beliefs through Confirmation Bias, resulting in a one-sided view. In Anchoring Bias, people tend to base their choices on the first information they receive when they make decisions. According to the Availability Heuristic, people tend to overestimate the occurrence of events that they can easily recall because these events tend to be vivid or recent in their memories. The representativeness heuristic makes people judge event probabilities by matching events to their mental prototypes or stereotypes. People experience loss aversion when they feel the negative impact of losing something more intensely than the positive effect of gaining an equal amount, thus tending to avoid situations where they are losing something, even when the gain is greater. People tend to follow the Bandwagon Effect when they observe numerous others performing the same action, leading to a loss of independent judgment. In Hindsight Bias, people tend to believe that after an event has occurred, they knew it would happen all along.

The ability to identify biases enables you to make more objective and rational decisions based on facts, which results in better decision outcomes. You can minimize the impact of biases, leading to fewer costly mistakes. Your ability to deliver effective communication will improve through bias understanding when you share information or discuss concepts with your colleagues and team members. Identifying your own biases helps you become a more reflective and thoughtful decision-maker. Recognizing biases within a team fosters a more collaborative and productive environment.

Daniel Kahneman in *Thinking, Fast and Slow* talks extensively about heuristics and biases in Part 2 of his book (Kahneman, 2013).

9.2.2 How Can You Mitigate the Impact of Biases

Figure 9.4 shows many techniques for avoiding and mitigating the impact of biases. The first requirement for bias mitigation is awareness. It requires people to recognize that biases can naturally arise and that anyone can develop them. Understanding the different types of biases, such as those mentioned here, allows you to determine situations where you may unconsciously start applying them. The next step is to build critical thinking abilities. Doubt your existing beliefs while questioning your current comprehension of everything. Engage in conversations with individuals who maintain different perspectives to seek diverse opinions. The decision-making process needs to use data evidence and facts as its foundation instead of depending on individual intuition. Use frameworks and checklists to ensure a systematic and structured approach. Make a conscious effort

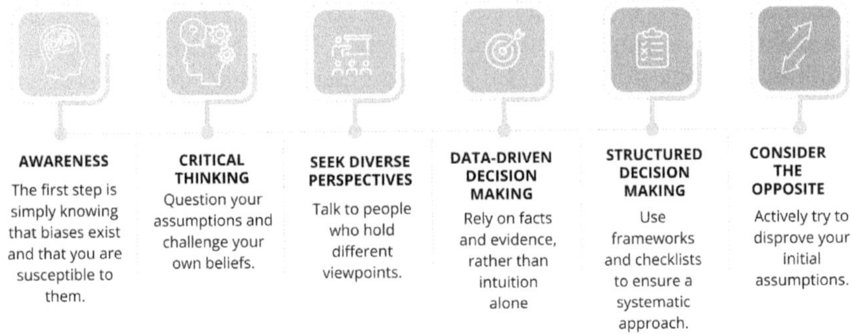

Figure 9.4 Avoiding biases

to prove your first assumptions wrong, possibly by testing the opposite view. These techniques can help you overcome biases and result in better decisions.

Charlie Munger, in his speech, "The Psychology of Human Misjudgment," shared his checklist of 25 standard causes of human misjudgment (Munger, 2005). The Brians, Behavior & Design group has published a well-designed toolkit of reference and strategy cards in the area of behavioral economics to assist in better-designed products and services (Brains, Behavior & Design Group, 2011).

9.2.3 *Frequent Biases Encountered in Complex IT Initiatives*

9.2.3.1 *Confirmation Bias*

Confirmation Bias has a wide-ranging impact on how people behave. Confirmation bias drives us to find, understand, and remember information that supports our current beliefs while we dismiss any evidence that contradicts them. An IT executive who believes an infrastructure system is reliable will actively seek supporting evidence while disregarding performance issues and increasing costs. People avoid testing current solutions and investigating new methods because they worry about producing mistakes or being thought of as coming off negatively.

In Run, Confirmation Bias may lead an IT executive to over-invest in a struggling system because they initially championed or sponsored it, and their well-meaning team of advisers echoed the sentiment without questioning it. Recognizing this bias requires objective data analysis through focusing on true operational costs and risks rather than sentimental attachment.

FinOps principles directly challenge these biases. The principle of having accessible, transparent data becomes even more critical, providing a factual basis to counteract biased judgments.

The champion of a Transform initiative may establish an echo chamber that perpetually repeats their proposed changes. Team members may tend to selectively pick data that supports their preferred direction, which makes them continue with their initial choice despite evidence showing otherwise. The most dangerous situation exists when working on complicated projects that involve significant risks. Innovate initiatives could face an obstacle to creativity and alternative solutions because of Confirmation Bias. If a team is invested in a particular technological direction, they might dismiss ideas that don't fit within that framework, missing out on potentially transformative opportunities.

The implementation of FinOps produces substantial effects on the organization. The accessibility of data is crucial, but simply providing data isn't enough. The interpretation of that data can be swayed by Confirmation Bias. A centralized FinOps function functions as a key element to reduce this bias. The process requires you to get multiple viewpoints through independent risk assessments and testing assumptions before you can make any decisions. A strong data governance system that maintains data precision and transparency will help reduce the impact of Confirmation Bias.

9.2.3.2 *Anchoring Bias – The Influence of Initial Numbers*

In Anchoring Bias, people base their following decisions on the very first information they get, which becomes ingrained in their minds as their anchor. The process of evaluating risks becomes severely affected due to this bias.

Within Run, a seemingly arbitrary initial cost estimate for a system upgrade can disproportionately influence subsequent budget decisions, even if that initial estimate is flawed. Subsequent calculations get unconsciously skewed toward that starting point.

In Transform, initial cost projections for a modernization project may get inflated to justify the business case. This can become an unshakeable benchmark, even if subsequent analyses reveal a more favorable ROI. The excitement surrounding new technology during Innovate, along with its first cost projection, creates an anchor effect that drives teams to spend large amounts on systems that might fail to generate expected value.

FinOps encourages accurate data and unbiased analytical methods for success. A centralized FinOps function can resist Anchoring Bias by actively testing first impressions and showing different cost projections and all possible results. Using benchmarking techniques can offset powerful and expensive renewal anchors set in your mind through earlier contracts.

Transparency makes a key difference. Stakeholders need to access detailed information on costs, risks, and benefits to make their own evaluation of the situation. Employing sensitivity analysis techniques lets you explore the impact of changes in key assumptions. It lets you identify the true range of potential outcomes and reduce the influence of the initial anchor. The analysis depends on strict data governance practices together with independent verification to maintain its integrity.

9.2.3.3 *Representativeness Heuristic – Judging by Appearance*

The representativeness heuristic leads us to judge the probability of an event based on how similar it seems to a prototype or stereotype. The problem impacts the complete portfolio selection process.

In Run, a system could present itself as simple and reliable, but may actually be inefficient. Yet people view it as low risk, so they continue to support it. The story gains credibility and support through its use of established storylines, which viewers can easily identify with. Transform initiatives can be affected when a project's scope or complexity is judged solely on its appearance and presentation to decision makers. A project that seems complex to reviewers may get rejected because of its perceived complexity, but a simple project may get accepted without proper evaluation of its effects. In Innovate, the representativeness heuristic can drive the adoption of technologies based on their "coolness" or market buzz, rather than their strategic alignment. This can lead to wasted investments in technologies with limited ROI.

FinOps can be challenged by this bias. The presentation of costs and risks often relies on simplifying complex data and is a tactic that can amplify the effect of the representativeness heuristic. The solution to this problem requires the FinOps principle of transparent data to be the main focus. Presenting data in a detailed, clear, and easy-to-understand manner helps to minimize bias. The centralized FinOps team needs to challenge overly simplistic or misleading interpretations by conducting a thorough impact analysis.

9.2.3.4 *Loss Aversion – The Pain of Loss*

The framework demonstrates that people experience the pain of a potential loss at a higher intensity than the pleasure they receive from equivalent gains.

In Run, if an IT executive in the CIO's team has invested significant time and resources over the years in a system that doesn't meet business needs anymore, the pain of "losing" that investment can create an aversion to making the difficult choice. Decommissioning it would be the optimal financial decision, but people tend to maintain support for outdated systems because they want to stay away from the emotional discomfort of losing something. Transform initiatives can be negatively affected. A team will avoid stopping a complicated modernization project even when initial signs show it is not working because they do not want to lose the money already spent. The fear of losing market position or competitive edge prevents Innovate from adopting new technologies because of perceived risks.

FinOps faces a high risk of this bias occurring. People become more loss-averse because of the focus on cost reduction. Employees may view cost reduction efforts as a loss of operational control and likely oppose the suggested modifications. A FinOps function needs to present cost optimization as a strategic advantage that brings operational efficiency and business alignment rather than a negative outcome. A communication plan and strong executive support from the CIO downwards need to deliver straightforward and open information that focuses on the beneficial elements of Enterprise FinOps.

9.2.3.5 *The Dunning-Kruger Effect – Overconfidence and Underestimation*

The Dunning-Kruger Effect reflects how people with minimal knowledge in a field believe they have more ability than they do, while experts may tend to undervalue their own competence (Dunning-Kruger Effect, 2025). The bias creates a major risk for decisions that need to be based on sound judgments.

A team with limited system performance knowledge under the Run pillar would most likely overestimate the efficiency of legacy systems. This could lead to longer or delayed times for necessary system updates. In Transform, the absence of technical expertise in project teams could lead to wrong assessments of transformation complexity, which causes projects to run late and costs to rise. Transform initiatives are particularly vulnerable. Teams that lack experience in modernizing complex systems tend to overestimate their capacity for new architecture implementation; this can result in unattainable targets and even risk the failure of the entire transformation effort. During Innovate, a team may be overly confident in its technical capabilities, perhaps driven by hype or a desire to appear innovative. They might pursue ambitious and unproven technologies, risking significant financial losses and risks from overcommitment and underperformance.

The implementation of FinOps principles requires objective decision-making, but the Dunning-Kruger Effect could work against achieving this goal. A centralized FinOps function needs to establish active methods for bias reduction through comprehensive training programs, independent verification of assumptions, and a team environment that promotes honesty. One of the most important factors is to cultivate a culture of humility that seeks outside expertise when necessary. The implementation of knowledge-sharing programs, together with formal lessons and open discussions, serves as an immediate solution to prevent this behavior. The emphasis should always be on data-driven assessment and continuous improvement, rather than perceived expertise.

9.2.3.6 Narrative Bias – The Power of Stories

Someone says in a meeting that a legacy CRM system is critical to their operations. They provide a description of how that system has supported their business through the years. But there is a thought at the back of your mind, wondering what the actual data behind that claim is, especially since the same team has had access to a modern SaaS CRM system for a couple of years now. That's Narrative Bias at work. It's the human tendency to cling to stories that feel right, even when the facts say otherwise.

Enterprise FinOps relies on data, not stories. But data alone may not be enough. How you frame it matters as well. 20% cost reduction feels different when it's framed as a win versus a necessary adjustment. But there's a downside to this as well, when Narrative bias twists even the best numbers into misleading conclusions.

In the Run phase, this can be a nightmare. A system might be labeled mission-critical because of a single success story from five years ago. But that doesn't mean it's still vital today. Yet, the narrative sticks. You keep funding it, delay decommissioning, and miss the chance to optimize. It's like holding onto a broken car because it once got you to work. In Innovate, a new SaaS tool comes in for your review. The story, often fueled by vendor marketing glitz, declares this to be the future that will revolutionize everything. But the real question is whether it aligns with your long-term goals. The narrative can drown out the data. You have to invest in strategy and outcomes, not hype. Transform initiatives are as vulnerable. A previous modernization project was a success, so the next one will be, too. But that ignores the unique challenges of the current project. The narrative becomes a rush to get resources funneled into the project, but the ones that actually deliver value may suffer.

This is where collaboration matters. Sharing data is important, and so is weaving it into a story that's honest, not manipulative. A centralized function that understands this bias can help. They can ensure every FinOps initiative is backed by a unified, unbiased, and accurate narrative. No more cherry-picked numbers or stories that ignore the facts. The goal to eliminate Narrative bias isn't to tell a good story but to tell the right one that aligns with reality.

9.2.3.7 The Fallacy of Sunk Costs

Sometimes people keep throwing good money after bad. That's the sunk cost fallacy, a trap where we convince ourselves that because we've already spent so much, we have to keep going. This bias is a silent killer.

Imagine a legacy system that's slow, insecure, and actively stifling innovation. It's been patched, rebranded, and repurposed over the years. But your team keeps funding it, not because it works, but because they already spent millions on it. It's a similar story with Transform. A project is months behind schedule, costs are spiraling, and the ROI is nowhere to be found. But the team pushes forward with implementation because they have already invested in the planning. It's like buying a car that's broken, then spending more to fix it instead of just walking away.

The sunk cost fallacy forces us to look backward, not forward. Rather than what could be, you focus on what was. FinOps can help you address this bias. Cost-benefit analyses don't care about biases. They show the numbers and the alignment to goals. And when the numbers point to a potential disaster, you need to consider whether stopping may be the right decision after all.

9.2.3.8 The Lemon Law (Risk Aversion and Sample Selection Bias)

If you have ever bought a car that's a lemon, you know what this bias can do. The car breaks down the second you drive it out of the lot. Now in the automobile industry, thanks to consumer laws, there's a Lemon Law where you can get a refund or a replacement (The Lemon Law, 2025). It's a rule that protects consumers from getting stuck in shady auto deals. In IT, we're not so lucky. We sometimes tend to ignore the red flags and convince ourselves that this time it'll work.

A new SaaS tool excites the team. It shows promise in early tests, and maybe shows a few wins. But the system is unstable, the data is messy, and the engineers are already whispering about technology limitations. The IT executive, swayed by those early successes, doubles down. They invest more. They ignore the engineers' warnings. And when the tool collapses under real-world load, it's a disaster. That's where you need a Lemon Law for IT. Sometimes we discount the negatives, focus on the rare wins, and convince ourselves we're getting a good deal. But in IT, a lemon may be a worse investment than tolerating the problem.

FinOps forces you to dig into the data and to ask what's actually working and what is not. It pushes for due diligence. Testing, monitoring, and governance support FinOps in identifying the lemons in your IT environment. It uses tooling to spot anomalies, like a service that's suddenly eating up 30% of the budget or a system that's consistently underperforming. If anomalies start getting regular, there's no ignoring that it's likely a lemon. Once a lemon is found, it's investigated. Logs are reviewed. Stakeholders are talked to. And if the evidence is clear, you can take the necessary actions. Invoke whatever "lemon clauses" your legal team may have had the foresight to build into the vendor contract. The cost is cut.

9.2.3.9 The Von Restorff Effect (Distinctiveness and Attention)

The odd one out in a group always grabs your attention. That's the Von Restorff Effect. It's the reason a single red sock in a drawer of black ones screams for your notice. Imagine a portfolio dominated by high-cost, mission-critical systems. They're the stars of the show. But buried in the mix is an outdated application, maybe a legacy HR tool that's eating up 15% of the budget. It's not even on the radar. But something about its usage patterns, like a sudden spike in errors or a weird spike in costs, makes it stand out. The Von Restorff Effect forces you to look and investigate.

FinOps is the perfect partner here. It tracks the usual suspects and then forces you to dig into the outliers as well. The ones that show glaring gaps between what's planned and what's actually happening. Most IT portfolios are a mess of complexity. The real danger may not be in the big systems. It's the small, hidden ones that no one's watching. The ones that quietly eat up budgets or quietly leak data. The Von Restorff Effect gives you a way to spot them, pin them down, and fix them before they become disasters.

9.2.3.10 Good Enough Decision-Making

In IT, we're always chasing the "perfect" solution. But that system that's flawless, scalable, and future-proof is rarely worth the time, money, or energy it takes to build it. Especially when the world around you is moving faster than your timelines. This is where "Good Enough" comes in. We're compromising, but we're being smart.

In the Run pillar, the CIO doesn't waste time waiting for the "perfect" system upgrade. They look at the current setup and an iterative implementation and go with it. Because trying to build the "perfect" system might take six months, drain the budget, and miss the window for a business opportunity that's already passing you by. We can use the 80-20 rule to focus on the 20% of issues that are taking up 80% of the efforts.

In the real world, "good enough" is often the best option. It avoids the paralysis of endless analysis, the sunk costs of over-engineering, and the delays that come from waiting for the "perfect" moment.

Figure 9.5 The tipping point model

9.3 Mental Models for Investment Decisions

9.3.1 The Tipping Point Model

Author Malcolm Gladwell talked about this in his book *The Tipping Point: How Little Things Can Make a Big Difference* (Gladwell, 2000). Applying the concepts to FinOps, the model, as shown in Figure 9.5, achieves its goal through initial spends that produce positive outcomes. These eventually reach a critical point and create a cascading effect that results in major long-term value. This model can be used for a large-scale transformation. Strategic upgrades unlock agility and innovation. This generates significant savings in the long run and needs only minimal efforts to maintain.

9.3.2 The "Momentum" Model

The "Momentum" Model is related. Investments produce momentum and enable faster improvement. Strategic investments create a crucial advantage, and smaller efforts are used to sustain and amplify that momentum. This model helps prioritize investments that will generate a self-reinforcing cycle of value creation. A single investment, done right, can unlock a chain reaction of faster decisions and teams that start seeing possibilities where they once saw dead ends.

A virtuous cycle where the value compounds can be the best thing for an IT transformation. I remember a client who migrated to the cloud. At first, it felt like a typical migration exercise, moving servers, updating protocols, and migrating applications. But within months, they were harnessing the advantage that the cloud offered. They were iterating faster, testing ideas in hours instead of weeks. That agility became a magnet for innovation. That's momentum in action.

There's a network effect at play as well. The first win gets you noticed. The second gets you more resources. The third gets you a culture that's hungry for more. It's like the early adopter who becomes the evangelist, pulling others in with them. I've seen this in AI projects that start small but grow into strategic cornerstones. They opened a door to the future.

But momentum is fragile. You have to adjust as you go. A tool that worked last year might be obsolete next month. A team that thrives on experimentation might need structure or else they will crash or forever stay in an experimentation mode that never reaches production in the live. The model needs a system that keeps the momentum alive.

9.3.3 The "Opportunity Cost" Model

Let's talk about the hard part of decision-making, the what-ifs. Every time you pick one project over another, you're saying no to something else. That's the Opportunity Cost (Fernando, 2025) model in a nutshell. It's slightly pessimistic, in my opinion, but it forces you to consider the alternatives. You naturally think only of what you gain from an investment, but you also consider what you lose by not choosing the other options.

The stark reality is that your time and money are finite. Resources are finite, and opportunity calls you. So, when you decide to fund a new data analytics platform, you're choosing a tool but you're also deciding to defer that server upgrade for your data center to the next year or cut back the planned investment in rolling out the new AI enterprise chatbot. Those are real trade-offs. The question is more than just whether the initiative delivers value. You know from ROI calculations that it will. But the real question is, what's the best use of your funds?

We go through this exact dilemma in almost every leadership decision. Recently, I had a choice: whether to spend $2 million on a platform modernization that promised to revolutionize our call center platform, or use that same budget to implement AIOps to improve our technology operations. In the end, we decided on a phased approach that let us achieve both. But if you have to choose only one, the Opportunity Cost model forces you to ask which of these is the bigger win in the long run. Is the call center platform a strategic leap forward, or is it a distraction from fixing the foundation and enabling efficient collaboration? It's about context.

The model doesn't apply only to big bets. It's applicable to every dollar you spend. That $50,000 you allocate to a new tool? What's the cost of not using that money to hire a specialist who could automate a bottleneck? That $100,000 you spend on a vendor? What's the cost of not investing in open-source solutions that could scale faster? Every investment is a choice. And the most informed choices are the ones that don't look at the upside and also influence you to look at the downside of what you're leaving behind.

9.3.4 *The S-Curve – The "Lifecycle" Perspective*

Timing is everything when it comes to tech investment. Picture the S-curve (Weidinger, 2025). As shown in Figure 9.6, it starts steep, flattens out, then stabilizes. Most organizations get stuck in the middle of the curve. They're chasing the next big thing but can't see the trap of maturity. Teams pour millions into platforms that are already saturated because they're safe. But safety here is a trap. It's like buying a car that's already been driven into the ground. You're not building for the future; you're just keeping the lights on. It's important to keep in mind the money you are spending when something is past the curve.

Any new innovation has sky-high expenses and low adoption in initial phases. Early adopters are your best friends. They give you feedback and boost your confidence that things are going to improve. Then comes growth. Costs drop and adoption takes off. It's the phase where you lean in and bet on the wave before it crashes. That's the power of timing.

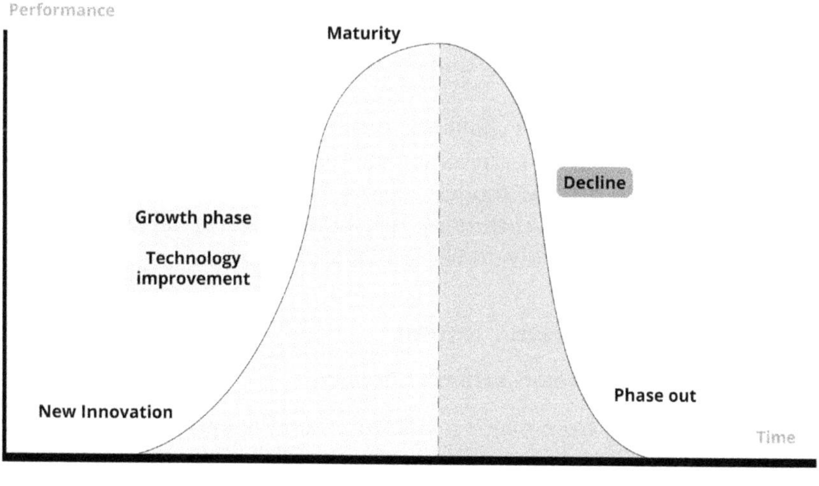

Figure 9.6 The S-curve provides a lifecycle perspective

Maturity is stable, but stagnant. It's the phase that keeps the lights on but won't light up the future. Your legacy systems are here. They're the ones that cost more to maintain than they're worth. The S-Curve forces you to ask whether we are satisfied with maintaining the present or wanting to build the future.

And then there's a decline in the curve's descent. This is where you draw the line. I've seen teams pour resources into dying technology. It's a costly mistake. The S-Curve helps you decide where to place your valuable bets.

9.3.5 *Why Do These Models Matter*

There are other models for making investment decisions.

- The "Phase-Shift" Model specifies that investments often trigger shifts in operational maturity. A large capital investment might establish a core foundational capability. Smaller efforts support its ongoing evolution and optimization. This can also guide decisions on whether to invest in a completely new system or incrementally improve an existing one.
- The "Staircase" Model demonstrates how investments advance through successive incremental steps that produce an increasing total impact. The initial development stage requires major capital expenditures for construction, but the following stages focus on operational expenses to achieve peak performance.
- In the "Utility Maximization" model, you aim to get the highest possible level of benefit from an investment. Value progression does not need to be linear or direct. Organizations can gain intangible benefits that boost employee productivity and customer satisfaction.

The mental models help you challenge assumptions by emphasizing understanding the specific circumstances surrounding an investment. The implementation of these mental models allows FinOps to move away from technical details and concentrate on delivering business value. The right choice requires organizations to change their thinking.

9.4 Avoiding Overcommitment

9.4.1 *Saying "No" to Non-essential Projects*

IT operations suffer from major inefficiencies and financial waste because of overcommitment. It often occurs when teams accept too many projects beyond their budgeted resources and operational limits. It strains their ability and compromises their quality. It's a hidden threat to financial control that hinders organizations from achieving successful FinOps operations.

The fundamental mental model that can work in this scenario is "Opportunity Cost." Every affirmative decision eliminates other possible outcomes. Within "Run," this means constantly evaluating the cost (not just monetary, but also in terms of time and effort) of supporting less critical projects. Evaluate proposed changes based on their ability to generate business value that matches the investment costs. The "Innovate" process needs scenario planning to assess new concepts properly before moving forward with resource allocation. The Pareto Principle enables organizations to maximize their value by concentrating on 20% of their projects, which produce 80% of their results, while preventing resource waste on non-productive initiatives.

9.4.2 *Managing Flexibility*

The "Systems Thinking" model is helpful in understanding the overall dynamics of your entire IT ecosystem. It can pinpoint how overallocation makes IT systems rigid and unable to adapt to changing business requirements because of the complexity and dependencies introduced by too many elements. The system becomes less able to respond to business requirements because of its excessive capacity and overlapping features. The "S-Curve" model shows that timing is of the essence. Putting too much money into technologies at their maturity stage makes it harder to develop new innovations. The Minimum Viable Product (MVP) method enables organizations to test and expand their changes step by step, which protects their ability to adapt in the long run.

The Lean Approach for IT management uses Lean Manufacturing principles to eliminate all non-value-adding activities that do not benefit the business. "Value Stream Mapping" helps "Run" operations to evaluate projects by removing or optimizing all non-essential processes and service complexities. The organization now prioritizes delivering correct outcomes over following correct procedures. The Lean principle guides "Transform" to implement "Kaizen," which means making small continuous improvements. In Innovate, it enables fast prototyping and experimental testing to speed up the launch of new services and technological solutions. The main goal is simplifying operations while cutting down on unnecessary costs and concentrating on delivering the highest possible value. A demand forecasting model can predict future IT needs based on projected business growth and changing priorities. These models help you build a flexible and resilient IT infrastructure that can adapt to future demands.

The Law of Social Exchange states that human relationships and cooperation are driven by mutual benefit. Individuals and groups engage in actions when they feel that the benefits of the exchange outweigh the costs. Similarly, successful IT initiatives depend on reciprocal relationships where stakeholders see value in exchanges such as those resulting in cost savings or innovation. Change requires collective ownership and shared incentives, where all parties benefit from transformation efforts. This law reinforces the chapter's emphasis on mental models as tools to design trust-based, accountable cultures where decisions are informed by collaboration rather than isolated biases. When teams internalize these mental models that help in decision-making or avoiding biases, they begin to create a positive environment that is able to use rationale, detect and avoid biases in judgment. It lets them make important decisions without creating animosity. Enterprise FinOps depends upon reciprocity, transparency, and shared goals in overcoming challenges. Social dynamics and mental models shape informed, unbiased, and collaborative decision-making and create a feedback loop that accelerates cultural shift. This becomes a catalyst for aligning behaviors and embedding FinOps into the organizational DNA.

Notes

1 FinOps refers to Enterprise FinOps and applies to the entire IT spend unless specifically mentioned with reference to the FinOps Framework from the FinOps Foundation.
2 "Run," "Transform" and "Innovate" refer to the run and maintenance operations, transformations and innovation pillars described in the RTI360 model in Chapter 1.

References

Brains, Behavior & Design Group. (2011). *Brains, behavior & design toolkit.* Retrieved from http://www.brainsbehavioranddesign.com/kit.html

Covey, R. S. (2004). *The 7 habits of highly effective people: Powerful lessons in personal change.* New York, NY: Free Press.

Dunning-Kruger Effect. (2025). Retrieved from https://en.wikipedia.org/wiki/Dunning%E2%80%93Kruger_effect

Feedback Loops. (2025). Retrieved from https://aboutmentalmodels.com/feedback-loops-mental-model/

Fernando, J. (2025). *Opportunity cost.* Retrieved from Investopedia.com: https://www.investopedia.com/terms/o/opportunitycost.asp

Gladwell, M. (2000). *The tipping point: How little things can make a big difference.* New York, NY: Little, Brown and Company.

Kahneman, D. (2013). *Thinking fast and slow.* New York, NY: Farrar, Straus and Giroux.

Martirosyan, A. (2021). *First principles thinking*. Retrieved from https://www.maray.ai/posts/first-principles-thinking
Munger, C. (2005). *The psychology of human judgement, revised*. Retrieved from https://fs.blog/great-talks/psychology-human-misjudgment/
Parrish, S. (2025). *The great mental models - Volumes 1 through 4; Boxed set*. New York, NY: Penguin Random House.
Ries, E. (2011). *The lean startup: How today''s entrepreneurs use continuous innovation to create radically successful businesses*. New York, NY: Crown Currency.
The Lemon Law. (2025). Retrieved from https://en.wikipedia.org/wiki/Lemon_law
Weidinger, D. (2025). *The S-curve*. Retrieved from https://www.indeed.com/career-advice/career-development/s-curve

Part IV

The Evolution of Enterprise FinOps

This part looks at the next steps in the evolution of Enterprise FinOps. Leveraging technologies like AI and automation can take you further up the maturity scale and accelerate the benefits from Enterprise FinOps. Enterprise FinOps becomes a silent but powerful engine ensuring continuous cost optimization and business alignment.

DOI: 10.4324/9781003682196-14

Chapter 10

The Future of Enterprise FinOps

DOI: 10.4324/9781003682196-15

10.1 A Strategic IT Capability

The modern IT landscape is a living, breathing ecosystem where agility and innovation are the oxygen. Enterprise FinOps redefines its role as a strategic partner, moving from cost control to value creation, from reactive firefighting to proactive alignment with business goals. Teams start by chasing cost overruns, fixing leaks and tears in the fabric of IT. With consistent progress along the FinOps[1] journey, it becomes a proactive force, weaving itself into the fabric of business strategy.

Enterprise FinOps demands a different lens. We evaluate investments on price, as well as on how well they align with business needs. You can turn IT into a value engine. That means spotting risks before they blow up, whether security gaps, compliance missteps, technology debt, or operational hiccups, and calculating their financial toll before commencing to fix them.

10.1.1 Enterprise FinOps Redefines Value

For years, IT financial management felt like a game of tug-of-war. You'd be handed a budget, told to keep it under control, and left to figure out how to make that happen without breaking anything. A significant part of the time was buried in spending percentages, budget overruns, cost reductions, and quarterly reports. The result was a disconnected, adversarial relationship between IT and the rest of the business. Enterprise FinOps changes the game. It changes the question from how much you can save to what IT investments do for the business. Tracking outcomes means that we follow up on whether that cloud or datacenter migration reduced costs, whether it cut down on customer complaints, or improved the time to market.

The metrics we use matter. If we're still fixated on total IT spend or percentage changes in the budget, we're looking at the wrong map. Enterprise FinOps introduces KPIs that actually matter because they are firmly aligned with business outcomes, such as how fast we can launch new features, how happy customers are, or how efficiently we're using resources. These are signals that tell us whether IT is fueling the business or just keeping the lights on.

Traditional budgeting cycles are annual, rigid, and typically based on what we spent last year. Enterprise FinOps lets you align spending with where the business is headed, not where it was. Smart forecasting goes way beyond just accounting. This shift changes how we measure success and also who we need to be. If we can't show how IT drives revenue, improves customer satisfaction, improves efficiency, or accelerates innovation, IT remains just another indistinct department in the enterprise. Figure 10.1

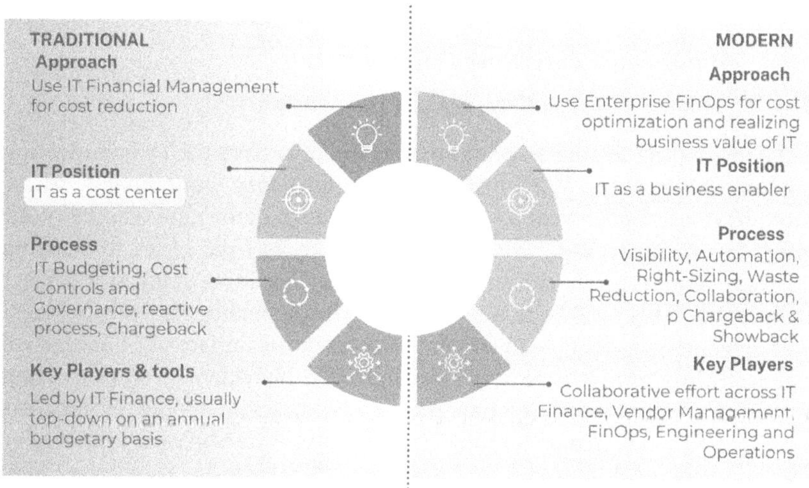

Figure 10.1 Traditional vs modern IT approaches

compares traditional approaches in IT to a modern, Enterprise FinOps-aligned approach.

10.2 The Power of AI and Machine Learning

AI/ML's power lies in its ability to learn from data to identify patterns and predict outcomes. The data can be either structured, such as in tables, system logs, or databases, or unstructured data, such as documents and manuals. You can even integrate domain or industry-specific knowledge. Once you have a trained model and working algorithms, it can assist you in identifying patterns and predicting outcomes. The models can be retrained and enhanced, adapting to new information, letting you make refined and more accurate decisions over time. AI/ML can automate repetitive tasks. It can even operate in real-time for instantaneous actions. These capabilities make AI/ML an indispensable tool for transforming Enterprise FinOps into an intelligent and strategic function.

The first part of this section looks into the ways AI can augment Enterprise FinOps processes such as cost and rate optimization, budgeting and forecasting, etc. Then we look at some AI tools and techniques such as GenAI, AIOps, and agentic AI that can let you implement it in your Enterprise FinOps workflow.

10.2.1 AI Augments Enterprise FinOps

10.2.1.1 AI and FinOps for Budgeting and Forecasting

At the heart of your financial and management system for IT is budgeting and forecasting costs. With historical spending data, your finance teams would have used statistical or other techniques to determine whether your budget is on track. With AI/ML, models such as time-series forecasting and regression analysis can analyze historical spending data and predict future costs. This is a huge aid to let teams align budgets with business goals. Scenario modeling can simulate the financial impact of IT initiatives such as scaling infrastructure or moving cloud providers. A FinOps team can use ML to forecast that a new product launch will increase cloud costs by 30% in Q4. The team can look for other optimization opportunities or work with the product team to determine if costs can be saved elsewhere to keep the budget on track.

10.2.1.2 AI-Powered Anomaly Detection

Your IT landscape is a complex maze of humming systems, transactions, information, and data flows. If something happens that is out of the ordinary, it can go undetected until too late. AI-powered anomaly detection is like a spotlight. It spots the weird stuff like sudden database spikes, storage leaks, or billing errors before they blow up. Usually, you'd wait impatiently for a post-mortem. But you can stop scrambling now. Unsupervised learning and pattern recognition sniff out unusual spending patterns such as sudden spikes, unauthorized resource usage, and help in fraud prevention. For FinOps, this means that you can be proactive and collaborate with engineering teams to quickly act on the problem area. Automated alerts flag anomalies for investigation. An ML model can detect that a team is using 10x more storage or compute than typical, revealing a misconfigured backup process that can be corrected. It's a system that knows what "normal" looks like and screams when it sees something different.

In the whitepaper, "AIOps for Log Anomaly Detection in the Era of LLMs: A Systematic Literature Review," the authors review LLM-based techniques for anomaly detection in AIOps systems and the use of Retrieval-Augmented Generation (RAG) to enhance LLMs' task-specific reasoning in IT operations (Cabello, Machado, & Sales, n.d.).

10.2.1.3 Continuous Cost Optimization with AI and FinOps

With Enterprise FinOps, cost optimization becomes an ongoing, continuous process, with teams routinely executing rightsizing, rate, and workload optimization actions. AI/ML can automate this. Imagine a system that goes beyond looking at metrics like CPU and memory usage but actually understands the workload. If your workload is a video rendering cluster, AI knows that GPU-heavy instances are the way to go. If it is a database with spiky traffic patterns due to variable transactions and batch programs, AL could suggest burstable instances. Optimization algorithms work continuously in the background to locate cost-effective resource allocations and also pinpoint them down to specific actions such as rightsizing VMs or switching to spot instances. AI/ML-enabled tools can monitor services across your IT landscape and offer recommendations on consolidating underutilized services. Imagine a FinOps team that can slice through their cloud spend and quickly determine that 30% of their costs are coming from a legacy app that's only used by 2% of the company. That's an immediate trigger for optimization.

Taking a step further, AI agents can execute actions such as automatically shutting down unused development environments during off-hours, reducing infrastructure and cloud costs. AI helps you allocate costs where they matter most.

10.2.1.4 AI-Powered Governance

Tagging automation is one of the most persistent headaches in FinOps. Manual tagging is error-prone, slow, and expensive. AI changes that. Algorithms suggest optimal tags and even apply them automatically as resources are provisioned, assigning the right cost centers and projects to resources.

Governance and policies are a necessary and essential part of IT. A SOX or GDPR audit is a critical but much-dreaded event for many companies. AI auto-applies tags as resources are created, ensuring compliance without slowing down developers. ML models can identify risks like unauthorized cloud usage or noncompliant configurations. Automated internal audits reduce the risk of extensive and urgent remediations from a failed audit by ensuring continuous adherence to regulatory requirements and internal policies. You can set up AI tools to flag exceptions that bypass guardrails, such as misconfigured databases or systems that violate data privacy policies, preventing potential fines resulting from an external audit.

10.2.1.5 *Optimize Vendor Management with AI*

Vendor management is typically a bottleneck in IT. Contracts and renewals take weeks to close. Legal teams are overwhelmed with the sheer number of contracts to go through. AI/ML can optimize your vendor management processes. I challenged my team to conduct a pilot where a model that was trained on standard legal contracts could red-flag clauses that didn't comply. Vendor contracts are no longer a black box. AI digs into granular usage data such as how many hours you're using reserved instances, how often you're hitting burst limits, or even how your workloads correlate with provider-specific discounts. Suddenly, rate optimization, a typical FinOps process, becomes supercharged. You're not just asking for a better rate. With evidence such as whether you used 95% of your reserved instances last quarter, you can confidently commit to a 12-month term.

You can train an ML model on benchmark prices and compare quotes with industry standards. An ML model can identify that your quote for that SaaS tool is 40% more expensive than the industry benchmark, and your VMO can renegotiate with the vendor. With real-time dashboards, you get visibility into spending trends. It becomes fairly routine to set up dynamic alerts powered by AI/ML. A finance team can set up an alert when a team's cloud spend exceeds a certain threshold, say, 80% of their budget, and this triggers a review to prevent overspending.

Think of AI as a financial analyst fine-tuned for your IT spend. It looks at usage patterns such as whether an application is generating $2 million in revenue per month and suggests that you prioritize its resources. Or, whether a tool is only used by three people and needs to be deprioritized. It's maximizing your return and unlocking value.

10.2.1.6 *Personalized Insights and Scenario Simulation*

AI/ML shines when it comes to offering personalized insights. GenAI translates complex data into recommendations that teams understand easily. AI-generated reports personalize information based on stakeholder roles. Finance teams can get ROI metrics while engineers see optimization suggestions.

AI/ML makes scenario simulation straightforward. Monte Carlo simulations can model the financial impact of strategic decisions. What-if analysis evaluates trade-offs between cost, performance, and innovation. A company can use ML to simulate the cost of migrating to a hybrid cloud model, balancing upfront investment with long-term savings. Your strategic planning becomes more accurate.

10.2.1.7 *Supercharge Operations with AI*

AI/ML takes operations to the next level. Capacity planning used to be a guessing game. Static estimates were based on last year's data. ML algorithms analyze historical usage, tie it to seasonality, marketing campaigns, and business cycles. Going beyond predicting demand, they understand the underlying causes. Reinforcement learning models, for example, don't just follow static rules. They adapt. Think of an e-commerce site that sees traffic spikes during Black Friday. A traditional auto-scaling policy might scale up aggressively, then scale back down, leaving resources idle for weeks. AI learns from past demand patterns, predicts the next spike, and scales just enough without over-provisioning.

Root cause analysis takes hours of digging through logs, tags, and service metrics. With AIOps, when an alert triggers, the system can narrow down to the root cause and suggest ways to fix it. With advanced AIOps techniques, you can even self-heal certain incidents. Your blind spots can be eliminated. The future of FinOps is about smarter decisions. Organizations that embrace this shift align IT spend with business goals, optimize every dollar, and build systems that adapt as fast as the world around them.

10.2.2 *AI Tools and Techniques*

10.2.2.1 *GenAI*

As you are well aware, Generative AI (GenAI) is a subset of AI that creates new, original content. Text, images, videos, data, or even code can be created using prompts. Many companies, as well as open-source groups and universities, have released Large Language Models (LLMs) that you can easily use. These models use techniques like deep learning to train on vast datasets. While traditional ML models extract insights from data, generative models create new content. GenAI uses synthesis rather than analysis.

In Enterprise FinOps, it can automate report generation, simulate scenarios, and translate complex data into actionable insights, bridging gaps between technical and non-technical stakeholders. You can further extend publicly available models with your own data using techniques like RAG and fine-tuning. GenAI doesn't spit out generic advice when it's fine-tuned with your data. It learns your business.

10.2.2.2 *AI for IT Operations (AIOps)*

As per Gartner, "An AIOps platform combines big data and machine learning functionality to support all primary IT operations functions through the scalable ingestion and analysis of the ever-increasing volume, variety and velocity of data generated by IT" (Gartner, 2025).

AIOps integrates AI/ML into IT operations. It automates processes, enhances decision-making, and optimizes system performance. There are several AIOps tools available from major vendors that integrate well with existing IT operations, service, and asset management systems.

AIOps starts with data integration. It aggregates and analyzes data from diverse sources in your IT landscape. These could be system logs from your cloud and datacenter VMs, servers and databases, application and security logs, metrics and KPIs, incident history, case history, and even user behavior synthesized from chats and call logs. AIOps automates incident detection, root cause analysis, and even remediation. It correlates alerts across multiple hardware, software, and services layers of an IT application or process, and reduces the noise, narrowing down to the root cause. From responding to alerts, you move to understanding the why and proactively preventing future incidents. Think of it as a detective who not only solves the crime but rewires the locks to stop the next one.

AIOps saves time and money. AIOps automation streamlines repetitive tasks and can speed up service requests, such as resource or access provisioning. Typical IT operational activities, such as incident resolution, clog up agent time and efforts. AIOps can be configured to create self-healing systems that automatically resolve issues without human intervention. The pattern detection in AIOps can detect things that humans may miss. If every time a certain change is made and a server crashes, AIOps could flag it, predict the next crash (letting you prevent it before the crash happens), and even suggest a long-term fix.

Predictive analytics in AIOps can forecast system failures and performance bottlenecks. It uses feedback loops to refine processes and models iteratively. It supercharges Enterprise FinOps by enabling real-time cost monitoring and identifying anomalies in spending. Without anomaly detection, FinOps teams are like firefighters, running to the scene of a cost spike only after the damage is done. AIOps is like a fire alarm. It spots a cost anomaly in real time, traces it back to a misconfigured VM or an overprovisioned server, and tells you how to fix it.

It can analyze change management data, predict how a new deployment might ripple through your infrastructure, and even suggest a safer rollout path. By integrating financial and operational data, AIOps provides actionable insights for cost governance, compliance, and strategic planning.

AWS has a great resource on AIOps that explores how AWS can support an AIOps implementation (Amazon AWS, 2025).

10.2.2.3 Retrieval-Augmented Generation (RAG)

Traditional LLMs are trained on massive datasets. You hear of staggering numbers such as GPT-4o being trained with over 1.8 trillion parameters.

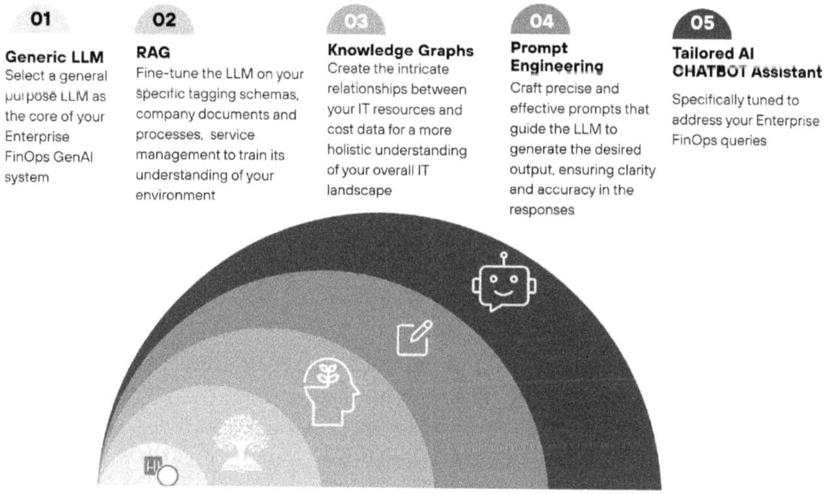

Figure 10.2 RAG for Enterprise FinOps

But even the most powerful LLMs have a simple basic gap. They struggle with the nuances of your particular organization's environment, the specific configurations of your IT infrastructure, the intricacies of your applications, and the unique business priorities that drive your IT spending. Retrieval-Augmented Generation (RAG) (retrieval-augmented-generation, 2025) addresses this limitation by bridging the gap between general knowledge and tailored insights, creating an AI assistant that understands and responds directly to the context of your enterprise. Figure 10.2 illustrates a high-level approach for RAG, and how other techniques can complement it.

You've got a superb chatbot service that's powered by the latest LLM. It's smart. It answers questions. But when you ask it why your cloud bill is 20% higher this quarter, it will respond with generic advice such as reducing instances or optimizing storage. It doesn't know your environment because it doesn't have your data. You'll come away with a general idea of what to do, but your teams will have to dig into your specific data to come up with insights. That's the gap. RAG is the bridge between AI's raw smarts and your company's unique DNA. Instead of relying solely on the LLM's general knowledge, RAG connects it to *your* data. It builds up a curated knowledge base on top of the LLM that contains a map of your IT spending, environment dependencies, resource configurations, and governance policies. The beauty of RAG lies in its ability to synthesize information from both a general LLM and a carefully curated knowledge base, resulting in responses that are far more accurate, relevant, and actionable than those produced by a standalone LLM. With RAG, your response would have to be,

> Your "prod" environment in region us-east-1 is running 15 instances of a batch application that was deployed this quarter. However, it's only used during off-hours for an average of 2 hours per day. Historical data since deployment shows that this pattern repeats monthly. Changing configurations to turn off the application during business hours, or using spot instances could reduce your cloud bill.

RAG takes effort to fine-tune. You have to feed it examples of your infrastructure code, your tagging schemes, and your cost data. You have to craft prompts that guide it. You have to build a knowledge graph that maps how your resources, applications, and costs are connected. If you skip the data quality part, it's going to lead to inconsistencies; you're in trouble. If your tagging is inconsistent, the AI will guess. If you have inaccurate cost data, the AI will misdiagnose. That's why deploying RAG is not the end. We need to audit our data. We need to clean our tags and document our policies.

I've experienced the power of RAG in action when my team used it to train our enterprise LLM with case history and incident resolution data. Our help desk agents were able to narrow down specific resolutions by querying the chatbot, speeding up incident resolution. RAG clears the gap between AI's potential and your business's needs. It turns a general-purpose tool into a dedicated assistant.

10.2.2.4 Knowledge Graphs

Knowledge graphs are structured, interconnected representations of entities such as people, organizations, systems, departments, or knowledge concepts, and their relationships. They organize information in a way that machines can understand context and answer complex queries. Knowledge Graphs function as a structured data source and allow RAGs to precisely retrieve contextually relevant information, thus improving the accuracy of answers.

The structured nature of Knowledge Graphs allows RAG to reduce ambiguity by looking up the context found in its relationships and nodes. When you need domain-specific expertise or have complex queries, Knowledge Graphs are critical to providing accuracy for the AI NLP Chatbots that use this trained and RAG and Knowledge Graph augmented

LLM model. Typically, they are implemented by embedding special tools like graph databases.

10.2.2.5 AI-Powered Enterprise FinOps Chatbot

The future of Enterprise FinOps is developing a private, secure, and data-aware chatbot that uses a fine-tuned, enterprise data-trained GenAI LLM in the background. Your teams can use this to query any FinOps activity, analyze documents, or generate code and recommendations. It stitches together data from server logs, app performance metrics, case management systems, system advisories, and even Slack or Teams messages. Your FinOps team gets responses to questions like, "Why is this database costing 30% more than last month? Is the team using a new tool? Could we restructure the queries?" What would previously have involved meetings with the database operations team now becomes an action that the database engineering team can add to their priority list.

Your FinOps team can model outcomes with the chatbot. They can construct scenarios like what if you were switched to a managed service rather than using the on-premises hosted service, or what would be the impact of changing vendors for a support contract. You can upload a software license contract, and the chatbot may spot a 40% drop in usage from Q3 to Q4. Your team can then draft a message to the vendor to ask them to adjust your licensing model. It can augment Enterprise FinOps automation efforts by writing Infrastructure-as-Code. If you need a server setup that meets compliance standards, it can write the code, check the security protocols, and deploy it. Your team is free to focus on the big picture.

This isn't a replacement for humans. It's a partner that augments their efforts. The AI might generate a plan, but it's up to you to validate it and determine if it aligns with your strategic goals or if it could disrupt operations. That's where your judgment comes in.

10.2.2.6 Agentic AI – From Insights to Automated Actions

Agentic AI systems are AI systems with advanced characteristics, unlike your typical AI systems. These characteristics, such as adaptability, autonomy, goal orientation, and collaboration, make them powerful tools for FinOps. It lets them make decisions, take actions, and learn from outcomes without constant human intervention. Agentic AI mimics humans. It dynamically interacts with environments and adjusts strategies based on feedback.

Autonomy guides it in independent decision-making. It can execute tasks like automating workflows or optimizing resources. It is adaptable. The agent keeps learning from new data and evolving strategies in real time. Goal orientation keeps the agent focused on specific objectives. You train the agent in the objectives that matter. It could be cost reduction, compliance, or efficiency. With collaboration, the agent is integrated with human workflows. Imagine a system that doesn't just tell you there's a problem but fixes it before you even know it exists. You're stuck in a meeting, and someone else handles a critical task without you needing to say a word. That's what agentic AI does. It's not only reacting; it's also acting. It sees a server struggling, and instead of sending an alert, it scales up resources. No human intervention or waiting. Just a problem solved.

Like AIOps, agentic AI supercharges FinOps by automating complex, repetitive tasks and enabling proactive resource optimization, such as dynamically scaling cloud infrastructure. But the technologies work differently. Agentic AI is a mix of technologies working in harmony. Think of it like training your dog. You give it a reward for doing the right thing. You correct it when it goes off track. That's reinforcement learning at work. Then there are the rules that act like traffic signs. They're not there to stop the AI but to guide it and provide alternatives. They keep things safe. Agentic AI uses orchestration across multiple systems and actions. That's why the AI goes further. It fixes it, spins up servers, adjusts configurations, and can even optimize code.

For IT teams, it means less manual work and fewer alerts to chase. Systems become more resilient. Agentic AI is the future of FinOps. Systems that can self-manage are finally feasible, but human oversight remains crucial for strategic direction and complex problem-solving. When the agentic AI handles the day-to-day optimization, it frees up valuable human resources to focus on higher-value tasks.

This informative article from Pega, "What is agentic AI?" explains the difference between agentic AI and traditional AI and its ability to run with little human intervention or completely autonomously (Pega, 2025).

10.3 The Power of Automation

Automation isn't a replacement for human insight. It's a multiplier. Your FinOps team has the brainpower to spot a cost-saving opportunity in a sea of data. But without automation, they're stuck sifting through spreadsheets, querying operations teams, chasing down Shadow IT, or manually resizing instances during a peak traffic hour. Several FinOps activities are repetitive and rule-based, but error-prone and tedious. Scaling up or down based on a single metric? Checking 100+ dashboards for a single integrated cloud bill? That's drudgery. Automation takes the weight off human shoulders, letting experts focus on the big picture, such as aligning IT spend with business goals, spotting inefficiencies in legacy systems, or even predicting where the next cost spike might come from. But automation is a living, breathing system that needs constant tuning and iteration. Your rules, policies, code, and algorithms must evolve as your business does. A policy that worked last year might be obsolete next quarter. An algorithm that predicted demand accurately in 2024 might need retraining in 2026.

10.3.1 Augmented FinOps

Automation in FinOps is like a toolkit of approaches that you use to automate FinOps processes for specific outcomes. Augmented FinOps uses intelligent automation and AI to evolve FinOps from a traditional manual process to a strategic approach.

10.3.1.1 Data Collection and Reporting

Manually pulling metrics from AWS, Azure, and GCP consoles is a nightmare. It's slow, error-prone, and utterly unsustainable. Automation is like having a 24/7 intern who pulls instance usage, storage costs, and network traffic from every corner of your cloud environment and transforms data as needed. It can be used to pull IT spend from other corners of your domain and give you a unified view. Allocating IT spend to the right department or project is a nightmare. Automation maps resource usage with billing data. It creates detailed reports and sends chargeback notifications to the right stakeholders. It's like having a single pane of glass for your entire FinOps operation.

10.3.1.2 Reactive Monitoring

Tools like AWS CloudWatch, Azure Monitor, or GCP Stackdriver are your first line of defense that alert you when something goes wrong, like a database instance hitting a cost or storage threshold. But this is firefighting, where you are always playing catch-up. Alerts flood in, and half of them turn out to be false positives. You spend hours digging through logs, only to find the real issue was a one-time spike in traffic. Reactive monitoring and alerts are just the first step in a much longer journey.

10.3.1.3 Rightsizing Automation

Imagine if your e-commerce site crashes during Black Friday because you scaled up inadequately. Automation learns from historical patterns. It scales up when demand spikes, scales down when traffic drops, and does it without a single human intervention.

A team provisions a "high-performance" instance for a simple app, only to realize it's 80% underutilized. Automation can monitor CPU, memory, and disk usage in real time, then automatically downsize underused instances. In rightsizing automation, machine learning meets FinOps. You analyze historical data, spot patterns, and adjust instance sizes in real time. A sudden spike in network traffic may not just be a cost issue, but it could be a security breach.

10.3.1.4 *Toolchain and Workflow Automation*

Orchestration takes things to the next level. Toolchain automation automates the entire SDLC lifecycle from provisioning infrastructure, deploying code, testing, to rolling back if something goes wrong. Automation gives teeth to policy enforcement. Let's say your security team sets a rule: "No developer instances can run outside of 6 AM to 11 PM." Without automation, that rule is just a suggestion. With it, the system automatically terminates any instance that violates the policy. It prevents budget overruns, stops security breaches, and ensures compliance without a single human needing to intervene. Workflow automation takes the stress out of tedious and slow tasks such as approving requests. No more back-and-forth emails when automation makes everything traceable.

10.3.1.5 *Rule-Based Automation*

This is where you start to move from being reactive to being proactive. You set up rules that determine actions to take on specific scenarios, like "If an instance is idle for 30 minutes, terminate it," or "If a cluster's CPU utilization hits 80%, scale up." These rules are simple, but they're powerful. They address common cost issues without waiting for a problem to blow up. But these rules are rigid and don't think. They blindly follow instructions as coded. If your workload patterns are unpredictable, you're going to get a lot of false positives.

10.3.1.6 *Tag-Based Automation*

We talked about tagging as an Enterprise FinOps lever previously. You can leverage tags for cost allocation and build up other automation approaches around it. You assign a "Marketing" tag to every resource used by that team, and suddenly you can track exactly how much they're spending. This only works if your tagging strategy is flawless. A mislabeled resource can throw your system off track.

Table 10.1 Automation approaches for Enterprise FinOps

Category	*Approach*	*Focus*	*Popular tools*	*Benefits*
Reactive monitoring	Cloud provider alerts	Immediate anomaly detection	AWS CloudWatch, Azure Monitor, GCP Stackdriver	Early warning, cost spikes
Rule-based automation	Predefined rules and alerts	Triggered actions based on rules	CloudHealth, Flexera One	Automated remediation, basic cost control
Tag-based automation	Leveraging tags for cost allocation	Automatic cost attribution	CloudHealth, Flexera One	Improved cost transparency, team accountability
Policy-as-code	Infrastructure-as-code (IaC) for cost optimization	Automated resource provisioning and deprovisioning	Terraform, CloudFormation, ARM Templates	Self-healing infrastructure, consistent policies
Rightsizing automation	Dynamic instance sizing based on workload	Automated adjustment of instance sizes	RightScale, Apptio Cloudability	Optimized resource utilization
Anomaly detection (ML-based)	Machine learning for predictive cost analysis	Proactive identification of cost trends	Apptio Cloudability, Flexera One, Datadog, ServiceNow	Reduced risk of cost overruns
Spend controls and budgets	Automated enforcement of spending limits	Automated blocking of overspending	CloudHealth, Flexera One	Budget adherence, risk mitigation

10.3.1.7 Policy-as-Code

Infrastructure-as-Code tools like Terraform or CloudFormation can let you automate maintenance tasks like provisioning or scaling. But you can also use these to embed governance policies, such as for cost optimization, into your configurations. An instance can automatically resize up to a maximum and down to a minimum based on workload.

10.3.1.8 Automation Tools

There are several platforms that can let you develop and deploy Infrastructure-as-Code for specific purposes. Table 10.1 outlines categories for automation, their benefits and some popular tools. This is a partial list only. Most enterprise systems and platforms, like AIOps or agentic AI that we discussed earlier in this chapter, have built-in hooks for automation. You can also evolve your own automation platform from scratch using tools provided by different vendors. When tools work together, they're symbiotic. Flexera One could collect granular cost data, while Apptio Cloudability analyzes it to identify strategic cost optimization opportunities. ServiceNow ties it all into workflows that actually do something. Ultimately, you are building an ecosystem. Each layer of automation feeds into the next. Reactive monitoring informs rule-based systems. Tag-based strategies enable policy-as-code. It's a constant, iterative process. You automate, refine, re-automate, and repeat. It's a long-term investment that ultimately leads you to more sophisticated tools like AIOps or agentic AI.

This article from NetBrain reflects on the stages involved in advancing automation along a maturity scale (NetBrain, 2025).

10.4 Emerging Technologies for Enterprise FinOps

10.4.1 How Will Blockchain Impact FinOps?

Blockchain can provide a foundational layer of trust and verifiable data. The concept of a permanent, unchangeable record of all financial transactions is a radical departure from the current reliance on centralized databases and reporting systems, which are inherently susceptible to alteration or subjective interpretation. With its inherent properties of immutability, transparency, and auditability, blockchain-based systems can directly address the shortcomings of current approaches.

Our current methods for tracking IT costs are riddled with gaps. Teams might mislabel a project, or a report gets lost in translation. It's how human systems work. But when you're trying to allocate $10 million in cloud spend across 500 teams, those gaps add up. Right now, cost attribution feels like playing 20 questions with a spreadsheet. You tag a server, but someone else tags the same server differently. A month later, you're staring at a report that says "Project X spent $25k," but can't prove it. Blockchain changes that. Every resource used gets logged in a way that's impossible to alter. It's like having a digital fingerprint on every dollar spent.

Service Level Agreement (SLA) compliance with blockchain can improve both governance and cost management. Traditionally, monitoring SLA performance requires continuous manual oversight. A blockchain-based system can automatically track resource utilization against SLAs, triggering automated cost adjustments when thresholds are breached. This ensures that organizations are not paying for resources that are not being utilized effectively and, conversely, are not being penalized for exceeding their allocated resources. Contracts are a complex interplay of usage tiers, SLA thresholds, penalty clauses, and license limits. Blockchain can watch your SaaS or cloud spend in real time, compare it to your contract, and adjust your bill automatically.

Blockchain can provide visibility and tracking across your supply chain. If you have a complex ecosystem of vendors, sub-vendors, and third-party services all contributing to your IT spend, tracking usage is like trying to follow a trail of breadcrumbs across three continents. Blockchain can show you exactly where your money is going, from the data center to the API call. You can spot inefficiencies, demand better rates, and hold providers accountable.

Solutions like Azure Confidential Ledger (Azure Confidential Ledger, 2025) provide a managed and decentralized ledger for data entries backed by blockchain to allow companies to maintain data integrity by preventing unauthorized or accidental modification. AWS offers the Amazon Managed Blockchain (Amazon Managed Blockchain, 2025), a fully managed service to build Web3 applications on both public and private blockchains.

However, blockchain is not as polished and ready for immediate use in Enterprise FinOps use cases as other AI tools we've talked about earlier. The technology is complex and needs specialized expertise, which can be a barrier to entry for organizations lacking the necessary technical skills. Cloud providers are experimenting with blockchain solutions for billing and service management. The fundamental shift offered by blockchain, which entails a system built on trust and verifiable data, is a significant step. It would operate as a foundational layer, providing a trusted and verifiable source of cost data, which would then be fed into other platforms to generate more informed insights and recommendations.

10.4.2 How Can AR/VR Assist in Enterprise FinOps?

Augmented Reality and Virtual Reality (AR/VR) can alter the way teams interact with, understand, and ultimately, optimize their IT investments. In AR, you overlay information over the real world. Think of walking through a data center and having performance and cost metrics pop up on your headset as you pass by racks and servers. An underutilized server shows up in red. You take the necessary action to right-size it.

Traditional 2D representations, such as graphs, charts, and dashboards, are pale in comparison to the intuitive and engaging possibilities afforded by an immersive, experiential approach. Users can "step into" a virtual representation of their IT infrastructure through a VR FinOps Dashboard. You point a virtual controller at a server cluster, and suddenly, the cost breakdown materializes like holograms floating in midair. The ability to "walk" through your virtual environment and correlate visual representation with cost data provides an immersive experience. You can feel the data and get a far more intuitive grasp of complex cost drivers.

Remote teams have always struggled with the problem of making abstract data feel real. In a VR environment, you're sharing a room, no matter where you are in the physical world. You and your team can stand in front of a 3D model of your IT portfolio, pointing out inefficiencies, dragging sliders to simulate cost cuts, and debating strategies in real time. The data becomes a shared language, and the barriers of distance vanish.

AR/VR can accelerate training. Throw someone into a VR tutorial where they're managing a simulated ERP environment, and now they can experiment with changed configurations and see the consequences without risking a production outage. It's a risk-free playground for building muscle memory around FinOps best practices. You give your team a sandbox to master them.

But AR/VR tools are expensive, and the UI design for these needs a complete reimagining. You can't just slap a 3D model onto a dashboard. It needs to be intuitive, immersive, and built for human hands, not just screens. The early days will likely see AR apps layered over existing consoles, offering quick insights like a heads-up display. But the real magic of true VR and the metaverse, where your FinOps teams meet up virtually with engineers on the other side of the country, is still in the future. For leaders, it's a chance to rethink how we interact with the very systems that power our businesses.

10.4.3 Enterprise FinOps Digital Twin for IT

Digital twins are usually associated with manufacturing systems. They mirror a physical asset, such as a machine or a production line, in a virtual environment. They duplicate a machine, track its vibrations, predict when it'll fail, and optimize its maintenance. This data is then used to simulate its performance, predict its failures, optimize its maintenance schedule, and ultimately, improve its overall efficiency.

Translating discrete physical assets to the intangible world of IT spend and operations requires a different approach. Imagine a world where your entire IT landscape is a living, breathing model that updates in real time, predicts where money might leak, and even suggests ways to plug those leaks before they form. That's the Enterprise FinOps Digital Twin, reimagined for the intangible world of IT. But IT is a complex dynamic system, a labyrinth of servers, licenses, processes, workflows, and people. Translating that model to IT means building something far more complex than a factory floor. You need to stitch together data from service providers, on-premises systems, SaaS tools, and the countless silos that litter modern enterprises.

But once you've got that living model, it evolves. Machine learning algorithms start watching server utilization, spotting underused resources, and suggesting cuts without breaking the system. You can see where a specific application is burning money, trace it back to a developer's workflow, or even predict how a new tool rollout will ripple through your infrastructure. The digital twin becomes a playground. A team simulates scaling up an application and estimates the cost spike before it happens, and adjusts accordingly to stay within budget. A developer deploys new code in the sandbox, spots potential bottlenecks, and avoids a production disaster.

You'll need data integration platforms that can handle the complexity of modern IT data, analytics tools that can parse through the chaos, and people who know how to make sense of it all. Starting off with an AIOps system would be a terrific first step. The future payoff would be a digital twin that becomes the nervous system of your enterprise.

The Law of Emergence states that complex systems exhibit properties that are not present in their individual components. It points to the future of Enterprise FinOps as a field that will generate enhanced capabilities through the interaction of its components. As organizations adopt advanced analytics, AI, and machine learning, the Enterprise FinOps framework will evolve intelligently to produce outcomes that were previously unattainable. For example, predictive modeling could emerge from the integration of real-time data, enabling CIOs to forecast IT spend with unprecedented accuracy. Similarly, AI-driven governance tools may emerge from the convergence of automation, compliance, policy enforcement, and risk management, creating a self-regulating system that optimizes IT spend without human intervention. RAG and Knowledge Graphs will enable powerful queries through an Enterprise FinOps chatbot. The CIO must embrace the potential for emergence, investing in the building blocks that will enable these new capabilities. This requires a forward-looking mindset, where the focus is not just on solving today's challenges but on creating the conditions for tomorrow's innovations to take root.

Note

1 FinOps refers to Enterprise FinOps and applies to the entire IT spend unless specifically mentioned with reference to the FinOps framework from the FinOps Foundation.

References

Amazon AWS. (2025). *What is AIOps*. Retrieved from https://aws.amazon.com/what-is/aiops/

Amazon Managed Blockchain. (2025). Retrieved from https://aws.amazon.com/managed-blockchain/

Azure Confidential Ledger. (2025). Retrieved from azure.microsoft.com: https://azure.microsoft.com/en-us/products/azure-confidential-ledger/

Cabello, M., Machado, M. R., & Sales, T. (n.d.). AIOps for log anomaly detection in the era of LLMs: A systematic literature review. *Intelligent Systems with Applications*, *28*. Retrieved from https://doi.org/10.1016/j.iswa.2025.200608

Gartner. (2025). *AIOps*. Retrieved from https://www.gartner.com/en/information-technology/glossary/aiops-platform

NetBrain. (2025). *Automation maturity*. Retrieved from https://www.netbraintech.com/blog/automation-maturity/

Pega. (2025). *What is agentic AI*. Retrieved from https://www.pega.com/agentic-ai

retrieval-augmented-generation. (2025). Retrieved from https://aws.amazon.com/what-is/retrieval-augmented-generation/

Author's Note

Your Enterprise FinOps journey may be fraught with obstacles and sudden turns. Your environment and challenges are going to be uniquely yours to solve. I hope *The CIO's Guide to Enterprise FinOps* has equipped you with some of the thinking tools and techniques that can be a reliable and informative guide through this journey. No doubt you will augment these with what you have learned from your experiences through the years. I can only hope that you persevere with these challenges, because your journey will inspire others to follow you, and the goal at the end is totally worth it. I wish you all the best as you continue on your mission to make IT the driver and Enterprise FinOps the engine powering business. I invite you to reach out to me at the website, through email and over LinkedIn with your queries, comments and suggestions.

Vineet Sawant
https://www.enterprisefinops.com
Houston, TX
January 2026

DOI: 10.4324/9781003682196-16

Appendix 1: The FinOps Foundation Framework

A1.1 The FinOps Framework

Enterprise FinOps as elaborated in this book, applies the principles of FinOps to the entire IT landscape. The FinOps framework (FinOps Framework, 2025) offered by the FinOps Foundation has evolved from being focused on the public cloud optimization space to encompass Cloud+, which allows the framework to be applied to other parts of the IT portfolio, such as AI, SaaS, and data centers. While you can define your own pathway using the information presented in this book, the FinOps framework from the FinOps Foundation can be used as a ready framework, supported by detailed training, resources, certification paths, and templates, to leverage in your Enterprise FinOps implementation journey.

The FinOps Foundation is a community comprised of over 60,000 members from over 15,000+ companies. The goal of this framework is to support you in maximizing business value from your IT landscape. It creates financial accountability through collaboration between engineering, finance, and business teams. It is vendor-neutral. It doesn't prescribe a one-size-fits-all solution and can be adapted as needed to your organization's size, landscape complexity, and goals. It provides a practical path that anyone involved in FinOps can adopt, such as training, process descriptions, activities, and assessment templates. The Maturity Model, which is part of the framework, allows you to plan your journey from stage to stage. By implementing the framework, you unlock cost savings, improved efficiency, and gain greater control over your IT investment.

But this is not a one-time project, unlike other transformation programs. The FinOps journey is continuous. Commitment, collaboration, and a willingness to learn are the key success factors for successful FinOps. Your ultimate goal is to realize a culture where cost efficiency is a shared responsibility. No matter what the size, industry, or maturity stage of your enterprise, whether you're a startup or a Fortune 500 company, the FinOps framework can help you unlock the full potential of your IT investments while keeping costs in check and achieving business alignment.

The complete framework is depicted in Figure A1.1. At the very top, the framework offers a bridge to tie together your business and technology strategy. Principles are the beacons that guide your entire journey. Scopes are equivalent to your IT portfolio. It's the units where you apply FinOps. While this originated as a Cloud FinOps framework, as of 2025, Scopes have expanded beyond the cloud portfolio. Personas are the roles that will be involved in implementing FinOps as well as supporting it. The four domains are the outcomes resulting from FinOps, while capabilities are the processes and activities within each domain. The FinOps framework also outlines a Maturity Model that you can use to progressively work toward a continuous FinOps culture.

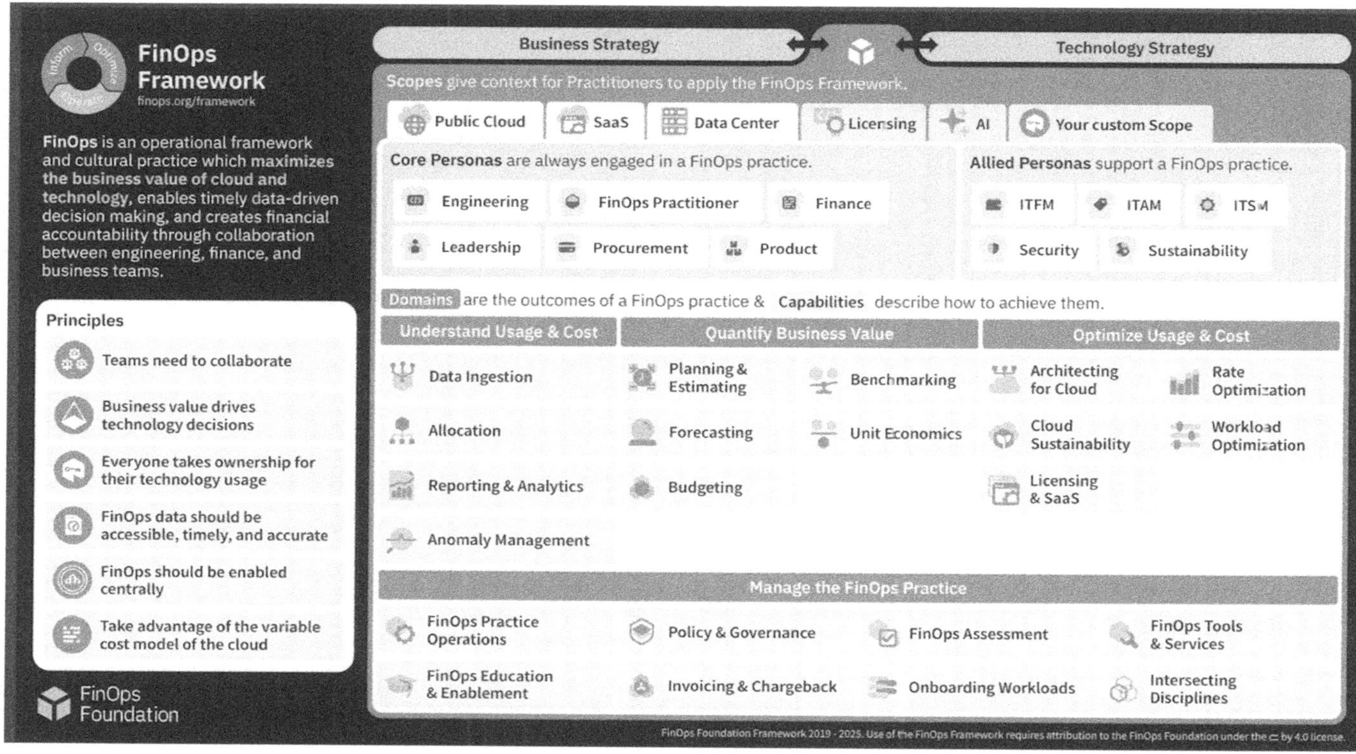

Figure A1.1 The FinOps framework 2025

Source: The FinOps Foundation, reproduced here as per the CC BY 4.0 attribution license.

A1.2 Scopes

Scopes (FinOps Framework Scopes, 2025) represent your IT portfolio. It's where you apply FinOps. You can customize Scopes for your own organization's model. I feel it is best aligned to the way you have structured your organization and the CIO+1 levels of VPs and Directors who are the decision makers in your team.

The FinOps framework often refers to Scopes as Cloud+. It's a nod to the fact that FinOps isn't limited to public cloud. It's about everything from the legacy systems in your data center, the SaaS tools your sales team swears by, and the custom apps that keep your business running. If your world is built on on-prem servers, FinOps lets you figure out how to make them work better.

Scopes are the boundaries that help you see where money is going and who's responsible for it. The Data Center Scope lets you use FinOps to plan for capacity, how you buy hardware, and how you track usage. Traditional models often rely on big upfront purchases, which can lead to over-provisioning or underutilized resources. But with FinOps, you can shift to a consumption-based model, where you pay only for what you actually use. When you apply FinOps principles to the Data Center Scope, teams could see which workloads are eating up resources and which ones are barely using anything. They can optimize their workload placement, move some apps to the cloud, and cut costs by 20% to 30% without sacrificing performance. But this is also about rethinking how you operate. In the Data Center Scope, teams can refine migration strategies, balance workloads between on-prem and cloud, and even improve how much value each server brings to the business.

A1.3 Principles

FinOps principles, as illustrated in Figure A1.2, serve as a guiding framework for the activities of a successful FinOps practice.

A1.3.1 *Teams Need to Collaborate*

Effective cost management requires collaboration across multiple teams, including engineering, finance, product, procurement, and others. Cross-functional teams need to work together, sharing knowledge and expertise toward common goals. I've seen too many organizations where finance and engineering speak different languages, and the result is chaos. When teams sit at the same table, you create value together.

A1.3.2 *Business Value Drives Technology Decisions*

The holy grail of IT is alignment with business goals. This means IT and business are in total synchronization, where every IT decision or activity

Figure A1.2 Principles of the FinOps framework 2025

Source: Infographic created by the author based on content from the FinOps Foundation, reproduced here as per the CC BY 4.0 attribution license.

can be traced back to a business requirement or priority. This is the same principle that Enterprise Architecture frameworks like TOGAF or the Zachman Framework have been screaming from the rooftops for years. Whether it's launching a new product, improving customer retention, or scaling operations, the FinOps framework needs to reflect that. I've worked with teams that treated cloud costs like an afterthought. Then they realized that if you don't align tech spend with business outcomes, you're just throwing money at problems without really solving anything that matters. When everyone knows how their work contributes to the bigger picture, decisions start being strategic, and IT starts becoming a driver of business value.

A1.3.3 *Everyone Takes Ownership for Their Technology Usage*

Technology is used by all layers across the organization. But ownership is often punted back to the IT department. Even within IT groups, the accountability issue is fragmented. I've seen teams where no one felt responsible for costs because they felt it was the finance team's job, or worse, they felt that their cloud provider contract already handled that. Developers use cloud and server resources indiscriminately because they think it's coming out of the infrastructure budget, and cost is not their responsibility. Everyone in the enterprise, whether a business user or developer or operations engineer, needs to take accountability for their technology usage. Chargeback and Showback models in Enterprise FinOps help stakeholders understand how they are using resources across IT. Assigning clear responsibilities to individuals or teams for managing specific aspects of technology spend ensures that everyone understands their role in maintaining financial control and compliance with organizational policies.

A1.3.4 FinOps Data Should Be Accessible, Timely, and Accurate

Teams often argue over costs because the data is stale or incomplete. Without transparency, building trust is a tall task. Transparency comes through visibility, and accurate and relevant data on technology spend. With this comes the ability to make informed decisions. It stops finger-pointing when problems are uncovered and turns questions on who's to blame to solutions on how it can be fixed.

A1.3.5 FinOps Should Be Enabled Centrally

Centralization or Decentralization has always been a perennial debate in organizational structures. Decentralization enables faster decision-making and agility, but also leads to duplication and redundancy. Centralization empowers standardization but can also slow down things. For FinOps, I'll argue for a hybrid approach, where the FinOps team is centralized, while decentralization is enabled through the collaboration principle. A centralized FinOps team can create guidelines that guide the organization in managing its technology investments. They set policies, share best practices, and ensure consistency. It results in a unified approach that saves time, reduces errors, and makes everyone more efficient. Actions to optimize costs can be taken by decentralized teams as best suited for their portfolio.

A1.3.6 Take Advantage of the Variable Cost Model of the Cloud

The cloud has introduced a whole new way of applying technology. The traditional Capex model, where you built in capacity for several years, has changed to an Opex model with pay-per-use and SaaS. This principle encourages organizations to leverage the pay-as-you-go nature of cloud computing, where costs are only incurred when resources are actually used. Teams can spin up or down resources on demand to match their needs. Variable costs are an opportunity to make your IT budgeting more resilient. But it can go out of hand quite rapidly, and that's where FinOps can apply the guardrails to keep you on track. As mentioned in the section on Scopes, this principle can be extended to other parts of your IT landscape, including data centers and SaaS.

A1.4 Maturity Levels – Crawl-Walk-Run

Any framework without a maturity level seems incomplete. You've seen the typical five-stage maturity levels with other IT frameworks that you may have implemented in your organization before. The FinOps framework has a simpler one: Crawl-Walk-Run (Maturity Model, 2025) that has been adapted from agile methodologies.

- The Crawl stage is where you start. You're mostly driven by spreadsheets. You have metrics but are trying to get basic KPIs defined. It's where the real work starts.
- The Walk phase is where things start to click. You're starting to see patterns. Forecasting becomes less of a guess and more of a science. You start applying levers like rightsizing, vendor negotiation, and others. Your data is becoming more accurate and real-time.
- Run is the part where automation, predictive analytics, and cross-departmental alignment become second nature. But you don't need to be "Run" level everywhere. Focus on the high-impact areas first. I've seen companies waste months trying to perfect every metric, only to realize their real leverage was in optimizing a single service. Prioritize what moves the needle.

Maturity levels are a guideline. Different portfolios or scopes could be at different stages of maturity levels, and that's OK. If you're in Crawl, don't rush. Start with one capability. If you're in Walk, find out and focus on the next bottleneck. And if you're in Run, ensure you're not chasing priorities that don't align with your goals.

A1.5 FinOps Phases

The FinOps framework consists of three iterative phases: Inform, Optimize, and Operate, as shown in Figure A1.3.

Inform is the starting line. You can't optimize what you don't understand. Teams need to dig into data sources such as cloud cost reports, usage metrics, server and efficiency logs. This builds the tools to budget smarter, predict trends, and track KPIs that actually matter. Often, teams get stuck because they didn't know where their money was going. One team spent weeks chasing down why their cloud bill spiked by 40%. Then they tagged their resources properly and could see which team was responsible for what. Accurate allocation brings clarity.

In Optimize, you take the data from Inform and start asking yourself how you could do better. Techniques like workload optimization, rate optimization, containerization, rightsizing, and software harvesting are levers you can apply. Rightsizing underutilized resources adjusts your cloud setup to match actual needs. One of my teams had 30% of its servers running at 10% capacity. We slashed costs by 20% just by moving workloads to more efficient instances. The next step is to adopt serverless, autoscaling, or containerized architectures. Look for automation possibilities.

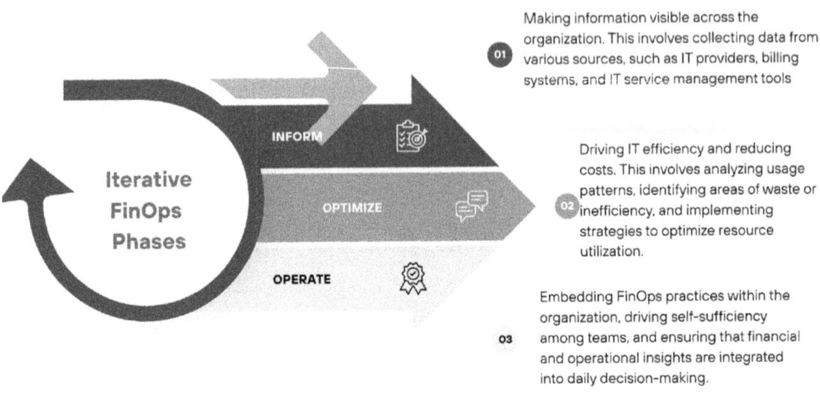

Figure A1.3 Phases of the FinOps framework 2025

Source: Infographic created by the author based on content from the FinOps Foundation, reproduced here as per the CC BY 4.0 attribution license.

In the Operate phase, you turn insights into action. Governance policies, compliance checks, and training programs are all part of the equation. FinOps gets embedded into daily workflows. Engineers tag resources properly, set up automated cost alerts, and align policies with business goals. The result is a culture where everyone owns their costs.

Teams don't all start at the same phase. Each of your portfolio areas may be at different phases. Some are still figuring out where their money goes. Others are already automating waste. The key is to keep moving. Also, it's a cycle. You inform, optimize, operate, and then start again, but faster. Build a system where everyone collaborates, data tells the truth, and every dollar spent moves the business forward.

A1.6 Core Personas

It takes a whole team to get it right.

- Leadership sets the culture, allocates resources, and ensures everyone's aligned with the organization's vision. They push for agility and business alignment and encourage continuous improvement.
- The FinOps practitioners bridge the gap between the tech teams and the finance folks, making sure everyone speaks the same language. They work with teams, no matter which phase they are in. They set up the systems to track costs, forecast budgets, and generally keep things under control. They're making sure the numbers make sense.
- The finance team is the strategic partner, working with the FinOps team to understand IT costs, aligning spending with business goals, and ensuring the spend is justified.

- Engineers and developers are the builders, making sure everything works. They tweak things, refactor code, right-size environments, automate stuff, and work with the FinOps folks to make sure it all adds up.
- Procurement is the deal-maker, negotiating contracts with IT providers. They find the best possible deals. They keep an eye on rate optimization and benchmarking. They're always asking if they can get a better price and making sure the requirements meet the business goals, and the solutions match the requirements.
- Product teams work with business users to make stuff that is needed, new products, services, and offerings that add direct value to the organization. Product development gets aligned with business strategy. They work with Engineering and FinOps to design efficient workflows and build the right things efficiently.
- Operations teams are deep into metrics, KPIs, software harvesting, incident resolution, and maintenance. They sense opportunities for both incremental and big improvements, automation of workflows, and ways to reduce inefficiencies and work with the FinOps team and engineering to generate a list of opportunities.

None of these roles work in a silo. They're all interdependent. Engineering needs finance to understand cost implications. FinOps needs Product to align resources. And Leadership needs Procurement to optimize contracts. When they all work together, FinOps develops a culture of accountability, innovation, and financial discipline. It's how organizations turn IT spending into a competitive advantage.

A1.7 Allied Personas

The teamwork around FinOps extends to other roles in the IT organization. These are the Allied Personas who support the initiatives and goals.

- The Information Technology Financial Management (ITFM) manages budgets, forecasts costs, and works hand-in-hand with finance to manage the IT spend. They are responsible for allocating costs to different departmental and business units through chargeback methods. Often ITFM is backed by a tool such as Apptio or ServiceNow that lets them collate costs across the organization, but more often than not, I've seen this team working with spreadsheets. With FinOps visibility and tagging, they can add enhanced showback and chargeback to the list, offering a more granular and transparent way to assign costs to business units. They are your allies in spotting waste and evaluating ROI.
- The Information Technology Asset Management (ITAM) team keeps track of what IT assets exist across the organization. They know what licenses you own and what the service life of any asset is. With FinOps,

they expand their purview to finding out which ones are underutilized and which ones are quietly duplicating work. They're the gatekeepers of your software inventory and can play a huge role in software harvesting and Application Rationalization. Often, this team already has tools in place, such as ServiceNow ITAM.

- The Information Technology Service Management (ITSM) goal is to deliver efficient IT services. They work closely with operations teams to ensure that services are delivered and continuously improved. They maintain tools like ServiceNow ITSM and provide visibility to service metrics like uptime and resolution time. They work with vendors to report SLAs and OLAs. They manage systems and also expectations. Whether it's ensuring uptime for mission-critical apps or running a competent change management approval process, or digging into the root cause of a recurring incident, ITSM teams keep operations running smoothly. With FinOps, they take on a broader role, focusing not only on service quality but also on service value. They help FinOps spot inefficiencies and redirect resources to high-impact areas.
- Security teams align risks with business objectives. They are the teams that protect the fortress, ensuring that breaches are detected and fixed. They take proactive measures to ensure that upgrades, new systems, and changes do not expose gaps in the armor. With FinOps, they ensure that security risks are prioritized for fixes and that compliance measures don't just add overhead.
- In many organizations, sustainability professionals are coming to the forefront. They monitor the environmental cost of the cloud infrastructure. In an era where ESG (Environmental, Social, Governance) metrics are increasingly being reported in the company reports, they're the voices of long-term value. They collaborate with FinOps to identify opportunities for energy efficiency, reduce carbon footprints, and turn cost savings into shared wins. They are helping you future-proof your business.

The true power is in collaboration, not silos. ITFM optimizes costs, ITAM aligns resources, ITSM improves efficiency, Security mitigates risk, and Sustainability future-proofs the business. When these Allied Personas work together with FinOps, the result is a culture of strategic alignment.

A1.8 Domains and Capabilities

The FinOps framework is comprised of four primary domains, as shown in Figure A1.4 (FinOps Domains, 2025): Understand Usage and Cost, Quantify Business Value, Optimize Usage and Cost, and Manage the FinOps Practice. Each domain represents a business outcome that organizations achieve from practicing FinOps. Domains are linked with capabilities that represent activities and processes needed to achieve the outcomes.

A1.8.1 *Understand Usage and Cost*

No one can optimize what they don't understand. This domain maps out where money is going now and where it might head next. Capabilities like cost estimation, budgeting, and forecasting are for anyone who wants to know why a team left 100 VMs running 24/7 for three months during off-hours when the application was not even being used during this time. It's your team's version of a "financial X-ray." For example, a company might use forecasting to spot a 30% spike in costs tied to a new project, then adjust budgets before the bill hits. That's preventing

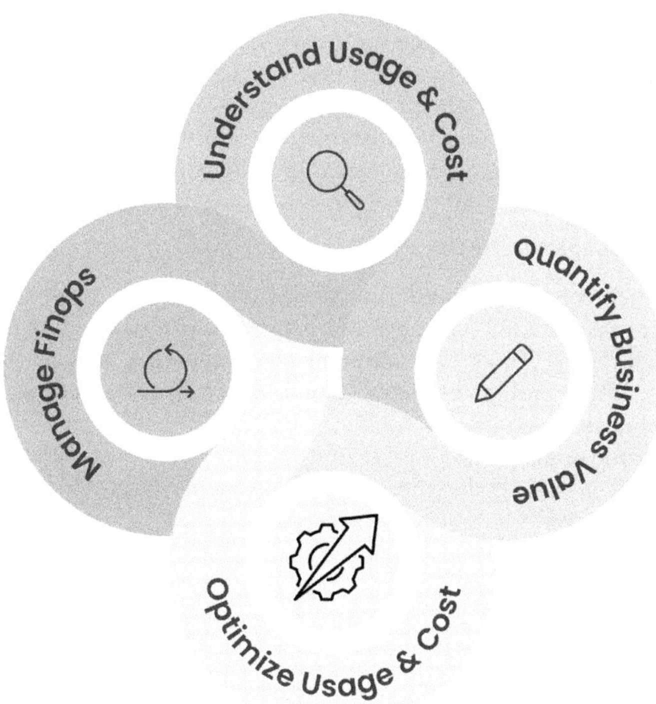

Figure A1.4 Domains of the FinOps framework 2025

Source: Infographic created by the author based on content from the FinOps Foundation, reproduced here as per the CC BY 4.0 attribution license.

a crisis. Tools like reporting and analytics detect patterns that may hint at waste.

A1.8.2 *Quantify Business Value*

No one cares about cost savings unless they see how they tie to revenue, efficiency, or risk reduction. This domain is where you translate numbers into meaning. Imagine setting a policy that mandates that every new workload be evaluated for cost efficiency before deployment. When you show that optimizing cloud spend improves service delivery, you instill confidence in your business peers that IT is continuously looking to maximize their assets and derive business value.

A1.8.3 *Optimize Usage and Cost*

You might use analytics to spot a team over-provisioning storage, then shift to a pay-as-you-go model for seasonal workloads. Or adopt autoscaling to match demand, freeing up resources for innovation. When you optimize, you're creating space for growth. That $500K in savings could fund a new project, a new feature, a new way to compete. Capabilities like resource optimization, rightsizing, and tagging are tools that help teams spot and eliminate waste. For instance, a team might use rightsizing to shrink a server from 16 cores to 4, saving $10K a month.

A1.8.4 *Manage the FinOps Practice*

When developers understand the cost implications of their code, and finance speaks the same language as operations, you're building a culture of accountability. Tools like planning and estimating lead to informed decisions. When FinOps becomes second nature, you're shaping a future where value always outpaces volume.

These four domains don't exist in isolation. They're an iterative cycle. Clarity leads to value, which fuels optimization, all supported by a culture that makes it stick.

A1.9 Certifications

Certification programs have several benefits. Think of popular certifications today, such as the AWS Certified Cloud Practitioner, Certified Scrum Master (CSM), or PMI's Project Management Professional (PMP). Structured and quality training is developed around the certification curriculum. Individuals look at certifications as a path to gain knowledge in a specific area and to boost their career prospects. Companies looking

Figure A1.5 FinOps certifications

Source: Infographic created by the author based on content from the FinOps Foundation.

to implement initiatives in specific areas prefer to hire candidates with proven and authentic certifications in that area. The FinOps Foundation has developed several certifications and supplemented them with training programs to help organizations and individuals embrace FinOps (FinOps Foundation, 2025).

There are several individual-level certifications, some of which are shown in Figure A1.5.

- When I was hiring for my FinOps team, I highly considered candidates who were FinOps Certified Practitioners and Professionals. Firstly, it demonstrates that individuals have foundational knowledge in areas like cost optimization, resource management, and accountability. It's also ideal for executive leaders wanting to know more about FinOps or senior managers looking to contribute to FinOps initiatives within their companies.
- The FinOps Certified Professional demonstrates the ability to design FinOps frameworks, integrate FinOps into governance models, and leverage tools for cost tracking. It's ideal for teams that will be leading FinOps programs.
- The FinOps Certified Enterprise program recognizes organizations that embed FinOps practices into their culture and foster a commitment to continuous improvement, community engagement, and knowledge sharing. Candidates equate this with your strong advocacy of FinOps. And when they join, they bring skills that align with your mission.

- The FinOps Certified Service Provider certification is for FinOps Foundation members who offer consulting or professional services in FinOps. It assures customers that their offerings meet practitioner needs.
  Company-level certifications
- For companies that develop, license, or deliver commercial software products in FinOps, the FinOps Certified Platform certification validates different capabilities in FinOps. No endorsement or ranking of tools is implied; the certification simply highlights alignment with established standards, not claims of superiority. The FinOps Foundation has further introduced the FOCUS specification to provide a single common specification for billing that cloud providers and tool vendors can adapt for greater data portability and transparency (FOCUS, The FinOps Foundation, 2025).

These programs create a clear path for individuals as well as organizations to adopt FinOps. They provide structured learning and a path to update teams on industry standards and best practices.

A1.10 FOCUS (FinOps Open Cost and Usage Specification)

The FinOps Open Cost and Usage Specification (FOCUS) (FOCUS, The FinOps Foundation, 2025) is a framework that aims to standardize cost and usage data management across providers. In plain words, it attempts to resolve the chaos of cloud billing into something coherent. Think of what the EDI (Electronic Data Interchange) specification did to integrate and standardize supply chain and logistics information across multiple companies. FOCUS aims to do that for the cloud.

Today, each provider speaks its own language, with metrics that don't align, formats that clash, and definitions that leave you scratching your head. You can't compare a compute hour on AWS to one on Azure without rewriting the data. FOCUS changes that. It's like giving everyone a shared dictionary, a universal format that maps resource hierarchies, cloud tech types, and pricing details across platforms. With FOCUS in place, your FinOps and finance teams aren't spending valuable cycles translating and normalizing data; instead, they can analyze data across multiple providers.

FOCUS provides consistent metrics that can be used to detect inefficiencies and identify opportunities across hybrid environments. The scope grows further – benchmark costs against competitors, track team-specific spending, and forecast budgets even if you are trying to change providers. FOCUS invites cloud providers, tool vendors, and enterprises to speak the same language. That collaboration sparks innovation. Startups can build

FinOps tools that work across platforms. With a common language and standard, you end up with a unified approach to cloud financial operations. The goal is to foster efficiency and accountability across teams, regardless of the cloud provider with which they have partnered.

A1.11 The State of FinOps

The latest "State of FinOps" report (The State of FinOps, 2025) throws a spotlight on the chaos and the opportunities hiding in plain sight. Last year, 31% of organizations were tracking AI-related spending. Now that's jumped to 63%. The cloud is now including algorithms, models, and the invisible costs of training those systems. This shift means FinOps is understanding where the money is flowing in ways that used to be invisible.

Organizations are throwing money at cloud, SaaS, and data centers faster than ever. Every new tool, every new service, every new layer of complexity adds to the workload. And yet, staffing hasn't kept up. The report doesn't mince words and emphasizes the necessary investment in upskilling, automation, and hiring expertise. FinOps is colliding with other tech management strategies like DevOps, SecOps, and even AI governance. The report offers insights into the challenges faced by organizations and how FinOps is helping them address it.

A1.12 Key Capabilities

This section provides an overview of the key capabilities in FinOps. Figure A1.6 provides a holistic view of the domains and their associated capabilities.

A1.13 Understand Usage and Cost

The four capabilities in this domain are the following: Data Ingestion, Allocation, Reporting and Analytics, and Anomaly Management.

Data ingestion is the activity of collecting and processing data from everywhere in the IT landscape. These could be billing statements, logs, sensors, you name it. You are building a complete picture of where your money is going and why. A company might use automated tools to pull data from AWS, Azure, and on-premises systems, then aggregate it into a single dashboard. Suddenly, they can see that 30% of their costs are tied to a single misconfigured server.

Allocation primarily assigns costs to departments, but it also holds people accountable. By mapping cloud resources to specific teams, projects, or even individuals through tagging, you create transparency. A marketing team might be charged for a server they didn't request, while the

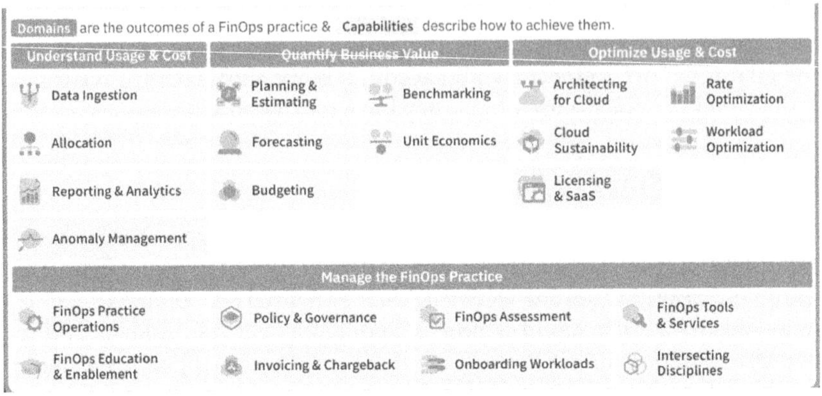

Figure A1.6 Domains and capabilities in the FinOps framework 2025

Source: Infographic created by the author based on content from the FinOps Foundation, reproduced here as per the CC BY 4.0 attribution license.

engineering team is left with a bill they can't explain. Allocation tools help you trace that back. Suddenly, the marketing team knows they need to justify their usage, and the engineering team can optimize what they're already paying for.

Reporting and Analytics asks the right questions and provides answers that matter in relevant formats for different stakeholders. A dashboard may reflect that 30% of this quarter's cloud costs are tied to instances with utilization levels of 25%. Immediately, you ask the engineering teams to right-size resources, move workloads, and cut waste. You've now unlocked savings for other priorities.

In Anomaly Management, the unexpected is what you're looking for. This could be anything out of the ordinary. It could be a sudden spike in costs, an API that's increased its transactions by 200% overnight, or a compliance issue hiding in plain sight. A tool might flag a 500% increase in storage costs overnight. Without anomaly detection, that could be a \$100K bill before anyone notices. With it, you can investigate, identify the cause (maybe a misconfigured backup job), and stop it in its tracks.

A1.14 Quantify Business Value

In this domain, capabilities tie cloud spending to business value.

Forecasting is a collaboration between engineering and product teams to build models that reflect real-world usage. Think of it as your team's version of a "financial radar."

A product team might flag a 300% increase in compute costs for a new feature, based on historical trends. Without forecasting, that could be a

$50K bill before anyone notices. With it, you can adjust the scope, reallocate resources, or secure funding early.

Budgeting aligns spend with priorities. This capability seeks baselines and estimates future costs. A team might use budgeting tools to cap cloud spend on a legacy system, redirecting funds to a new AI-driven application.

Benchmarking establishes a customized standard for what "good" looks like for your company. A company might set a benchmark that no team should exceed 15% of its budget on unoptimized instances. Suddenly, teams are held accountable. Note that this is different from the benchmarking we do in vendor management to establish a sense of industry rates and pricing for services and products.

Unit Economics is where you get granular. You zoom in on individual units such as apps, services, or features to see where your money is actually working. A team might discover that a specific microservice is eating up 40% of their cloud budget, despite only handling 10% of user traffic. With unit economics, they can reallocate resources, cut waste, and reinvest savings.

With the right FinOps team in place, you get people who understand the data, processes that enforce accountability, and leaders who prioritize visibility.

A1.15 Optimize Usage and Cost

In Architecting for the cloud, you are building systems designed to take advantage of the cloud. You've got a team that's been burning through compute costs because their app demands are going through the roof. Then someone says, "What if we split this into microservices and let them sleep when they're not needed?" Suddenly, costs drop by 30%, and the app still works.

Sustainability lets you ensure your cloud spend is making the right choices for the environment. You've got a CTO who's been told, "We're too small to care about carbon footprints." Then they find a cloud provider that runs on 100% renewable energy and cut costs by 20% on energy-intensive workloads.

Licensing lets you optimize your software spend. Why pay for 100 licenses when you only need 20? You're stuck with 30 SaaS tools you don't use. Then someone audits and says, "We're wasting $50K a year on this." Now that the budget gets reallocated to a much-delayed integration between your ERP and CRM system.

In rate optimization, you are using insights from your data and market pricing to know when to haggle, when to commit, and when to walk away. Negotiation becomes an art form. You're stuck with a vendor charging $2 per hour for compute. Then you find out they've cut prices by 20%

for multi-year contracts. You sign and save $500K annually because you know you'll need this for at least two years.

Workload optimization places your workloads where they'll do the best with the least waste. You've got a batch job that runs during peak hours, burning through $10K a month. Then someone says, "What if we move this to a spot instance during off-peak times?" Suddenly, costs drop by 60%.

A1.16 Manage the FinOps Practice

Effective FinOps Practice Operations lets you build a culture where cost decisions are made with clarity and purpose.

Policy and Governance avoid the chaos of a team that thinks "we'll fix it later." A dev team spins up a new instance, no one tracks it, and suddenly you're paying for a server that's forgotten in a corner. Effective governance ensures that teams create and follow guardrails to innovate without burning through the budget.

FinOps assessment identifies blind spots in your cloud environment, like a team that's using spot instances but hasn't set up alerts for unexpected costs. FinOps Tools and Services encourage you to use the right tools for providing visibility and controlling your cloud spend. The right tools give you visibility, control, and the ability to act before costs spiral.

FinOps Education and Enablement focus on training your teams in the right FinOps practices. Education creates a shared language, so the dev team knows what "reserved instances" mean, and the finance team understands why "cost allocation" matters.

Invoicing and chargeback seek accountability. They ensure that every team knows where their money is going when they are using cloud assets.

Onboarding Workloads creates workflows that prevent mistakes before they happen. It lets your teams set up guardrails to move fast without breaking things.

References

FinOps Domains. (2025). Retrieved from finops.org: https://www.finops.org/framework/domains/

FinOps Foundation. (2025). *Training and certifications*. Retrieved from finops.org: https://www.finops.org/training-certification/

FinOps Framework. (2025). Retrieved from finops.org: https://www.finops.org/framework/

FinOps Framework Scopes. (2025). Retrieved from finops.org: https://www.finops.org/framework/scopes/

FOCUS, The FinOps Foundation. (2025). *FOCUS*. Retrieved from https://focus.finops.org/

Maturity Model. (2025). Retrieved from finops.org: https://www.finops.org/framework/maturity-model/

The State of FinOps. (2025). *The State of FinOps*. The FinOps Foundation. Retrieved from https://data.finops.org/

Glossary

80-20 rule (Pareto principle) The observation that 80% of consequences or results come from 20% of causes or efforts.

abstraction level The process of removing physical, spatial, or temporal details in the study of systems to focus on relevant information.

ACV (annual contract value) The average annual revenue value of a single customer contract.

ADM (application development & maintenance) The ongoing process of creating, deploying, and supporting software applications within an organization.

agentic AI Advanced artificial intelligence systems capable of taking autonomous actions and making decisions without constant human intervention.

Agile An iterative approach to software development and project management that emphasizes flexibility and customer feedback.

AI (artificial intelligence) Systems or machines that mimic human intelligence to perform tasks and improve themselves through iteration.

AIOps (artificial intelligence for IT operations) The application of AI and machine learning to automate and enhance IT operations and incident response.

Amortization The process of spreading the cost of a one-time purchase, such as a cloud reservation, over the period it is used.

anomaly detection An analytical technique used to spot unusual spending patterns or technical deviations from a baseline.

API (application programming interface) A set of rules and protocols that allow different software applications to communicate with each other.

application rationalization The practice of strategically identifying which business applications to keep, replace, retire, or consolidate.

ARB (architectural review board) A committee that reviews IT designs to ensure compliance with enterprise standards and financial goals.

B2B (business-to-business) Commercial transactions and interactions between two or more business entities.

B2C (business-to-consumer) Commercial transactions conducted directly between a business and individual consumers.

Benford's law A mathematical observation used in forensic analytics to detect anomalies in financial datasets by analyzing leading digits.

bimodal IT An organizational model that separates IT into two modes: one focused on stability (Mode 1) and the other on agility (Mode 2).

BYOL (bring your own license) A model where a customer purchases a software license independently and deploys it on their choice of infrastructure.

Capex (capital expenditure) Funds used by a company to acquire, upgrade, and maintain physical assets such as servers and data centers.

CFO (chief financial officer) The senior executive responsible for managing the financial actions and strategy of a company.

Chargeback A practice where the costs of IT services are billed back to the specific business units or departments that consumed them.

CI/CD (continuous integration/continuous deployment) A method to frequently deliver apps to customers by introducing automation into the stages of app development.

CIO (chief information officer) The executive responsible for the management, implementation, and usability of information and computer technologies.

cloud FinOps A practice focused specifically on managing and optimizing public cloud consumption and spending.

COBIT A framework for the governance and management of enterprise IT developed by ISACA.

CRM (customer relationship management) Technology and strategies used for managing a company's relationships and interactions with customers.

CUD (committed use discount) A discount model where a customer commits to a certain amount of usage in exchange for lower rates.

CXO (chief (any executive position) officer) The executive responsible for a specific role, business or function within a company, such as CEO for Chief Executive Officer, or CMO for Chief Marketing officer, or CTO for Chief technology Officer, etc.

DDD (domain-driven design) A software development approach that focuses on modeling software based on the reality of the business domain.

DevOps A set of practices that combines software development (Dev) and IT operations (Ops) to shorten the development life cycle.

EBITDA Earnings before interest, taxes, depreciation, and amortization; a measure of a company's overall financial performance.

enterprise FinOps Financial optimization across the entire IT spend, as defined in this book. It includes a holistic framework and transformative roadmap to align IT spending with strategic enterprise and business goals and optimize operations across all IT assets, improving cost utilization and business alignment across the entire IT spend.

ERP (enterprise resource planning) Software used by organizations to manage day-to-day business activities like accounting and procurement.

ETL (extract, transform, load) A data integration process that combines data from multiple sources into a single data store.

FinOps Financial optimization, as defined in this book, where strategy and techniques are applied to optimize costs and reduce unnecessary consumption. Also defined in some contexts as Financial Operations.

FOCUS (FinOps Open Cost & Usage Specification) An open standard for cloud cost, usage, and billing data to ensure consistency across providers.

GenAI (generative AI) A type of artificial intelligence that can create new content, such as text, images, or code, based on training data.

IaaS (infrastructure as a service) A form of cloud computing that provides virtualized computing resources over the internet.

IaC (infrastructure as code) The managing and provisioning of infrastructure through code rather than manual processes.

ITIL A set of detailed practices for IT service management (ITSM) that focuses on aligning IT services with the needs of the business.

IVD (IT value delivered) A composite metric introduced in this book that bundles cost savings, efficiency gains, and strategic impact to measure IT success.

KPI (key performance indicator) A quantifiable measure used to evaluate the success of an organization or activity in reaching performance targets.

LLM (large language model) AI trained on vast amounts of data to understand and generate human-like text.

Opex (operating expenditure) The ongoing costs for running a product, business, or system, including cloud subscriptions and maintenance.

PaaS (platform as a service) A cloud computing model where a provider delivers a platform for customers to develop and run applications without managing infrastructure.

RACI A matrix used to assign and clarify roles and responsibilities (Responsible, Accountable, Consulted, Informed) in a project.

RI (reserved instance) A billing model that offers a significant discount in exchange for a commitment to use a specific level of resources over a set term.

ROI (return on investment) A performance measure used to evaluate the efficiency or profitability of an IT investment.

RPA (robotic process automation) Software technology used to build and deploy software robots that emulate human actions within digital systems.

RTI360 (Run-Transform-Innovate 360) A foundational model introduced in this book, and used to categorize IT services through a holistic 360-degree viewpoint into Run(maintenance), Transform(modernization), and Innovate(value creation).

SaaS (software as a service) A software distribution model in which a third-party provider hosts applications and makes them available to customers over the internet.

Showback A practice of reporting IT costs to business units for awareness without actually billing them.

SLA (service level agreement) A commitment between a service provider and a client regarding the standards and uptime of a service.

TCO (total cost of ownership) An estimation of all direct and indirect costs associated with an IT asset over its entire life cycle.

tech debt (technology debt) The implied cost of technical (software), infrastructure, services, or other IT debt that builds up over time due to various factors

zero-trust A security framework requiring all users to be continuously authenticated and authorized before gaining access to applications and data.

Index

For Product Safety Concerns and Information please contact our EU representative GPSR@taylorandfrancis.com
Taylor & Francis Verlag GmbH, Kaufingerstraße 24, 80331 München, Germany

www.ingramcontent.com/pod-product-compliance
Ingram Content Group UK Ltd.
Pitfield, Milton Keynes, MK11 3LW, UK
UKHW022347190926
475702UK00015B/2156